J

CW01083426

THE TRAᖴᖴᴵᴄ ᴏᖴᖴᴵᴄᴇᴿ'ᔆ
COMPANION

17th Edition

Gordon Wilson

BA (Law), MSc

Further titles available:

● Promotion Crammer for Sergeants' and Inspectors' Part I Exams
● Pass for Promotion for Sergeants' and Inspectors' Part II Exams
● Beat Officer's Companion
● Scottish Beat Officer's Companion

To order or for further details phone +44 (0) 20 8700 3700 or fax +44 (0) 20 8763 1006

By the same author:
The Beat Officer's Companion

7th edition 1992
8th edition 1993
9th edition 1995
10th edition 1997
11th edition 1999
12th edition 2002
13th edition 2003
14th edition 2005
15th edition 2006
16th edition 2007
17th edition 2008

ISBN 978-0-7106-2862-6

Jane's Information Group
Sentinel House
163 Brighton Road
Coulsdon
Surrey CR5 2YH

Edited by Mike McGrath

Printed and bound in Great Britain by
Hobbs the Printers - www.hobbs.uk.com

PREFACE

The present-day police officer engaged in the enforcement of traffic law is faced with the onerous task of interpreting, committing to memory and, whenever the situation demands, instantaneously recalling and making decisions upon, an immense field of technical legislation. This manual attempts to assist in handling the problems encountered, by presenting the more practical aspects of traffic policing in a fashion which facilitates speedy reference and easy interpretation.

In recent years a myriad of text books have been published, many of which contain a comprehensive coverage of traffic legislation. Their authors are to be congratulated in their presentation of a subject which is renowned for its complexity and obscurity. But in the majority of cases such works, whilst ideally suited to the legal practitioner engaged in the wider aspects of the law, are not in keeping with the more urgent demands of the operational police officer dealing with incidents.

The problems experienced in compiling this guidebook have surrounded the need to balance the selection of material thought to be a possible source of assistance, with an easily read and understood format whilst, at the same time, maintaining a system which would facilitate speedy reference. With this in mind material has been presented in almost every case in a diagrammatic or pictorial manner.

Because the book is intended to serve merely as a guide to the operational police officer, the relevant legislation has been subjected to a practical interpretation. It should not, therefore be regarded as a definitive work of reference and specific technical details may require further research.

In this edition the main changes have been brought about by:

1. **The Driving Licences (Exchangeable Licences) Order 2007**, which added the Faroes Islands to the list of countries included in the 'exchangeable licences' scheme.
2. **The Vehicle Drivers (Certificates of Professional Competence) Regulations 2007**, which introduced a new requirement for bus and lorry drivers to acquire a CPC in order to allow them to drive relevant vehicles.

3. **The Community Drivers' Hours and Recording Equipment Regulations 2007** which, together with **Regulation (EC) 561/2006**, amended the provisions relating to drivers' hours, deleting the old Regulation 3820/85. Some amendments were also made to Reg 3821/85 which deals with records of work.

4. **The Carriage of Dangerous Goods and Use of Transportable Pressure Equipment Regulations 2007**, which, together with the **European Agreement concerning the International Carriage of Dangerous Goods by Road (ADR) 2007** and the 2007 version of the **Dangerous Goods Emergency Action Code List 2007**, made various changes to the carriage of dangerous goods.

5. **The Welfare of Animals (Transport) (England) Order 2006** which enforces the requirements of **Council Regulation 1/2005** in relation to transport and transporters of animals. It also revokes the Welfare of Animals (Transport) Order 1997.

6. **The Road Safety Act 2006** (Commencement No 2) which inserted a new section 3ZA into the Road Traffic Act 1988, clarifying the meaning of 'without due care and attention' and 'without reasonable consideration'. It also extended the offence of causing death by careless driving while under the influence of drink or drugs. By Commencement Order No. 3 it amended Section 28 of The Vehicles (Crime) Act 2001 relating to the sale of registration plates. By Commencement Order No 4 it created the offences of causing death whilst driving without a licence, driving whilst uninsured, driving whilst disqualified, and by driving carelessly or inconsiderately.

7. **The Passenger and Goods Vehicles (Recording Equipment) (Downloading and Retention of Data) Regulations 2008** which require transport undertakings to download data from vehicle units and driver cards within specified periods to ensure that data is not overwritten. Also, drivers are now required to produce records made under the Transport Act 1968 within 42 days, rather than 21 days as required previously.

8. **Motor Cars (Driving Instruction) (Amendment) Regulations 2008** which amended the manner in which licences must be displayed in the vehicle.

9. **Vehicles Crime (Registration of Registration Plate Suppliers) Regulations 2008** which extended the provisions to cover the whole of the UK.

At the time of going to press, whilst the Road Safety Act 2006 had received Royal Ascent, very few provisions had been brought into force.

The following relevant Sections are awaiting commencement orders:

S4 (Fixed penalty points to be graduated depending on the nature and seriousness of the offence, the venue, and previous record of the offender).
Ss 8 & 9 (The creation of 'driving records' into which particulars of endorsements awarded to unlicensed and foreign drivers may be entered).
S11 (The introduction of a police power to impose a financial penalty deposit requirement where the offender has failed to provide his address).
S12 (Power to immobilise vehicles where driving has been prohibited).
S15 (The introduction of alcohol ignition interlock programme orders).
S18 (Creating the offence of failing to comply with a Construction and Use requirement as to speed assessment equipment detection devices).
S22 (A new offence by the registered owner of keeping a vehicle which does not meet insurance requirements).

CONTENTS

Part 1: CONSTRUCTION AND USE   1

VEHICLE DEFINITIONS	2 – 5
INTERNATIONAL CATEGORIES	6
MAXIMUM LENGTH	8
CALCULATION OF LENGTH	11
OVERHANG	12
TURNING CIRCLES	13
MINIMUM GROUND CLEARANCE	14
MAXIMUM WIDTH	15
CALCULATION OF WIDTH	16
MAXIMUM HEIGHT – BUSES	17
WEIGHT	18 – 34
TRAVELLING HEIGHT	35
HIGH-LEVEL EQUIPMENT	36 – 37
TRAILERS	38 – 43
DANGEROUS VEHICLES	44
SILENCERS	45
EMISSIONS OF SMOKE etc.	46 – 47
TYRES	48 – 53
WARNING INSTRUMENTS	54 – 55
SPEEDOMETER	56
SEAT BELTS	57 – 68
MIRRORS	69 – 73
VISION, WINDOWS, TRANSMISSION OF LIGHT	74
GLASS, WINDSCREEN WIPERS AND WASHERS	74
SPECIAL TYPES VEHICLES	75 – 106
SIDEGUARDS	107
REARGUARDS	108
SPRAY SUPPRESSION DEVICES	109
MISCELLANEOUS	110 – 113
MOBILE TELEPHONES	113

Part 2: DOCUMENTATION 115

HGV DOCUMENTATION 116
DRIVING LICENCES 117 – 143
CERTIFICATES OF PROFESSIONAL
   COMPETENCE 144–146
INSURANCE 147
SEIZURE OF VEHICLES 148
OPERATORS' LICENCES 149 – 157
EXCISE LICENCES 158 – 162
REGISTRATION MARKS 163 – 168
REGISTRATION OFFENCES 169 – 171
TESTING OF VEHICLES OTHER THAN GOODS
   VEHICLES 172 – 174
PLATING AND TESTING OF GOODS VEHICLES 175 – 178
MOTORCYCLE PLATES 179
TRADE LICENCES 180 – 181
PUBLIC SERVICE VEHICLES 182 – 185
MINIBUSES 186 – 188
HACKNEY CARRIAGES 190
BUSES CARRYING CHILDREN 191

Part 3: LIGHTING AND MARKING 195

INTERNATIONAL OPERATIONS 192 – 193
OBLIGATORY LAMPS etc. 196 – 201
GENERAL EXEMPTIONS 202 – 203
USE OF LAMPS 204 – 205
MOVEMENT OF LAMPS 206 – 207
COLOUR OF LIGHTS 208 – 209
HEADLAMPS 210 – 211
FRONT POSITION LAMPS 212 – 213
REAR POSITION LAMPS 214 – 215
REAR REFLECTORS 216 – 217
FRONT REFLECTORS 218
SIDE REFLECTORS 219
DIRECTION INDICATORS 220 – 221
STOP LAMPS 222 – 223
REAR FOG LAMPS 224 – 225

FRONT FOG LAMPS 226
REVERSING LIGHTS 227
HAZARD WARNING 228
REAR REGISTRATION PLATE LAMP 228
WARNING BEACONS 229
SIDE MARKER LAMPS 230 – 231
END-OUTLINE MARKER LAMPS 232
REAR REFLECTIVE MARKERS 233 – 236
LAMPS ON PROJECTING LOADS 237
PROJECTION MARKERS 238
TRAILER PLATES – REAR REFLECTORS 239
RESTRICTIONS ON USE OF LAMPS 240

Part 4: DRIVER'S HOURS AND RECORDS 241

DRIVERS' HOURS AND RECORDS 242 – 247
DRIVERS' HOURS, COMMUNITY 248 – 252
DRIVERS' HOURS, DOMESTIC 253 – 258
RECORDS, APPLICATION 259 – 262
RECORDING EQUIPMENT 263 – 278
PROHIBITION OF DRIVING FOREIGN VEHICLES 279 – 281
WORKING TIME 282

Part 5: MISCELLANEOUS 283

TESTING ON ROADS 284 – 285
TESTING ON PREMISES 286
REMOVAL OF VEHICLES 287
MOTOR SALVAGE OPERATORS 288
TAKING A CONVEYANCE WITHOUT AUTHORITY 289
VEHICLE INTERFERENCE 290
DRINK/DRIVING 291 – 299
SPEED LIMITS 300 – 303
SPEED LIMITERS 304 – 305
DANGEROUS SUBSTANCES 306 – 330
ANIMALS IN TRANSIT 331 – 333
REPORTING OF ACCIDENTS 334
DUTY TO GIVE INFORMATION AS TO DRIVER 335
POWERS OF ARREST 336 – 338
ROAD CHECKS 339
STOP AND SEARCH 340

POWER TO STOP VEHICLES 341
SEIZURE OF VEHICLES 342
TAXI TOUTS 343
BUILDERS' SKIPS 344
NOTICE OF INTENDED PROSECUTION 345
CRASH HELMETS 346
EYE PROTECTORS 347
MOTORWAYS 348
EYESIGHT 349
PHYSICAL HEALTH 349
STOPPING DISTANCES 349
DRIVER INSTRUCTION 350
PEDESTRIAN CROSSINGS 351
MISCELLANEOUS DRIVING OFFENCES 352
PARKING 354

Part 6: SUPPLEMENT FOR SCOTLAND 355

INTRODUCTION 356
DEFINITION (ROAD) 357
BUILDER'S SKIPS 358 – 359
OBSTRUCTION OF ROADS 360
PLACING BRIDGES 361
MUD ON ROAD 362
DAMAGE TO ROADS 363
ROPES, etc. IN ROAD 364
AIDING AND ABETTING 365
TAKING VEHICLE WITHOUT AUTHORITY 366
USE OF TELEPHONES 367
POWER OF ARREST 368
PEDAL CYCLES 369 – 370
DRINK, DRUGS & DRIVING 371 – 372
RESTRICTION ON USE OF RIGHT-HAND LANE 373

CONVERSION TABLES 375–376

TABLE OF LEGISLATION 377–388

INDEX 389–394

PART 1

CONSTRUCTION
AND USE

In Part 1 we will start with relevant vehicle
definitions, and then go on to consider some
of the more complex issues of Construction
and Use (C&U) Regulations in
summarised form, aided by a series of
diagrams

VEHICLE DEFINITIONS

Before we go on to consider the main contents of this book, we should consider some of the more important vehicle definitions you are likely to encounter.

MOTOR VEHICLE

Mechanically propelled vehicle intended or adapted for use on the roads.

REG 3 ROAD VEHICLES (CONSTRUCTION AND USE) REGULATIONS 1986

NOTE

The term **'mechanically propelled'** includes all known means of propulsion, e.g. petrol, diesel, gas, electricity. The test for whether a mechanically propelled vehicle is a motor vehicle is simply that of establishing if the vehicle in question is intended or adapted for use on a road. If the vehicle meets that criteria it is a motor vehicle, if it does not it is a mechanically propelled vehicle.

The Road Traffic Act 1991 made amendments to the Road Traffic Act 1988 which resulted in many (but not all) offences which related to motor vehicles being extended to the wider term of mechanically propelled vehicle.

MOTOR CAR

Under the C&U Regulations, a **'motor car'** is a mechanically propelled vehicle, not being a motor tractor, motor cycle or invalid carriage, constructed and adapted for load or passengers, unladen weight (UW) not exceeding:

- if not more than seven passengers and effects, 3,050 kg;
- if for goods or burden, 3,050 kg; and
- in any other case, 2,540 kg.

REG 3 ROAD VEHICLES (CONSTRUCTION AND USE) REGULATIONS 1986

However, under the RTA 1988 a **'motor car'** is a mechanically propelled vehicle, not being a motor cycle or invalid carriage, which is constructed itself to carry a load or passengers and of which the UW:

- does not exceed 3,050 kg if constructed solely for the carriage of not more than seven passengers and their effects and is fitted with pneumatic tyres;
- does not exceed 3,050 kg (3,500 kg if gas propelled) if constructed or adapted for the conveyance of goods or burden of any description;
- does not exceed 2,540 kg in cases falling within neither of the above descriptions.

SECTION 185 ROAD TRAFFIC ACT 1988

You will have noted that there is little difference between the two definitions. However, you must apply the C&U definition to vehicles coming within the scope of those Regulations and the RTA definition to vehicles coming within the scope of that legislation.

Matters are further complicated by the insertion of a third definition by S 141A of the RTA 1988 for the purposes of Part V of the Act (Driving Instruction):
'a motor vehicle (other than an invalid carriage or motor cycle)
(a) not constructed or adapted to carry more than 9 persons inclusive of the driver, and
(b) which has a maximum gross weight not exceeding 3.5 tonnes' (S.I. 1996/1974).

HEAVY MOTOR CAR

Under the C&U Regulations, a heavy motor car is a mechanically propelled vehicle, not being a locomotive, motor tractor or motor car, which is constructed itself to carry a load or passengers, UW exceeds 2,540 kg,

REG 3 ROAD VEHICLES (CONSTRUCTION AND USE) REGULATIONS 1986

Under the RTA 1988 it is a mechanically propelled vehicle, not being a motor car, which is constructed itself to carry a load or passengers and the UW exceeds 2,540 kg.

SECTION 185 ROAD TRAFFIC ACT 1988

MOTOR TRACTOR

Mechanically propelled vehicle not constructed itself to carry a load other than equipment for propulsion, loose tools and loose equipment, UW not exceeding 7,370 kg.

SECTION 185 ROAD TRAFFIC ACT 1988

LIGHT LOCOMOTIVE

Mechanically propelled vehicle not itself constructed to carry load other than equipment for propulsion, loose tools and loose equipment, UW exceeding 7,320 kg but not exceeding 11,690 kg.

SECTION 185(1) ROAD TRAFFIC ACT 1988

HEAVY LOCOMOTIVE

Mechanically propelled vehicle not itself constructed to carry load other than equipment for propulsion, loose tools and loose equipment, UW exceeding 11,690 kg.

SECTION 185(1) ROAD TRAFFIC ACT 1988

GOODS VEHICLE

Motor vehicle or trailer constructed or adapted for use for carriage or haulage of goods or burden of any description.

REG 3 ROAD VEHICLES (CONSTRUCTION AND USE) REGULATIONS 1986

(See later for large and medium-sized goods vehicle.)

ARTICULATED VEHICLE

Under the C&U Regulations 1986, an articulated vehicle is a heavy motor car, or motor car not being an articulated bus, with trailer so attached that part of the trailer is superimposed upon the drawing vehicle and not less than 20 per cent of weight of load is borne by drawing vehicle.

REG 3 ROAD VEHICLES (CONSTRUCTION AND USE) REGULATIONS 1986

Under the RTA 1988 an articulated vehicle is:
a)   a vehicle so constructed that it can be divided into two parts
- both of which are vehicles, and one of which is a motor vehicle
- and shall (when not so divided) be treated as that motor vehicle with the part attached as a trailer; or
b)   a passenger vehicle (i.e. a vehicle constructed or adapted for use solely or principally for carriage of passengers) so constructed that it can be divided into two parts
- both of which are vehicles and one of which is a motor vehicle
- but cannot be so divided without the use of facilities normally available only at a workshop
- and passengers carried by it, when not so divided can at all times pass from either part to the other, and
- it shall, when not so divided, be treated as a single motor vehicle.

SECTION 187 ROAD TRAFFIC ACT 1988

DUAL PURPOSE VEHICLE

A vehicle constructed and adapted for both the carriage of passengers and goods UW not exceeding 2,040 kg and:
a)   is so constructed or adapted that the driving power of the engine is, or by appropriate use of the controls can be, transmitted to all wheels of the vehicle, or
b)   it is constructed so that:
- it has a rigid roof, with or without a sliding roof panel,
- the area of the vehicle to the rear of the driver's seat must have at least one row of properly upholstered transverse seats (fixed or folding) capable of carrying at least two persons,
- the distance between the steering wheel and the backrest of the rear most seats must not be less than one third of the distance between the steering wheel and the rearmost part of the floor, and
- the windows to rear of drivers seat must have an area of not less than 1,850 sq cm on either side and not less than 770 sq cm at the rear.

REG 3 ROAD VEHICLES (CONSTRUCTION AND USE) REGULATIONS 1986

MEDIUM-SIZED GOODS VEHICLE

A motor vehicle which is constructed or adapted to carry or to haul goods and is not adapted to carry more than nine persons inclusive of the driver and the permissible maximum weight of which exceeds 3.5 but not 7.5 tonnes.   SECTION 108(1) ROAD TRAFFIC ACT 1988

SMALL VEHICLE

NOTE: The terms 'small goods' and 'small passenger vehicles' have now been replaced by the new term 'small vehicle'.

A small vehicle is a motor vehicle, other than an invalid carriage, moped or motor bicycle which:
a) is not constructed to carry more than nine passengers inclusive of the driver; and
b) has a maximum gross weight not exceeding 3.5 tonnes; and includes a combination of such motor vehicle and trailer.

INVALID CARRIAGE

A mechanically propelled vehicle, the weight of which unladen does not exceed 254 kg and which is specially designed and constructed – not merely adapted – for use of a person suffering from some physical defect or disability and is used solely by such a person.

REG 3 ROAD VEHICLES (CONSTRUCTION AND USE) REGULATIONS 1986
AND SECTION 185(1) ROAD TRAFFIC ACT 1988

LARGE GOODS VEHICLE

A motor vehicle (not being a medium-sized goods vehicle) which is constructed or adapted to carry or to haul goods and the maximum permissible weight of which exceeds 7.5 tonnes.

SECTION 121 ROAD TRAFFIC ACT 1988

MOTOR CYCLE

Mechanically propelled vehicle, not being an invalid carriage, with less than four wheels and the weight unladen does not exceed 410 kg.

REG 3(1) ROAD VEHICLES (CONSTRUCTION AND USE) REGULATIONS 1986
AND SECTION 185(1) ROAD TRAFFIC ACT 1988

MOPED
first used on or after 1.8.77

This is a motor cycle, not being a mowing machine or a pedestrian controlled vehicle, which has a maximum design speed which does not exceed 30 mph, a kerbside weight which does not exceed 250 kg and, if propelled by an internal combustion engine, an engine which does not exceed 50 cc. Alternatively;

first used before 1.8.77

A motor cycle which has an engine with a cylinder capacity not exceeding 50cc and is equipped with pedals by means of which the cycle is capable of being propelled.

REG 3 MOTOR VEHICLES (DRIVING LICENCES) REGULATIONS 1987

PASSENGER CARRYING VEHICLE

(a) **large passenger carrying vehicle**, that is to say, a vehicle used for carrying passengers which is contructed or adapted to carry more than 16 passengers, or
(b) **a small passenger carrying vehicle**, that is to say, a vehicle used for carrying passengers for hire or reward which is constructed or adapted to carry more than 8 but not more than 16 passengers, and includes a combination of such a motor vehicle and a trailer.

SECTION 121 ROAD TRAFFIC ACT 1988

INTERNATIONAL CATEGORIES
COMMUNITY DIRECTIVE 70/156

The following categories of vehicle had been defined and are referred to in various S.I.s. Where a reference is made to 'maximum mass' this means 'technically permissible maximum laden mass'.

Category	Description
M	Motor vehicles having at least 4 wheels, designed and constructed for the carriage of passengers.
M_1	Vehicles designed and constructed for the carriage of passengers and comprising no more than 8 seats in addition to the driver's seat.
M_2	Vehicles designed and constructed for the carriage of passengers, comprising more than 8 seats in addition to the driver's seat, and having a maximum mass not exceeding 5 tonnes.
M_3	Vehicles designed and constructed for the carriage of passengers, comprising more than 8 seats in addition to the driver's seat, and having a maximum mass exceeding 5 tonnes.
N	Motor vehicles having at least 4 wheels, designed and constructed for the carriage of goods.
N_1	Vehicles designed and constructed for the carriage of goods and having a maximum mass not exceeding 3.5 tonnes.
N_2	Vehicles designed and constructed for the carriage of goods and having a maximum mass exceeding 3.5 tonnes but not exceeding 12 tonnes.
N_3	Vehicles designed and constructed for the carriage of goods and having a maximum mass exceeding 12 tonnes.

In the case of a towing vehicle designed to be coupled to a semi-trailer or centre-axle trailer, the mass to be considered for classifying the vehicle is the mass of the tractor vehicle in running order, increased by the mass corresponding to the maximum static vertical load transferred to the tractor vehicle by the semi-trailer or centre-axle trailer and, where applicable, by the maximum mass of the tractor vehicle's own load.

O	Trailers (including semi-trailers).
O_1	Trailers with a maximum mass not exceeding 0.75 tonnes.
O_2	Trailers with a maximum mass exceeding 0.75 tonnes but not exceeding 3.5 tonnes.
O_3	Trailers with a maximum mass exceeding 3.5 tonnes but not exceeding 10 tonnes.
O_4	Trailers with a maximum mass exceeding 10 tonnes.

In the case of a semi-trailer or centre-axle trailer, the maximum mass to be considered for classifying the trailer corresponds to the static vertical load transmitted to the ground by the axle or axles of the semi-trailer or centre-axle trailer when coupled to the towing vehicle and carrying its maximum load.

MAXIMUM LENGTH

REG 7 ROAD VEHICLE (CONSTRUCTION AND USE) REGULATIONS 1986
If the maximum is exceeded refer to 'special types' (see later)

Vehicle combinations

(1) Motor vehicle (not mentioned in (2) below) drawing one trailer which is not a semi-trailer – **18.75 m.**

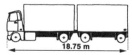

(IF SHOWMAN'S VEHICLE AND LIVING ACCOMMODATION TRAILER – 22 **m**)

(2) Until 31.12.2006, motor vehicle manufactured before 1.6.98 drawing one trailer where:
  (a) distance from foremost point of loading area behind the drivers cab to rear of trailer (marked 'A' below) less distance between rear of motor vehicle and the front of the trailer ('B') exceeds 15.65 m, and
  (b) distance (A) does not exceed 16.4 m, and the trailer is not a semi-trailer – **18 m.**

> **Notes** (1) The thickness of any wall at the forward end of the loading area shall be regarded as part of the loading area
> (2) any towing attachment in area 'B' shall be disregarded.

(3) Articulated bus – **18.75 m**
Bus drawing a trailer – **18.75 m**

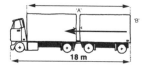

(4)

Articulated vehicle, where:
  (a) distance from king pin to rear of semi-trailer (A) does not exceed –
    (i) 12.5 m in the case of a car transporter, or
    (ii) 12 m in any other case; and
  (b) distance between king pin to front of trailer (B) does not exceed –
    (i) 4.19 m in the case of a car transporter or
    (ii) 2.04 m in any other case, and is not a low loader – **16.5 m.**

> Notes Where there is more than 1 king-pin, where the vehicle was manufactured after 1.1.99, the measurement is taken from the foremost king-pin, otherwise the rearmost is used.

(5) Articulated vehicle where the semi-trailer does not meet the above requirements and is not a low loader – **15.5 m.**

(6) Articulated vehicle where semi-trailer is a low loader – **18 m.**

Motor Vehicles

(7) A wheeled motor vehicle other than a bus – **12 m**.

(IF TRACK-LAYING 9.2 m)

(8) A bus with 2 axles – **13.5 m.**
(9) A bus with more than 2 axles – **15 m.**

Trailers (See also notes on following page)

(10) Agricultural trailed appliance manufactured on or after 1.12.1985 – **15 m**.
(11) Semi-trailer manufactured on or after 1.5.1983 which does not meet the requirements mentioned in item (4) above and is not a low loader – **12.2 m**.

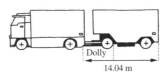

12.2 m

(12) Composite trailer (combination of converter dolly and trailer) drawn by
   (a) a goods vehicle over 3,500 kg maximum gross weight or
   (b) an agricultural motor vehicle – **14.04 m.**

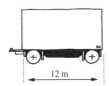

Dolly

14.04 m

(13) Trailer (not being a semi-trailer or composite trailer) with at least 4 wheels, which is
   (a) drawn by a goods vehicle over 3,500 kg gross vehicle weight or
   (b) an agricultural trailer – **12 m**.

12 m

(14) Any other trailer not being an agricultural trailed appliance or semi-trailer – **7 m**.

Notes:

(1) Items 1, 2, 4, 5, & 6 do not apply to indivisible load trailers, to broken down vehicles being towed, nor to an articulated vehicle with low loader semi-trailer manufactured before 1.4.91.

(2) Items 10 to 14 do not apply to indivisible load trailers, to broken down vehicles being towed, nor to a trailer being drying or mixing plant for tarmacadam, etc. used for road construction, or a road planing machine so used.

(3) Item 11 does not apply to a semi-trailer which is a car transporter, or normally used for international journeys.

(4) Where a motor vehicle is drawing –
   (a) 2 trailers, only 1 may exceed 7 m
   (b) 3 trailers, none may exceed 7 m
   Note: A broken down articulated vehicle being towed is regarded as being only 1 trailer.

(5) Where a motor vehicle is drawing –
   (a) 2 or more trailers, or
   (b) 1 trailer for indivisible loads of exceptional length, then
       (i) overall length of motor vehicle not to exceed 9.2 m, and
       (ii) overall length of combination not to exceed 25.9 m unless 2 days notice is given to the police and at least 1 attendant is carried.

(6) A motor vehicle drawing a trailer which is not a semi-trailer must not exceed the requirements mentioned in item 2.

(7) A trailer over 18.65 m may only be used if 2 days notice is given to the police and an attendant is carried.

CALCULATION OF LENGTH

ROAD VEHICLES (CONSTRUCTION AND USE) REGULATIONS 1986
REGS 7 & 81

The overall length of a combination of vehicles is calculated in accordance with the following:

(1) Where there are 1 or more trailers being drawn, the combination includes any other motor vehicle which is assisting in the propulsion of the trailer(s).

(2) Measurement of the foremost and rearmost points of the combination are taken in the same vertical plane:

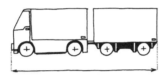

(3) References to the front of the vehicle, rear of the vehicle and king-pin means the transverse plane passing through each:

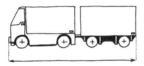

(4) References to the front and rear of the vehicle includes all parts of the vehicle, any receptacle which is a permanent fitting and strong enough for repeated use, and any fitting on or attached to the vehicle but excluding:

(a) driving mirror
(b) expanding or extending turntable fire escape
(c) snow plough
(d) customs clearance seals
(e) tailboard let down when vehicle is stationary for loading/unloading
(f) tailboard let down to accommodate long loads
(g) fittings etc, on vehicles or receptacles to enable it/them to be transferred to or from a road vehicle to or from a railway vehicle
(h) bridging plate on trailer to allow vehicles to be moved between that trailer and the attached drawing motor vehicle
(i) sheeting or other flexible means for covering or securing a load
(j) empty receptacle forming a load
(k) receptacle containing indivisible load of exceptional length
(l) receptacle manufactured before 30.10.85 not being a maritime container
(m) special appliance (crane, etc) which is a permanently fitted fixture
(n) rearward projecting buffer
(o) in the case of a semi-trailer, any part designed to attach it to another vehicle (but not the drawbar, etc, of an agricultural trailed appliance).

OVERHANG

REGS 3(1) AND 11(1) ROAD VEHICLES (CONSTRUCTION AND USE) REGS 1986

Overhang **'x'** (see diagrams showing categories 1–4 below) must not exceed:	**EXCEPT**

FOR MOTOR TRACTOR
1.83 m (except track-laying vehicle and agricultural motor vehicle)

FOR HEAVY MOTOR CAR AND MOTOR CAR
60% of **'y'**

EXCEPT
(a) bus
(b) refuse vehicle
(c) works truck
(d) track-laying vehicle
(e) agricultural motor vehicle
(f) motor car which is an ambulance
(g) vehicle disposing of its load to the rear (max 1.15 m overhang)
(h) vehicle first used before 2.1.33
(i) vehicle first used before 1.1.66 if (i) distance between rearmost and foremost axles does not exceed 2.29 m, and (ii) overhang does not exceed 76 mm
(j) heating plant on road surface heating vehicle
(k) heavy motor car meeting the turning circle requirements of Comm Directive 97/27, para 7.6.2 of Annex I

1. motor vehicle with not more than three axles – and only one is not a steering axle

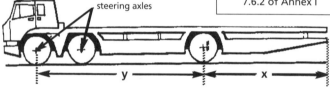

steering axles

y   x

2. motor vehicle with three axles if only front one steers, and
3. motor vehicle with four axles if only front two steer:

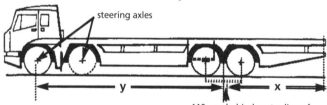

steering axles

y   x

110 mm behind centre line of two rearmost axles

4. any other case

y

'y'= the distance between the centre of the foremost wheel and a point along the length of the vehicle from which a line drawn at right angles would pass through the centre of the minimum turning circle of the vehicle.

TURNING CIRCLES
ROAD VEHICLES (CONSTRUCTION AND USE) REGULATIONS 1986

Subject to the provisions mentioned below, buses, articulated vehicles and heavy motor cars must be able to turn on either lock, both with and without all its wheels in contact with the ground, so that no part of the vehicle projects outside the area between concentric circles with radii of 12.5 m and 5.3 m. If manufactured before 1.6.98, the reference to 'with and without all wheels on the ground' does not apply.

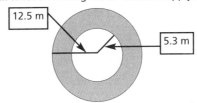

(1) **Buses. (Reg.13)** Only applies to buses first used on or after 1.4.82.

(2) **Articulated vehicles other than car transporters. (Reg.13A)** Does not apply to:
   a) semi-trailer manufactured before 1.4.90 and has not been lengthened since then;
   b) car transporter;
   c) low loader;
   d) semi-trailer constructed for indivisible long loads;
   e) vehicle with overall length not over 15.5 m and either the drawing vehicle or trailer was first used before 1.6.98;
   f) vehicle when axle is raised to add traction; or
   g) projections set out in paras. (a) to (m) in definition of 'overall width' (see later) or in paras. (4)(a) to (o) in 'Calculation of Length' page (see earlier).

(3) **Articulated vehicles incorporating a car transporter. (Reg.13B)** Applies to vehicles with overall length over 15.5 m. Regs. do not apply to:
   a) semi-trailer manufactured before 1.4.90 and has not been lengthened since then;
   b) low loader;
   c) stepframe low loader; or
   d) projections set out in paras. (a) to (m) in definition of 'overall width' (see later) or in paras. (4)(a) to (o) in 'Calculation of Length' (see earlier).

(4) **Heavy motor car. (Reg.13C)** Manufactured after 31.5.98. Includes when drawing a trailer which is not a semi-trailer. Does not apply to vehicles included in one of the above categories; to a vehicle with 4 or more axles where distance between front and rear axles exceeds 6.4 m; to vehicles constructed for indivisible long loads; or to projections set out in paras. (a) to (m) in definition of 'overall width' (see later) or in paras. (4)(a) to (o) in 'Calculation of Length' (see earlier).

MINIMUM GROUND CLEARANCE

ROAD VEHICLES (CONSTRUCTION AND USE) REGULATIONS 1986
REG 12.

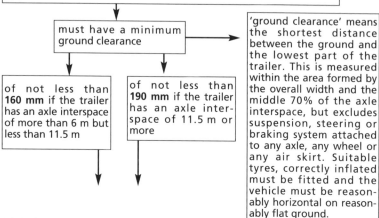

A wheeled trailer which is a goods vehicle manufactured on or after 1.4.84.

must have a minimum ground clearance

of not less than **160 mm** if the trailer has an axle interspace of more than 6 m but less than 11.5 m

of not less than **190 mm** if the trailer has an axle interspace of 11.5 m or more

'ground clearance' means the shortest distance between the ground and the lowest part of the trailer. This is measured within the area formed by the overall width and the middle 70% of the axle interspace, but excludes suspension, steering or braking system attached to any axle, any wheel or any air skirt. Suitable tyres, correctly inflated must be fitted and the vehicle must be reasonably horizontal on reasonably flat ground.

"Axle interspace" means:

(a) **Semi-trailer**, the distance between the point of support of the semi-trailer at its forward end and the centre of the rear axle (or if more than 1 rear axle, the point half way between the centres of the foremost and rearmost axles).

(b) **Any other trailer**, the distance between the centre of the front axle (or if more than one, the point halfway between the foremost and rearmost axles) and the centre of the rear axle (or if more than one, the point halfway between the centre of the foremost and rearmost axles).

SEMI-TRAILER

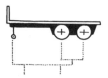

measurement taken in middle 70%

ANY OTHER TRAILER

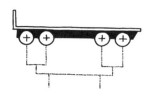

measurement taken in middle 70%

Exemptions

The requirement does not apply to a trailer –

(a) fitted with adjustable suspension to lower the trailer to clear bridges etc, while being operated, (but must not touch the ground), or

(b) while being loaded or unloaded.

MAXIMUM WIDTH

REG 8 (CONSTRUCTION AND USE) REGULATIONS 1986

If the maximum is exceeded, refer to 'Special Types' (see later).

Locomotive	**2.75 m**
Refrigerated vehicle A vehicle specially designed for the carriage of goods at low temperatures and the thickness of each side-wall including insulation is at least 45 mm	**2.6 m**
Any other motor vehicle	**2.55 m**
Trailer drawn by a motor vehicle (having max gross weight exceeding 3,500 kg) **Agricultural trailer,** **Agricultural trailed appliance,** **or an off-set combination of an agricultural motor vehicle drawing a wheeled trailer**	**2.55 m**
Any other trailer drawn by a vehicle other than a motor cycle	**2.3 m**
Trailer drawn by motor cycle	**1.5 m**

CALCULATION OF WIDTH
ROAD VEHICLES (CONSTRUCTION AND USE) REGULATIONS 1986

'Lateral projection' (Reg.81) means that part of the load which extends beyond a side of the vehicle. The width of any lateral projection is to be measured between longitudinal planes passing through the extreme projecting point on that side and that part of the projection furthest from that point:

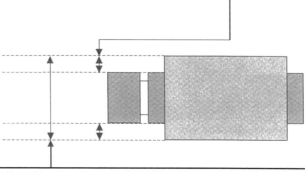

'Overall width' (Reg.3) means the distance between longitudinal planes passing through the extreme lateral projecting points of the vehicle including all parts of the vehicle, any permanent receptacle which is strong enough for repeated use, and any fitting on, or attached to, the vehicle except-

a) Driving mirror;
b) Snow plough fixed to the front;
c) Distortion of the tyre caused by the weight of the vehicle;
d) Customs seals;
e) Lamp or reflector fitted in accordance with the Lighting Regulations;
f) Sideboard let down while vehicle is stationary, for loading or unloading;
g) Any fitting or receptacle which does not increase the carrying capacity of the vehicle, but which allows it to be transferred to or from a railway vehicle; is secured to a railway vehicle by a locking device; and carried on a railway vehicle by the use of stanchions;
h) Sheeting or other flexible means of covering or securing the load;
i) Receptacle with external width not over 2.5 m;
j) Empty receptacle which itself forms a load;
k) A receptacle which contains an indivisible wide load;
l) A receptacle manufactured before 30.10.85, not being a maritime container;
m) A permanent crane, special appliance or apparatus, which does not increase the carrying capacity of the vehicle;
n) Apparatus fitted to a bus to guide it by wheels bearing outwards provided it does not project more than 75 mm beyond the side of the bus.

MAXIMUM HEIGHT – BUSES

REG.9 ROAD VEHICLES (CONSTRUCTION AND USE) REGULATIONS 1986

DEFINITION

A bus is a motor vehicle constructed or adapted to carry more than eight seated passengers in addition to the driver.

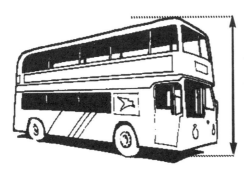

The overall height of a bus shall not exceed **4.57 m**

NOTE: See later this section for overall travelling heights

WEIGHT

Regulations prohibiting excess axle weight are designed primarily to prevent damage to the road surfaces and foundations, while those relating to excess overall weight are aimed at ensuring the design limits are not exceeded and that the vehicle can stop within the distance for which its brakes were designed. There are therefore separate offences of:

excess axle weight and
excess overall weight.

> All locomotives, motor tractors, and heavy motor cars must have the unladen weight (UW) marked on the near side of the vehicle.

Vehicles should be equipped with a

Manufacturer's plate and a
Ministry plate*

containing details of the maximum axle, gross and train weights.

Offences may be committed if the maximum permitted weight contained in C&U Regulations 1986, the manufacturer's plate or the Ministry plate are exceeded. *The following chart may be a guide to procedure:*

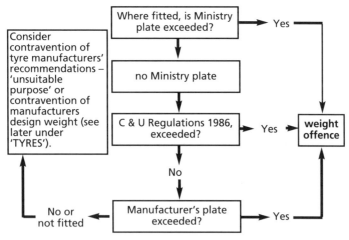

NOTE: *For further details see Plating of goods vehicles, in Part 2.

POWER TO WEIGH VEHICLES
ROAD TRAFFIC ACT 1988

Failure to comply or obstructing the exercise of functions is an offence
(S 78(3))

On production of his authority **a constable authorised by the chief constable** may require a person in charge of a motor vehicle to
1. proceed to a weighbridge (or other machine for weighing vehicles)
2. allow the vehicle or trailer to be weighed, either laden or unladen and the weight transmitted to the road by any part of the vehicle or trailer in contact with the road to be tested.
S 78(1)

NOTE: An authorised officer has no power to require the person in charge of a motor vehicle to unload the vehicle or trailer or to cause or allow it to be unloaded in order to have it weighed unladen. S 78(4)

Where a goods vehicle or a motor vehicle adapted to carry more than eight passengers has been weighed under the provision of S 78, and it appears to the authorised officer that the weights imposed by the C&U Regulations 1986 have been exceeded – or would be exceeded were it used on a road – he may give notice* in writing to the person in charge of the vehicle prohibiting it being driven on a road until
(a) the weight is reduced to the limit, and
(b) the person in charge has been notified in writing that it is allowed to proceed. S 70(2)

* This notice may be withheld until the vehicle has been weighed to satisfy the constable that the weight has been sufficiently reduced.
S 70(4)

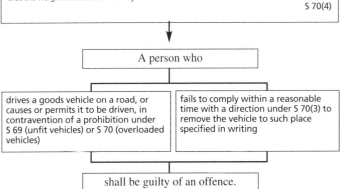

A person who

| drives a goods vehicle on a road, or causes or permits it to be driven, in contravention of a prohibition under S 69 (unfit vehicles) or S 70 (overloaded vehicles) | fails to comply within a reasonable time with a direction under S 70(3) to remove the vehicle to such place specified in writing |

shall be guilty of an offence.

S 71(1) (AS SUBSTITUTED BY S 14 RTA 1991)

MAXIMUM OVERALL WEIGHT
ROAD VEHICLES (CONSTRUCTION AND USE) REGULATIONS 1986

If the maximum is exceeded, refer to 'Special Types' (see later).

Most of the maximum weight for combinations, vehicles and axles are contained in regulations 75 to 79. However, under certain circumstances the maximum weight may be exceeded, as authorised by the Road Vehicles (Authorised Weight) Regulations 1998 (see later under Additional Authorised Weights).

LOCOMOTIVE   REG 75

If fitted with suitable tyres & springs:

with less than 6 wheels	22,360 kg
with 6 wheels	26,420 kg
more than 6 wheels	30,490 kg

Not conforming as above   20,830 kg

Total weight of all trailers laden or unladen, drawn by a locomotive   44,000 kg

BUS   REGS 75 & 78

The maximum permitted laden weight is the same as a heavy motor car or motor car but the weight is calculated when the vehicle is complete and fully equipped for service with:

roof luggage space – uniformly distributed load at 75 kg per sq m

63.5 kg per person who could legally be carried (65 kg if bus first used after 1.4.88)

100 kg per cubic metre of luggage space or 10 kg per person who could legally be carried whichever is less

full supply of water, oil and fuel

MAXIMUM OVERALL WEIGHT cont
ROAD VEHICLES (CONSTRUCTION AND USE) REGULATIONS 1986

If the maximum is exceeded, refer to 'Special Types' (see later).

VEHICLE WITH TRAILER   (REG 76)

The **total laden weight** of a trailer together with that of any motor tractor, heavy motor car or motor car drawing such trailer

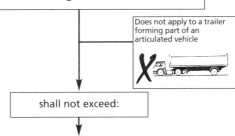

Does not apply to a trailer forming part of an articulated vehicle

shall not exceed:

if trailer and vehicle both have wheels and: combination has total of 4 axles; and drawing vehicle first used on or after 1.4.73 and has relevant brakes	35,000 kg
as above but with total of 5 or more axles	38,000 kg
if trailer and vehicle are not mentioned above and both have wheels – and brakes as below a) power assisted brakes b) brakes can be operated by driver of drawing vehicle c) brakes will not become ineffective when engine is switched off d) drawing vehicle has warning device, visible to driver, to indicate impending failure of braking system	32,520 kg
a wheeled trailer manufactured on or after 27.2.77 and fitted with automatic brakes, drawn by a vehicle first used on or after 1.4.73 and has relevant brakes	29,500 kg
if trailer and vehicle are not mentioned above and both have wheels	24,390 kg
if trailer or vehicle is track laying	22,360 kg

MAXIMUM OVERALL WEIGHT cont

RIGID VEHICLES (REG 75)

The sum of the weights transmitted to the road surface by all the wheels of a heavy motor car, motor car or trailer, — in each case not forming part of an articulated vehicle,

which:
a) complies with the relevant braking requirements;
b) every driving axle other than a steering axle has twin tyres; and
c) either every driving axle has road-friendly* suspension or does not exceed 9,500 kg;

shall not exceed:

*Road-friendly suspension means air suspension or equivalent.

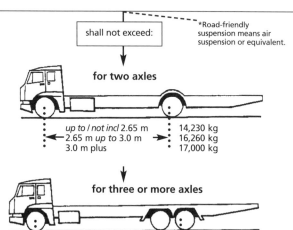

for two axles

up to / not incl 2.65 m	14,230 kg
2.65 m *up to* 3.0 m	16,260 kg
3.0 m plus	17,000 kg

for three or more axles

Distance between foremost and rearmost axles (m)

Distance between foremost and rearmost axles (m)	Maximum axle weight	Maximum permitted laden weight
up to but not incl 3.0 m	10,170 kg	16,260 kg
3.0 m *up to* 3.2 m	10,170 kg	18,290 kg
3.2 m *up to* 3.9 m	10,170 kg	20,330 kg
3.9 m *up to* 4.9 m	10,170 kg	22,360 kg
4.9 m *up to* 5.2 m	10,170 kg	25,000 kg
5.2 m *plus*	10,170 kg	26,000 kg

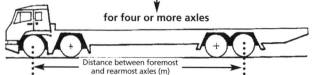

for four or more axles

Distance between foremost and rearmost axles (m)

Distance between foremost and rearmost axles (m)	Maximum permitted laden weight
5.2 m *up to / not incl* 6.4 m	distance (m) x 5,000 rounded up to next 10 kg
6.4 m *plus*	32,000 kg

MAXIMUM OVERALL WEIGHT cont
ROAD VEHICLES (CONSTRUCTION AND USE) REGULATIONS 1986

If the maximum is exceeded, refer to 'Special Types' (see later).

RIGID VEHICLES cont (REG 75)

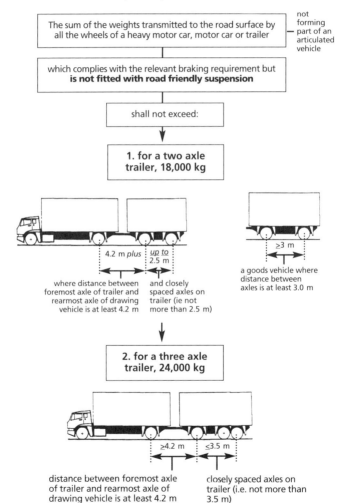

The sum of the weights transmitted to the road surface by all the wheels of a heavy motor car, motor car or trailer

not forming part of an articulated vehicle

which complies with the relevant braking requirement but **is not fitted with road friendly suspension**

shall not exceed:

1. for a two axle trailer, 18,000 kg

4.2 m *plus* | *up to* 2.5 m

where distance between foremost axle of trailer and rearmost axle of drawing vehicle is at least 4.2 m

and closely spaced axles on trailer (ie not more than 2.5 m)

≥3 m

a goods vehicle where distance between axles is at least 3.0 m

2. for a three axle trailer, 24,000 kg

≥4.2 m | ≤3.5 m

distance between foremost axle of trailer and rearmost axle of drawing vehicle is at least 4.2 m

closely spaced axles on trailer (i.e. not more than 3.5 m)

continued on following page

MAXIMUM OVERALL WEIGHT cont
ROAD VEHICLES (CONSTRUCTION AND USE) REGULATIONS 1986

If the maximum is exceeded, refer to 'Special Types' (see later).

RIGID VEHICLES cont   (REG 75)

continued from previous page

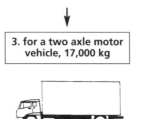

> **3. for a two axle motor vehicle, 17,000 kg**

≥3 m

a goods vehicle where distance
between axles is at least 3.0 m

If the vehicle is not within the description of the above three categories, max weight is as follows:

No of axles	Distance between foremost and rearmost axles	Max laden weight
2	*up to/not incl* 2.65 m	14,230 kg
2	2.65 m *plus*	16,260 kg
3 or more	*up to* 3.0 m	16,260 kg
3 or more	3.0 m *up to* 3.2 m	18,290 kg
3 or more	3.2 m *up to* 3.9 m	20,330 kg
3 or more	3.9 m *up to* 4.9 m	22,360 kg
3	4.9 m *plus*	25,000 kg
4 or more	4.9 m *up to* 5.6 m	25,000 kg
4 or more	5.6 m *up to* 5.9 m	26,420 kg
4 or more	5.9 m *up to* 6.3 m	28,450 kg
4 or more	6.3 m *plus*	30,000 kg

MAXIMUM OVERALL WEIGHT cont
REGS 75 & 77 & SCHED 11 ROAD VEHICLES (C&U) REGS 1986

If the maximum is exceeded, please refer to 'Special Types' (see later).
GVW=Gross Vehicle Weight, GCW=Gross Combined Weight

ARTICULATED

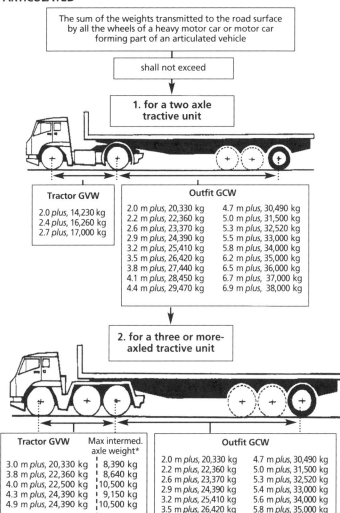

The sum of the weights transmitted to the road surface by all the wheels of a heavy motor car or motor car forming part of an articulated vehicle

shall not exceed

1. for a two axle tractive unit

Tractor GVW

2.0 *plus*, 14,230 kg	
2.4 *plus*, 16,260 kg	
2.7 *plus*, 17,000 kg	

Outfit GCW

2.0 m *plus*, 20,330 kg	4.7 m *plus*, 30,490 kg
2.2 m *plus*, 22,360 kg	5.0 m *plus*, 31,500 kg
2.6 m *plus*, 23,370 kg	5.3 m *plus*, 32,520 kg
2.9 m *plus*, 24,390 kg	5.5 m *plus*, 33,000 kg
3.2 m *plus*, 25,410 kg	5.8 m *plus*, 34,000 kg
3.5 m *plus*, 26,420 kg	6.2 m *plus*, 35,000 kg
3.8 m *plus*, 27,440 kg	6.5 m *plus*, 36,000 kg
4.1 m *plus*, 28,450 kg	6.7 m *plus*, 37,000 kg
4.4 m *plus*, 29,470 kg	6.9 m *plus*, 38,000 kg

2. for a three or more-axled tractive unit

Tractor GVW | **Max intermed. axle weight***

Tractor GVW	Max intermed. axle weight*
3.0 m *plus*, 20,330 kg	8,390 kg
3.8 m *plus*, 22,360 kg	8,640 kg
4.0 m *plus*, 22,500 kg	10,500 kg
4.3 m *plus*, 24,390 kg	9,150 kg
4.9 m *plus*, 24,390 kg	10,500 kg

Outfit GCW

2.0 m *plus*, 20,330 kg	4.7 m *plus*, 30,490 kg
2.2 m *plus*, 22,360 kg	5.0 m *plus*, 31,500 kg
2.6 m *plus*, 23,370 kg	5.3 m *plus*, 32,520 kg
2.9 m *plus*, 24,390 kg	5.4 m *plus*, 33,000 kg
3.2 m *plus*, 25,410 kg	5.6 m *plus*, 34,000 kg
3.5 m *plus*, 26,420 kg	5.8 m *plus*, 35,000 kg
3.8 m *plus*, 27,440 kg	6.0 m *plus*, 36,000 kg
4.1 m *plus*, 28,450 kg	6.2 m *plus*, 37,000 kg
4.4 m *plus*, 29,470 kg	6.3 m *plus*, 38,000 kg

* Maximum intermediate axle weight, as shown in column 2 of the DTP plate, or, where the vehicle has not been fitted with a DTP plate, on the manufacturer's plate.

continued on following page

MAXIMUM OVERALL WEIGHT cont

ARTICULATED cont

HOWEVER

Articulated vehicles with relevant braking requirements must comply with whichever is the lower of those weights listed on the previous page, or those below:

Motor vehicle first used on or after 1.4.73 and semi trailer having total of 5 or more axles:	38,000 kg
Motor vehicle with 2 axles first used on or after 1.4.73 and semi trailer with 2 axles used on international transport:	35,000 kg
Motor vehicle with 2 axles first used on or after 1.4.73 with driving axles having twin tyres and friendly suspension, and semi trailer with 2 axles:	35,000 kg
Motor vehicle and semi trailer not listed above, with 4 or more axles:	32,520 kg
Motor vehicle with 2 or more axles first used on or after 1.4.73 with twin tyres and friendly suspension on driving axles, and semi trailer with 1 axle:	26,000 kg
Motor vehicle with 2 axles and semi trailer with 1 axle, not described above:	25,000 kg

Articulated vehicles not complying with the relevant braking requirements are permitted the following maximum laden weight:

less than 4 wheels	20,330 kg	
4 wheels or more	24,390 kg	REG 77

ARTICULATED VEHICLE MATCHING

- Tractive units and semi-trailers are plated separately.
- When loading articulated outfits the plated weights of both the tractive unit and the trailer must be taken into consideration.
- Difficulties may arise where various trailers covering a range of plated weights are used with a tractive unit.
- The same problem arises in relation to excise duty rating where incorrect matching may result in excise offences being committed.

Examples:

Tractive unit plated for operation at 32 tons gross weight when used with a long tandem-axle semi-trailer

For the same tractive unit linked with a short single-axle trailer, a lower weight must be observed, limited by the shorter trailer's gross plated weight.

MAXIMUM OVERALL WEIGHT cont

ROAD VEHICLES (CONSTRUCTION AND USE)
REGULATIONS 1986. REGS 15, 16, 75 & 87

TRAILERS

Qualification		Max weight (kg)
Does the trailer have brakes? | Yes ↓	→ No →	1) laden weight not to exceed max gross weight 2) kerbside weight of drawing vehicle must be at least twice weight of trailer plus load. 3) 750
Manufactured on or after 27.2.77 having overrun brakes except (agricultural trailer) No ↓	→ Yes →	3,500
Manufactured before 27.2.7 having overrun brakes No ↓	→ Yes →	3,560
Track laying No ↓	→ Yes →	12,210
Balanced agricultural No ↓	→ Yes →	See previous pages, but subject to max of 18,290
Unbalanced agricultural No ↓	→ Yes →	18,290
Drawn by motor tractor, heavy motor car or motor car, and having pressure brakes (but not semi-trailer) No ↓	→ Yes →	See previous pages, depends upon number and spacing of axles.
Less than 6 wheels or agricultural trailed appliance	→ Yes →	14,230

COMBINED TRANSPORT OPERATIONS

REGULATIONS 76 (1A), 77 (2A) AND SCHED. 11A ROAD VEHICLES
(CONSTRUCTION & USE) REGS 1986

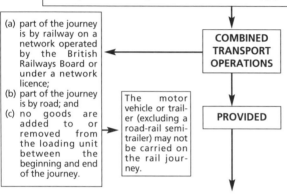

The maximum overall weight for vehicles and trailers, and for articulated vehicles, laid down in regulations 76 and 77 do not apply in the case of

COMBINED TRANSPORT OPERATIONS

(a) part of the journey is by railway on a network operated by the British Railways Board or under a network licence;

(b) part of the journey is by road; and

(c) no goods are added to or removed from the loading unit between the beginning and end of the journey.

The motor vehicle or trailer (excluding a road-rail semi-trailer) may not be carried on the rail journey.

PROVIDED

DEFINITIONS:

Relevant receptacle (not being a vehicle) having length of at least 6.1 m designed and constructed for repeated use on road and railway vehicles

Loading unit means a bi-modal vehicle, road-rail semi-trailer or relevant receptacle.

Bi-modal vehicle means a semi-trailer which can be adapted for use as a railway vehicle

Road-rail semi-trailer constructed or adapted so as to be capable of use both on roads and railway.

Road Friendly suspension means air suspension or equivalent.

(1) The drawbar and trailer must each be carrying a RELEVANT RECEPTACLE or, in the case of an articulated vehicle, a LOADING UNIT, on a journey to a railhead under contract made before the journey began or from a railhead to which the load has been transported by railway.

(2) A document must be carried in the cab of the vehicle specifying (a) if going to a railhead, the railhead and the date the contract was made and the parties thereto; and (b) if from a railhead, the railhead and the time and date the load was collected.

(3) The motor vehicle must comply with the relevant braking requirements.

(4) Every driving axle not being a steering axle must have twin tyres.

(5) Either every driving axle has road friendly suspension or no axle exceeds 8,500 kg.

(6) The motor vehicle and trailer (or articulated vehicle) must have at least 6 axles.

DRAWBAR COMBINATIONS must not exceed 44,000 kg.

ARTICULATED VEHICLES
The motor vehicle must have at least 3 axles. The laden weight must not exceed the number of kg. which result from multiplying the distance in metres between the kingpin and the centre of the rearmost axle of the semi-trailer by 5,500 rounded up to the nearest 10 kg (max 44 tonnes).

MAXIMUM GROSS AXLE WEIGHT

REG 78 ROAD VEHICLES (CONSTRUCTION AND USE) REGULATIONS 1986

If the maximum is exceeded, refer to 'Special Types' (see later).

For wheeled heavy motor cars, motor cars and trailers, complying with relevant braking requirements, max gross axle weights are as follows:

One wheeled axles REG 78	No other wheel in the same line transversely and	
	single tyred not less than 300 mm wide or double tyred not less than 300 mm apart	**5,090 kg**
	otherwise	**4,600 kg**
More than 2 wheels in line transversely REG 78	• Manufactured before 1.5.83 where the wheels are on one axle of a group of closely spaced axles (see later for definition)	**10,170 kg**
	• Manufactured on or after 1.5.83	**10,170 kg**
	• Any other case	**11,180 kg**

Two wheels in line transversely
single tyred not less than 300 mm wide
or
double tyred not less than 300 mm apart

If wheels are on the sole driving axle	**10,500 kg**
Not as above	**10,170 kg**
not tyred as above	**9,200 kg**

For wheeled heavy motor cars, motor cars and trailers not falling within the above

More than 2 wheels transmitting weight to a strip of road between 2 parallel lines at right angles to the longitudinal axis of the vehicle

up to 1.02 m	**11,180 kg**
1.02 m *up to* 1.22 m	**16,260 kg**
1.22 m *up to* 2.13 m	**18,300 kg**

Two wheels in line transversely	**9,200 kg**
One wheel, where no other wheel is in the same line transversely	**4,600 kg**

For wheeled locomotives

Two wheels in line transversely (except road roller, or vehicle with not more than 4 wheels first used before 1.6.55)	**11,180 kg**
Any two wheels of vehicle having not more than 4 wheels first used before 1.6.55 (not being a road roller or agricultural motor vehicle driven at more than 20 mph)	**three quarters of total weight of locomotive**

MAX GROSS AXLE WEIGHT cont

REG 79 and SCHED 11 ROAD VEHICLES (CONSTRUCTION AND USE) REGS 1986

This Regulation applies to:

(a) a wheeled motor vehicle which complies with the relevant braking requirements; (b) a wheeled trailer drawn by such a vehicle; and (c) an agricultural motor vehicle, trailer or appliance, as follows

Two closely spaced axles *	Motor vehicle	Trailer
	up to 1.3 m **16,000 kg**	*up to* 1.3 m **16,000 kg**
	1.3 m *plus* **18,000 kg**	1.3 m *up to* 1.5 m **18,000 kg**
	1.3 m *plus* and (a) driving axles other than steering axles has twin tyres and (b) either every axle has road friendly suspension or neither has an axle weight over 9,500 kg **19,000 kg**	Both axles driven from drawing vehicle and fitted with twin tyres; and either have road friendly suspension or neither has axle weight over 9,500 kg **19,000 kg**
		1.5 m *up to* 1.8 m **19,320 kg**
		1.8 m *plus* **20,000 kg**

	Three closely spaced axles *	*up to* 1.3 m **21,000 kg**
	Distance between any 2	1.3 m *plus* and at least one axle does not have air suspension **22,500 kg**
		1.3 m plus and all three axles have air suspension **24,000 kg**

	Four or more closely spaced axles *	
		24,000 kg

* 'Closely spaced axles' means
(a) 2 axles not falling within (b) or (c) below, spaced not more than 2.5 m apart;
(b) 3 axles not falling within (c) below, the outermost placed not more than 3.25 m apart; or
(c) 4 or more axles, the outermost placed not more than 4.6 m apart.

Exemptions

(a) vehicles first used before 1.6.73 (provided it complies with the requirements of Reg 78 relating to vehicles not complying with braking requirements);
(b) plating certificate issued immediately before 1.1.93 (provided no axle weight exceeds the weight on the certificate) as being the weight not to be exceeded in Great Britain for that axle.

NOTIONAL GROSS WEIGHT

GOODS VEHICLES (ASCERTAINMENT OF MAXIMUM GROSS WEIGHTS)
REGULATIONS 1976

A notional gross weight can be obtained from an unladen weight by multiplying the unladen weight by the following prescribed factor:

This can be used where the appropriate gross weight or train weight is not marked on the vehicle in accordance with C&U Regulations, 1986.

Class of Vehicle   Multiplier

Motor Vehicles

Class of Vehicle	Multiplier
Dual Purpose Vehicle	1.5
Break-down Vehicle	2
Works Trucks	2
Electrically Propelled	2
Salt/grit Spreader	2
Hauling Lifeboats	2
Living Vans	1.5
Vehicle with permanently affixed equipment for medical, dental, veterinary, health, display or clerical purposes	1.5
3 wheeled street cleaners	2
Steam-propelled vehicles	2
Aircraft Servicing vehicles	2
Permanently attached equipment and not mentioned above	1
Heavy motor cars and motor cars first used before 1.1.68 and not mentioned above	2
Locomotives and motor tractors first used before 1.4.73	2
Any motor vehicle not mentioned above	4

Class of Vehicle   Multiplier

Trailers

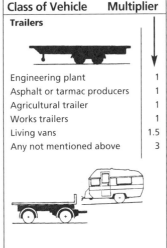

Class of Vehicle	Multiplier
Engineering plant	1
Asphalt or tarmac producers	1
Agricultural trailer	1
Works trailers	1
Living vans	1.5
Any not mentioned above	3

Articulated

Class of Vehicle	Multiplier
Goods combinations with trailer of a type listed above	1.5
Any other	2.5

ADDITIONAL AUTHORISED WEIGHTS
ROAD VEHICLES (AUTHORISED WEIGHT) REGS 1998
(AS AMENDED BY S.I. 2000/3224)

The maximum weights authorised by Construction and Use regulations are increased by these regulations provided certain conditions are complied with.

The regulations apply to the following types of vehicle:

Category	Type
M2	Passenger vehicle with more than 8 seats in addition to the drivers' with max mass not over 5 tonnes.
M3	Passenger vehicles with more than 8 seats in addition to the drivers' and with max mass over 5 tonnes
N2	Goods vehicles with max mass over 3.5 tonnes but not over 12 tonnes
N3	Goods vehicles having max mass over 12 tonnes
O3	Trailers with max mass over 3 tonnes but not over 12 tonnes
O4	Trailers with max mass over 12 tonnes

The regulations do not apply to "Combined Transport Operations" (see earlier).

The new authorised weights are determined according to

(a) vehicle M_2, M_3, N_2, N_3, O_3, O_4. (For definitions see under 'Vehicle Categories')

(b) combinations

(c) number of axles but in each case there is a weight not to be exceeded in any circumstances and a weight determined by axle spacing. Where the weight by axle spacing is greater than that according to vehicle combination or number of axles, the latter will restrict the maximum weight.

Weight by reference to axle spacing
Multiply the distance in metres between the foremost and rearmost axles by the factor specified below to give the maximum weight in kg. (rounded up to nearest 10 kg if above weight would not be exceeded)

Type of vehicle	Number of axles	Factor
Rigid motor vehicle	2	6,000
	3	5,500
	4 or more	5,000
Tractor unit	2	6,000
	3 or more	6,000
Trailer not being semi-trailer or centre-axle trailer	2	6,000
	3 or more	5,000
Articulated bus	Any number	5,000

VEHICLE COMBINATIONS
(SCHEDULE 2)

Weight not to be exceeded in any circumstances

Combination	Conditions	No. of axles	Max weight (kg)
Articulated vehicle	None	3	26,000
"	(a) 2 axle tractor unit and 2 axle trailer, (b) tractor unit not over 18,000 kg, (c) sum of semi-trailer axles not over 20,000 kg, and (d) driving axle has twin tyres and road friendly suspension	4	38,000
"	Not complying with above	4	36,000
"	None	5 or more	40,000
"	(a) no driving axle over 10,500 kg (b) either (i) all driving axles have twin tyres and road friendly suspension, or (ii) all driving axles not being steering axles have twin tyres and not over 8,500 kg (c) all trailer axles have road friendly suspension and, (d) each vehicle in combination has at least 3 axles	6 or more	41,000
	In addition to (a) and (d) above, the vehicle is fitted with a low pollution engine.	6 or more	44,000
Rigid vehicle towing a trailer	Distance between rear axle of motor vehicle and front axle of trailer not less than 3 m.	3	26,000
"	"	4	36,000
"	"	5 or more	40,000
"	Not complying with previous condition	3	22,000
"	"	4	30,000
"	"	5 or more	34,000
"	Complying with conditions applicable to articulated vehicles with 6 or more axles	6 or more	41,000
	Complying with the above conditions and the vehicle is fitted with a low pollution engine	6 or more	44,000

Weight by reference to axle spacing

This only applies to articulated vehicles with 3 or more axles. The maximum weight (in kg) is ascertained by multiplying the distance in metres between the kingpin and the centre of the rearmost axle of the semi-trailer by a factor of 5,500. The answer may be rounded up to the nearest 10 kg provided this is less than the above weights.

MAXIMUM AXLE WEIGHTS

Weight not to be exceeded in any circumstances

Description of axle	Max weight (kg)
Single driving axle	11,500
Single non-driving axle	10,000
Driving tandem axle meeting either of the below conditions	19,000
Driving tandem axle not meeting either of the below conditions	18,000
Non-driving tandem axle	20,000
Triaxle	24,000

Conditions

Either (a) driving axle has twin tyres and road friendly suspension, or
(b) each driving axle has twin tyres and no axle is over 9,500 kg.

Weight by reference to axle spacing

Description of axle	Dimension	Length (m)	Max weight (kg)
Driving tandem axle	Distance between the two axles	Less than 1	11,500
"		Not less than 1 but less than 1.3	16,000
Non-driving "		Less than 1	11,000
"		Not less than 1 but less than 1.3	16,000
"		Not less than 1.3 but less than 1.8	18,000
Triaxle	Distance between any 2 adjacent axles	1.3 or less	21,000

RETRACTABLE AND LOADABLE AXLES

A vehicle first used on or after 1.1.2002 which is fitted with one or more retractable or loadable axles may have maximum authorised axle weight in accordance with the above tables under all driving conditions if the retractable or loadable axle is automatically lowered to the ground when the front axle (or nearest if in a group) is laden to that maximum authorised weight. However this will not apply (subject to further conditions) if the vehicle is in slippery road conditions and it is necessary to raise the axle in order increase the traction of the remaining tyres.

DEFINITIONS

"centre axle trailer" – having only a single axle or single group of axles positioned at or near to the centre of gravity so that the load transmitted to the drawing vehicle does not exceed 10 per cent or 1,000 kg whichever is the less.

"loadable axle" – the load on which can be varied without the axle being raised by an axle-lift device.

"retractable axle" – raised or lowered by an axle-lift device.

"road friendly suspension" – at least 75 per cent of the spring effect is produced by air or other compressible fluid under pressure, or suspension recognised as being equivalent within the community.

"steering axle" – positively steered by the actions of the driver

"tandem axle" – 2 axles not more than 2.5 m apart sharing the load

"triaxle" – (a) 3 axles where none is more than 3.25 m apart from any other, or (b) more than 3 axles where none is more than 4.6 m from any other. The load is shared by them all.

TRAVELLING HEIGHT – CAB NOTICES

ROAD VEHICLES (CONSTRUCTION AND USE) REGS 1986 REG 10
(for interpretation of terms see definitions page)

A motor vehicle with an overall travelling height over 3 m must display a notice in the cab indicating the vehicle height.

Requirements of the notice:
(a) height expressed in feet and inches or both feet and inches and in metres;
(b) if in feet and inches, numbers to be at least 40 mm tall;
(c) the height expressed is the overall travelling height (or, if a vehicle to which the next regulation applies (warning device required), the 'overall travelling height' or 'predetermined height', whichever is the greater);
(d) if not a 'relevant vehicle' the height expressed must not exceed the 'overall travelling height' by more than 150 mm.
(e) if a 'relevant vehicle' the height expressed must not exceed the 'overall travelling height' by more than 1 m;
(f) if the height is expressed in both feet and inches and metres they must not differ by more than 50 mm.
(g) no other letters or numbers which could be understood as an indication of height may be displayed in the notice.

Exemptions:
(a) Highly unlikely driver would encounter a bridge, etc, which was not at least 1m higher than the 'overall travelling height', (or, if applicable, the 'maximum travelling height' for vehicles needing a warning device);
(b) Driver has documentation giving information regarding a risk-free route and the driver is following the route or an unforeseen diversion;
(c) Driver has bridge height information for a particular route indicating structures under which the vehicle will/will not pass;
(d) Vehicles not over 4 m 'overall travelling height', registered in an EEA state being used in international traffic.

HIGH LEVEL EQUIPMENT – WARNING DEVICE

ROAD VEHICLES (CONSTRUCTION AND USE) REGULATIONS 1986. REGS 10A AND 10B

(For interpretation of terms see definitions page)

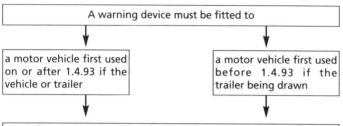

Requirements of the warning device:

Constructed, maintained, adjusted and connected so that it gives a visible warning to the driver if, while vehicle is being driven, the height of the 'high level equipment' exceeds a 'predetermined height'. The 'predetermined height' shall not exceed the 'overall travelling height' by more than 1 m.

Exemptions:

(a) Unlikely driver would encounter a bridge, etc. which was not at least 1m higher than the 'maximum travelling height';

(b) 'Overall travelling height' of not more than 4 m and registered in an EEA state being used on international traffic;

(c) agricultural motor vehicle;

(d) industrial tractor;

(e) works truck;

(f) naval, military or air force vehicle;

(g) fire brigade vehicle;

(h) vehicle constructed and normally used for carrying at least two other vehicles;

(i) motor vehicle drawing a car transporter;

(j) motor vehicle where 'maximum travelling height' does not exceed its 'overall travelling height'.

CAB NOTICES AND WARNING DEVICES – DEFINITIONS

ROAD VEHICLES (CONSTRUCTION AND USE) REGULATIONS 1986. REG 10C

High Level Equipment is equipment so fitted that –
(a) it can be raised by means of a power operated device, and
(b) the raising or lowering is capable of altering the overall travelling height when the vehicle and every trailer is unladen.

In relation to a tipper which is (a) a motor vehicle first used before 1.4.98, or (b) a trailer manufactured before that date, "high level equipment" does not include the relevant part of the tipper.

Where (a) the equipment is so designed and constructed that it can be fixed in a stowed position by a locking device and it is not possible for a person in the cab to interfere with the locking device; and (b) the equipment is fixed in that position by the locking device, the equipment shall not be regarded as "high level equipment".

Maximum Height in relation to high level equipment means the height of the highest point of that equipment when it is raised as far as possible and the vehicle is unladen.

Maximum Travelling Height means (i) if the overall travelling height could be increased by raising the high level equipment, the highest level to which it could be raised, or (ii) in any other case, the overall travelling height.

Overall Travelling Height means the overall height for the time being of the vehicle (or combination of vehicles), its equipment and load.

Tipper means a vehicle which can be unloaded by part of the vehicle (the relevant part) being tipped sideways or rearwards.

TRAILERS

REG 83 ROAD VEHICLES (CONSTRUCTION AND USE) REGULATIONS 1986

Description of vehicle	Max no of trailers
Motor tractor If both tractor and See definition at front of book– trailer are unladen basically a motor vehicle for hauling trailers with wide load etc. 	1 2
Locomotive	3
Motor car or heavy motor car (not being a straddle carrier, articulated bus or a bus) (for buses see following page)	1
If one of the trailers being drawn is a towing implement (i.e. a 'dolly') and the other is an articulated type semi trailer secured to and resting on, or suspended from, the dolly *The following diagram shows a conventional six-wheel rigid vehicle drawing a dolly mounted semi-trailer.* 	2

Agricultural motor vehicle
This is a motor vehicle constructed
and adapted for use off roads for
agricultural, horticultural or forestry
and which is primarily used for one
or more of those purposes – not
being a dual purpose vehicle
 	
1. With non-
   agricultural trailers
   or appliances
	As for
	locomotive
	motor tractor or
	heavy motor car
	above

2. With agricultural trailers or trailed appliances An agricultural trailer is a trailer constructed or adapted for the purpose of agriculture, horticulture or forestry and only used for one or more of those purposes An agricultural trailed appliance is a trailer which is an implement constructed or adapted for the use off roads for the above purposes	**2** unladen agricultural trailers; or **1** agricultural trailer and **1** agricultural trailed appliance; or **2** agricultural trailed appliances

TRAILERS cont

ROAD VEHICLES (CONSTRUCTION AND USE) REGULATIONS 1986

ARTICULATED TRACTIVE UNIT
DRAWING TWO SEMI-TRAILERS   REG 83

An articulated tractive unit drawing two semi-trailers
(a double bottom) will be permitted by the DTP subject
to special ministerial permission

subject to a 30 mph limit
(40 mph on motorways) and prescribed routes.

Must comply with C&U Regs 1986 but carry additional lights and mirrors.
No maximum weights and lengths are specified.

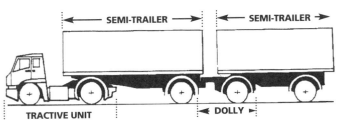

← SEMI-TRAILER → ← SEMI-TRAILER →

TRACTIVE UNIT ← **DOLLY** →

NOTES

● *'Trailer' does not include a water carrying vehicle drawn for the
purpose of a steam powered drawing vehicle.*

● *A broken down unladen articulated vehicle being towed will be
counted as only one trailer.*

MOTOR VEHICLE DRAWING A TRAILER BY ROPE OR CHAIN

REG 86

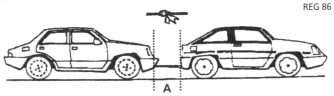

A

'A' must not exceed 4.5 m. If it exceeds 1.5 m the
rope or chain must be made clearly visible

TRAILERS cont

ROAD VEHICLES (CONSTRUCTION AND USE) REGULATIONS 1986

MOTOR CYCLES   REG 84

A person using, or causing or permitting **ANY MOTOR CYCLE** to be used, on a road, may not:

1. draw more than one trailer;
2. draw a trailer carrying a passenger (unless broken down);
3. draw a trailer with UW over 254 kg.

A **TWO-WHEELED MOTOR CYCLE**, (not with a sidecar)

and engine cc not over 125cc shall not

with engine capacity over 125cc may draw a trailer subject to the following

draw a trailer except a broken-down motor cycle being ridden.

trailer must not exceed 1 m wide; distance between rear axle of motor cycle and rear of trailer not to exceed 2.5 m;
- motor cycle to be marked with kerbside weight (unless broken down);
- trailer to be marked with unladen weight (unless broken down);
- laden weight of trailer not to exceed 150 kg or two-thirds kerbside weight of motor cycle, whichever the less (unless broken down).

TRAILERS cont
ROAD VEHICLES (CONSTRUCTION AND USE) REGULATIONS 1986

Leaving trailers at rest (Reg. 89)

It is an offence to cause or permit a trailer to stand on a road when detached from the drawing vehicle unless at least one of its wheels (or if track-laying, its tracks) is prevented from revolving by the setting of a parking brake or the use of a chain, chock or other efficient device.

Maximum weight of unbraked trailers (Reg. 87)

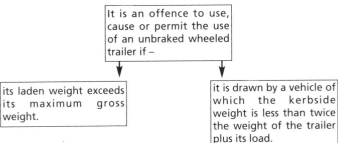

It is an offence to use, cause or permit the use of an unbraked wheeled trailer if –

its laden weight exceeds its maximum gross weight.

it is drawn by a vehicle of which the kerbside weight is less than twice the weight of the trailer plus its load.

Except

(a) street cleansing trailer not carrying a load
(b) agricultural trailer manufactured before 1.7.47 drawn by motor tractor or agricultural motor vehicle at not more than 10 mph, with unladen weight not over 4,070 kg, and being the only trailer drawn
(c) trailer drawn by a motor cycle in accordance with Reg 84.
(d) agricultural trailed appliance
(e) agricultural trailed appliance conveyor
(f) broken down vehicle
(g) gritting trailer with max gross weight not over 2,000 kg

TRAILERS cont

ROAD VEHICLES (CONSTRUCTION AND USE) REGULATIONS 1986

PASSENGERS IN TRAILERS (REG 90)

> no person shall use, cause or permit to be used on a road

> any trailer for the carriage of passengers for hire or reward

> except a wheeled trailer which is, or is carrying, a broken down motor vehicle if
> (a) not exceeding 30 mph; and
> (b) if the trailer is, or is carrying, a broken down bus, it is attached by a rigid draw bar. (Reg 90(1))

> a wheeled trailer in which any person is carried and which is a living van having either –
> (a) less than 4 wheels; or
> (b) 4 wheels consisting of two close-coupled* wheels on each side
>
> * 'close-coupled' means wheels on the same side having their centres not more than 1 m apart.

> except if being tested by its manufacturer, repairer, distributor or dealer in trailers. (Reg 90(2))

REG 90

A BUS

> A bus – not being an articulated bus or mini-bus – may draw:

> a broken-down bus – where no person other than the driver is carried on either vehicle – or

> one trailer.

REG 83
BUT REFER TO REG 7 FOR MAXIMUM LENGTH

TRAILERS cont

SECONDARY COUPLING (REG 86A)

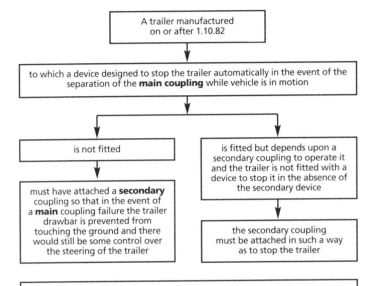

A trailer manufactured on or after 1.10.82

to which a device designed to stop the trailer automatically in the event of the separation of the **main coupling** while vehicle is in motion

is not fitted

must have attached a **secondary** coupling so that in the event of a **main** coupling failure the trailer drawbar is prevented from touching the ground and there would still be some control over the steering of the trailer

is fitted but depends upon a secondary coupling to operate it and the trailer is not fitted with a device to stop it in the absence of the secondary device

the secondary coupling must be attached in such a way as to stop the trailer

Except:
Agricultural trailer or appliance not exceeding 20 mph. Vehicle with max speed not over 25 km/h. Works trailer. Public works vehicle. Trailer designed, constructed or adapted to be drawn by a locomotive, motor tractor, vehicle with max speed not exceeding 25 km/h, works truck or public works vehicle. Street cleansing trailer. Max total design axle weight not over 750 kg. Motor cycle trailer. Broken down vehicle. Gritting trailer with max gross weight not over 2,000 kg.

THESE EXCEPTIONS TO REG 86A ARE CONTAINED WITHIN REG 15 C&U REGS 1986

SIDECARS (REGS 92 & 93)

The sidecar wheel must not be wholly outside this space.

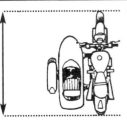

It is an offence to use, cause or permit to be used a two-wheeled motor cycle registered on or after 1.8.81 (other than one brought temporarily into Great Britain by a person resident abroad) if the sidecar is attached to the right (or offside) of the motor cycle.

DANGEROUS VEHICLES

REG 100 ROAD VEHICLES (CONSTRUCTION AND USE) REGULATIONS 1986
SECTION 40A ROAD TRAFFIC ACT 1988

A motor vehicle, every trailer drawn thereby and all parts and accessories shall at all times be such

that no danger is caused or is likely to be caused to any person

in or on the vehicle or trailer, or on a road, by reason of:

condition or unsuitable purpose

number of passengers
(may not apply to vehicles subject to PSV (Carrying Capacity) Regs 1984)

manner passengers carried

weight, distribution, packing and adjustment of load

The load shall be so secured by physical restraint and be in such a position that

neither danger nor nuisance is likely to be caused to any person or property

by reason of the load moving or being blown or falling from the vehicle.

SILENCERS

ROAD VEHICLES (CONSTRUCTION AND USE) REGULATIONS 1986

MOTOR CYCLE SILENCER AND EXHAUST SYSTEM REGS 1995

Every vehicle propelled by an internal combustion engine shall be fitted with an **exhaust system including a silencer**

suitable and sufficient for reducing, as far as may be reasonable, the noise caused by the escape of the exhaust gases from the engine.

No person shall use, cause or permit to be used, a vehicle on a road if exhaust gases from the engine escape into the atmosphere without first passing through the silencer, etc.

The silencer etc. shall, at all times when the vehicle is used on a road, be maintained in good and efficient working order and shall not, after the date of manufacture, have been altered in any way which makes the noise of escaping gases greater.

REG 54 C&U REGS 1986

Motor cycle and moped silencers must now meet requirements of specified EC Directives with a distinction being made between those first used before 1.2.96 and those first used after that date.

A silencer marked 'not for road use' may not be used on a road by such a vehicle.

REG 57A C&U REGS 1986

Using a motor cycle or moped on a road if it does not meet noise limit requirements and it is not in good or efficient working order or has been altered and the noise is therefore greater is an offence.

REG 57B C&U REGS 1986

Supply of motor cycle silencers: In the course of a business, no person may supply or offer or agree to supply or expose or have in his possession for the purpose of supplying, an exhaust system, silencer or component for such a system unless it is clearly and indelibly marked with the relevant British Standard Specification or EEC Directive. The above does not apply if the silencer or exhaust system is clearly and indelibly marked 'NOT FOR ROAD USE' or 'PRE-1985 MC ONLY'.

S1 MOTOR CYCLE NOISE ACT 1987
AND REGS 3, 4 & 5 MOTOR CYCLE SILENCER AND EXHAUST SYSTEM REGS 1995

As to sound levels generally, see Reg 55, C&U Regulations 1986

No motor vehicle shall be used on a road in a manner which causes any excessive noise which could have been avoided by reasonable care by the driver.

REG 97 C&U REGS 1986

EMISSIONS OF SMOKE ETC.

REGS. 61 & 61A ROAD VEHICLES (CONSTRUCTION AND USE) REGULATIONS 1986

1) All Vehicles

Emission of Smoke or Vapour

Unless complying with a relevant instrument (Community Directive, ECE Regulation, or the table below), every vehicle shall be constructed and maintained so as not to emit any avoidable smoke or visible vapour.

Emission of Ashes, Cinders, etc.

Every motor vehicle using solid fuel shall be fitted with a tray or shield to prevent ashes or cinders from falling onto the road; and an appliance to prevent any emission of sparks or grit.

Emissions likely to cause Damage or Injury

No person may use, cause or permit the use of a motor vehicle from which any smoke, visible vapour, grit, sparks, ashes, cinders or oily substance is emitted if it causes, or may cause, damage to any property or injury or danger to any person who is, or may be, on the road.

Carbon Monoxide and Hydrocarbon

(1) No person may use, cause or permit the use of a 4-stroke spark ignition engine vehicle first used on or after 1.8.75 if
  1. when idling, the carbon monoxide content of the exhaust exceeds 4.5% (if first used before 1.8.86) or 3.5% (if first used on or after that date);
  2. when running without load at 2000 rpm the hydrocarbon content of the exhaust exceeds 0.12%.

This requirement does not apply (a) to vehicles which, when manufactured, could not comply, (b) to vehicles to which the following provision applies, or (c) to vehicles contained in the 'exemptions' box below.

(2) No person may use, cause or permit the use of –
  1. a passenger car first used on or after 1.8.92 and before 1.8.95, and is mentioned in the emissions publication (a DETR document);
  2. a vehicle which is not a passenger car, is first used on or after 1.8.94, and is mentioned in the emissions publication;
  3. a passenger car first used on or after 1.8.95; or
  4. a vehicle which is not a passenger car, is first used on or after 1.7.02 and has a maximum gross weight not exceeding 3,500 kg.

if, **when the engine is idling,** the carbon monoxide content of the exhaust exceeds the level mentioned in the emissions publication or, if the vehicle is not mentioned in the publication, 0.5 %, if first used before 1.7.02, or 0.3 % if used on or after 1.7.02 or if, **when the engine is at fast idle**, (a) carbon monoxide exceeds the amount mentioned in the publication, or, if the vehicle is not mentioned in the publication, 0.3 %, if first used before 1.7.02, or 0.2 % if first used on or after 1.7.02; (b) the hydrocarbon content exceeds 0.02 %; or (c) the lambda value (ratio of air to petrol vapour) is outside limits.

This requirement does not apply to vehicles which, when manufactured, could not comply, nor to vehicles contained in the 'exemptions' box below.

Exemptions

(a) vehicle being taken for repairs, (b) vehicle constructed by a person not in the vehicle manufacturing business and first used before 1.7.98, (c) a vehicle with: less than 4 wheels; max. gross weight less than 400 kg; max. speed less than 25 km/hr; or an agricultural motor vehicle, (d) goods vehicle with max. gross weight over 3,500 kg, (e) engineering plant, industrial tractor or works truck, (e) vehicle with rotary piston engine first used before 1.8.87.

EMISSIONS OF SMOKE ETC. cont
REGS. 61 & 61A ROAD VEHICLES (CONSTRUCTION AND USE) REGULATIONS 1988

No person shall use, cause or permit the use of a compression ignition vehicle if the coefficient of absorption of the exhaust emissions exceeds-
1. if first used before 1.7.08 and turbo-charged, 3.0 per metre, or if not turbo charged, 2.5 per metre; or
2. if first used on or after 1.7.08, 1.5 per metre.

This requirement does not apply to (a) vehicles which, when manufactured, could not comply, (b) vehicle going for repairs, (c) a vehicle with: less than 4 wheels; max. gross weight less than 400 kg; max. speed less than 25 km/hr; or an agricultural motor vehicle, (d) engineering plant, industrial tractor or works truck, or (e) vehicles subject to the testing regs. in class lll, IV, V or Vll.

2) Vehicles used before 1.1.2001
Every wheeled vehicle shall be constructed so as to comply with the following:

Item	Class of Vehicle	Requirements	Exemptions
1	Vehicles with compression ignition engine fitted with a device to facilitate starting by supplying excess fuel.	The device must not be operable by a person inside the vehicle.	(a) Works truck (b) Vehicle with device designed so that (i) its use after the engine has started cannot cause the engine to be supplied with excess fuel, or (ii) it does not cause any increase in the smoke or visible vapour emitted.
2	Vehicles first used on or after 1.4.73 with compression ignition engine.	Must have a type test certificate in accordance with BS AU 141a; 1971.	(a) vehicle manufactured before 1.4.73 with a Perkins 6.354 engine, (b) vehicle with not more than 2 cylinders, being an agricultural vehicle (first used before 1.6.86), an industrial tractor, a works truck or engineering plant.
3	Vehicles first used on or after 1.1.72 with a spark ignition engine other than a 2-stroke engine.	Must have a means to ensure that when the engine is running, any vapours or gases in the crank case or other part of the engine are prevented from passing into the atmosphere except through the combustion chamber.	Two-wheeled motor cycle with or without a sidecar attached. A vehicle to which any item in Table 2 in the Regulations applies (which requires compliance with Community Directives or ECE Regulations).

Readers are referred to a further table in Reg. 61 containing details of the various Community Directives and ECE Regulations with which vehicles must comply.

3) Vehicles first used on or after 1.1.2001
Reg. 61A contains details of Directives and ECE Regs. which impose further requirements for certain motor vehicles first used on or after 1.1.01.

TYRES

REGS 26 AND 27 ROAD VEHICLES (CONSTRUCTION AND USE) REGULATIONS 1986

must

BE SUITABLE having regard to the use to which the vehicle or trailer is being put or to the types of tyres fitted to its other wheels.

BE INFLATED so as to be fit for use to which vehicle is being put.

Have no portion of the **PLY OR CORD EXPOSED.**

have **NO LUMP, BULGE OR TEAR** caused by separation or partial failure of its structure.

HAVE THE BASE OF ANY GROOVE which showed in the original tread pattern **CLEARLY VISIBLE.**

does not apply to:
1. a 3-wheeled motor cycle UW not over 102 kg and incapable of more than 12 mph on level; or
2. a pedestrian-controlled works truck.

NOT BE A 'TEMPORARY USE SPARE TYRE' (for use only if normal tyre fails and used at lower speed.

unless either:
1. a passenger vehicle first used before 1.4.87, or
2. complying with ECE Reg 64 or Community Directive 92/93.

(REG 24(3))

TYRES cont

REGS 26 AND 27 ROAD VEHICLES (CONSTRUCTION AND USE) REGULATIONS 1986

must

FOR TWO AXLE-VEHICLES – not have:
1. diagonal ply or bias-belted on rear with radial ply on front;
2. diagonal ply on rear and bias belted on front.

NOT BE RECUT TYRES if:
1. ply or cord has been cut or exposed, or
2. wholly or partially different pattern to manufacturer's recut tread pattern.

HAVE NO CUT in excess of 25 mm or 10 per cent of width, whichever is greater, measured in any direction on outside of tyre, deep enough to reach the ply or cord.

HAVE EITHER:
1. depth of groove of tread pattern at least 1 mm throughout continuous band of at least three quarters of breadth round entire circumference, or
2. where original tread did not extend beyond three quarters of breadth, whole of original tread to have depth of at least 1 mm.

does not apply to:
1. 3-wheeled motor cycle UW not exceeding 102 kg and incapable of more than 12 mph on level:
2. pedestrian controlled works truck; or
3. motor cycle not over 50cc.

in the case of:
1. passenger vehicles for not more than eight passengers in addition to the driver (other than motor cycles)
2. goods vehicles under 3,500 kg,
3. and light trailers,
for 1 mm read 1.6 mm in the central three quarters of breath and round the entire outer circumference of the tyre.

continued on following page

TYRES cont

REGS 26 AND 27 ROAD VEHICLES (CONSTRUCTION AND USE) REGULATIONS 1986

must

↓

continued from previous page

BE MAINTAINED in such condition as to be fit for the use to which they are being put and free from any defect which might cause damage to the road surface or danger to persons in or on the vehicle or using the road.

NOT HAVE DIFFERENT TYPES OF STRUCTURE where fitted to the same axle.

FOR VEHICLES WITH MORE THAN 1 STEERABLE AXLE – not have different type of structure on different steerable axles; or

FOR VEHICLES WITH MORE THAN 1 DRIVEN AXLE NOT BEING STEERABLE AXLES – not have different type of structure on different non-steerable axles.

SUPPLY OF TYRES
MOTOR VEHICLE TYRES (SAFETY) REGULATIONS 1994

No person shall supply a tyre designed to be fitted to a

It is an offence to supply a tyre bearing a false mark for a

passenger car, light trailer, moped (not low performance), motor cycle, motor tricycle, three-wheel moped, or quadricycle

passenger car, commercial vehicle or trailer

moped, motor cycle, motor tricycle, three-wheel moped, or quadricycle on or after 1.1.04

or commercial vehicle

which is a **NEW TYRE**

which is a **PART-WORN TYRE**

which is a **RETREADED TYRE** (not part-worn)

unless it is marked to indicate that it complies with ECE Regulations or EC Directives as a new tyre

unless it does not have-
a) a cut in excess of 25 mm or 10 per cent of the width (whichever is the greater) deep enough to reach the ply or cord;
b) any lump, bulge or tear caused by seaparion or failure of its structure;
c) ply or cord exposed;
d) penetration damage which has not been repaired;
e) tread less than 2 mm
It must bear the word "PART-WORN"

unless it is not marked as a new tyre; it is marked as a retreaded tyre in accordance with B.S., ECE Regs. or EC Directives; and, after 1.1.04, has ECE type approval.

unless either-
(a) it is not marked as a new tyre and ECE type approval has been granted; or
(b) the following are met-
(i) not marked as a new tyre; (ii) carcass not more than 7 yrs. old and conforms to ECE Regs. or Directives; (iii) not previously retreaded; (iv) marked with original manufacturer's details; (v) complies with ECE dimension & performance requirements; (vi) bears word "RETREAD"; (vii) has 'e' mark; (viii) if repaired, has been done properly; and (ix) must not show higher speed rating or load index than original carcass.

If it has not been retreaded it must bear an approval mark and the original speed category symbol and load capacity index.

If it has been retreaded it must bear the appropriate B.S. or ECE approval mark, or be marked (by code or otherwise) with the original manufacturer's name and tyre model, and the word "RETREAD". If it bears the mark "BS AU 144e" it must show the original speed category and load index.

EXEMPTIONS

New or retreaded (including part-worn retreaded)
Bias belted or diagonal ply for pre-1.1.49 vehicle or trailer; 'competition' tyres; 'off-road' tyres; tyres for pre-1.1.33 vehicles; tyres for test or trial; tyres for other than retail sale; and tyre sizes 185R16, 125R400, 135R400, 145R400, 155R400, 165R400, 175R400 or 185R400.

Part-worn
Where complete vehicle is supplied. If (a) for vehicle manufactured before 1.1.33; (b) limited run-flat tyre; or for agricultural use, need not bear approval marks etc.

TYRES – SIDEWALL SYMBOLS

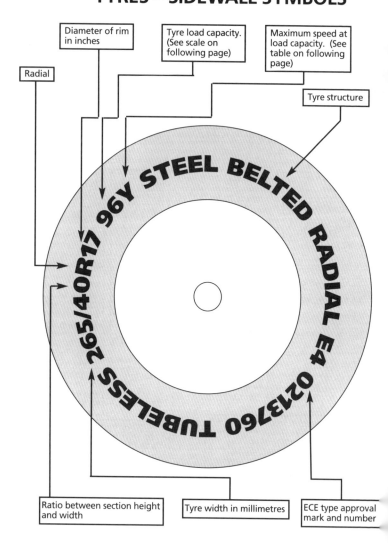

Diameter of rim in inches

Tyre load capacity. (See scale on following page)

Maximum speed at load capacity. (See table on following page)

Radial

Tyre structure

Ratio between section height and width

Tyre width in millimetres

ECE type approval mark and number

TYRES – LOAD AND SPEED LIMITATIONS

CAR, VAN AND TRUCK LOAD CAPACITY PER WHEEL IN kg

INDEX	LOAD	INDEX	LOAD	INDEX	LOAD	INDEX	LOAD	INDEX	LOAD
60	250	88	560	116	1,250	144	2,800	172	6,300
61	257	89	580	117	1,285	145	2,900	173	6,500
62	265	90	600	118	1,320	146	3,000	174	6,700
63	272	91	615	119	1,360	147	3,075	175	6,900
64	280	92	630	120	1,400	148	3,150	176	7,100
65	290	93	650	121	1,450	149	3,250	177	7,300
66	300	94	670	122	1,500	150	3,350	178	7,500
67	307	95	690	123	1,550	151	3,450	179	7,750
68	315	96	710	124	1,600	152	3,550	180	8,000
69	325	97	730	125	1,650	153	3,650	181	8,250
70	335	98	750	126	1,700	154	3,750	182	8,500
71	345	99	775	127	1,750	155	3,875	183	8,750
72	355	100	800	128	1,800	156	4,000	184	9,000
73	365	101	825	129	1,850	157	4,125	185	9,250
74	375	102	850	130	1,900	158	4,250	186	9,500
75	387	103	875	131	1,950	159	4,375	187	9,750
76	400	104	900	132	2,000	160	4,500	188	10,000
77	412	105	925	133	2,060	161	4,625	189	10,300
78	425	106	950	134	2,120	162	4,750	190	10,600
79	437	107	975	135	2,180	163	4,875	191	10,900
80	450	108	1,000	136	2,240	164	5,000	192	11,200
81	462	109	1,030	137	2,300	165	5,150	193	11,500
82	475	110	1,060	138	2,360	166	5,300	194	11,800
83	487	111	1,090	139	2,430	167	5,450	195	12,150
84	500	112	1,120	140	2,500	168	5,600	196	12,500
85	515	113	1,150	141	2,575	169	5,800	197	12,850
86	530	114	1,180	142	2,650	170	6,000	198	13,200
87	545	115	1,215	143	2,725	171	6,150	199	13,600

MAXIMUM SUSTAINABLE SPEED FOR THE TYRE AT THE LOAD CAPACITY GIVEN (NORMAL USE)

SYMBOL	SPEED (kph)	SPEED (mph)
CAR		
S	180	111.8
T	190	118.1
U	200	124.3
H	210	130.5
V	240	149.1
W	270	167.8
Y	300	186.4
VR*	210+	130+
ZR*	240+	150+
WINTER/REINFORCED		
Q	160	99.4
R	170	105.6
VAN		
N	140	87
P	150	93.2
TRUCK		
J	100	62.1
K	110	68.4
L	120	74.6
M	130	80.8
* Old designation		

WARNING INSTRUMENTS

REG 37 ROAD VEHICLES (CONSTRUCTION AND USE) REGULATIONS 1986

Requirement

Every vehicle which has a maximum speed of more than 20 mph shall be fitted with a horn, not being a reversing alarm or two-tone horn.

Exception

Agricultural motor vehicle unless it is being driven at more than 20 mph.

Sound emitted

Other than a reversing alarm, a boarding aid alarm (for a power operated lift or ramp fitted to a bus for wheelchairs) or a two-tone horn, fitted to a wheeled vehicle first used on or after 1.8.73 shall be continuous and uniform and not strident. A reversing alarm or boarding aid alarm fitted to a wheeled vehicle shall not be strident.

Bells, gongs, sirens and two-tone horns

No vehicle shall be fitted with a bell, gong, siren or two-tone horn (emits a sound which alternates at regular intervals between 2 fixed notes), except vehicles used for:

(a) fire, ambulance, police or Serious Organised Crime Agency
(b) fire salvage
(c) forestry commission or local authority fire fighting
(d) bomb or explosive disposal
(e) blood transfusion
(f) coastguard
(g) mine rescue
(h) RAF mountain rescue
(i) RNLI lifeboat launching
(j) Revenue and Customs serious crime investigation; or
(k) radiation accident or emergency.

Sale of goods

None of the above provisions will make it unlawful for a motor vehicle to be fitted with an instrument or apparatus (not being a two-tone horn) designed to emit a sound to inform the public that goods are on the vehicle for sale.

Theft prevention or summoning help

A bell, gong or siren may be fitted for the purpose of:

(a) preventing theft of the vehicle or contents (but if fitted to a vehicle first used on or after 1.10.82 it must have a device to stop the noise being emitted for more than 5 minutes); or
(b) to summon help for the driver, conductor or inspector of a bus.

WARNING INSTRUMENTS cont

REG 37 ROAD VEHICLES (CONSTRUCTION AND USE) REGULATIONS 1986

EEC

Instead of complying with the above provisions, a vehicle may comply with the equivalent Community Directive or ECE Regulation.

Restrictions on sounding

No person shall sound, or cause to be sounded, any horn, gong, bell or siren fitted to or carried on a vehicle which is:
(a) stationary on a road, at any time, other than at times of danger due to another moving vehicle on or near the road (other than a reversing alarm or boarding aid alarm); or
(b) in motion on a restricted road (subject to 30 mph limit), between the hours of 11.30 pm and 7 am.

Reversing alarm or boarding aid alarm

Shall not be sounded:
(a) unless it is a goods vehicle with a maximum gross weight not less than 2,000 kg, a bus, engineering plant, a refuse vehicle or a works truck; or
(b) if the sound of the alarm is likely to be confused with a sound emitted in the operation of a pedestrian crossing.

Gongs, bells, sirens and two-tone horns

No person shall sound, or cause or permit to be sounded, any gong, bell, siren or two-tone horn fitted to or carried on a vehicle (whether stationary or not).

Exemptions

(a) a vehicle listed in the exemptions under "Gongs, bells, sirens and two-tone horns" on the previous page, and it is necessary to do so either to indicate to other road users the urgency of the purposes for which the vehicle is being used, or to warn of the presence of the vehicle on the road; or
(b) a horn (not being a two-tone horn), bell gong or siren (i) to raise alarm as to the theft or attempted theft of the vehicle or its contents; or (ii) to summon help for the driver, conductor or inspector of a bus;
(c) between 12 pm and 7 pm, other than a two-tone horn, for the purpose of informing members of the public that the vehicle is conveying goods for sale.

SPEEDOMETER

REGS. 35 AND 36 ROAD VEHICLES (CONSTRUCTION AND USE) REGULATIONS 1986

A speedometer must be fitted to all vehicles,
with the following exceptions

- maximum speed not exceeding 25 mph
- unlawful to drive at more than 25 mph
- agricultural vehicle not driven at more than 20 mph
- motor cycle first used before 1.4.84 not exceeding 100cc
- invalid carriage first used before 1.4.84
- works truck first used before 1.4.84
- vehicle first used before 1.10.37
- vehicle fitted with approved recording equipment indicating the speed.

A speedometer must be fitted in such a position that the driver can see speed of vehicle

and if vehicle first used on or after 1.4.84, must be capable of indicating speed in mph and kph

Must be maintained in good working order
and must be kept free from any obstruction
which may prevent it being read but:

defence:
- if defect occurred during journey on which contravention detected
- if steps have already been taken to have defect remedied with reasonable expedition.

SEAT BELT ANCHORAGE POINTS
ROAD VEHICLES (CONSTRUCTION AND USE) REGULATIONS 1986

Anchorage points must be fitted in accordance with the table on the following page.

This regulation applies to a vehicle which is not an excepted vehicle and which is:
- bus first used on or after 1.4.82
- wheeled motor car first used on or after 1.1.65
- 3-wheeled motor cycle with unladen weight over 255 kg first used on or after 1.9.70
- heavy motor car first used on or after 1.10.88.

Excepted vehicles are:
- goods vehicle (other than a dual purpose vehicle) –
    1. first used before 1.4.67,
    2. first used on or after 1.4.80 and before 1.10.88 having a gross maximum weight over 3,500 kg. or
    3. first used before 1.4.80 or, if manufactured before 1.10.79, first used before 1.4.82 and, in either case, with unladen weight over 1,525 kg;
- agricultural motor vehicle;
- motor tractor;
- works truck;
- electrically propelled goods vehicle first used before 1.10.88;
- pedestrian controlled vehicle;
- vehicle which has been used outside G.B., being driven from its place of arrival in G.B. to the owner's or driver's home, or to a place to be fitted with anchorage points and seat belts;
- vehicle having maximum speed not over 16 mph;
- motor cycle with seat for sitting astride, and which is constructed or assembled by a person not ordinarily engaged in the trade of manufacturing such vehicles;
- locomotive.

Definitions
Exposed forward-facing seat means:
1. a forward-facing front seat (including any crew seat) and the driver's seat;and
2. any other forward-facing seat which is not immediately behind and on the same horizontal plane as a forward-facing high-backed seat.

Non-protected seat – not a front seat and the screen zones within the protected area have a combined surface of less than 800 sq cm.

Urban bus – a bus designed for urban use with standing passengers.

Community Directives or ECE Regulations (in item 2 of the table overleaf) means
- Community Directive 76/115, 81/575, 82/318, 90/629 or 96/38, or
- ECE Regulation 14, 14.04 or 14.05

whether or not those instruments apply to the vehicle

Specified passenger seat means the forward-facing front seat alongside the driver or, if there is more than 1 such seat, the 1 furthest away. If there are no seats as above, the foremost forward-facing front passenger seat furthest from the driver (unless there is a fixed partition in front of it).

SEAT BELT ANCHORAGE POINTS cont

ROAD VEHICLES (CONSTRUCTION AND USE) REGULATIONS 1986, REG.46

Item	Description of Vehicle	Seats for which anchorage points must be fitted (mandatory)	Installation Requirement
1	Any vehicle first used before 1.4.82	Driver's seat and specified passenger seat (if any)	Designed to hold seat belts securely in position
2	Minibus constructed or adapted to carry not more than 12 in addition to driver, motor ambulance or motor caravan, in any case first used on or after 1.4.82 but before 1.10.88	As item 1	In accordance with Community Directives or ECE Regulations
3	Minibus (not falling within items 7 or 8) with gross weight not over 3,500 kg, motor ambulance or motor caravan, in any case first used on or after 1.10.88	Driver's seat and each forward-facing front seat	As item 2
4	Goods vehicle first used on or after 1.10.88 but before 1.10.01 with gross weight over 3,500 kg	As item 3	2 or 3 anchorage points to hold seat belts securely
5	Goods vehicle first used on or after 1.10.01 with gross weight over 3,500 kg	All forward-facing front seats	In accordance with Community Directive 96/38 or ECE Reg. 14.04 or 14.05
6	Coach first used on or after 1.10.88 but before 1.10.01	All exposed forward-facing seats	As item 2 or, if fitted before 1.10.01 and forming part of a seat, must not become detached from the seat when horizontal force is applied
7	Bus (other than urban bus) with gross weight over 3,500 kg and first used on or after 1.10.01	Every forward-facing and rearward-facing seat	As item 5
8	As item 7 but with weight not exceeding 3,500 kg	As item 7	As item 5
9	Passenger or dual purpose vehicle (other than a bus) first used on or after 1.4.82 and not falling within items 2 to 8	Every forward-facing seat constructed or adapted for not more than 1 adult	As item 2
10	Vehicle (other than a bus) first used on or after 1.4.82 and not falling within items 2 to 9	Every forward-facing front seat and every non-protected seat	As item 2

Where a vehicle to which this regulation applies is fitted with non-mandatory anchorage points, those points must comply with the requirements applicable to mandatory anchorage points, unless they are –

- anchorage points fitted to a minibus before 1.4.86, or
- anchorage points fitted to any other vehicle before 1.10.88

SEAT BELTS – FITTING
ROAD VEHICLES (CONSTRUCTION AND USE) REGULATIONS 1986, REG.47

This regulation applies to every vehicle to which Reg.46 applies (see previous pages for application and definitions).

Seat belts must be provided in accordance with the following table:

Vehicle (reference to an item means an item in the table on the previous page)	Requirement
First used before 1.4.81	1. Adult body restraining seat belt for the driver's seat; and 2. Body restraining seat belt for specified passenger seat (if any).
First used on or after 1.4.81	3-point belts for the driver's seat and the specified passenger seat (if any).

Item 9 or 10 first used on or after 1.4.87	In addition to the item above,
	1. For any forward-facing front seat alongside the driver's seat, not being a specified passenger seat, a 3-point belt, lap belt or disabled person's belt;
	2. If a passenger or dual purpose vehicle having not more than 2 forward-facing seats behind the driver's seat must have either –
	  (A) an inertia reel belt for at least 1 of those seats, or
	  (B) a 3-point belt, a lap belt, a disabled person's belt or a child restraint for each seat;
	3. If a passenger or dual purpose vehicle having more than 2 forward-facing seats behind the driver's seat, must have either –
	  (A) an inertia reel belt for 1 of those 2 seats being an out board seat and a 3-point belt, a lap belt, a disabled person's belt or a child restraint for at least one other of those seats;
	  (B) a 3-point belt for 1 of those seats and either a child restraint or a disabled person's belt for at least one other of those seats; or
	  (C) a 3-point belt, a lap belt, a disabled persons belt or a child restraint for each of those seats.

Item 3	1. For the driver's seat and the specified passenger seat (if any) a 3-point belt; and 2. For any forward-facing front seat which is not a specified passenger seat, a 3-point belt or a lap belt.
Item 6	3-point belts, lap belts, or disabled person's belts.
Item 5	1. For the driver's seat, a 3-point belt or a lap belt; and 2. For every other forward-facing front seat, a 3-point belt, a lap belt, or a disabled person's belt.
Item 7	For every forward-facing and rearward-facing seat, an inertia reel belt; a retractable lap belt; a disabled person's belt, or a child restraint.
Item 8	For every forward-facing seat, an inertia reel belt, a disabled person's belt, or a child restraint; For every rearward-facing seat, an inertia reel belt, a retractable lap belt, a disabled person's belt, or a child restraint.

SEAT BELTS – FITTING cont
ROAD VEHICLES (CONSTRUCTION AND USE) REGULATIONS 1986, REG. 47

Exemptions

The requirement to fit seat belts in accordance with this regulation do not apply:

- to a vehicle while it is being used under a trade licence;
- to a vehicle to which Type Approval Regs. do not apply and the vehicle is being delivered from the manufacturer, distributor or dealer to a distributor, dealer, purchaser or hirer.
- to a seat in relation to which there is a seat belt:
  - (i)   bearing the mark BS AU 183: 1983 and 'kite' mark,
  - (ii)   which comprises a lap belt and shoulder straps bearing the mark BS 3254: 1960 or BS 3254; Part 1: 1988 and 'kite' mark or approval mark,
  - (iii) the standard of which corresponds with BS AU 183:1983, or
  - (iv)   which is an adult belt comprising a lap belt and shoulder straps and which satisfies the standard referred to in (ii) above
- in relation to the driver's seat or the specified passenger's seat (if any) specially designed, constructed or adapted for a person suffering from a defect or disability
- to a vehicle to which item 4 of the table under 'Anchorage Points' applies.
- to a vehicle constructed or adapted for the transport of prisoners, in relation to seats for persons other than the driver and any front seat passenger provided those seats have anchorage points.

Padding

Where a lap belt is fitted to a forward-facing front seat of a minibus, motor ambulance or motor caravan, or to an exposed forward-facing seat of a coach (other than the driver's seat) either:

1. at least 50 mm padding shall be provided for any bar and any screen or partition which would be likely to be struck by the head of a passenger wearing the lap belt in the event of an accident, or
2. the requirements of Annex 4 of ECE Reg. 21 shall be met in respect of any such bar, screen or partition but padding will not be required by (1) above on any surface more than 1m from the backrest or more than 150 mm to either side or on any instrument panel of a minibus.

Securing to anchorage points

Seat belts must be secured to the anchorage points or, in the case of a child restraint, to specially provided anchorage points or, in the case of a disabled person's belt first fitted before 1.10.01, secured to the vehicle or to the seat being occupied.

BS Mark

Every seat belt except:

1. a disabled person's seat belt
2. a seat belt bearing such marks as are mentioned above
3. an adult seat belt or a child restraint that satisfies
   the requirements of a standard corresponding to the appropriate British Standard (recognised as such by any EEA State)

shall be legibly and permanently marked either with a BS mark or with an EC Component Type-Approval Mark.

SEAT BELTS AND ANCHORAGE POINTS – MAINTENANCE
ROAD VEHICLES (CONSTRUCTION AND USE) REGULATIONS 1986, REG. 48

This regulation applies to all seat belts and anchorage points which are required to be provided by Regs 46 and 47 of these regulations.

Use of anchorage points
Anchorage points for seat belts must only be used for anchorages for the seat belts for which they are intended to be used or are capable of being used.

Integral seat belts
Where a seat incorporates integral belt anchorages, the term 'anchorages' includes the system by which the seat assembly itself is secured to the vehicle structure.
The following maintenance requirements will not apply if the requirement ceased to be complied with after the start of that journey and steps have been taken for such compliance to be restored with all reasonable expedition.

Vehicle structure
All load-bearing members of the vehicle structure or panelling within 30 cm of each anchorage point shall be maintained in a sound condition and free from serious corrosion, distortion or fracture.

Adjusting device
The adjusting device and any retracting mechanism of the seat belt shall be so maintained that the belt may be readily adjusted to the body of the wearer, according to its design.

General defects
The seat belt, anchorages, fastenings and adjusting device shall be maintained free from any obvious defect which would be likely to adversely affect its performance.

Buckles, etc.
The buckle or other fastening of the seat belt shall be
- so maintained that it can be readily fastened or unfastened;
- kept free from any temporary or permanent obstruction, and;
- readily accessible to a person sitting in the seat (except in the case of a disabled person's seat belt).

Seat belt material
The webbing or other material which forms the seat belt shall be maintained free from cuts or other visible faults which would be likely to adversely affect its performance.

Securing to anchorages
The ends of every seat belt, other than a disabled person's seat belt, shall be securely fastened to the anchorage points.

Disabled person's seat belt
The ends of such belts when in use shall be securely fastened either to the structure of the vehicle or to the occupied seat so that the body would be restrained in the event of an accident.

SEAT BELTS – MINIBUSES AND COACHES REG 48A

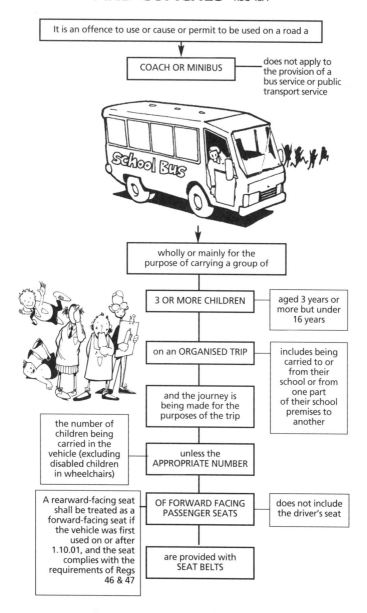

It is an offence to use or cause or permit to be used on a road a

COACH OR MINIBUS — does not apply to the provision of a bus service or public transport service

wholly or mainly for the purpose of carrying a group of

3 OR MORE CHILDREN — aged 3 years or more but under 16 years

on an ORGANISED TRIP — includes being carried to or from their school or from one part of their school premises to another

and the journey is being made for the purposes of the trip

the number of children being carried in the vehicle (excluding disabled children in wheelchairs) — unless the APPROPRIATE NUMBER

A rearward-facing seat shall be treated as a forward-facing seat if the vehicle was first used on or after 1.10.01, and the seat complies with the requirements of Regs 46 & 47 — OF FORWARD FACING PASSENGER SEATS — does not include the driver's seat

are provided with SEAT BELTS

SEAT BELTS – NOTIFICATION TO BUS PASSENGERS

ROAD TRAFFIC ACT 1988 S 15B

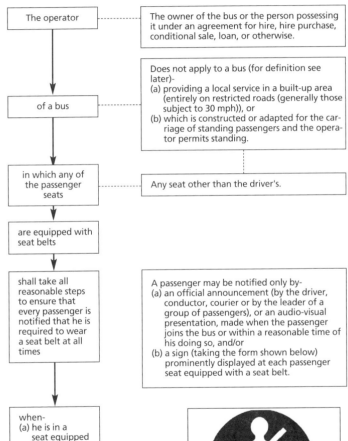

| The operator | ┄┄┄ | The owner of the bus or the person possessing it under an agreement for hire, hire purchase, conditional sale, loan, or otherwise. |

| of a bus | ┄┄┄ | Does not apply to a bus (for definition see later)-
(a) providing a local service in a built-up area (entirely on restricted roads (generally those subject to 30 mph)), or
(b) which is constructed or adapted for the carriage of standing passengers and the operator permits standing. |

| in which any of the passenger seats | ┄┄┄ | Any seat other than the driver's. |

| are equipped with seat belts |

| shall take all reasonable steps to ensure that every passenger is notified that he is required to wear a seat belt at all times | | A passenger may be notified only by-
(a) an official announcement (by the driver, conductor, courier or by the leader of a group of passengers), or an audio-visual presentation, made when the passenger joins the bus or within a reasonable time of his doing so, and/or
(b) a sign (taking the form shown below) prominently displayed at each passenger seat equipped with a seat belt. |

| when-
(a) he is in a seat equipped with a seat belt, and
(b) the bus is in motion. |

| An operator who fails to comply commits an offence |

Form of seat belt symbol for buses (white figure on blue background).

SEAT BELTS – WEARING BY ADULTS

REGS 5 & 6 MOTOR VEHICLES (WEARING OF SEAT BELTS) REGULATIONS 1993

EVERY PERSON
(of 14 years and over)

driving a

riding in the front or rear seat of

motor vehicle
(other than a two-wheeled motor cycle with or without a sidecar)

Shall wear an adult belt

except

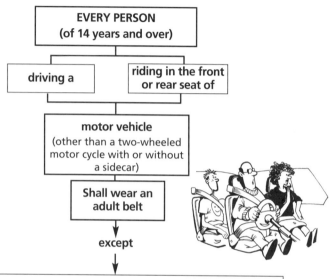

(a) person holding a medical certificate
(b) driver or passenger in a motor vehicle constructed or adapted for carrying goods, while on a journey which does not exceed 50 m and which is undertaken for the purpose of delivering or collecting any thing
(c) person driving whilst reversing
(d) qualified driver supervising a provisional licence holder while reversing
(e) person conducting a test of competence to drive if wearing a seat belt would endanger himself or others
(f) person driving or riding in a vehicle being used for fire brigade, police or Serious Organised Crime Agency purposes, or carrying a person in lawful custody
(g) driver of a licensed taxi or private hire vehicle
(h) person riding in a vehicle, being used under a trade licence, for the purpose of investigating or remedying a mechanical fault
(i) disabled person wearing a disabled person's belt
(j) person riding in a vehicle whilst taking part in a procession organised by or on behalf of the crown
(k) person riding in a vehicle whilst taking part in a possession which is either commonly held in the area, or in respect of which notice has been given under the Public Order Act 1986
(l) person driving a vehicle if the driver's seat is not provided with a belt; or
(m) person riding in the vehicle if no belt is available.
(n) (i) person riding in a small or large bus–
(ii) providing a local service in a built-up area (entirely on restricted roads (generally those subject to 30 mph)), or
(iii) which is constructed or adapted for the carriage of standing passengers and the operator permits standing.
For definitions of small and large bus, see later.

SEAT BELTS – WEARING BY CHILDREN IN FRONT SEATS

MOTOR VEHICLES (WEARING OF SEAT BELTS BY CHILDREN IN FRONT SEATS)
REGULATIONS 1993, AND SECTION 15(1) & (1A) ROAD TRAFFIC ACT 1988

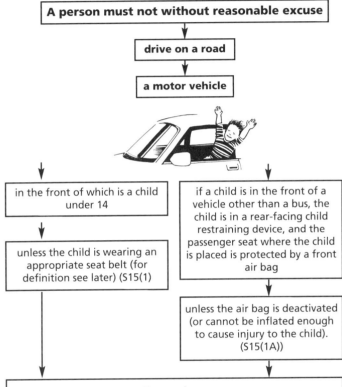

A person must not without reasonable excuse

↓

drive on a road

↓

a motor vehicle

in the front of which is a child under 14	if a child is in the front of a vehicle other than a bus, the child is in a rear-facing child restraining device, and the passenger seat where the child is placed is protected by a front air bag

↓ (left column)

unless the child is wearing an appropriate seat belt (for definition see later) (S15(1))

↓ (right column)

unless the air bag is deactivated (or cannot be inflated enough to cause injury to the child). (S15(1A))

Exemptions

(a) a small child (for definition see later) aged 3 years or more in a bus, and wearing an adult belt if an appropriate belt is not available for him in the front or rear of the vehicle;

(b) a child for whom there is a medical certificate;

(c) a disabled child wearing a disabled person's belt;

(d) a child riding in a bus being used to provide a local service in a built up area (entirely on restricted roads (generally those subject to 30 mph)), or which is constructed or adapted for the carriage of standing passengers and the operator permits standing; and

(e) a large child (for definition see later) if no appropriate belt is available for him in the front of the vehicle.

SEAT BELTS – WEARING BY CHILDREN IN REAR SEATS

MOTOR VEHICLES (WEARING OF SEAT BELTS) REGS 1993, AND S 15 RTA 1988

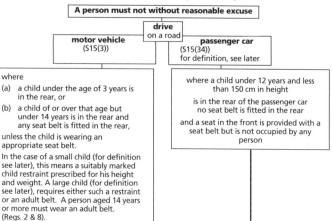

A person must not without reasonable excuse

drive on a road

motor vehicle (S15(3))

passenger car (S15(3A)) for definition, see later

where

(a) a child under the age of 3 years is in the rear, or

(b) a child of or over that age but under 14 years is in the rear and any seat belt is fitted in the rear,

unless the child is wearing an appropriate seat belt.

In the case of a small child (for definition see later), this means a suitably marked child restraint prescribed for his height and weight. A large child (for definition see later), requires either such a restraint or an adult belt. A person aged 14 years or more must wear an adult belt. (Regs. 2 & 8).

where a child under 12 years and less than 150 cm in height

is in the rear of the passenger car no seat belt is fitted in the rear

and a seat in the front is provided with a seat belt but is not occupied by any person

Vehicles

The following vehicles are exempt:

(a) large buses (for definition see later); and

(b) licensed taxis and hire cars in which the rear seats are separated from the driver by a fixed partition.

Exceptions to S 15(3) and (3A)

(a) a child for whom there is a medical certificate;

(b) a small child under 3 years in a licensed taxi or hire car if no appropriate seat belt is available;

(c) a small child aged 3 years or more in a licensed taxi, hire car or small bus, wearing an adult belt if no appropriate seat belt is available;

(d) a small child aged 3 years or more wearing an adult belt in a passenger car or light goods vehicle (maximum laden weight not exceeding 3.5 tonnes) where 2 child occupants in the rear are using the child restraints and there is no appropriate seat belt available in the front;

(e) a small child riding in a police, security or emergency services vehicle;

(f) a small child aged 3 years or more wearing an adult belt and who, because of unexpected necessity, is travelling a short distance in a passenger or light goods vehicle in which no appropriate belt is available; or

(g) a disabled child wearing a disabled person's belt or whose disability makes it impracticable to wear a seat belt where no disabled person's belt is available.

Exceptions to S15(3) only

(a) a child under 3 years riding in the rear seat of a small bus (for definition see later);

(b) a small child aged 3 years or more riding in the rear seat of a small bus if neither an appropriate seat belt or an adult belt is available in the front or rear of the vehicle;

(c) a large child in any vehicle if no appropriate seat belt is available in the rear;

(d) a child riding in a small bus - (i) providing a local service in a built-up area (entirely on restricted roads (generally those subject to 30 mph), or (ii) which is constructed or adapted for the carriage of standing passengers and the operator permits standing.

Exception to S15(3A) only

A child if no appropriate seat belt is available in the front of the vehicle.

SEAT BELTS – DEFINITIONS

Passenger car

A passenger car is a motor vehicle which:

- is constructed or adapted for the carriage of passengers and is not a goods vehicle
- has no more than 8 seats in addition to the driver's
- has 4 or more wheels
- has a maximum design speed exceeding 25 kph and
- has a maximum laden weight not exceeding 3.5 tonnes.

SECTION 15 ROAD TRAFFIC ACT 1988

Available

A seat belt will be regarded as being available unless:

- another person is wearing the relevant belt
- a child is occupying the relevant seat and wearing a child restraint which is an appropriate child restraint for that child
- another person, being a person holding a medical certificate, is occupying the relevant seat
- a disabled person (not being the person in question) is occupying the relevant seat and wearing a disabled person's belt
- by reason of his disability, it would not be practicable for the person in question to wear the relevant belt
- the person in question is prevented from occupying the relevant seat by the presence of child restraint which could not readily be removed without the aid of tools; (unless the person in question is a child and the child restraint is appropriate for him) or
- the relevant seat is specially designed so that –
  (i) its configuration can be adjusted in order to increase the space in the vehicle available for goods or personal effects, and
  (ii)when it is so adjusted the seat cannot be used as such, and the configuration is adjusted in the manner described in sub-paragraph (i) and it would not be reasonably practicable for the goods and personal effects being carried in the vehicle to be so carried were configuration not so adjusted.

SCHED 2 MOTOR VEHICLES (WEARING OF SEAT BELTS) REGULATIONS 1993

SEAT BELTS – DEFINITIONS cont
ROAD TRAFFIC ACT 1988 & MOTOR VEHICLES (WEARING OF SEAT BELTS)
REGULATIONS 1993

Bus
A motor vehicle that has at least 4 wheels, is constructed or adapted for the carriage of passengers, has more than 8 seats in addition to the driver's, and has a maximum design speed exceeding 25 kph.

Large bus
A motor vehicle having at least 4 wheels, is constructed or adapted for the carriage of passengers, has more than 8 seats in addition to the driver's, has a maximum design speed exceeding 25 kph, and has a maximum laden weight exceeding 3.5 tonnes.

Small bus
A motor vehicle having at least 4 wheels, is constructed or adapted for the carriage of passengers, has more than 8 seats in addition to the driver's, has a maximum design speed exceeding 25 kph, and has a maximum laden weight not exceeding 3.5 tonnes.

Light goods vehicle
A motor vehicle which has 4 or more wheels, has a maximum design speed exceeding 25 kph and a maximum laden weight not exceeding 3.5 tonnes.

Appropriate seat belt
   (a)   For a small child, a child restraint of a description prescribed for a child of his height and weight and marked that it is suitable for his weight (or a child restraint which complies with the corresponding requirements of a member State).

   (b)   For a large child, a child restraint of a description prescribed for a child of his height and weight and marked that it is suitable for his weight; or an adult belt

   (c)   For a person aged 14 years or more, an adult belt.

Small child
A child under 12 years and under 135 cm in height.

Large child
A child who is not a small child.

Child
A person under the age of 14 years.

MIRRORS

REG 33 ROAD VEHICLES (CONSTRUCTION AND USE) REGULATIONS 1986

Requirement

A motor vehicle (not being a road roller) specified in column 2 of the table below shall be fitted with mirrors or other devices for indirect vision, if any, as are specified in column 3. Any such mirror or device shall, whether or not it is required to be fitted, comply with the relevant Community Directive of Regulation.

Exterior mirrors

Each exterior mirror mentioned in items 2 or 8 of the table shall, if the vehicle has a permissible maximum weight over 3,500 kg, be a class II mirror, and in any other case, a class II or III mirror.

Interior mirrors

In the case of a wheeled motor vehicle mentioned in items 1, 2, 10 or 11 of the table, first used on or after 1.4.69, the edges of any interior mirror shall be surrounded by some material such as will render it unlikely that severe cuts would be caused if the mirror or that material were struck by any occupant of the vehicle.

Community Directives

Instead of complying with this regulation, vehicles may comply with the relevant Community Directive or ECE Regulation.

'Devices for indirect vision' mean to observe the traffic area adjacent to the vehicle which cannot be observed by direct vision and may include conventional mirrors, camera-monitors or other devices able to present information about the indirect field of vision to the driver.

'Mirror' means any device with a reflecting surface, excluding devices such as periscopes, intended to give a clear view to the rear, side or front of the vehicle.

Trailers

In the case of (a) an agricultural vehicle or (b) a vehicle described in items 2 or 8 in the table, when drawing a trailer the references to a vehicle in the definitions above shall include references to that trailer.

1 Item	2 Class of vehicle	3 Mirrors, etc. to be fitted
1	A motor vehicle which is (a) drawing a trailer if a person is carried on the trailer so that he has an uninterrupted view to the rear and has an efficient means of communicating to the driver the effect of signals given by the drivers of other vehicles to the rear; (b) (i) a works truck; (ii) a track-laying agricultural motor vehicle; and (iii) a wheeled agricultural motor vehicle first used before 1.6.78, if, in each case, the driver can easily obtain a view to the rear; (c) a pedestrian controlled vehicle; (d) a chassis being driven from its place of manufacture to a place to receive a body; or (e) an agricultural motor vehicle which has an unladen weight exceeding 7,370 kg and which- (i) is a track-laying vehicle or (ii) is a wheeled vehicle first used before 1.6.78.	No requirement.

MIRRORS cont

REG 33 ROAD VEHICLES (CONSTRUCTION AND USE) REGULATIONS 1986

1 Item	2 Class of vehicle	3 Mirrors, etc. to be fitted
2	A motor vehicle not included in item 1, which is: (a) a wheeled locomotive or a wheeled motor tractor first used in either case on or after 1.6.78; (b) an agricultural motor vehicle, not being a track-laying vehicle with an unladen weight not exceeding 7,370 kg (which falls in item 11) or a wheeled agricultural motor vehicle first used after 1.6.86 which is driven at more than 20 mph (which falls in item 8); or (c) a works truck.	At least one exterior mirror fitted on the offside.
3	A wheeled motor vehicle not included in items 1 or 4 first used on or after 1.4.83 which is: (a) a bus; or (b) a goods vehicle with a maximum gross weight exceeding 3,500 kg (not being an agricultural motor vehicle or one which is not driven at more than 20 mph) other than a vehicle described in item 5.	See note 1 below or, except in the case of a goods vehicle first used on or after 1.4.85, note 5.
4	A wheeled motor vehicle not included in item 1 first used on or after 26.1.2007 which is: (a) a bus; (b) a goods vehicle with a maximum gross weight: (i) exceeding 3,500 kg but not exceeding 7,500 kg; or (ii) exceeding 7,500 kg but not exceeding 12,000 kg; (not being an agricultural motor vehicle or one which is not driven at more than 20 mph).	(a) and (b)(ii), (see note 2 below. (b)(i), see note 3.
5	A goods vehicle not being an agricultural motor vehicle with a maximum gross weight exceeding 12,000kg which is first used on or after 1.10.88 and before 26.1.2007.	See note 4 below.
6	A goods vehicle not being an agricultural motor vehicle with a maximum gross weight exceeding 12,000kg which is first used on or after 26.1.2007.	See note 2 below.
7	A two-wheeled motor cycle with or without a sidecar attached.	No requirement.
8	A wheeled motor vehicle not in items 1 to 7, which is first used on or after 1.6.78 (or, in the case of a Ford Transit 10.7.78) and before 26.1.2010.	See note 5 below.
9	A wheeled motor vehicle not in items 1 to 7, which is first used on or after 26.1.2010.	See note 2 below.
10	A wheeled motor vehicle not in items 1 to 7, first used before 1.6.78 (or in the case of a Ford Transit, 10.7.78) and a track-laying motor vehicle which is not an agricultural motor vehicle first used on or after 1.1.58, which in either case is: (a) a bus; (b) a dual-purpose vehicle; or (c) a goods vehicle.	See note 6 below.
11	A motor vehicle whether wheeled or track-laying, not in items 1 to 10.	See note 7 below.

Note 1. Must comply with Community Directive 79/795, 86/562, 88/321 or ECE Regulation 46.01. Exterior mirrors fitted to M2, M3, N2 & N3 vehicles must be class II; M1 & N1 vehicles must have class II or III.

MIRRORS cont

REG 33 ROAD VEHICLES (CONSTRUCTION AND USE) REGULATIONS 1986

M1 & N1 vehicles must have both an interior and an exterior mirror fitted to the left side of the vehicle on a right hand side rule of road country, and vice versa. If the interior mirror does not meet the prescribed field of vision, an additional exterior mirror must be fitted on the opposite side to the existing one.

M2, M3, N2, N3 vehicles must have 2 exterior mirrors – one on each side, to be visible through the side windows or that portion of the windscreen which is swept by the wipers (except, in the case of M2 & M3 vehicles, the right side exterior mirror in right hand rule of road countries, and vice versa). Exterior mirrors must not extend beyond the external bodywork of the vehicle substantially more than necessary. The interior mirror must be capable of being adjusted by the driver from his driving position. The exterior mirror on the driver's side must be capable of being adjusted from inside the vehicle with the door closed, although the window may be open. It may be capable of being locked in position from the outside (but this does not apply if, having been knocked out of alignment, it can be returned to its former position without being adjusted).

Note 2. Must comply with Community Directive 2003/97, 2005/27 or ECE Reg. 46.02. The required field of vision must be obtained by the minimum number of mandatory mirrors laid down in the following table, where 'C' = compulsory, 'O' = optional, 'NP' = not permitted. Reference should also be made to the relevant footnotes. Definitions of vehicle categories may be found under 'Vehicle Categories'.

Vehicle Category	Interior Class I (Inside)	Class II (Main) (large)	Class III (Main) (small)	Exterior Class IV (Wide angle)	Class V (Close proximity)	Class VI (Front)
M_1	C^1	O	C^2	O^3	O^4	O^5
M_2	O	C^6	NP	O^3	O^4	O^5
M_3	O	C^6	NP	O^3	O^4	O^5
N_1	C^1	O	C^2	O^3	O^4	O^5
N_2 7.5 t	O	C^6	NP	O^6	O^4	O^7
N_2 > 7.5 t	O	C^6	NP	C^6	C^8	C^7
N_3	O	C^6	NP	C^6	C^8	C^7

Table footnotes:

1 Unless it would not provide rearward vision, in which case it is optional.
2 One on each side. Class II may be fitted instead.
3 One on driver's side and/or one on passenger's side.
4 One on each side. Both must be at least 2 m above the ground.
5 Must be at least 2 m above the ground.
6 One on each side.
7 One front mirror (must be at least 2 m above the ground).
8 One on passenger's side. Optionally one may also be fitted on the driver's side. In all cases they must be at least 2 m above the ground.

MIRRORS cont

REG 33 ROAD VEHICLES (CONSTRUCTION AND USE) REGULATIONS 1986

General

An indirect vision device may be fitted instead of a mirror. A camera/monitor device may be used. Mirrors must be placed so that the driver has a clear view to the rear, side or front. Mirrors must be visible through the side windows or that portion of the windscreen which is swept by the wipers (except, in the case of M2 & M3 vehicles). Exterior mirrors must not extend beyond the external bodywork of the vehicle substantially more than necessary. If the lower edge is less than 2 m above the ground when loaded, it must not project more than 250 mm beyond the overall width. The interior mirror must be capable of being adjusted by the driver from his driving position. The exterior mirror on the driver's side must be capable of being adjusted from inside the vehicle with the door closed, although the window may be open. It may be capable of being locked in position from the outside (but this does not apply if, having been knocked out of alignment, it can be returned to its former position without being adjusted).

Note 3. The same as for note 2, above, but Class V mirrors for N2 7.5 t vehicles are compulsory and footnote 8 beneath the table applies.

Note 4. Must comply with Council Directive 86/562, 88/321 or ECE Regulation 46.01 (Council Directive 71/127). The required field of vision must be obtained by the minimum number of mandatory mirrors laid down in the following table. Reference should also be made to the relevant footnotes. For definitions of vehicle categories see under 'Vehicle Categories'.

Vehicle Category	Interior Class I (Inside)	Class II (Main) (large)	Class III (Main) (small)	Exterior Class IV (Wide angle)	Class V (Close proximity)
M_1	1^1	$_2$	$1^{3\ \&\ 4}$	–	–
M_2	–	2^5	–	$_6$	$_7\ \&\ 8$
M_3	–	2^5	–	$_6$	$_7\ \&\ 8$
N_1	1^1	$_2$	$1^{3\ \&\ 4}$	$_6$	–
N_2 7.5 t	$_9$	2^5	$_{10}$	$_{11}$	$_7\ \&\ 8$
N_2> 7.5 t	$_9$	2^5	$_{10}$	1	$_8$
N_3	$_9$	2^5	$_{10}$	1	1^8

Table footnotes:

1   If the interior mirror does not satisfy the requirements for field of vision, a second exterior mirror must be fitted on the opposite side to the compulsory mirror. If the interior mirror does not provide any rear view, it is not required. Class II mirrors are permissible.
2   Class II exterior mirrors are permissible.
3   On the side opposite to the direction followed by traffic.

MIRRORS cont

REG 33 ROAD VEHICLES (CONSTRUCTION AND USE) REGULATIONS 1986

4 A second exterior mirror may be fitted on the opposite side to the compulsory mirror.

5 One on the left and one on the right.

6 A class IV exterior mirror is acceptable for N^2 7.5 t and for M^2 and M^3 vehicles.

7 A class V exterior mirror is acceptable for N^2 7.5 t and for M^2 and M^3 vehicles.

8 No part of the mirror is to be less than 2 m from the ground when the vehicle is carrying its maximum load.

9 An interior mirror may be fitted.

10 If it is not possible to acquire the required field of vision when a class IV mirror is fitted to a class II mounting, a class III mirror may be used instead of the latter.

11 A class IV mirror is required if the mandatory class II mirror is not convex.

Note 5. It must be fitted with:

(i) at least one exterior mirror fitted on the offside; and

(ii) at least one interior mirror, unless it would give the driver no view of the rear; and

(iii) at least one exterior on the nearside unless an interior mirror gives the driver an adequate view to the rear.

Mirrors must be fitted as follows:

(a) each mirror must remain steady under normal driving conditions

(b) each exterior mirror on a vehicle fitted with windows and a windscreen shall be visible to the driver, when in his driving position, through a side window or through the portion of the windscreen which is swept by the windscreen wiper

(c) where the bottom edge of an exterior mirror is less than 2 m above the road surface when the vehicle is laden, that mirror shall not project more than 20 cm (or 25 cm where the mirror complies with the relevant Community Directive) beyond the overall width of the vehicle, or, where drawing a trailer which is wider than the drawing vehicle, not more than 20 cm (or 25 cm) beyond the overall width of the trailer

(d) each interior mirror shall be capable of being adjusted by the driver when in his driving position; and

(e) except in the case of a mirror which, if knocked out of its alignment, can be returned to its former position without needing to be adjusted, each exterior mirror on the driver's side shall be capable of being adjusted by the driver when in his driving position. However, this shall not prevent such a mirror from being locked into position from the outside.

Note 6. It must be fitted with at least one exterior mirror on the offside and either one interior mirror or one exterior mirror fitted on the nearside.

Note 7. It must be fitted with at least one interior or exterior mirror.

VISION

View to the front (REG 30)

Every motor vehicle shall be designed and constructed so that the driver can at all times have a full view of the road and traffic ahead of the vehicle.

All glass or other transparent material shall be maintained in such condition that it does not obscure the vision of the driver while the vehicle is being driven on a road.

Transmission of light (REG 32)

Windows and windscreens which are required to be fitted (including any tint, film or other substance or material applied to a windscreen) must be capable of transmitting light not less than-
• motor vehicles first used before 1.4.85, 70% for all windows,
• motor vehicles first used on or after 1.4.85 and trailers, 75% for windscreens and 70% for all other windows.

Windscreen Wipers and Washers (REG 34)

Every vehicle fitted with a windscreen shall, unless the driver can see to the front without looking through the windscreen, be fitted with one or more efficient **automatic windscreen wipers** capable of clearing the screen so the driver can see the road in front on both sides of the vehicle and the front.

Every wheeled vehicle required to be fitted as above, must also have a windscreen washer capable of clearing mud etc. (except agricultural vehicles first used on or after 1.6.86 driven at not more than 20 mph; track laying vehicles; vehicles with max speed not over 20 mph; or local transport service vehicles).

Glass (REG 32)

Caravans first used on or after 1.9.78 and wheeled motor vehicles and trailers first used on or after 1.6.78 shall have windows as follows:

Windows	Requirement
Windscreens and other windows wholly or partly on either side of the driver's seat.	Glass complying with British Standard Specification or ECE Regulations and bearing the relevant marking.
All other windows, windscreens of motor cycles, temporary replacements for windscreens or windows wholly or partly in front of or on either side of the driver's seat.	Materials other than glass which is so constructed or treated that if fractured it does not fly into fragments likely to cause severe cuts.
Screen or door in interior of a bus first used on or after 1.4.88.	Either of the above.
Police or security vehicles, engineering plant, etc; upper deck of buses; roof windows.	Either of the above or safety glass.

SPECIAL TYPES VEHICLES – GENERAL
THE ROAD VEHICLES (AUTHORISATION OF SPECIAL TYPES)(GENERAL) ORDER 2003

This order applies only to motor vehicles and trailers which do not comply in all respects with standard construction and use regulations, and which are a **recognised category** of special vehicle as specified in the list below. Such vehicles may be used on roads only if they comply with the **authorised requirements** applicable to that category. It should be noted that there may be addition requirements applicable to a group of vehicle categories. These requirements may be found in respective pages referred to in the list –

Category	Requirements specific to the category Page	Additional requirements specific to the group (see relevant pages)				
		Police	Attendants	Sec. of State	Roads/bridges	Marking
Abnormal indivisible load	74	x	x	x	x	x
Mobile crane	80	x	x	x	x	x
Engineering plant	83	x	x	x	x	x
Road recovery vehicle	86	x	x	x	x	x
Agricultural motor vehicle	88	x	x	x	x	x
Wide load over 4.3 metres	89	x	x	x	x	
Local excavation vehicle	90	x	x	x	x	
Vehicle for test, trial or non-U.K. use	92	x			x	
Track-laying vehicle	92				x	
Straddle carrier	94	x				
Vehicle with moveable platform	95					
Pedestrian-controlled road maintenance	96					
Vehicle/trailer for cutting grass/ hedges	96					
Operational military vehicle	98					
R.N.L.I. track-laying vehicle	98					
Highway testing vehicle	99					
Vehicle propelled by natural gas	99					

SPECIAL TYPES VEHICLES – ABNORMAL LOADS

SCHED 1 ROAD VEHICLES (AUTHORISATION OF SPECIAL TYPES) (GENERAL) ORDER 2003

Definition

An **abnormal indivisible load** is one which can not, without undue expense or risk of damage, be divided into 2 or more loads for the purpose of carriage, and on account of its length, width, height or weight cannot be carried on a normal vehicle. (Para. 2)

An **abnormal indivisible load vehicle (AILV)** is:

(a) a goods vehicle having a mass over 12 tonnes (cat. N3), specially designed or constructed for abnormal loads
(b) a trailer having a mass over 12 tonnes (cat. O4), specially designed or constructed for abnormal loads
(c) a locomotive specially designed to tow such trailers; or
(d) a motor vehicle with a mass over 12 tonnes (cat. N3), not itself designed to carry a load, but which is specially designed and constructed to tow such trailers. (Para. 3)

A **'category 1' AILV** is a vehicle which does not exceed the vehicle and axle weights applicable to it in paragraphs 28 & 29 (see later), and it also complies with any other requirements imposed by those paragraphs. (Para. 4)

A **'category 2' AILV** is a vehicle which is not in cat. 1 and does not exceed the vehicle and axle weights applicable to it in paragraphs 30 & 31 (see later), and it also complies with any other requirements imposed by those paragraphs. (Para. 4)

A **'category 3' AILV** is a vehicle which is not in cat. 1 or 2 and does not exceed the vehicle and axle weights applicable to it in paragraphs 32 & 33 (see later), and it also complies with any other requirements imposed by those paragraphs. (Para. 4)

Construction

(a) must be **wheeled** and fitted with **pneumatic tyres** (paras. 5 & 6);
(b) must have a **braking system** which complies with the relevant requirements for the type of vehicle (paras. 7–12)
(c) a cat. 2 or 3 vehicle (see later) must have a **"SPECIAL TYPES VEHICLE"** plate fitted to the vehicle in a readily accessible and conspicuous position, containing the **maximum axle, gross and train weight** (or, in the case of a trailer, the maximum weight which may be imposed on the towing vehicle) for the following speeds of the vehicle: 20, 25, 30, 35 & 40 mph, at which the vehicle may be travelling (does not apply to vehicles manufactured before 29.7.83) (para. 13)
(d) must have a clean and unobscured sign vertically mounted in a clearly visible position on the front of the vehicle indicating the category into which the vehicle or combination falls. The sign contains white letters on a black background as follows (para. 15):

SPECIAL TYPES VEHICLES – ABNORMAL LOADS cont

Conditions relating to use.

(a) **may not be used to carry a load** which may safely be carried on a vehicle which complies with Con. & Use and Authorised Weights Regulations (para.16)

(b) an AILV falling within para. (a) or (b) under "definition" on the previous page **may only be used for the carriage of abnormal loads** or wide loads (does not apply to a disassembled AILV combination not carrying an abnormal load, where one module is carrying the other) (para. 17)

(c) where the **overall width of the such an AILV exceeds 3 m**, it may not be used to carry a load other than one which can only be safely carried on such a vehicle (para. 17)

(d) an AILV falling within para. (c) or (d) under "definition" on the previous page **may only be used for the towing of an AILV which is a trailer** (does not apply to a disassembled AILV combination not carrying an abnormal load, where one module is carrying the other) (paras. 18 & 19)

(e) where the overall width of such an AILV exceeds 3 m, it **may not be used unless the trailer it is towing has a width exceeding 3 m** and the load can only safely be carried on such a trailer (para. 18)

(f) an AILV or AILV combination **may normally only carry one abnormal load at a time** but two or more may be carried if certain conditions are met e.g. cannot safely be carried if separated, maximum width or length of AILV not to exceed that of widest/longest load, weight restrictions not exceeded (paras. 20–23).

Maximum width. The maximum width plus any lateral projections is not to exceed 6.1 m (para. 24).

Maximum length. The maximum length is not to exceed 30 m measured as follows (para. 25):

Description	Measuring Criteria
Weight rests wholly on an N3 AILV	Overall length of vehicle plus any rearward or forward projection
AILV combination where weight rests solely on an O4 trailer	Overall length of trailer plus any rearward or forward projection
AILV combination consisting of only a motor vehicle and trailer, where load rests on both vehicles (whether or not articulated)	Overall length of trailer plus any projection in front of the foremost part of the trailer plus the length of any rearward projection of the load
AILV combination other than as mentioned above and the load rests on at least 2 vehicles	Overall length of the vehicles which bear the load plus the length of any distance between them plus the length of any rearward or forward projection of the load

SPECIAL TYPES VEHICLES – ABNORMAL LOADS cont

Maximum weight

1. General

(a) No AILV or AILV combination may exceed the weight restrictions which apply to a cat. 3 AILV or AILV combination (para. 26);

(b) A cat. 1 AILV may not exceed the weight specified on any plate required by Reg. 66 of the Con. & Use Regs (para. 27);

(c) A cat. 2 or 3 AILV must not exceed any of the maximum weights (for the speed at which it is travelling) specified on the plate with which it is required to be fitted by para. 13 (does not apply to trailers first used before 29.7.83) (para. 27).

2. Category 1 AILVs and combinations

Such vehicles must not exceed the weights in the table below (paras. 28 & 29). For "Authorised Weight Regs." see under "Additional Authorised Weights".

Description of Vehicle	Maximum Weight	Article
Cat. 1 AILV to which Authorised Weight Regs. apply	Weights laid down in Sched. 1 to the regulations. But see note below.	28
Cat.1 AILV combinations to which the above regs. apply	Total weight of vehicles carrying a load – 46,000 kg But see note below	28
Cat. 1 AILV or AILV combination to which the above regs. do not apply	Must comply with the equivalent Con. & Use Regs.	28
Any cat. 1 AILV or AILV combination (including a vehicle to which the note below applies)	If carrying a load, each vehicle must have 5 or more axles. The axle weight must not exceed the weights laid down in Sched. 3 of the Authorised Weight Regs.	29
Cat. 1 AILV or AILV combination to which the above regs. do not apply	Must comply with the equivalent Con. & Use Regs.	29

Note

Where this note applies, the relevant weights may be exceeded by a combination if –

(a) the combination has at least 6 axles;

(b) total weight does not exceed 50,000 kg; and

(c) it otherwise complies with the Authorised Weight Regs. as they apply to a combination of 44,000 kg.

SPECIAL TYPES VEHICLES – ABNORMAL LOADS cont

Maximum weight, continued

3. Category 2 AILVs and combinations

Total weight (para. 30)
Any cat. 2 AILV or vehicle in an AILV combination must not exceed 80,000 kg total weight. But if the weight calculated in accordance with the following formula (rounded up to the nearest 10 kg) is less than 80,000 kg then the lesser weight becomes the maximum. The formula is –

Max. weight (kg) = D × 7,500, where D is the distance in metres between –
(a) in the case of an AILV, the foremost and rearmost axle;
(b) in the case of a combination which is an articulated vehicle, the kingpin and the rearmost axle of the semi-trailer; or
(c) in the case of any other AILV combination, the foremost axle and the rearmost axle of the group of vehicles carrying a load.

Axles and wheels (para. 31)
The total weight must be transmitted to the road by 6 or more axles.
The distance between any 2 adjacent axles must not be less than 1 m.
The distance between adjacent axles as per the following table determines the maximum axle and wheel weight.

Distance between axles	Axle weight	Wheel weight
Less than 1.35 m	12,000 kg	6,000 kg
1.35 m or more	12,500 kg	6,250 kg

But where the vehicle has groups of axles, the distance between any 2 adjacent axles in a group is less than 2 m, and the distance between adjacent axles in different groups is more than 2 m, the sum of the weights of all the wheels in a group must not exceed 50,000 kg.

"Group of axles" means 2 or more axles that are so linked together that the load applied to 1 axle is applied to the other.

"Distance between axles" is the shortest distance between the centres of contact of an axle wheel with the road surface and the similar point of another axle wheel.

SPECIAL TYPES VEHICLES – ABNORMAL LOADS cont

Maximum weight, continued

4. Category 3 AILVs and combinations (Sched. 1, para 32)

Total weight (para. 32)

The total weight of a cat.3 AILV or AILV in a combination must not exceed 150,000 kg total weight. But if the weight calculated in accordance with the following formula (rounded up to the nearest 10 kg) is less than 150,000 kg then the lesser weight becomes the maximum. The formula is –

Max. weight (kg) = $D \times 12{,}500$, where D is the distance in m between –

(a) in the case of an AILV, the foremost and rearmost axle;
(b) in the case of a combination which is an articulated vehicle, the kingpin and the rearmost axle of the semi-trailer; or
(c) in the case of any other AILV combination, the foremost axle and the rearmost axle of the group of vehicles carrying a load.

Axles and wheels (para. 31)

The total weight must be transmitted to the road by 6 or more axles.
The distance between any 2 adjacent axles must not be less than 1 metre.
The distance between adjacent axles as per the following table determines the maximum axle and wheel weight.

Distance between axles	Axle weight	Wheel weight
Less than 1.35 m	15,000 kg	7,500 kg
1.35 m or more	16,500 kg	8,250 kg

But where the vehicle has groups of axles, the distance between any 2 adjacent axles in a group is less than 1.5 m, and the distance between adjacent axles in different groups is more than 1.5 m, the sum of the weights of all the wheels in a group must not exceed 90,000 kg if the distance between any 2 adjacent axles in a group is less than 1.35 m, or 100,000 kg in any other case.
"Group of axles" and "distance between axles" – see previous page.

Speed restrictions

A cat. 2 or 3 AILV must not exceed the speed contained in the plate required by para. 13 (see earlier). A cat. 1, 2 or 3 AILV must not exceed the speed in the following table –

AILV	Motorway	Dual carriageway	Other road
Cat. 1	60	50	40
Cat. 2 or 3	40	35	30

Other special requirements. Where limits relating to length, width, projections, or weight are exceeded, there may be a requirement to notify the police, the road and bridge authorities, the Secretary of State, and to carry attendants. For details of *when* and *how* these are required, see respectively under "Additional Requirements" and "Notification of Police, etc.". For details of when and how to provide markers, see under "Marking of Projections".

SPECIAL TYPES VEHICLES – ABNORMAL LOADS cont

Application of regulations.

An AILV manufactured before 1.10.89 continues to be subject to the requirements of the old 1979 regulations, otherwise the following applies –

1. Category 1 AILV & AILV combinations.

Must comply with –

(a) the Road Vehicles (Construction and Use) Regulations 1986 except for the following –

Non-applicable regulations	Subject
7	Length
8	Width
80	Over-riding weight regulations
82	Restrictions on use of vehicles carrying long or wide loads

(b) the Road Vehicles (Authorised Weight) Regulations 1998; and
(c) the Road Vehicles Lighting Regulations 1989. (para. 35)

2. Category 2 and 3 AILVs & AILV combinations.

Must comply with –

(a) the Road Vehicles Lighting Regulations 1989; and
(b) the Construction and Use Regulations 1986 except for the following –

Non-applicable regulations	Subject
7	Length
8	Width
15,16	Braking systems
18(1A) to (9)	Maintenance and efficiency of brakes
25	Tyre loads and speed ratings
64	Spray suppression devices
65	Maintenance of spray suppression devices
75(1), in so far as it relates to items 1–4, 6–11, 15 & 16 of the table	Maximum permitted laden weight of vehicle. See earlier under "Maximum Overall Weight".
76–80	Other maximum permitted weights of non-articulated vehicles and trailers. See earlier under "Maximum overall weight".
82	Restrictions on vehicles carrying wide or long loads
83(1)	Number of trailers

SPECIAL TYPES VEHICLES – MOBILE CRANES

SCHED 2 ROAD VEHICLES (AUTHORISATION OF SPECIAL TYPES) (GENERAL) ORDER 2003

Definition

A mobile crane is a motor vehicle which –

1. is specially designed and constructed, or adapted for the special purpose of lifting operations that cannot safely be carried out by a motor vehicle or trailer that complies in all respects with the Construction and Use Regulations, the Authorised Weights Regulations and the Goods Vehicles Type Approval Regulations;
2. has a gross weight which exceeds 12,000 kg;
3. has crane apparatus permanently mounted as part of the vehicle chassis design;
4. is operated by a driver or other person riding on it; and
5. meets the requirements for registered use as a mobile crane under the Vehicle and Excise Registration Act 1994.

Any other vehicle which meets the above criteria but does not comply with the authorisation requirements for mobile cranes (see below) may nevertheless fall within the category of 'engineering plant' if it complies with the requirements of sched. 3 in the following section.

Mobile cranes fall within 3 categories – A, B and C.

Category A – does not exceed the plated vehicle or axle weight for that category, and complies with the conditions applicable to it.

Category B – does not fall within cat. A and does not exceed the plated vehicle or axle weight for its category, and complies with the conditions applicable to it.

Category C – does not fall within cat. A or B and does not exceed the plated vehicle or axle weight for its category, and complies with the conditions applicable to it.

Construction. A mobile crane must be a wheeled vehicle fitted with pneumatic tyres. It must have suspension on all axles and an efficient braking system.

Design speed. It must be able to travel on roads at 25 mph or more.

Warning beacon. Must be fitted with an amber warning beacon. When used on a road it must be kept lit when stationary at a site, or when, for whatever reason, it is unable to maintain speeds appropriate to the road. But it may be switched off if there is no reasonable prospect of it causing a hazard, or if it might mislead or confuse other road users.

Plates. (This requirement comes into operation on 1.12.04). It must be fitted with a plate securely affixed to the vehicle in a conspicuous and readily accessible position, indelibly marked in numbers and letters not less than 6 mm high with the maximum gross weight and maximum axle weight for each axle. The plate must be marked "SPECIAL TYPES USE". But such a plate is not required if the vehicle is already equipped with a plate in accordance with regs. 66 or 71 of the Construction and Use Regulations, and those weights are not exceeded.

Restrictions on use. It is only allowed to be used on roads for the purposes of testing, demonstration, delivery on sale, proceeding to or from a manufacturer or repairer, proceeding to or from the site of lifting operations, or carrying out such operations.

SPECIAL TYPES VEHICLES – MOBILE CRANES cont

Cranes more than 3 m wide. May only be used on roads in connection with lifting operations for which intended.

Carriage of loads. When used on roads may not carry any load except its own necessary gear and equipment, or transport any goods or burden except in the course of lifting operations.

Trailers. Must not tow any trailer.

Maximum width. Width, including any projections must not exceed 6.1 m.

Maximum length. Length, including any forward or rearward projections must not exceed 30 m.

Maximum weight. No crane may exceed any weight applicable to a cat. C crane, nor the maximum weight as specified in the plate fitted to that particular crane. The maximum weights applicable to each category are contained in the table below.

Category A		
Maximum axle weight (may not have more than 4 axles)	(a) 11,500 kg for a single driving axle, and (b) 10,000 kg for a single non-driving axle	
Maximum gross weight	**Number of axles**	**Distance between**	**Max gross weight**

Maximum gross weight	Number of axles	Distance between	Max gross weight
	2	3 m	20,000 kg
	3	5 m	30,000 kg
	4	6 m	36,000 kg

Category B	
Maximum axle weight	12,500 kg
Maximum gross weight	Max. gross wt. = **n x 12,500 kg** (rounded up to the nearest 10), where n = the number of axles

Category C	
Maximum axle weight	16,500 kg
Maximum gross weight	(a) 150,000 kg, or (b) **n x 16,500 kg** (rounded up to the nearest 10), where n = the number of axles

Speed restrictions. A mobile crane may not travel at a speed in excess of that in the following table (expressed in mph) –

Category	Motorway	Dual carriageway	Other road
A	60	50	40
B	50	45	40
C	40	35	30

SPECIAL TYPES VEHICLES – MOBILE CRANES cont

Application of regulations

Category A mobile cranes must comply with –

(a) the Road Vehicles (Construction and Use) Regulations 1986 except for the table below, and

(b) the Road Vehicles Lighting Regulations 1989.

Non-applicable regulations	Subject
8	Width
80	Over-riding weight regulations

Category B or C mobile cranes must comply with –

(a) the Road Vehicles (Construction and Use) Regulations 1986 except for the table below, and

(b) the Road Vehicles Lighting Regulations 1989.

Non-applicable regulations	Subject
7	Length
8	Width
15,16	Braking systems
18(1A) to (9)	Maintenance and efficiency of braking systems
25	Tyre loading and speed ratings
49	Rear under-run protection
51	Sideguards
64	Spray suppression devices
65	Maintenance of spray suppression devices
75 to 80	Other maximum permitted weight limits other than articulated vehicles
82	Restriction on use of vehicles carrying wide or long loads

But regs. 49, 51, 64 & 65 are disapplied only to the extent that it is not possible to comply on account of the need to perform the lifting operation.

Other special requirements. Where limits relating to length, width, projections, or weight are exceeded, there may be a requirement to notify the police, the road and bridge authorities, the Secretary of State, and to carry attendants. For details of *when* and *how* these are required, see respectively under "Additional Requirements" and "Notification of Police, etc.". For details of *when* and *how* to provide markers, see under "Marking of Projections".

SPECIAL TYPES VEHICLES – ENGINEERING PLANT

SCHED 3 ROAD VEHICLES (AUTHORISATION OF SPECIAL TYPES) (GENERAL) ORDER 2003

Definition

Engineering plant is any moveable plant or equipment which is a motor vehicle or trailer, and which –

(a) if it is a mobile crane as defined in sched. 2 (see earlier), satisfies conditions 1 to 4 below; or

(b) in any other case, satisfies conditions 1 to 3 below.

Condition 1. It is specially designed and constructed for the purpose of engineering operations which could not safely be carried out by a vehicle which complied in all respects with the Construction and Use Regulations and the Goods Vehicle Type Approval Regulations.

Condition 2. The vehicle or trailer is not constructed to carry any load apart from that allowed (see later).

Condition 3. The vehicle or trailer is operated by a driver or other person riding on it.

Condition 4. The vehicle does not comply in all respects with the authorisation requirements for mobile cranes as laid down in sched. 2 (see earlier).

Construction. It must be wheeled, tracked, or a wheel-track combination. If it does not have pneumatic tyres it must have smooth tyres with rounded edges (except gritting machines which may have diagonal cross bars). The tyres must be marked with speed and load ratings if it may travel in excess of speeds laid down for 'slow vehicles' (see later).

Brakes. If it is designed and constructed to travel in excess of 12 mph it must have a braking system which complies with reg. 16 of Construction and Use Regs. Any other vehicle must have an efficient braking system capable of stopping the vehicle when it is travelling at the maximum speed allowed by these regs. (If it is steam driven, this will be deemed to have been met if it can be reversed). It must also have a parking brake. (If steam driven it will not need one if the engine can be set to hold the vehicle stationary). If it is not reasonably practicable to fit a parking brake, the provision of 'scotches' or similar devices to hold the vehicle stationary will suffice.

Restrictions on use. It may not be used on operations which could be carried out by a vehicle which complies with Construction and Use and Type Approval Regulations. It may only be used for testing, demonstration, delivery on sale, proceeding to or from a manufacturer or repairer, proceeding to or from the site of engineering operations, or carrying out such operations. Plant over 3 m wide may only be used for operations for which it was designed and constructed.

Loads. It must not carry any load except its own necessary gear and equipment. It must not transport goods or burden except materials that have been excavated by the plant or materials that it is designed to process while on the plant.

Trailers. It must not tow a trailer except, if it is a motor vehicle not over 8 m long, a trailer which is engineering plant or a living van or office hut used in connection with road repair etc.

Maximum width. The vehicle, together with any lateral projections, must not exceed 6.1 m.

SPECIAL TYPES VEHICLES – ENGINEERING PLANT cont

Maximum length. The overall length, together with any forward or rearward projections must not exceed 30 m.

Maximum weight. The gross weight, together with any load must not exceed 150,000 kg. The weight transmitted to the road by any wheel must not exceed 11,250 kg. In addition, there is a limit to the weight that may be transmitted to a strip of road surface (measured as the distance between any 2 parallel lines drawn at right angles to the longitudinal axis of the plant) as follows –

Size of Strip	Maximum Weight
Wheeled vehicle	
0.5 m or less	45,000 kg
Between 0.5 and 2 m	45,000 kg + 30,000 kg per m over 0.5 m
Over 2 m	The weight as above up to 2 m + 10,000 kg per m over 2 m
Track-laying or wheel-track combination	
0.5 m or less	11,500 kg
Between 0.5 and 2 m	11,500 kg + 7,500 kg per m over 0.5 m
Over 2 m	The weight as above up to 2 m + 2,500 kg per m over 2 m

Speed restrictions. Generally, motorway – 30 mph; any other road – 12 mph. (Referred to as 'slow plant'). However, plant (except mobile cranes which fall within this schedule) which complies with the following conditions have revised speed restrictions as per the table below. The conditions are those referred to in schedule 1 (see earlier) as described in the relevant paragraphs of that schedule: 7 to 15 (brakes, plates and signs); 26 to 33 (weight); and 35 or 36 (requirements of Con. & Use, Authorised weight and Lighting Regs.) Any plant with complies with the requirements for an Abnormal Indivisible Road Vehicle (AILV) falling within category 1, 2 or 3 is regarded, for the purposes of the below table to be a vehicle of that category.

Vehicle	Motorway	Dual carriageway	Other road
Cat. 1	60 mph	50 mph	40 mph
Cat. 2 or 3	40 mph	35 mph	30 mph
But where the plant does not have suspension on all axles, it must not exceed 20 mph			

Other special requirements. Where limits relating to length, width, projections, or weight are exceeded, there may be a requirement to notify the police, the road and bridge authorities, the Secretary of State, and to carry attendants. For details of *when* and *how* these are required, see respectively under "Additional Requirements" and "Notification of Police, etc.". For details of *when* and *how* to provide markers, see under "Marking of Projections".

SPECIAL TYPES VEHICLES – ENGINEERING PLANT cont

Application of regulations

1. **Engineering plant which falls within cat. 1, 2 or 3 Abnormal Indivisible Load Vehicle** (AILV) (see previous page) must comply with –
(a) the Road Vehicles (Construction and Use) Regulations 1986,
(b) the Road Vehicles Lighting Regulations 1989, and
(c) the Road Vehicles (Authorised Weight) Regulations 1998 to the same extent as an AILV falling within the same category. (See Sched. 1 paras. 35 and 36 earlier under "Abnormal Indivisible Loads").

2. **Slow plant** (see previous page) must comply with –
(a) the Road Vehicles (Construction and Use) Regulations 1986, apart from those provisions in the table below, and
(b) the Road Vehicles Lighting Regulations 1989.

Non-applicable regulations	Subject
7	Length
8	Width
10A to 14	Other provisions as to dimensions and manoeuvrability
15 & 16	Braking systems (but reg. 16 *does* apply to slow plant which is wheeled)
17	Vacuum or pressure brake warning devices
18(1A) to (9)	Maintenance and efficiency of brakes
19	Application of brakes of trailers
20 to 22, 24 to 26	Wheels, springs, tyres and tracks
23	Wheel loads (but only in relation to wheeled slow vehicles used for road repair, etc. if the weight of any 2 wheels in line transversely does not exceed 11,180 kg)
27(1)(f)	Tyre treads (but only in relation to wheeled slow vehicles and trailers used for road repair, etc. if fitted with pneumatic tyres with smooth treads and incapable of exceeding 20 mph)
27(1)(b)	Tyre inflation (but only in relation to wheeled slow trailers used for road repair, etc. if fitted with pneumatic tyres with smooth treads)
28	Tracks (but only in relation to slow plant that is a track-laying trailer or track-laying road roller)
31	Glass (but only in relation to slow plant that is track laying first registered on or before 31.12.51)
34	Windscreen wipers and washers (but only in relation to slow plant that is track laying first registered on or before 31.12.51)
35 to 36C	Instruments and equipment
39A, 39B	Fuel
49 to 53B	Protective systems
62 to 65	Control of emissions
66 to 74	Plates, markings, testing and inspections
75	Maximum laden weight
76 to 80	Other maximum weight of vehicle other than articulated
82	Restrictions on wide or long loads

SPECIAL TYPES VEHICLES – ROAD RECOVERY VEHICLES

SCHED 4 ROAD VEHICLES (AUTHORISATION OF SPECIAL TYPES) (GENERAL) ORDER 2003

Definition. A 'road recovery vehicle' is a vehicle that is –
a locomotive; an N3 motor vehicle; or a combination of an N3 motor vehicle and an O4 trailer; which is –

(a) specially designed and constructed for the recovery of disabled road vehicles, or which is permanently adapted for such purpose;
(b) fitted with a crane, winch or other lifting system specially designed for recovering another vehicle; and
(c) meets the requirements for registration under the Vehicle Excise and Registration Act 1994.

Wheels. It must be a wheeled vehicle with pneumatic tyres.
Warning beacon. An amber warning beacon must be fitted. It must be kept lit when stationary at the scene of a breakdown, or when unable, for whatever reason to maintain a speed appropriate to the road. However, it may be switched off if there is no reasonable prospect of it causing a hazard, or if it might cause confusion or mislead other road users.
Plates. It must be fitted with a plate specifying the maximum weight that may be lifted by its crane, winch or other lifting system.
Loads. It must not carry or tow any load other than its own necessary gear and equipment or a disabled vehicle.
Towing/lifting vehicles. If using a tow-bar or lift-and-tow method, it may only tow or lift the vehicle as far as is necessary to clear the road. The braking system of a towed disabled vehicle must not be operated other than by an approved brake connection point fitted to both vehicles. The weight of the recovery vehicle plus the weight of the towed vehicle must not exceed the maximum train weight as stated on the plate required to be fitted by reg. 66 of the Con. & Use Regs.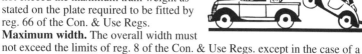
Maximum width. The overall width must not exceed the limits of reg. 8 of the Con. & Use Regs. except in the case of a trailer not over 3 m wide, used to recover vehicles which can only safely be done by a trailer which exceeds those limits.
Maximum length. Must not exceed 18.75 m, not including the disabled vehicle.
Maximum gross weight. Must not exceed that in the table below –

Number of Axles	Gross weight
3	36,000 kg
4 or more	50,000 kg
Vehicle and trailer with 6 or more axles	80,000 kg
Any other case	The maximum allowed by the Authorised Weight Regulations

SPECIAL TYPES VEHICLES – ROAD RECOVERY VEHICLES cont

Maximum axle and wheel weights. The distance between and 2 adjacent axles must not exceed 1.3 m. The axle weight must not exceed 12,500 kg. The wheel weight must not exceed 6,250 kg. Where it has axles in 2 or more groups the distance between adjacent axles in any group must not be less than 1.3 metres and the sum of weights of any group must not exceed 25,000 kg (but this does not apply to a combination of N3 vehicle and O4 trailer). If it has only one front steer axle, that axle must carry at least 40% of the maximum axle weight shown on the reg. 66 plate. If it has 2 or more front steer axles, all those axles together must carry 40% of such weight.

Speed restrictions. When towing or carrying a disabled vehicle it must not exceed motorway, 40 mph; dual carriageways and other roads, 30 mph.

Application of regulations. It must comply with –

(a) the Road Vehicles (Construction and Use) Regulations 1986, apart from the provisions in the table below,
(b) the Road Vehicles Lighting Regulations 1989, and
(c) the Road Vehicles (Authorised Weight) Regulations 1998, but only to the extent mentioned under 'maximum gross weight' on the previous page.

Non-applicable regulations	Subject
36A, 36B, 36C	Speed limiters
51	Sideguards
70, 70B	Plates
70A	Speed limiters - plates
72	Additional markings
73	Test date disc
75, 76, 77	Maximum permitted laden weight
78	Maximum permitted wheel and axle weights
79	Maximum permitted weight for closely-spaced axles
79A	Savings for Authorised Weight Regulations
82	Restrictions on long or wide loads
83(1)	Number of trailers

Other special requirements. Where limits relating to length, width, projections, or weight are exceeded, there may be a requirement to notify the police, the road and bridge authorities, the Secretary of State, and to carry attendants. For details of *when* and *how* these are required, see respectively under "Additional Requirements" and "Notification of Police, etc.". For details of *when* and *how* to provide markers, see under "Marking of Projections".

SPECIAL TYPES VEHICLES – AGRICULTURAL VEHICLES

ROAD VEHICLES (AUTHORISATION OF SPECIAL TYPES) (GENERAL) ORDER 2003

Categories. The following recognised categories are referred to as 'Special Type Agricultural Vehicles' –

(a) agricultural motor vehicles;
(b) agricultural trailers;
(c) agricultural trailed appliances.

"Agricultural motor vehicle" means a motor vehicle (not being a dual purpose vehicle) which is constructed or adapted for off-road use for the purpose of agriculture, horticulture or forestry, and is primarily used for one or more of those purposes. "Agricultural trailer" and "agricultural trailed appliance" have similar meanings and are fully defined in Con. & Use Regs. (art. 19)

Authorisation requirements (art. 20). Before such vehicles may be used on roads, they must comply with the following –

(a) the conditions listed in articles 21 to 27 below;
(b) the Road Vehicles (Construction and Use) Regulations 1986, apart from reg. 8 (width), reg. 75(1) (maximum laden weight of track-laying vehicles), and reg. 82 (restrictions on wide or long loads);
(c) the Road Vehicles Lighting Regulations 1989, and
(d) the Road Vehicles (Authorised Weight) Regulations 1998.

Construction and use (art. 21). If track-laying, the tracks must be covered in rubber or other composite material so as not to cause damage to the road surface. The overall width, together with any lateral projections, must not exceed 4.3 m. If track-laying the gross weight together with any load, must not exceed 30,000 kg. All spikes, cutting blades or other sharp protruding objects must be removed or guarded so as not to cause danger to any person. If the overall width is more than 2.55 m but less than 3.5 m, it must not travel in excess of 20 mph. If the width is over 3.5 m, the maximum speed is 12 mph.

Towing trailers (art. 22). If the vehicle is over 3 m it must not tow any trailer. Where it is towing a trailer or appliance and the overall width, if measured as 1 vehicle, exceeds 3 m it must not tow any other trailer other than –

(a) a 2-wheeled trailer for carrying equipment for use on the towing vehicle;
(b) an agricultural trailed appliance; or
(c) an unladen trailer specially designed for use with the vehicle when harvesting.

Forward and rear projections (art. 23). The action to be taken depends on the type and length of the projection, as per the following table –

Type and length	Action
Forward or rearward over 4 m	Notify the police in accordance with sched. 5 (see later)
Forward or rearward over 6 m	In addition to the above, must be accompanied by attendants in accordance with sched. 6 (see later)
Rearward over 12 m	In addition to the above, obtain the consent of the Secretary of State in accordance with sched. 7 (see later)

SPECIAL TYPES VEHICLES – AGRICULTURAL VEHICLES cont

Width (art. 24). The action to be taken depends on the circumstances and width as per the following table –

Circumstances and width	Action to be taken
Width exceeds 3 m and either there is a 40 mph limit or less on the road, or the journey exceeds 5 miles	Notify the police in accordance with sched. 5 (see later)
Width exceeds 3.5 m	In addition to the above, it must be accompanied by attendants in accordance with sched. 6 (see later)

Visibility and marking (art. 25). All forward, rearward and lateral projections must be marked in accordance with sched. 8 (see later).

Track-laying vehicles (arts. 26 & 27). Where a track-laying vehicle does not comply with reg. 75(1) of Con. & Use Regs. (maximum laden weight of track-laying vehicles) the relevant bridge and road authorities must be notified and given an indemnity in accordance with sched. 9. If the vehicle is caused to stop on a bridge for any reason, the driver must ensure that it is moved as soon as possible and that no concentrated load is applied to the road surface before seeking advice from the authority regarding the use of spreader plates.

SPECIAL TYPES VEHICLES – EXCEPTIONALLY WIDE LOADS
ROAD VEHICLES (AUTHORISATION OF SPECIAL TYPES)(GENERAL) ORDER 2003

These are motor vehicles or trailers carrying a load with a lateral projection where the overall width of the vehicle together with the projection exceeds 4.3 metres. They are a recognised category of special vehicles. (Art. 28).
Authorisation requirements (art. 29). Before such vehicles may be used on roads, they must comply with the following –

(a) the conditions listed in articles 30 & 31 below;
(b) the Road Vehicles (Construction and Use) Regulations 1986, apart from reg. 82(1) & (2) (restrictions on wide loads);
(c) the Road Vehicles Lighting Regulations 1989, and
(d) the Road Vehicles (Authorised Weight) Regulations 1998.

Maximum width (art. 30). The vehicle, together with any lateral projection must not exceed 6.1 m.

Speed restrictions (art. 30). Motorway – 40 mph; dual carriageway – 35 mph; other road – 30 mph.

SPECIAL TYPES VEHICLES – EXCEPTIONALLY WIDE LOADS cont

Width (art. 32). The action to be taken depends on the width as per the following table –

Width	Action to be taken
All loads over 4.3 m	Notify the police in accordance with sched. 5 (see later) and be accompanied by attendants in accordance with sched. 6 (see later)
Width exceeds 5 m	In addition to the above, obtain the consent of the Secretary of State in accordance with sched. 7 (see later)

SPECIAL TYPES VEHICLES – LOCAL EXCAVATION VEHICLES
ROAD VEHICLES (AUTHORISATION OF SPECIAL TYPES) (GENERAL) ORDER 2003

Definition (sched. 10). Any moveable plant or equipment which is a heavy motor car, trailer or articulated vehicle which –

(a) is intended for use on a work site on private premises
(b) specially designed and constructed for moving excavated material
(c) fitted with a tipping body, moveable platform or similar device for discharging its load; and
(d) does not fall within the definition of engineering plant (see earlier).

Authorisation requirements (art. 33). Must comply with the following –
Width
(a) if the overall width of the vehicle, together with any lateral projection, exceeds 3 m, the police must be notified in accordance with sched. 5 (see later);
(b) if the width exceeds 3.5 m, attendants must also be carried in accordance with sched. 6 (see later);
(c) if the width exceeds 5 m the consent of the Secretary of State must also be obtained in accordance with sched. 7 (see later).
Weight
(d) if the vehicle does not comply with the Authorised Weight Regulations (or, if they do not apply, the requirements of regs. 75 to 79 of Con. & Use Regs. (maximum weights)), the relevant bridge and road authority must be notified and an indemnity given in accordance with sched. 9.
Wheels
(e) wheels must be fitted with pneumatic tyres.
Restrictions on use
(f) may only be used on roads to proceed between different parts of the same private premises, or between the private premises and a port (but in either case not more than 3 miles).

SPECIAL TYPES VEHICLES - LOCAL EXCAVATION VEHICLES cont

Loads

(g) must not carry loads or transport any goods or burden other than its own necessary gear and equipment.

Towing trailers

(h) if a heavy motor car (not being part of an articulated vehicle), must not tow any trailer.

(i) a motor vehicle towing a trailer, where the motor vehicle or trailer is a local excavation vehicle, must not tow any other trailer.

Maximum width

(j) must not exceed 6.1 m.

Maximum length

(k) the overall length must not exceed –

Type of vehicle	Maximum length
Heavy motor car	Maximum permitted by reg. 7 Con. & Use Regs.
Trailer	8.54 m
Articulated vehicle	13.4 m

Maximum weight

(l) the maximum weight must not exceed –

Type of vehicle	Maximum gross weight	Maximum axle weight
Heavy motor car not being an articulated vehicle; or an articulated vehicle	50,800 kg	22,860 kg
Trailer	As per Authorised Weight Regulations (AWR) for a trailer of that description	
Trailer to which AWR does not apply	The equivalent provisions of regs. 75 to 79 of Con. & Use Regs.	

Speed restrictions

(m) must not exceed: motorway – 40 mph, other roads – 12 mph.

Authorisation requirements (art. 29). Before such vehicles may be used on roads, they must comply with the following –

(a) the Road Vehicles (Construction and Use) Regulations 1986, apart from the provisions in the table on the following page applicable to the description of vehicle

(b) the Road Vehicles Lighting Regulations 1989; and

(c) the Road Vehicles (Authorised Weight) Regulations 1998 (but the vehicle will be excluded if it is either a heavy motor car not forming part of an articulated vehicle, or an articulated vehicle).

SPECIAL TYPES VEHICLES – LOCAL EXCAVATION VEHICLES cont

The regulations in the table below do not apply to local excavation vehicles according to the description of vehicle in question –

Non-applicable regulations	Subject
Heavy motor car not forming part of an articulated vehicle	
8	Width
16(4) item 8	Braking system
18(1A) to (9)	Maintenance and efficiency of brakes
22	Springs and resilient material
63	Wings
66	Plates for goods vehicles
75 to 80	Maximum weights
Articulated vehicle (all of the above plus:)	
7	Length
Trailer not forming part of an articulated vehicle	
8	Width
18(1A) to (9)	Maintenance and efficiency of brakes
22	Springs and resilient material
63	Wings
66	Plates for goods vehicles

SPECIAL TYPES VEHICLES – VEHICLE FOR TEST, TRIAL OR NON-UK USE

ROAD VEHICLES (AUTHORISATION OF SPECIAL TYPES) (GENERAL) ORDER 2003

The following are recognised categories of special vehicles –

(a) a motor vehicle or trailer, or type of motor vehicle or trailer, constructed for use outside the UK.

(b) a new or improved type of motor vehicle or trailer constructed for tests or trials

(c) a motor vehicle or trailer equipped with new or improved equipment, or types of new or improved equipment.

But it does not include a motor vehicle or trailer which is not wheeled; nor abnormal indivisible load vehicles, mobile cranes, engineering plant or road recovery vehicles.

Before such vehicles may be used on the roads they must comply as follows –
Length (art. 38). In relation to a motor vehicle or trailer constructed for use outside the UK, if the overall length of the vehicle or combination exceeds that laid down in reg. 7 of Con. & Use Regs. the police must be notified in accordance with sched. 5 (see later).
Width (art. 39). In relation to a motor vehicle or trailer constructed for use outside the UK, if the overall width of the vehicle , together with any lateral projection, exceeds 3 m the police must be notified in accordance with sched. 5 (see later).

SPECIAL TYPES VEHICLES – VEHICLE FOR TEST, TRIAL OR NON-UK USE cont

Weight (art. 40). In relation to a motor vehicle or trailer constructed for use outside the UK, if the Authorised Weight Regulations are not complied with (or, if they do not apply, regs 75 to 79 of Con. & Use Regs.) the relevant bridge or road authority must be notified and an indemnity given in accordance with sched. 9.

General restrictions on use (sched. 11). The vehicle may only be used for testing, demonstration, delivery on sale, and proceeding to or returning from a manufacturer or repairer (except where it is being used by a person authorised by the Secretary of State for the purpose of making an evaluation of it, and the vehicle is registered under the Vehicle and Excise Act in that person's name). The vehicle must not be used in such a way as to cause danger to any person.

Loads (sched. 11). It must not carry a load or transport goods or burden except its own necessary gear and equipment, and apparatus or ballast necessary for the test or trial. In such circumstances it must comply with the Authorised Weight Regulations (or if they do not apply, the equivalent Con. & Use Regs.).

Conditions relating to use (sched. 11). Before being used on a road it must comply with –

(a) the Road Vehicles (Construction and Use) Regulations 1986 as specified in the table below;

(b) the Road Vehicles Lighting Regulations 1989 specified in the table below; and

(c) the Road Vehicles (Authorised Weight) Regulations 1998.

	Construction & Use Regs.	97	Excessive noise
10	Indication of travelling height	98	Stopping of engine
16	Braking systems	99	Use of horn
18(1)	Maint. & efficiency of brakes	100	Vehicle not to cause danger
20	Wheels and tracks	101	Parking in darkness
26	Mixing of tyres	102	Motor cycle passengers
27	Condition of tyres	103	Obstruction
29	Maint. of steering gear	104	Driver's control
30	View to the front	105	Opening of doors
34	Windscreen wipers and washers	106	Reversing
37	Audible warning instrument	107	Leaving vehicle unattended
53	Mascots	108	Securing suspended implements
54	Silencers	109	Television sets
61	Emissions		**Lighting Regs.**
62	Closets	11	Colour of lamps and reflectors
81, 82	Wide or long loads	13	Lamps to show steady light
83	Number of trailers	16	Blue warning beacons
84	Trailers drawn by motor cycles	17	Obligatory warning beacons
86	Vehicle/trailer distance	18	Obligatory lamps and reflectors
89	Leaving trailers at rest	19	Obstruction of lamps
90	Passengers in trailers	21	Projections
92	Sidecars	22	Side marker lamps

SPECIAL TYPES VEHICLES – TRACK-LAYING VEHICLES

ROAD VEHICLES (AUTHORISATION OF SPECIAL TYPES) (GENERAL) ORDER 2003

These provisions do not apply to any track-laying vehicle that falls within any other category of special vehicle (art. 41).

Authorisation requirements (art. 42). Before being used on roads, track-laying vehicles must comply with –

(a) Reg. 100 of the Road Vehicles (Construction and Use) Regulations 1986 (maintenance and use so as not to be a danger)
(b) the Road Vehicles Lighting Regulations 1989
(c) the Road Vehicles (Authorised Weight) Regulations 1998; and
(d) the requirements specified in articles 43 & 44 below.

Restrictions on use (art. 43). May only be used for demonstration, proceeding to the nearest railway station for conveyance to a port for shipment, or where no suitable railway facilities are available, proceeding to a port for shipment. It must not be used for hire or reward. It must not be used in such a way as to cause danger to anyone.

Consent of road authorities (art. 44). Written consent for the vehicle to be used on roads must be obtained from each road authority prior to commencement of a journey.

SPECIAL TYPES VEHICLES – STRADDLE CARRIERS

Authorisation requirements (art. 46). Before being used on a road, straddle carriers must comply with –

(a) the Road Vehicles (Construction and Use) Regulations 1986 apart from regs. 7 (length), 8 (width), 11 (overhang), 16(4) (braking systems), 18(1A) to (9) (braking maintenance), 22 (springs), and 66 (plates)
(b) the Road Vehicles Lighting Regulations 1989
(c) the Road Vehicles (Authorised Weight) Regulations 1998; and
(d) the requirements specified in article 47 below.

Restrictions on use, speed and width (art. 47). It may only be used for demonstration, delivery on sale, proceeding to or returning from a manufacturer or repairer. If it does not comply with reg. 11, but does comply with regs. 8 & 22, it may also be used for proceeding between different parts of the same private premises or between private premises in the neighbourhood (but not over 3 miles).

Load (art. 47). It must not carry any load apart from its own necessary gear and equipment, but may be laden where it is authorised to travel between different parts of the same private premises or between private premises in the neighbourhood, as above.

Speed (art. 47). It must not travel at more than 12 mph.

Width (art. 47). Must not exceed 3 m.

Length (art. 47). If overall length plus any forward or rearward projection exceeds 9.2 m, police must be notified in accordance with sched. 5 (see later).

SPECIAL TYPES VEHICLES – VEHICLE WITH MOVEABLE PLATFORM

ART. 49 ROAD VEHICLES (AUTHORISATION OF SPECIAL TYPES)
(GENERAL) ORDER 2003

Authorisation requirements. Before being used on a road, vehicles with a moveable platform must comply with –

(a) the Road Vehicles (Construction and Use) Regulations 1986 apart from regs. 7 (length), 8 (width), 11 (overhang), 20 (wheels and tracks), 23 (wheel loads), and 82 (wide or long loads);
(b) the Road Vehicles Lighting Regulations 1989;
(c) the Road Vehicles (Authorised Weight) Regulations 1998; and
(d) the following requirements
  (i) the special equipment must be retracted at all times except when it is at a place to facilitate overhead working;
  (ii) when equipment is retracted, regs. 7, 8 & 11 of Con. & Use Regs. must be complied with (except a locomotive which need not comply with reg. 11); and
  (iii) any jacks which protrude from the side of the vehicle must be made clearly visible from a reasonable distance.

SPECIAL TYPES VEHICLES – PEDESTRIAN CONTROLLED ROAD MAINTENANCE VEHICLES (ART. 50)

These vehicles are not constructed or used to carry a driver or
passenger, and which are specially constructed or adapted for gritting roads, laying road markings, clearing frost, snow or ice from roads, or any other maintenance work.

Authorisation requirements. Before being used on a road, pedestrian controlled road maintenance vehicles must comply with –

(a) the road Vehicles (Construction and Use) Regulations 1986 apart from 16 (braking systems), 18 (1A) to (9) (maintenance and
efficiency of brakes), 23 (wheel loads), and 61 (emission of smoke);
(b) the Road Vehicles Lighting Regulations 1989;
(c) the Road Vehicles (Authorised Weight) Regulations 1998; and
(d) the following requirements
  (i)   the weight of the vehicle (laden or unladen) must not exceed 410 kg;
  (ii)   must have an efficient braking system capable of stopping and holding the vehicle;
  (iii) if it does not have a braking system, it must have some other means of achieving the same result.

SPECIAL TYPES VEHICLES – MOTOR CUTTERS

ART. 51 ROAD VEHICLES (AUTHORISATION OF SPECIAL TYPES) (GENERAL) ORDER 2003

Definition. A motor cutter is a motor vehicle that is specially
constructed to be used as a grass cutter and hedge trimmer, and to be used by a person other than a pedestrian.

Authorisation requirements. Before being used on a road, a motor cutter must comply with –

(a) the Road Vehicles (Construction and Use) Regulations 1986 apart from regs. 8 (width) and 82(11) (restrictions on wide or long loads);
(b) the Road Vehicles Lighting Regulations 1989;
(c) the Road Vehicles (Authorised Weight) Regulations 1998; and
(d) the following requirements
  (i)   overall width, together with any equipment, not to exceed 2.55 m except when cutting grass or trimming hedges; and
  (ii)   all cutting or trimming blades to be guarded so as not to cause danger, except when cutting grass or trimming hedges

SPECIAL TYPES VEHICLES – CUTTER TRAILER

ART. 52 ROAD VEHICLES (AUTHORISATION OF SPECIAL TYPES)
(GENERAL) ORDER 2003

Definition. A cutter trailer is a vehicle that is specially constructed or adapted to be used as a grass cutter and hedge trimmer.

Authorisation requirements. Before being used on a road, a cutter trailer must comply with –

(a) Regs. 27 (condition and maintenance of tyres) and 100 (maintenance and use so as not to be a danger) of the Road Vehicles (Construction and Use) Regulations 1986;

(b) the Road Vehicles Lighting Regulations 1989;

(c) the Road Vehicles (Authorised Weight) Regulations 1998; and

(d) the following requirements

    (i) overall width of the motor vehicle towing the cutter trailer or the cutter trailer, not to exceed 2.6 m except when cutting grass or trimming hedges;

    (ii) all cutting or trimming blades to be guarded so as not to cause danger, except when cutting grass or trimming hedges;

    (iii) unladen weight not to exceed 1020 kg. When being towed by a loco-motive, motor tractor or heavy motor car, or 815 kg. In any other case; and

    (iv) must not travel at a speed in excess of 20 mph.

SPECIAL TYPES VEHICLES – OPERATIONAL MILITARY VEHICLES

ART. 53 ROAD VEHICLES (AUTHORISATION OF SPECIAL TYPES) (GENERAL) ORDER
2003

Definition. Means a motor vehicle or trailer intended for
(a) operational use for military action or the carrying out of strategic, tactical, service or administrative military mission, the process of carrying on combat, including movement, supply, attack, defence and manoeuvres needed to gain the objectives of any battle or campaign or use for military support to the civil community;
(b) training in connection with such operational use; or
(c) the carrying or recovery of vehicles or equipment in connection with such operational use or training.

Such vehicles are a recognised category of special vehicle where compliance with regulations would compromise the vehicle's operational capability.

Authorisation requirements. Before being used on a road, an operational military vehicle must comply (apart from the provisions specified in the certificate mentioned below) with
(a) the Road Vehicles (Construction and Use) Regulations 1986;
(b) the Road Vehicles Lighting Regulations 1989;
(c) the Road Vehicles (Authorised Weight) Regulations 1998; and
(d) the following requirements
  (i) the vehicle must be certified by the Secretary of State as being, for operational reasons, unable to comply with the regulations contained in the certificate; and
  (ii) must be the property of, or under the control of, the Secretary of State or of a procurement contractor (or sub-contractor) who has obtained the Secretary of State's permission for use on roads.

SPECIAL TYPES VEHICLES – TRACK-LAYING VEHICLES BELONGING TO THE R.N.L.I.

ART. 54 ROAD VEHICLES (AUTHORISATION OF SPECIAL TYPES)
(GENERAL) ORDER 2003

These are track-laying vehicles that are the property of the Royal National Lifeboat Institution.

Authorisation requirements. Before being used on a road, an R.N.L.I. track-laying vehicle musts comply with –
(a) comply with reg. 100 (maintenance and use so as not to be a danger) of the Road Vehicles (Construction and Use) Regulations 1986; and
(b) may only be used on roads to tow lifeboats, or in connection with their launching.

SPECIAL TYPES VEHICLES – HIGHWAY TESTING VEHICLES

ART. 54 ROAD VEHICLES (AUTHORISATION OF SPECIAL TYPES) (GENERAL) ORDER 2003

Definition. Means any motor vehicle or trailer used in the conduct of experiments or trials of roads or bridges under S 283 of the Highways Act 1980.
Authorisation requirement. The only requirement is reg. 100 (maintenance and use so as not to be a danger) of the Road Vehicles (Construction and Use) Regulations 1986.

SPECIAL TYPES VEHICLES – VEHICLES PROPELLED BY COMPRESSED NATURAL GAS

ART. 55 AND SCHED. 12 ROAD VEHICLES (AUTHORISATION OF SPECIAL TYPES) (GENERAL) ORDER 2003

Sched. 12 contains a comprehensive list of technical authorisation requirements, which are too lengthy and detailed to fully reproduce here. However, a general overview is provided below –

1. **"Compressed natural gas"** means natural gas stored at a pressure above 30 bar.
2. **Plate.** Every vehicle running on natural gas must be fitted with a metal identification plate in a readily accessible and visible position to identify that the vehicle has been constructed or adapted to run on natural gas; and the maximum system filling pressure.
3. **Gas containers** must be pressure tested before use and then every 3 years or less, and marked with the dates of the original and periodic test dates. It must not be used for more than 30 years and must be marked with the date of manufacture and a "DO NOT USE AFTER" date. It must be securely attached to the vehicle with suitable mountings and be placed in such a position as to minimise the risk of impact damage, flying debris or heat. There must be adequate ventilation to prevent the accumulation of gas, or otherwise sealed to prevent gas leakage. It must be fitted with a clearly marked isolation valve by which it can be isolated from the supply pipework. A pressure relief valve must be fitted.
4. **Pipelines.** Must be fitted so the heat of the engine exhaust system or any other source of heat will not adversely affect them. It must be so placed that the risk from flying debris is minimised.
5. **Unions and joints.** Must be fitted so they will not work loose or leak, and be in a position where they can be inspected.
6. **Filling connectors.** Must be compatible for use with the filling nozzle without the use of an adapter. The connector must be fitted with a dust cap secured permanently to the vehicle. It must be located in a well-ventilated area outside the driver or passenger compartment.
7. **Cut-off valve.** There must be an automatic valve to stop the flow of gas to the engine when the engine is stopped, when the engine is not running on natural gas, or when the ignition is turned off. In addition, the supply of gas must be automatically cut off at a point as near as possible to the gas container in the event of rapid deceleration of the vehicle in an accident, etc.
8. **Regulators.** Regulator(s) must be fitted with a pre-set pressure and flow rating.
9. **Buses.** Must be fitted with a valve to automatically stop the flow of gas in the event of an excessive tilt of the vehicle.
10. **Articulated vehicles.** An approved articulating connector must be fitted between the motor vehicle and the trailer.

SPECIAL TYPES VEHICLES – GROUP ADDITIONAL REQUIREMENTS

THE ROAD VEHICLES (AUTHORISATION OF SPECIAL TYPES) (GENERAL) ORDER 2003

The requirements below apply to the following categories of vehicles in addition to those detailed in their respective pages-

(a) abnormal indivisible loads
(b) mobile cranes
(c) engineering plant; and
(d) road recovery vehicles.

But the requirements of articles 12–17 below do not apply to **engineering plant or road recovery vehicles** where they are assisting at a civil emergency or road traffic accident and there is a danger to the public, provided they are being used within 24 hours of the request for their use by the police.

1. Length: police notification and attendants.
Where the length limits set out below are exceeded, the user must notify the police (see later) and carry attendants (see later).
The specified lengths are-

(a) overall length of a single rigid unit together with any forward or rearward projection - 18.75 m; and
(b) overall length of a combination – 25.9 m. (Art. 12)

2. Forward and rearward projections: police notification.
Where the length of any forward or rearward projection exceeds 3.05 m the user must notify the police (see later). (Art. 13)

3. Forward and rearward projections: attendants.
Where the length of any forward projection of the load exceeds 2 m, or the length of any rearward projection of the load exceeds 3.05 m, the user must carry attendants (see later). (Art. 14)

4. Width and lateral projections: police notification, secretary of state notification and attendants
Where 1 or more of the following widths is exceeded, the corresponding action must be taken by the user (Art. 15) –

Width exceeded	Action to be taken
The overall width of the vehicle together with any lateral projections of the load is **3 m or less**, but any lateral projection exceeds **305 mm**.	Notify the police (see later).
The overall width of the vehicle together with any lateral projections of the load exceeds **3 m**.	Notify the police (see later).
The overall width of the vehicle together with any lateral projections of the load exceeds **3.5 m**.	Notify the police (see later) and carry attendants (see later).
The overall width of the vehicle together with any lateral projections of the load exceeds **5 m**.	Notify the police (see later), carry attendants (see later) and notify the Secretary of State (see later).

SPECIAL TYPES VEHICLES – GROUP ADDITIONAL REQUIREMENTS cont

5. Visibility and marking of forward, rearward and lateral projections of loads etc.

Such marking is required in accordance with sched. 8 (see later). (Art. 16)

6. Weight: police notification and road and bridge authority notification and indemnity.

1. Where the vehicle or combination, laden or unladen –
   (a) exceeds 44,000 kg, or
   (b) the requirements of sched. 3 of the Authorised Weight Regulations regarding axle weights (or where this does not apply, the equivalent Construction and Use Regulations) are not complied with, the user must notify each road or bridge authority for each road or bridge on which the vehicle is to be used, and give each an indemnity. Where the gross weight of the vehicle or vehicle combination exceeds 80,000 kg, 5 days notice is required. In any other case, 2 days is needed. The notice must contain details similar to those required by the police (see later).

2. Where the vehicle or combination, laden or unladen exceeds 80,000 kg. the user must, in addition to complying with the requirements of para. 1 above, notify the police (see later). (Art. 17)

7. Use on bridges

The driver of the foremost vehicle or vehicle combination –

1. must not cause or permit any part of the vehicle to enter on any bridge if he knows, or could be reasonably expected to ascertain, that the whole or part of another such vehicle or combination is already on the bridge;

2. must not cause or permit any vehicle or combination to remain stationary on a bridge, except in circumstances beyond his control;

3. where the vehicle is one to which paragraph 6(1) or (2) above applies, and it is caused to stop on a bridge for any reason, must ensure that the vehicle is moved clear of the bridge as soon as possible, and that no concentrated load is applied to the road;

4. where it is not possible to comply with the previous sub-pasragraph, must seek advice from the bridge authority regarding spreader plates to reduce damage, and must comply with that advice before applying concentrated load. (Art. 18)

NOTICES TO THE POLICE

SCHED. 5 ROAD VEHICLES (AUTHORISATION OF SPECIAL TYPES) (GENERAL) ORDER 2003

A notice must be given to the chief constable of **each area** in which the vehicle is used –

(a) at least **24 hours** before use in the case of-

- a special type agricultural vehicle with forward projection exceeding 4 m (art. 23)
- a special type agricultural vehicle over 3 m to be used on any road which has a 40 mph limit or less, or to be used on a journey over 5 miles long (art. 24); or
- a straddle carrier with overall length together with any forward or rearward projection exceeding 9.2 m (art. 48); or

(b) at least **2 days** before use in any other case.

The notice must contain –

(a) a list of all police forces to which notice has been given;

(b) details of the user including contact details and licence number;

(c) details of intended use of the vehicle including points of departure and destination, times and dates, and load particulars; and

(d) details of the vehicle(s) including reg. no., type, dimensions, weight, wheels, axles and axle spacings.

The vehicle must be used in accordance with the particulars given in the notice, and in compliance with police directions as to times, dates, routes and places to halt.

ATTENDANTS

SCHED. 6

An attendant must be employed to accompany and attend to the vehicle or vehicle combination and its load, and to give warning to the driver and any other persons of any likely danger to such other persons owing to the presence of the vehicle on the road.

The attendant must be appropriately trained or experienced. He may travel in a different vehicle provided he can see the other vehicle and is in direct radio voice link with the driver.

Where three or more vehicles are travelling in convoy, only the foremost and rearmost vehicles need to be accompanied by an attendant.

NOTICES TO THE SECRETARY OF STATE

SCHED. 7

A notice to the Secretary of State must be in writing, containing details similar to those required by the police. But where it is (a) an abnormal load, or (b) a load of exceptional width to which art. 28 applies and which is over 5 m wide, details must also be given of the number of separate pieces, approximate value, implications of dividing the load, approximate cost of alternatives to road movement which have been considered, approximate cost of road movement, and any proposed movement of load additional to that for which consent is applied.

If granted, the written consent must be carried on the vehicle and the vehicle must be used in accordance with any requirements.

MARKING OF PROJECTIONS
SCHED. 8 ROAD VEHICLES (AUTHORISATION OF SPECIAL TYPES) (GENERAL)
ORDER 2003

"End marker" and "side marker" means a marker fitted to the a forward, rearward or lateral projection of a load, and which complies with the below design and dimensions, or is one approved for that purpose by another state.

FRONT OR REAR END MARKER

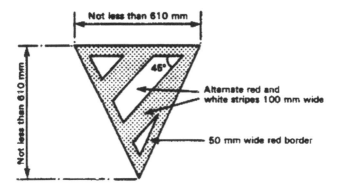

SIDE MARKER

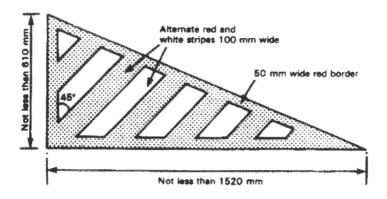

MARKING OF PROJECTIONS cont

The type, number and manner of fitting is determined by the length and nature of the projection as follows –

Length/type of projection	Requirement
Forward or rearward exceeding 1 m	Must be clearly visible from the end from which it projects, and from the side.
Forward or rearward exceeding 2 m	In addition to the above, must be fitted with an end marker – as near as possible in a transverse plane; not more than 0.5 m from the extreme end; the bottom of the marker not more than 2.5 m above the road surface; impeding the view of the driver as little as possible; and clearly visible from a reasonable distance from the end.
Forward or rearward exceeding 3 m	In addition to the above, must be fitted with a side marker – as near as possible in a longitudinal plane; not extending beyond the end of the projection; the bottom of the marker not more than 2.5 m above the road surface; horizontal distance between side and end marker not to exceed 1 m; and clearly visible from a reasonable distance from the side.
Forward exceeding 4.5 m or rearward exceeding 5 m	In addition to the above, additional side markers must be fitted to the sides so that the horizontal distance between the extreme projecting point of the vehicle and the nearest point of any adjacent side marker does not exceed 2.5 m for a forward projection, or 3.5 m for a rearward projection. They must be fitted so that it is as near as possible in a longitudinal plane; the bottom of the marker not more than 2.5 m above the road surface; and is clearly visible from the side. *Any part of a crane or special appliance or apparatus is to be disregarded.*
Lateral exceeding 305 mm on either side	In addition to the above side markers must be fitted to the lateral projection so that one marker is visible from the front, and one from the rear. At least part of it must be within 50 mm from the edge. If the fitting of markers is not reasonably practicable, tape must be fitted to the edge so that is clearly visible from the front, rear and side of the vehicle. The tape must be red, yellow or white (or any combination) and made of day-glow, fluorescent or retro-reflective material to BSI standard (or equivalent EEA, etc. state approval). Such tape will not contravene reg. 11 of the Lighting Regulations regarding retro-reflective material.

Any marker must be kept clean and unobscured. Between sunset and sunrise, and at times of seriously reduced visibility, markers must be kept illuminated by a shielded light which is not visible to other road users.

SIDEGUARDS

REG 51 ROAD VEHICLES (CONSTRUCTION AND USE) REGULATIONS 1986

The following vehicles are to be fitted with sideguards to give protection on any side of the vehicle – no sideguard to be outside vehicle's normal width nor more than 30 mm inboard of outer wall of rearmost tyre.

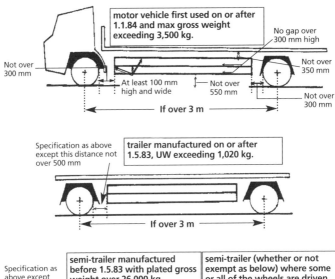

motor vehicle first used on or after 1.1.84 and max gross weight exceeding 3,500 kg.

No gap over 300 mm high

Not over 300 mm

Not over 350 mm

At least 100 mm high and wide

Not over 550 mm

Not over 300 mm

If over 3 m

Specification as above except this distance not over 500 mm

trailer manufactured on or after 1.5.83, UW exceeding 1,020 kg.

If over 3 m

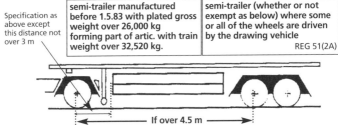

Specification as above except this distance not over 3 m

semi-trailer manufactured before 1.5.83 with plated gross weight over 26,000 kg forming part of artic. with train weight over 32,520 kg.

semi-trailer (whether or not exempt as below) where some or all of the wheels are driven by the drawing vehicle
REG 51(2A)

If over 4.5 m

Exemptions

- Incapable of over 15 mph on flat
- Agricultural trailer
- Engineering plant
- Fire engine
- Agricultural motor vehicle
- Rear and side tippers
- Defence
- Chassis for testing or fitting

- Used for fitting sideguards
- Street cleaning etc
- Trailer for lengthy beams etc
- Articulated tractive unit
- Vehicle for carrying vehicles
- Trailers not over 750 mm high
- Trailer temporarily in GB within 12 months of entry

Shall be maintained free from any defect likely to affect effectiveness.
REG 52

REARGUARDS

REG 49 ROAD VEHICLES (CONSTRUCTION AND USE) REGULATIONS 1986

Rearguards generally consists of a cross-member and linking components connected to the chassis side-members or whatever replaces them.

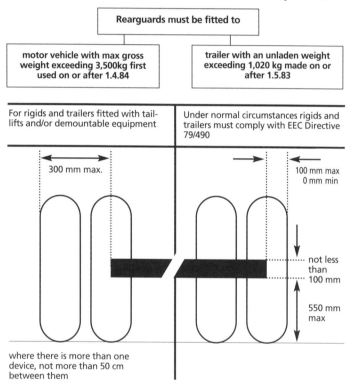

Rearguards must be fitted to

| motor vehicle with max gross weight exceeding 3,500kg first used on or after 1.4.84 | trailer with an unladen weight exceeding 1,020 kg made on or after 1.5.83 |

For rigids and trailers fitted with tail-lifts and/or demountable equipment

Under normal circumstances rigids and trailers must comply with EEC Directive 79/490

300 mm max.

100 mm max
0 mm min

not less than 100 mm

550 mm max

where there is more than one device, not more than 50 cm between them

Rearguards need not be fitted to

- Incapable of over 15 mph on flat
- Articulated tractive unit
- Engineering plant
- Fire engine
- Agricultural motor vehicle
- Agricultural trailer
- Road spreader
- Rear tipper
- Defence
- Chassis for testing or fitting
- For fitting guards
- For carrying other vehicles
- Trailer for lengthy beams etc
- Tail lifts over one metre long
- Concrete carrier/mixer
- Trailer temp. in GB within 12 months of entry

Must be maintained free from any obvious defect which would be likely to adversely affect performance in the event of an impact from the rear.

REG 50

SPRAY SUPPRESSION DEVICES

REG 64 ROAD VEHICLES (CONSTRUCTION AND USE) REGULATIONS 1986

Spray suppression devices
are required by goods
vehicles which are:

→

*The device must be fitted to
the wheels on each axle and
conform to the British
standard specification.*

1. motor vehicles first used on or after 1.4.86 with max gross
   weight exceeding 12,000 kg
2. trailers manufactured on or after 1.5.85 with max gross weight
   exceeding 3,500 kg
3. trailers whenever manufactured with max gross weight
   exceeding 16,000 kg and 2 or more axles.

Exemptions

- Motor vehicles of which no part in
  the area consisting the middle 80%
  of the width (measured between
  the insides of the wheels) and the
  entire length is less than 400 mm
  above the ground.

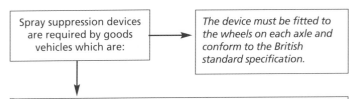

400 mm

middle 80%

- Agricultural motor vehicle
- Agricultural trailed appliance
- Agricultural trailer
- Broken down vehicles
- Concrete mixer
- Engineering plant
- Fire engine
- Four-wheel drive vehicles
- Max speed not exceeding 30mph
- Military etc vehicles
- Refuse vehicle
- Tipper vehicles (side or rear)

- Trailer leased outside GB which
  has been in this country in
  previous 12 months.
- Vehicle being taken for spray
  suppression device to be fitted.
  Vehicle already fitted with spray-
  suppression device in accordance
  with EC Directive 91/226.
- Vehicle without a body being
  taken for testing, body fitting or
  delivery to a dealer.
- Works trailers
- Works trucks

At all times when the vehicle is on a road the device must be maintained
free from defects which would adversely affect the efficiency of the device.

REG 65

MISCELLANEOUS CONSTRUCTION AND USE OFFENCES

MASCOTS (REG 53)

No mascot, emblem or other ornamental object shall be carried by a motor vehicle first used on or after 1.10.37 in any position where it is likely to strike any person with whom the vehicle may collide unless the mascot is not liable to cause injury.

MOTOR CYCLE SIDESTANDS (REG 38)

No motorcycle first used on or after 1.4.86 shall be fitted with any sidestand which is capable of:
1. disturbing stability or direction when in motion; or
2. closing automatically if the angle of inclination of the motor cycle is inadvertently altered when it is stationary.

RADIO INTERFERENCE SUPPRESSION (REG 60)

Every wheeled motor vehicle first used on or after 1.4.74 which is propelled by a spark ignition engine shall comply at the time of its first use with EEC or Community Directives relating to suppression. This does not apply to vehicles constructed or assembled by persons not normally in the business of manufacturing such vehicles.

STOPPING OF ENGINE WHEN STATIONARY (REG 98)

The driver of a vehicle shall, when the vehicle is stationary, stop the action of any machinery attached to or forming part of the vehicle so far as may be necessary for the prevention of noise or of exhaust emissions. Does not apply when stationary due to traffic, when the working of the machinery is necessary for other than driving the vehicle, or gas propelled vehicle producing gas.

MISCELLANEOUS CONSTRUCTION AND USE OFFENCES cont

AVOIDANCE OF EXCESSIVE NOISE (REG 97)

No motor vehicle shall be used on a road in such a manner as to cause any excessive noise which could have been avoided by the exercise of reasonable care on the part of the driver.

PARKING IN DARKNESS (REG 101)

A motor vehicle must, between sunset and sunrise, when standing on a road, have the nearside of the vehicle as close as may be to the edge of the carriageway. This does not apply with permission of a police officer in uniform; fire, police, ambulance or defence purposes; building, demolition repair of buildings or roads etc; on a one-way street; parking place or taxi or bus stand; or setting down or picking up passengers in accordance with regulations.

MOTOR CYCLES – FOOTRESTS (REG 102)

Footrests shall be available for any passenger carried astride a two-wheeled motor cycle (whether a sidecar is attached or not).

OBSTRUCTION (REG 103)

No person in charge of a motor vehicle or trailer shall cause or permit the vehicle to stand on a road so as to cause any unnecessary obstruction of the road.

MISCELLANEOUS CONSTRUCTION AND USE OFFENCES cont

DRIVER'S CONTROL (REG 104)

No person shall drive or cause or permit any other person to drive, a motor vehicle on a road if he is in such a position that he cannot have proper control of the vehicle or have a full view of the road and traffic ahead.

OPENING OF DOORS (REG 105)

No person shall open, or cause or permit to be opened, any door of a vehicle on a road so as to injure or endanger any person.

REVERSING (REG 106)

No person shall drive, or cause or permit to be driven, a motor vehicle backwards on a road further than may be requisite for the safety or reasonable convenience of the occupants of the vehicle or other traffic, unless for road repairs, etc.

LEAVING VEHICLE UNATTENDED (REG 107)

No person shall leave, or cause or permit to be left, on a road a motor vehicle which is unattended by a licensed driver unless the engine is stopped and the parking brake is set. This does not apply to police, ambulance or fire, or if the engine is needed to drive machinery, etc.

TELEVISION SETS (REG 109)

The driver must not be in a position to see, whether directly or by reflection, any television or other like apparatus used to display anything other than information about the state of the vehicle, location, to assist the driver to see the adjacent road, or to assist the driver to reach his destination.

MISCELLANEOUS CONSTRUCTION AND USE OFFENCES cont

Mobile telephones (REG 110)

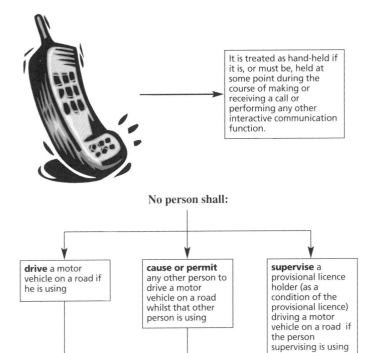

It is treated as hand-held if it is, or must be, held at some point during the course of making or receiving a call or performing any other interactive communication function.

No person shall:

drive a motor vehicle on a road if he is using	**cause or permit** any other person to drive a motor vehicle on a road whilst that other person is using	**supervise** a provisional licence holder (as a condition of the provisional licence) driving a motor vehicle on a road if the person supervising is using

a hand-held mobile telephone or a hand held device other than a two-way radio.

Defence: Calling the police, fire, ambulance or other emergency service using 112 or 999, responding to a genuine emergency and it is unsafe or impracticable to cease driving in order to make the call.

Failure to comply with any of these requirements is an offence under S41D of the Road Traffic Act 1988 (inserted by S 26 Road Safety Act 2006 (Commencement No.1)).

PART 2

DOCUMENTATION

This part of the book aims to highlight the various types of formal documentation required, including driving licences, insurance, operator's licences, vehicle excise duty, registration plates, plating and testing, trade licences, the operation of passenger carrying vehicles, and foreign vehicles.

HGV DOCUMENTATION

The following 'check list' may prove to be a guide to the legal requirements for the use of a heavy goods vehicle. Depending on the type of vehicle, reference should be made to the relevant pages as indicated.

	PAGE
records of work	259
hours of work	242 – 258
operators' licence	147 – 157
LGV and PCV driving licences	125
ordinary driving licences	118 – 136
plating and testing of vehicles	170 – 176
certificate of insurance	147
excise licence	153 – 166
manufacturer's plate	175 – 177
Ministry plate	176
trailer disc	175
plating certificate	175
trailer plate	175 – 177
unladen weight markings	150
rear reflective markers	233 – 236

DRIVING LICENCES – DEFINITIONS

MOTOR VEHICLES (DRIVING LICENCES) REGULATIONS 1999

LARGE MOTOR BICYCLE

(a) If without sidecar, the bicycle engine has a maximum net power exceeding 25 kW or a power-to-weight ratio exceeding 0.16 kW per kg, or
(b) if with sidecar, the combination has a power-to-weight ratio exceeding 0.16 kW per kg.

STANDARD MOTOR BICYCLE

Not a large motor bicycle.

PASSENGER CARRYING VEHICLE RECOVERY VEHICLE

A vehicle other than an articulated goods vehicle which:
(a) has unladen weight not exceeding 10.2 tonnes
(b) is being operated by the holder of a PSV Operator's Licence, and
(c) is proceeding to, returning from or giving assistance to, a damaged or disabled passenger-carrying vehicle.

INCOMPLETE LARGE VEHICLE

(a) Typically consisting of a chassis and a complete or incomplete cab which, when complete, is capable of becoming a medium-sized or large goods vehicle or a passenger-carrying vehicle, or
(b) a vehicle which would be an articulated goods vehicle but for the absence of a 5th wheel coupling.

WORKING WEIGHT

The weight of a vehicle in working condition on a road but exclusive of the weight of any liquid coolant and fuel used for its propulsion.

MAXIMUM AUTHORISED MASS

(a) in relation to a goods vehicle means its permissible maximum weight (as marked on the plate of the vehicle, or the notional maximum gross weight (see general definitions))
(b) in relation to an incomplete large vehicle, means its working weight
(c) in relation to any other motor vehicle or trailer, its maximum gross weight as shown on the Ministry plate or (if none), manufacturer's plate or (if none), the design weight.

Continued on following page

DRIVING LICENCES - DEFINITIONS cont

MOTOR VEHICLES (DRIVING LICENCES) REGULATIONS 1999

AMBULANCE

A motor vehicle which –

(a) is constructed or adapted for, and used for no other purpose than, the carriage of sick, injured or disabled people to or from welfare centres or places where medical or dental treatment is given, and

(b) is readily identifiable as such a vehicle by being marked "Ambulance" on both sides.

EXEMPTED GOODS VEHICLE (S51)

Steam-driven vehicle; road construction vehicle for conveying built-in road construction machinery (with or without articles or materials used for the purpose of the machinery); engineering plant (other than a mobile crane); works truck; industrial tractor; agricultural motor vehicle (not being an agricultural or forestry tractor); digging machine; vehicle not used on public roads or, if so used, is only passing between pieces of land in the occupation of the person keeping the vehicle and not used for more than 9.7 km in any calendar week; any vehicle – not being an agricultural motor vehicle – only used for agriculture, horticulture or forestry and used on public roads for not more than 1.5 km to pass between different areas of land occupied by the same person; vehicle for hauling lifeboats; unladen vehicle manufactured before 1.1.60 not drawing a trailer; articulated goods vehicle with UW not over 3.05 tonnes; visiting Forces vehicles; vehicle driven by a constable to protect life and property, etc; vehicle with UW not over 3.05 tonnes for raising and drawing disabled vehicles, used solely for that purpose and not carrying goods other than those required for its operation; passenger-carrying vehicle recovery vehicle; and a mobile project vehicle. 'Public road' in this definition means a road repairable at public expense (or in Scotland, as defined in the Roads (Scotland) Act 1984).

EXEMPTED MILITARY VEHICLE

Defence fire vehicle, urgent national defence work, and defence armoured vehicle not being a tracked vehicle.

MOBILE PROJECT VEHICLE

Vehicle having a maximum authorised mass exceeding 3.5 tonnes, constructed or adapted to carry not more than 8 persons in addition to the driver, carrying

(a) play or educational equipment, or

(b) articles required for the purposes of display or of an exhibition, and the primary purpose when stationary is recreational, educational or instructional.

DRIVING LICENCES – DEFINITIONS cont

MOTOR VEHICLES (DRIVING LICENCES) REGULATIONS 1999 REG. 17

QUALIFIED DRIVER

For the purpose of supervising a provisional licence holder, the supervising driver must:

(a) be over 21 years of age (unless member of the Armed Forces acting as such)

(b) hold a <u>relevant licence</u> (includes the Northern Ireland or Community Licence)

(c) have the <u>relevant driving experience</u> (unless member of the Armed Forces acting such), and

(d) in the case of a disabled driver who is supervising a provisional licence holder in a category B, C, D, C+E, or D+E vehicle, be able in an emergency to take control of the steering and braking of the vehicle.

"Relevant licence" means (subject to the provision below relating to disabled drivers) a full licence authorising:

(a) the driving of vehicles of the same class as the vehicle being driven by the provisional licence holder, and

(b) where: (i) a person holds a full licence authorising the driving of vehicles of the same class as that being driven by the provisional licence holder; (ii) that class is included in a category or sub-category in column 1 of the table below; and (iii) that person has held that licence for **less than** a minimum period of 3 years, then:

(aa) where that class of vehicle is included within any sub-category specified in column 1, the driving of vehicles in column 2 opposite that sub-category, or

(bb) where sub-para (aa) above does not apply, the driving of vehicles in the category specified in column 2 which is opposite the category in column 1 that includes the class of vehicle being driven by the provisional licence holder.

In the case of a **disabled driver** who holds a licence authorising the driving of vehicles in category B, a relevant licence must authorise the driving of vehicles other than vehicles in sub-category B1 or B1 (invalid carriages).

"Relevant driving experience" means:

(i) where only paragraph (a) under "relevant licence" above applies, he has held the relevant licence for a period of 3 years, or

(ii) where paragraph (b) under "relevant licence" above applies, he has held the relevant licence authorising the driving of vehicles of the same class as that being driven by the provisional licence holder for a minimum of 1 year, AND in the category or sub-category specified in column 2 in the table below for a minimum of 3 years.

DRIVING LICENCES – DEFINITIONS cont

MOTOR VEHICLES (DRIVING LICENCES) REGULATIONS 1999 REG. 17

The minimum period of time may be met either by holding a licence continuously or for periods amounting in aggregate to not less than that period.

Column 1 Categories and sub-categories of vehicle being driven by the provisional licence holder	Column 2 Categories and sub-categories authorised by the relevant licence
C	D
C1	D1
C+E	D+E
C1+E	D1+E
D	C
D1	C1
D+E	C+E
D1+E	C1+E

DRIVING LICENCES – GRANTING
REG 5 MOTOR VEHICLES (DRIVING LICENCES) REGULATIONS 1999

A driving licence may be granted to a person entitled to drive by virtue of:

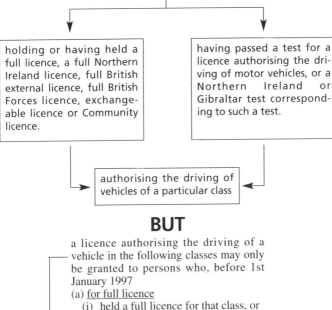

holding or having held a full licence, a full Northern Ireland licence, full British external licence, full British Forces licence, exchangeable licence or Community licence.

having passed a test for a licence authorising the driving of motor vehicles, or a Northern Ireland or Gibraltar test corresponding to such a test.

authorising the driving of vehicles of a particular class

BUT

a licence authorising the driving of a vehicle in the following classes may only be granted to persons who, before 1st January 1997

(a) <u>for full licence</u>
   (i) held a full licence for that class, or
   (ii) passed a test authorising the driving of a vehicle in that class

(b) <u>for provisional licence</u>
   held a provisional licence for that class.

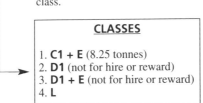

<u>CLASSES</u>

1. **C1 + E** (8.25 tonnes)
2. **D1** (not for hire or reward)
3. **D1 + E** (not for hire or reward)
4. **L**

A Sub-category B1 (Invalid Carriages) licence may not be granted unless before 12.11.99
(a) in an application for a full licence, a full B1 (Invalid Carriages) licence (or corresponding sub-category) was held, or
(b) in the case of a provisional licence application he held a provisional B1 (Invalid Carriages) Licence (or corresponding sub category)

CATEGORIES & SUB-CATEGORIES OF VEHICLE FOR LICENSING PURPOSES

REGS 4, 40 AND SCHED 2 MOTOR VEHICLES (DRIVING LICENCES) REGULATIONS 1999

Category or sub-category	Classes of vehicle included
A	Motor bicycles but excluding any motor vehicle in category K.
A1	A sub-category of category A comprising learner motor bicycles.
B	Any motor vehicle, other than a vehicle included in category A, F, K or P, having a maximum authorised mass not exceeding 3.5 tonnes and not more than 8 seats in addition to the driver's seat, including: (i) a combination of such a vehicle and a trailer where the trailer has a maximum authorised mass not exceeding 750 kg, and (ii) a combination of such a vehicle and a trailer where the maximum authorised mass of the combination does not exceed 3.5 tonnes and the maximum authorised mass of the trailer does not exceed the UW of the tractor vehicle.
B + E	Combination of a motor vehicle and trailer where the tractor vehicle is in category B but the trailer may be over 750 kg.
B1	A sub-category of category B comprising motor vehicles having three or four wheels and an UW not exceeding 550 kg.
B1 (invalid carriages)	A sub-category of category B comprising motor vehicles which are invalid carriages.
C	Any motor vehicle having a maximum authorised mass exceeding 3.5 tonnes, other than a vehicle falling within category D, F. G or H, including such a vehicle drawing a trailer having a maximum authorised mass not exceeding 750 kg.
C + E	Combination of a motor vehicle and trailer where the tractor vehicle is in category C but the trailer may be over 750 kg.
C1	A sub-category of category C comprising motor vehicles having a maximum authorised mass exceeding 3.5 tonnes but not exceeding 7.5 tonnes, including such a vehicle drawing a trailer having a maximum authorised mass not exceeding 750 kg.
C1 + E	A sub-category of category C + E comprising any combination of a motor vehicle and trailer where: (a) the tractor vehicle is in sub-category C1, (b) the maximum authorised mass of the trailer exceeds 750 kg but not the UW of the tractor vehicle, and (c) the maximum authorised mass of the combination does not exceed 12 tonnes.

continued on following page

CATEGORIES & SUB-CATEGORIES OF VEHICLE FOR LICENSING PURPOSES cont

MOTOR VEHICLES (DRIVING LICENCES) REGULATIONS 1999

Category or sub-category	Classes of vehicle included (cont from previous page)
C1 + E (8.25 tonnes)	A sub-category of category C + E comprising any combination of a motor vehicle and trailer in sub-category C1 + E where (a) the maximum authorised mass of the trailer exceeds 750 kg and may exceed the unladen weight of the tractor vehicle, and (b) the maximum authorised mass of the combination does not exceed 8.25 tonnes.
D	Any motor vehicle constructed or adapted for the carriage of passengers having more than 8 seats in addition to the driver's seat, including such a vehicle drawing a trailer having a maximum authorised mass not exceeding 750 kg.
D + E	Combination of a motor vehicle and trailer where the tractor vehicle is in category D but the trailer may be over 750 kg.
D1	A sub-category of category D comprising motor vehicles having more than 8 but not more than 16 seats in addition to the driver's seat and including such a vehicle drawing a trailer with a maximum authorised mass not exceeding 750 kg.
D1 (not for hire or reward)	A sub-category of category D comprising motor vehicles in sub-category D1 where (a) the motor vehicles are driven otherwise than for hire or reward, and (b) the maximum authorised mass of the trailer exceeds 750 kg and may exceed the unladen weight of the tractor vehicle.
D1 + E	A sub-category of category D + E comprising any combination of a motor vehicle and trailer where: (a) the tractor vehicle is in sub-category D1, (b) the maximum authorised mass of the trailer exceeds 750 kg but not the UW of the tractor vehicle, (c) the maximum authorised mass of the combination does not exceed 12 tonnes, and (d) the trailer is not used for the carriage of passengers.
D1 + E (not for hire or reward)	A sub-category of category D + E comprising motor vehicles in sub-category D1 + E where (a) the motor vehicles are driven otherwise than for hire or reward, and (b) the maximum authorised mass of the trailer exceeds 750 kg and may exceed the unladen weight of the tractor vehicle.
F	Agricultural or forestry tractor, but excluding any motor vehicle included in category H.
G	Road roller.
H	Track-laying vehicle steered by its tracks.
K	Mowing machine or vehicle controlled by a pedestrian.
L	Motor vehicle propelled by electrical power.
P	Moped.

NOTE: Persons authorised to drive the former groups M (trolley vehicles with not more than 16 seats) and N (vehicles used for short distances) will be able to continue to drive those vehicles (Regs 71 & 71A).

LICENCES ISSUED BEFORE 1.1.97
REG 76 MOTOR VEHICLES (DRIVING LICENCES) REGULATIONS1999

A person who before 1 January 1997 passed a test in respect of a class in an old category shall be regarded as having passed a test in the new category as shown in the table below:

("Old category" includes those groups in existence before 1 January 1990.)

Old Category or Class	Corresponding New Category or Class
A	**A**
B1	**B1**
B1, limited to invalid carriages	**B1,** (invalid carriages)
B	**B**
B plus **E**	**B + E**
C1	**C1**
C1 plus **E**	**C1 + E** (8.25 tonnes)
C	**C**
C plus **E**	**C+ E**
C plus **E,** limited to drawbar trailer combination only	Vehicles in cat **C + E** which are drawbar trailer combinations
D1	**D1** (not for hire or reward)
D1 plus **E**	**D1** plus **E** (not for hire or reward)
D, limited to 16 seats	**D1**
D, limited to vehicles not more than 5.5 m in length	**D1** and vehicles in cat. **D** not more than 5.5 m in length
D, limited to vehicles not driven for hire or reward	Vehicles in cat. **D** which are either driven while being used in accordance with a Section 19 permit or, if not being so used, driven otherwise than for hire or reward
D	**D**
D plus **E**	**D + E**
F	**F**
G	**G**
H	**H**
K	**K**
L	**L**
P	**P**

LICENCES – LGV/PCV EXEMPTIONS

REG 50 MOTOR VEHICLES (DRIVING LICENCE) REGULATIONS 1999

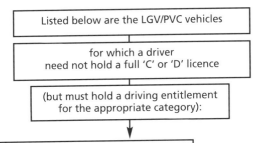

Listed below are the LGV/PVC vehicles

for which a driver
need not hold a full 'C' or 'D' licence

(but must hold a driving entitlement
for the appropriate category):

large goods vehicles *
1. included in categories
    F – agricultural or forestry tractor;
    G – road roller;
    H – track-laying vehicle steered by its tracks;
    C1 + E (8.25 tonnes) – motor vehicle and
    trailer; or
2. which are exempted goods vehicles
    or exempted military vehicles: ******

passenger-carrying vehicles *
1. manufactured more than 30 years before
    the date when driven and not used for
    hire or reward or for the carriage of more
    than 8 passengers; or
2. driven by a constable for the purpose of
    removing or avoiding obstructions, or
    protecting life or property, etc.

dual purpose vehicles *
These are treated for the purpose of
LGV/PCV licences as PCVs
                    except:
(a) adapted to carry not more than 24 persons
    in addition to the driver,
(b) driven by a member of the armed forces of
    the crown, and
(c) carrying passengers for naval, military or
    airforce purposes
will be regarded as LGVs.

* see definition at the start
  of the book
** see definitions page at
  start of this section

DRIVING LICENCES – ADDITIONAL ENTITLEMENTS

Regs 19, 43, 44A and Sched. 2 Motor Vehicles (Driving Licences) Regulations 1999

● The holder of a full licence for a category specified in the table below is also authorised to drive vehicles in the column alongside as if he held a provisional licence to do so.

● In addition the classes of vehicle mentioned alongside in the 3rd column may be driven as if a full licence for that category was held.

● For convenience, the corresponding old groups are shown.

CATEGORY ENTITLEMENT	PROVISIONAL ENTITLEMENT	ADDITIONAL FULL ENTITLEMENT	OLD GROUP
A	B & F	B1 (but see next page), K & P	D
A1	A, B, F & K	P (but see note next page)	
B	A, B + E, G & H	F, K & P	A
B1	A, B & F	K & P	C, J
B1 (inv.)			
B + E			A
C	C1 + E, C + E		HGV 2 & 3
C1			A
D	D1 + E, D + E		PSV
D1	D1 + E		PSV
C + E		B + E	HGV 1 & 2
C1 + E		B + E	A
D + E		B + E	PSV
D1 + E		B + E	PSV
F	B & P	K	F
G	H		G
H	G		H
K			K
P (but see note next page)	A, B, F + K		E
L			L

DRIVING LICENCES – ADDITIONAL ENTITLEMENTS cont

Note

- Where a full licence authorises only vehicles with automatic transmission, it will act as a provisional licence for manual vehicles in that category.

- Category entitlement A – will not include additional category B1 if test passed on or after 1.2.2001.

- If a licence authorises only A1 category motor cycles or standard motor cycles, large motor cycles may not be driven by a person under 21.

- Category entitlement B – only includes additional category P if – (a) test was passed before 1.2.2001; (b) at the time test was passed he had completed an approved course for motor cycles. Where the approved course was for 3-wheeled mopeds, the category P authorisation only covers such vehicles.

- Similarly, where a test is passed for category P on a 3-wheeled moped the authorisation is restricted to such vehicles.

- For provisional entitlement of LGV trainee driver's licence, see that section, later.

- The holder of a Community licence may claim the provisional entitlements in the table above as if he held a full licence of the appropriate category.

ADDITIONAL CLASSES COVERED BY EXISTING LICENCE

REG 6 AND SCHED 2. MOTOR VEHICLES (DRIVING LICENCES) REGULATIONS 1999

Licence Held	Additional Classes Covered
'C' for at least 2 years (other than C1)	Vehicles in Category 'D' (a) damaged or defective and being driven to a place for repair or being road tested following repair, and (b) not carrying any person not connected with its repair or road testing. But if licence is restricted to automatic transmission, may only drive automatic vehicles.
'C' (other than C1)	Dual Purpose Vehicle if (a) a member of the Armed Forces of the Crown; and (b) the vehicle is adapted to carry not more than 24 persons in addition to the driver, and being used for naval, military or air force purposes. Incomplete large vehicle with working weight exceeding 7.5 tonnes (unless licence restricts driving to automatic transmission in which case vehicle must be automatic.)
C1	Incomplete large vehicles with working weight exceeding 3.5 tonnes but not exceeding 7.5 tonnes (unless licence restricts driving to automatic transmission in which case vehicle must be automatic).
Full 'D' licence (other than D1 or D1 (not for hire or reward))	Passenger-carrying vehicle recovery vehicle. (But if licence is restricted to automatic vehicles then recovery vehicle must be automatic.)
'B' except if restricted to B1 and B1 (invalid carriages)	Exempted goods vehicle other than a passenger-carrying vehicle recovery vehicle, or a mobile project vehicle. Exempted military vehicle. Passenger carrying vehicle (a) manufactured more than 30 years ago and not used for hire or reward or for the carriage of more than 8 passengers; or (b) being driven by a constable for removing or avoiding obstruction, protecting life or property or other similar purposes. (Unless licence is restricted to automatic transmission, in which case the above vehicles must also be automatic.) B+E if trailer is damaged or defective and presenting hazard or obstruction, driven only to remove it and no consideration is received.
'B' except if restricted to B1 and B1 (invalid carriages), has held the licence for not less than 2 years and aged 21 or over	Mobile project vehicle for a non-commercial body: (a) to or from a place where the equipment, display or exhibition is used, or (b) to or from a place where a defect is being remedied, or (c) vehicle is exempt from excise duty due to it being subject to a compulsory test or weight test. (Unless licence is restricted to automatic transmission, in which case above vehicles must also be automatic.)

ADDITIONAL CLASSES COVERED BY EXISTING LICENCE cont

Licence Held	Additional Classes Covered
'B' except if restricted to B1 and B1 (invalid carriages), and has held the licence for not less than 2 years, aged 21 years or over, aged 70 years or over and not suffering from any relevant disability which would result in refusal of a licence to drive this category of vehicle, and receives no payment except expenses	D1 without trailer and maximum authorised mass not exceeding: (a) 3.5 tonnes (excluding specialised equipment for disabled passengers), and (b) 4.25 tonnes otherwise. (But if licence is restricted to automatic transmission, the above vehicles must also be automatic.) Vehicles must be driven for a non-commercial body for social purposes but not for hire or reward.

NOTE:

If a test is passed,

(a) on a vehicle with automatic transmission, only classes of vehicle with automatic transmission are authorised to be driven (except where the additional category is F, K or P);

(b) on an invalid carriage, only they are authorised; and

(c) on a vehicle adapted for a disabled person, only vehicles so adapted are authorised.

The above additional classes covered may be claimed by persons holding a full licence granted under the Road Traffic Act, a corresponding Northern Ireland licence or a Community licence.

DUAL PURPOSE VEHICLES – ARMED FORCES DRIVING

REG 8 MOTOR VEHICLES (DRIVING LICENCES) REGULATIONS 1999

A member of the armed forces may drive a dual purpose vehicle whilst carrying passengers for armed forces purposes provided –

(a) vehicle does not exceed 3.5 tonnes maximum authorised mass and a full Category B licence is held,

(b) if maximum authorised mass is over 3.5 tonnes but under 7.5 tonnes, a full sub-category C1 licence is held,

(c) in any other case, a full Category C licence is held.
    If authorised only for automatic transmission, may only drive such vehicles.

PROVISIONAL LICENCES – CONDITIONS

REG 16 MOTOR VEHICLES (DRIVING LICENCES) REGULATIONS 1999

Provisional licence-holders must comply with the following conditions:

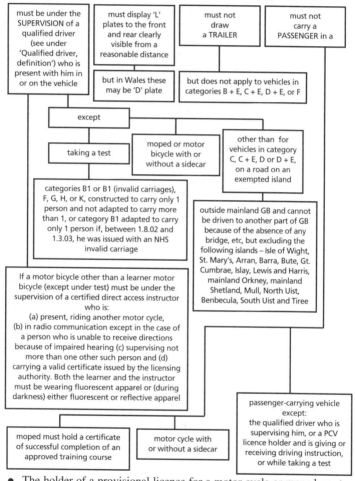

must be under the SUPERVISION of a qualified driver (see under 'Qualified driver, definition') who is present with him in or on the vehicle

must display 'L' plates to the front and rear clearly visible from a reasonable distance

but in Wales these may be 'D' plate

must not draw a TRAILER

must not carry a PASSENGER in a

but does not apply to vehicles in categories B + E, C + E, D + E, or F

except

taking a test

moped or motor bicycle with or without a sidecar

other than for vehicles in category C, C + E, D or D + E, on a road on an exempted island

categories B1 or B1 (invalid carriages), F, G, H, or K, constructed to carry only 1 person and not adapted to carry more than 1, or category B1 adapted to carry only 1 person if, between 1.8.02 and 1.3.03, he was issued with an NHS invalid carriage

outside mainland GB and cannot be driven to another part of GB because of the absence of any bridge, etc, but excluding the following islands – Isle of Wight, St. Mary's, Arran, Barra, Bute, Gt. Cumbrae, Islay, Lewis and Harris, mainland Orkney, mainland Shetland, Mull, North Uist, Benbecula, South Uist and Tiree

If a motor bicycle other than a learner motor bicycle (except under test) must be under the supervision of a certified direct access instructor who is:
(a) present, riding another motor cycle, (b) in radio communication except in the case of a person who is unable to receive directions because of impaired hearing (c) supervising not more than one other such person and (d) carrying a valid certificate issued by the licensing authority. Both the learner and the instructor must be wearing fluorescent apparel or (during darkness) either fluorescent or reflective apparel

moped must hold a certificate of successful completion of an approved training course

motor cycle with or without a sidecar

passenger-carrying vehicle except:
the qualified driver who is supervising him, or a PCV licence holder and is giving or receiving driving instruction, or while taking a test

- The holder of a provisional licence for a motor cycle or moped must take Compulsory Basic Training before they may ride on a road. Upon successful completion, a certificate will be issued and must be produced to the police if requested. (S 164(4A) RTA 1988)
- When motor cyclists pass their test, they are restricted to standard motor cycles for the first 2 years unless, if over 21 years, they take a further test.

MOTOR CYCLE/MOPED LICENCES – IN A NUTSHELL

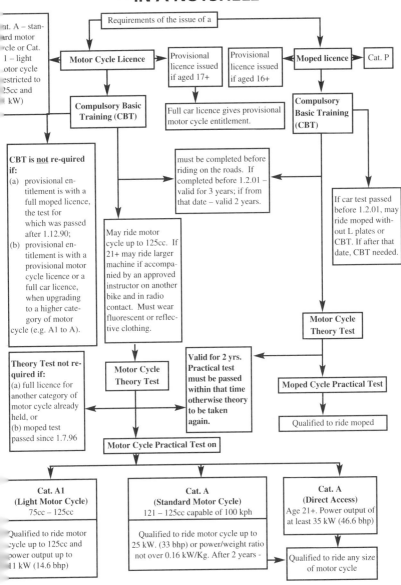

Requirements of the issue of a

Cat. A – standard motor cycle or Cat. A1 – light motor cycle restricted to 125cc and 11 kW)

Motor Cycle Licence

Provisional licence issued if aged 17+

Provisional licence issued if aged 16+

Moped licence ► Cat. P

Compulsory Basic Training (CBT)

Full car licence gives provisional motor cycle entitlement.

Compulsory Basic Training (CBT)

CBT is not re-quired if:
(a) provisional entitlement is with a full moped licence, the test for which was passed after 1.12.90;
(b) provisional entitlement is with a provisional motor cycle licence or a full car licence, when upgrading to a higher category of motor cycle (e.g. A1 to A).

must be completed before riding on the roads. If completed before 1.2.01 – valid for 3 years; if from that date – valid 2 years.

If car test passed before 1.2.01, may ride moped without L plates or CBT. If after that date, CBT needed.

May ride motor cycle up to 125cc. If 21+ may ride larger machine if accompanied by an approved instructor on another bike and in radio contact. Must wear fluorescent or reflective clothing.

Motor Cycle Theory Test

Theory Test not re-quired if:
(a) full licence for another category of motor cycle already held, or
(b) moped test passed since 1.7.96

Motor Cycle Theory Test

Valid for 2 yrs. Practical test must be passed within that time otherwise theory to be taken again.

Moped Cycle Practical Test

Qualified to ride moped

Motor Cycle Practical Test on

Cat. A1 (Light Motor Cycle) 75cc – 125cc

Qualified to ride motor cycle up to 125cc and power output up to 11 kW (14.6 bhp)

Cat. A (Standard Motor Cycle) 121 – 125cc capable of 100 kph

Qualified to ride motor cycle up to 25 kW. (33 bhp) or power/weight ratio not over 0.16 kW/Kg. After 2 years -

Cat. A (Direct Access) Age 21+. Power output of at least 35 kW (46.6 bhp)

Qualified to ride any size of motor cycle

PROVISIONAL LICENCES – PREREQUISITES FOR ISSUE

REG 11 MOTOR VEHICLES (DRIVING LICENCES) REGS 1999

- Before a provisional licence for a particular category of vehicle can be issued, a relevant full licence must be held in the appropriate category.

- The table below shows the category of full licence needed for a particular provisional licence.

- Licences for sub-categories D1 (not for hire or reward), D1 + E (not for hire or reward) and C1 + E (8.25 tonnes) shall not be treated as a licence authorising the driving motor vehicles of a class included in sub-categories D1, D1 +E and C1 + E.

CATEGORY OF LICENCE APPLIED FOR	FULL LICENCE NEEDED
B + E	B
C	B
C1	B
D	B
D1	B
C1 + E	C1
C + E	C
D1 + E	D1
D + E	D
G	B
H	B

NOTE: The above provisions do not apply to full-time members of the armed forces.

LARGE GOODS VEHICLE LICENCES – TRAINEE DRIVERS

REG 54 MOTOR VEHICLES (DRIVING LICENCES) REGULATIONS 1999.
(AS SUBSTITUTED BY THE MOTOR VEHICLES (DRIVING LICENCES)
(AMENDMENT) (NO.3) REGULATIONS 2003

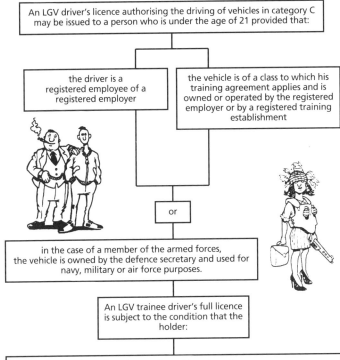

An LGV driver's licence authorising the driving of vehicles in category C may be issued to a person who is under the age of 21 provided that:

the driver is a registered employee of a registered employer

the vehicle is of a class to which his training agreement applies and is owned or operated by the registered employer or by a registered training establishment

or

in the case of a member of the armed forces, the vehicle is owned by the defence secretary and used for navy, military or air force purposes.

An LGV trainee driver's full licence is subject to the condition that the holder:

(a) must be a registered employee of a registered employer;

(b) may drive only vehicles of a class to which his training agreement applies and which is owned by that registered employee or registered training establishment;

(c) may not draw a trailer otherwise than under the supervision of the holder of a full LGV licence for that class of vehicle; and

(d) may only drive C + E as a provisional licence holder after 6 months from passing the category C test. (Does not apply to C1 + E if max. authorised mass does not exceed 7.5 tonnes).

LICENCES –
NEWLY QUALIFIED DRIVER
ROAD TRAFFIC (NEW DRIVERS) ACT 1995

- A driver who acquires 6 or more penalty points within two years of passing his test may have his driving licence revoked and will then have to take another driving test. Newly qualified drivers are on a 2-year probationary period starting from the day on which the driving test is passed.

SECTION 1

- If a newly qualified driver acquires 6 or more penalty points, the Secretary of State will be informed by the convicting court and must revoke the licence by notice to the driver which will state the date of revocation (cannot be earlier than the date of service of the notice). There is provision for the licence to be restored without re-testing where the driver successfully appeals against the conviction and where he gives notice of appeal.

SECTION 5

- Until the driver passes a driving test he is in the position of a learner driver.

SECTION 4

LICENCES – MINIMUM AGES
REG 9 MOTOR VEHICLES (DRIVING LICENCES) REGULATIONS 1999
AND SECTION 101 ROAD TRAFFIC ACT 1988

CATEGORY	AGE	REMARKS
A	21 (17)	Large motor bicycle, 21 years. But will not apply if: (a) If test passed on or after 1.1.97 for category A (but not A1), and 2 years have elapsed since passing the test, or (b) large motor bicycle owned by defence secretary or being driven subject to the orders of the armed forces, and being used for naval, military or air force purposes,17 years, or (c) test passed for large motor bicycle before 1.1.97
A1	17 years	Other motor cycles, 17 years.
B	17 (16)	Generally 17 but if in receipt of a disability living allowance and no trailer drawn, then16.
B + E	17 years	
B1	17 years	
B1 (invalid carriages)	16 years	
C1, C1 + E and C1 + E (8.25 tonnes)	21 years (17, 18)	Generally 21 years except: (a) max authorised mass not over 7.5 tonnes (18 years), or (b) owned by defence secretary or being driven under orders of the armed forces (17 years).
C and C + E	21 years (17, 18)	Generally 21 but if on LGV training scheme,18 years. If owned by defence secretary and driven under orders of the armed forces, 17 years. If incomplete large vehicle (a) with working weight not exceeding 3.5 tonnes, 17 years, (b) with working weight exceeding 3.5 tonnes but not exceeding 7.5 tonnes, 18 years.
D1 (not for hire or reward) D1 + E (not for hire or reward)	21 (18) 21 years	Generally 21 but if an ambulance which is a category D1 vehicle owned or operated by a health service, national health service trust, or primary care trust, 18 years
D1, D1 + E, D and D + E	21 years (17, 18)	Generally 21 except: (a) provisional licence and not carrying passengers except supervisor and other trainees,18 years. (b) used under PSV operator's licence or community bus permit and (i) carrying passengers on a regular service with route not over 50 km, or (ii) where not carrying passengers as aforementioned and the vehicle is in category D1,18 years, or (c) vehicle owned by defence secretary and driven subject to the orders of the armed forces, 17 years.
F	17 (16)	Agricultural or forestry tractor generally 17 but if a wheeled vehicle with overall width not over 2.45 m and not drawing a trailer other than one which is either 2-wheeled or close-coupled 4-wheeled in either case with width not over 2.45 m; and used only in connection with a category 'F' test, 16 years
G	17 – 21	Road roller which is not steam propelled, does not have pneumatic soft or elastic tyres, unladen weight does not exceed 11.69 tonnes, is not constructed or adapted to carry a load other than water, fuel or accumulator used for propulsion, loose tools and objects for increasing the weight of the vehicle – 17 years. Otherwise 21 years.
H K L P	21 years 16 years 17 years 16 years	

LICENCES – UNDER AGE DRIVING
ROAD TRAFFIC ACT 1988

● A person who drives under age may be prosecuted for driving otherwise in accordance with the conditions of a licence.   S 87 RTA 1988

DRIVING LICENCES – MISCELLANEOUS
RENEWAL

A person may drive even when he has not received his licence provided that a valid application for the grant or renewal of the licence has been received by the driving licence computer centre at Swansea, except where the application relates to:

(a) the first provisional licence

(b) further classes of vehicle not covered in existing licence

(c) a replacement more than 10 years after the expiry of the previous one

(d) an applicant suffering from a relevant disability and this is declared in the application

(e) an applicant disqualified until he passes a test of competence

S 88 (1-2) RTA 1988

PHOTOCARD LICENCES

The licence includes details of driver number, signature, name and address, date of birth and categories of vehicle. A paper counterpart shows categories for provisional entitlement, previous history, endorsements (see following page), penalty points and disqualification period.

Both photocard and paper counterpart must be produced when required by a police officer or other authorised person.

DRIVING WHILST DISQUALIFIED

A person is guilty of an offence under the Road Traffic Act 1988, Ss 101 & 103, if, while disqualified from holding or obtaining a licence, he –

(a)   obtains a licence; or

(b)   drives a motor vehicle on a road.

However, the above provision does not apply to persons disqualified by reason of their age. Such persons should be dealt with under S.87 (driving otherwise than in accordance with a licence). For minimum ages for driving, see under 'Driving Licences – Minimum Ages'.

ENDORSEMENT OFFENCE CODES AND PENALTY POINTS

ROAD TRAFFIC OFFENDERS ACT 1988

Code	Offence	Points
AC10	Failing to stop after accident	5-10
AC20	Fail to report accident	5-10
AC30	Undefined accident offence	4-9
BA10	Driving while disqualified	6
BA30	Attempted BA10	6
CD10	Careless driving	3-9
CD20	Inconsiderate driving	3-9
CD30	Careless or inconsiderate driving	3-9
CD40	Death by careless driving – unfit through drink	3-11
CD50	Death by careless driving – unfit through drugs	3-11
CD60	Death by careless driving – alcohol above limit	3-11
CD70	Death by careless driving – fail to provide specimen (alcohol)	3-11
CD71	Death by careless driving – fail to provide specimen (drugs)	3-11
CU10	Defective brakes	3
CU20	Vehicle unsuitable or dangerous	3
CU30	Defective tyres	3
CU40	Defective steering	3
CU50	Causing danger by load or passengers	3
DD40	Dangerous driving	3-11
DD60	Manslaughter by vehicle	3-11
DD80	Death by dangerous driving	3-11
DR10	Driving with alcohol above limit	3-11
DR20	Driving -unfit through drink	3-11
DR30	Fail to supply specimen (alcohol)	3-11
DR31	Fail to supply specimen (drugs)	3-11
DR40	In charge – alcohol above limit	10
DR50	In charge – unfit through drink	10
DR60	Fail to supply specimen – not driving or attempting (alcohol)	10
DR61	Fail to supply specimen – not driving or attempting (drugs)	10
DR70	Fail to supply breath test	4
DR80	Driving – unfit through drugs	3-11
DR90	In charge – unfit through drugs	10
IN10	No insurance	6-8
LC20	No driving licence	3-6
LC30	False declaration to obtain licence	3-6
LC40	Fail to notify a disability	3-6

ENDORSEMENT OFFENCE CODES AND PENALTY POINTS cont

Code	Offence	Points
LC50	Driving after licence revoked on medical grounds	3-6
MS10	Vehicle in dangerous position	3
MS20	Unlawful pillion riding	3
MS30	Play street offences	2
MS50	Motor racing on highway	3-11
MS60	Offences not covered by other codes	
MS70	Uncorrected defective eyesight	3
MS80	Refusing eyesight test	3
MS90	Fail to give information as to identity of driver	3
MW10	Special roads offences	3
PC10	Pedestrian crossing offence	3
PC20	Pedestrian crossing offence – moving vehicle	3
PC30	Pedestrian crossing offence – stationary vehicle	3
SP10	Speed limit – goods vehicle	3-6
SP20	Speed limit – type of vehicle	3-6
SP30	Statutory speed limit	3-6
SP40	Speed limit – passenger vehicle	3-6
SP50	Speed limit – motorway	3-6
SP60	Speed limit – undefined	3-6
TS10	Traffic light signals	3
TS20	Double white line	3
TS30	Stop sign	3
TS40	Direction of a constable	3
TS50	Traffic sign (not stop sign, traffic lights or white lines)	3
TS60	Traffic sign – undefined	3
TT99	Disqualified under totting up	
UT50	Aggravated taking of vehicle	3-11

Aiding and abetting – all '0's above changed to '2'.
Causing or permitting – '0' changed to '4'.
Inciting – '0' changed to '6'

PRODUCTION OF DRIVING LICENCE etc.

ROAD TRAFFIC ACT 1988, S 164

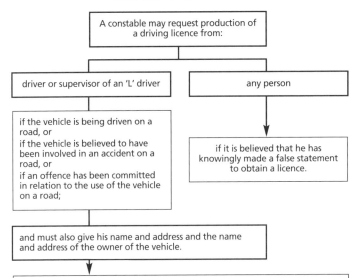

A constable may request production of a driving licence from:

| driver or supervisor of an 'L' driver | any person |

driver or supervisor of an 'L' driver:

if the vehicle is being driven on a road, or
if the vehicle is believed to have been involved in an accident on a road, or
if an offence has been committed in relation to the use of the vehicle on a road;

any person:

if it is believed that he has knowingly made a false statement to obtain a licence.

and must also give his name and address and the name and address of the owner of the vehicle.

If a driving licence is not produced; suspected not to be granted to him; granted in error; or altered with intent to deceive, where the driver number has been altered, removed or defaced; or (if supervising a provisional licence holder) he is suspected to be under 21 years of age, he must also give his date of birth.

REG 83 MV (DL) REGS 1999

The driver → must also produce Insurance, Test certificate, Plating certificate and this includes where an accident has occurred on a road or <u>other public place.</u>

S 165

For production of registration documents see under 'Registration Offences'

NOTE:

- If this licence is not produced at the time, it may be produced at a police station within seven days S 164(8)

- Upon a licence being granted it must be signed in ink forthwith

REG. 20 MV(DL) REGS 1999

DRIVING LICENCES –
VISITORS AND NEW RESIDENTS IN GB

MOTOR VEHICLE (DRIVING LICENCES) REGULATIONS 1999. REG 80
MOTOR VEHICLES (INTERNATIONAL CIRCULATION) ORDER 1975
ROAD TRAFFIC ACT 1988, S 108
DRIVING LICENCE (COMMUNITY DRIVING LICENCE) REGULATIONS 1996
DRIVING LICENCES (EXCHANGEABLE LICENCES) ORDER 2007

The rules governing driving in GB by persons from foreign countries depends upon the country from which the person originated and whether they are a visiting or new resident.

Originating countries may be conveniently grouped as follows:

European Community and the European Economic Area (EC/EEA)
Northern Ireland
Gibraltar and Designated Countries
Jersey, Guernsey and Isle of Man
Faroe Islands, South Africa and Canada
All other countries

European Community Countries:
Austria, Belgium, Czech Republic, Denmark, Estonia, Finland, France, Germany Greece, Hungary, Iceland, Ireland, Italy, Latvia, Liechtenstein, Lithuania Luxembourg, Malta, Netherlands, Norway, Poland, Portugal, Cyprus, Slovakia Slovenia, Spain, Sweden, UK.

European Economic Area Countries:
All EC countries.

Designated Countries:
Australia, Barbados, British Virgin Islands, Canada, Cyprus Republic, Falkland Islands, Hong Kong, Japan, Monaco, New Zealand, Republic of Korea Singapore, South Africa, Switzerland, Zimbabwe.

Ordinary Licence
Generally cars or vans with up to 8 passenger seats up to 3.5 tonnes and moto cycles.

Vocational Licence
Generally medium/large goods vehicles, minibuses and buses.

Where authorised, the use of a non-GB licence is subject to it remaining valid an containing the appropriate group/category of vehicle. All drivers must compl with the British minimum age requirements.

Students
If a community licence, may drive cars and motor cycles until licence expires, c until age 70. If a non-community licence or an international driving permit, ma drive for up to 12 months. If from a designated country may exchange up to years after becoming resident.

THE CHART ON THE FOLLOWING PAGE EXPLAINS THE DRIVING ENTITLEMENT FOR VISITORS/RESIDENTS FROM EACH OF THE ABOVE COUNTRIES.

VISITORS AND NEW RESIDENTS cont

	VISITORS		RESIDENTS	
	ORDINARY LICENCE	VOCATIONAL LICENCE	ORDINARY LICENCE	VOCATIONAL LICENCE
EC/EEA	Provided licence issued in EC/EEA may drive _any_ vehicle shown on licence.		May drive until 70 years of age or 3 years after becoming resident whichever is longer.	May drive until age 45 or for 5 years after becoming resident, whichever longer. If aged 45 but under 65 may drive until 66th birthday or for 5 years after becoming resident whichever shorter. Aged 65 or over – for 12 months after becoming resident.
			After these periods a British licence must be obtained, but may apply for one at any time.	
NORTHERN IRELAND	May use licence until it expires or may exchange for British one.			
GIBRALTAR AND DESIGNATED COUNTRIES	May drive vehicles up to 7.5 tonnes and with up to 16 passenger seats for up to 12 months from date of last entering GB.	May only drive temporarily imported vehicles for 12 months but may travel in and out indefinitely.	May drive for up to 12 months from date of becoming resident but may exchange for GB one.	Must exchange for GB licence before driving. But may drive for 12 months and may exchange for up to 5 years after becoming resident with a Gibraltar licence.
JERSEY, GUERNSEY, ISLE OF MAN	May drive for 12 months.	May drive GB registered or temporarily imported vehicle for up to 12 months. Guernsey licence restricted to temporary imports.	May drive for 12 months from becoming resident but may exchange for GB one.	May drive for 12 months and may exchange for GB one.

VISITORS AND NEW RESIDENTS cont

FAROE ISLANDS, SOUTH AFRICA AND CANADA	A licence authorising category A, B, B1, B+E, F, K or P, (for Faroe Islands omit Cat A) which has been granted by that country (a) to a person who has passed a test there, or (b) which has been exchanged for a licence granted in the UK, in an EEA State, in a designated country, or in Guernsey, Isle of Man, Jersey, Faroe Islands, South Africa or Canada, may exchange the licence for a UK one authorising the driving of vehicles of the above-mentioned categories. However, if the test was passed on an automatic vehicle, the licence is exchangeable only for automatic entitlement.			
ALL OTHER COUNTRIES	May drive vehicles up to 7.5 tonnes and with up to 16 passenger seats for 12 months from date of entering GB.	May drive only temporarily imported vehicles.	May drive for 12 months. To drive continually must pass test within 12 months. If not must comply with provisional licence conditions.	Must take relevant GB test.

COMMUNITY DRIVING

DRIVING LICENCES (COMMUNITY DRIVING LICENCE) REGS. 1996

Exchange for British Licence

The holder of a licence issued within the European Economic Area (EEA) – a 'Community Licence', who become resident in GB need not now exchange it for a British one within 12 months. There remains, however, a right to exchange. But exchange of licences is mandatory for the purpose of periods of validity, health standards and disqualification, where applicable.

Period of Validity of licence held by British residents

Community licences held by Britons are valid for the same period as a British licence unless it would have expired earlier had the holder remained in the State of issue or would otherwise have become invalid in that State.

Health and Fitness

Community licence holders resident in GB are subject to the same health and fitness standards and medical checks as persons holding British licences.

LGV and PCV Licences

Resident community licence holders who are entitled to drive large goods and passenger carrying vehicles are subject to the requirements of Part IV of the Road Traffic Act (hours of work and records, etc.) For certain classes, details must be submitted to the Secretary of State within 1 year of becoming resident.

Endorsements

Counterpart licences will be issued to provide evidence of convictions and fixed penalties.

Modification of Vehicle Categories and Ages

Provision is made in the Road Traffic Act for the re-categorisation of vehicles for licensing purposes and for changes to the minimum age for driving motor cycles.

Right to Issue of British Licence

This is restricted to persons normally resident in GB or the UK.

Other Benefits

Certain statutory benefits such as taxi and community bus licences are extended to the holders of community motor car licences.

CERTIFICATES OF PROFESSIONAL COMPETENCE

VEHICLE DRIVERS (CERTIFICATES OF PROFESSIONAL COMPETENCE)
REGULATIONS 2007

These regulations require the drivers of certain road vehicles for the carriage of goods or passengers to take an initial practical and theoretical driving test (CPC). The test is more extensive than the current driving test and may be taken at the same time as that driving test.

Persons to whom the regulations apply (Reg. 3).
They apply to

    (a)   any person who is a national of a member state (EEA) or a national of a third country employed or used by an undertaking in a member state, and

    (b)   who drives a vehicle which requires a driving licence of category C, C+E, D or D+E or equivalent (a relevant vehicle).

But the regulations do not apply to a vehicle-

    (a)   which it is an offence for that person to drive on a road in GB at a speed greater than 45 kph;

    (b)   being used by, or under the control of any of the following-

        (i)   the armed forces;

        (ii)   the police force;

        (iii)   a local authority in the discharge of any function under the Civil Contingencies Act 2004;

        (iv)   a fire and rescue authority;

    (c)   undergoing road tests for technical development, repair or maintenance purposes, or that is a new or rebuilt vehicle not yet put into service;

    (d)   being used in a state of emergency or assigned to a rescue mission;

    (e)   being used in the course of a driving lesson or driving test for a driving licence or CPC;

    (f)   being used for the non-commercial carriage of passengers or goods for personal use;

    (g)   which is carrying material or equipment to be used by that person in the course of his work, providing that driving the vehicle is not his principal activity.

CERTIFICATES OF PROFESSIONAL COMPETENCE cont

VEHICLE DRIVERS (CERTIFICATES OF PROFESSIONAL COMPETENCE)
REGULATIONS 2007

Persons who must take the initial CPC test (Reg. 4)

Subject to the exceptions below, a person to whom the regulations apply is not permitted to drive a relevant vehicle on a road on or after the date specified below unless he has successfully completed the appropriate CPC test for vehicles of that category.

Specified dates:

    (a)   Category D or D+E, 10/9/2008;

    (b)   Category C or C+E, 10/9/2009.

A person may take an initial CPC test whether or not he has been granted a licence for a relevant vehicle.

Exceptions:

    (a)   Drivers undergoing an approved vocational training course lasting at least six months, leading to a professional qualification relevant to the carriage of passengers or goods may be exempted for up to 12 months from taking the test. During that time he may drive a relevant vehicle within the UK. He will be issued with a document authorising him to drive.

    (b)   Drivers who hold a bus or lorry licence (D, D+E, C or C+E) before the specified date (see above) ('drivers with acquired rights') are exempt from taking the initial CPC test (but see below for periodic training requirements).

    (c)   A person who holds a CPC certifying an initial qualification awarded on the basis of course attendance and test.

Driver qualification card (Reg. 8)

A person who has passed the initial CPC test, or who has completed 35 hours of periodic training is issued with a driver qualification card. This card is the 'CPC'. It is valid for five years.

Time limits for obtaining a CPC (Reg. 9)

A person is prohibited from driving a bus or lorry unless that person has passed the initial CPC test within the previous five years or has completed 35 hours of periodic training within the previous five years. Drivers with 'acquired rights' (see above) who do not need to take the initial CPC test must complete 35 hours periodic training by 10th September 2013 in respect of bus drivers and by 10th September 2014 in respect of lorry drivers.

Offence of driving without a CPC (Reg. 10)

A person who drives or causes or permits a person to drive a relevant vehicle on a road without a current CPC commits an offence.

CERTIFICATES OF PROFESSIONAL COMPETENCE cont

VEHICLE DRIVERS (CERTIFICATES OF PROFESSIONAL COMPETENCE)
REGULATIONS 2007

Requirement to carry and produce evidence of CPC (Reg.11)
A person who is required to hold a CPC and does not carry with him in the vehicle evidence of that CPC commits an offence.
That evidence may be any of the following documents-
- (a) a driver qualification card;
- (b) a community licence with the community code;
- (c) a driver's certificate granted to him by a member state other than the UK; or
- (d) any other document issued to the driver by a member state other than the UK certifying an initial or periodic CPC.

A person who is undergoing a vocational training course must carry with him in the vehicle the document authorising him to drive (see above). He commits an offence if he fails to do so.

A police constable or vehicle examiner may at any time require a person to produce to him the evidence or document referred to above. A person failing to do so commits an offence.

Forgery and false statements (Reg. 13)
A person is guilty of an offence if, with intent to deceive he-
- (a) forges, alters or uses any document or evidence referred to above;
- (b) lends to, or allows to be used by, any other person such a document; or
- (c) makes or has in his possession any document so closely resembling such a document as to be calculated to deceive.

A person who knowingly makes a false statement for the purpose of obtaining a driver qualification card is guilty of an offence.

Power to seize documents (Reg. 14)
If a constable or vehicle examiner has reasonable cause to believe that a document carried in a motor vehicle or by the driver of the vehicle is a document in relation to which an offence has been committed under Reg. 13, he may seize it.

New minimum age requirements (Reg. 15)
Bus and lorry drivers who have passed the initial CPC test have new minimum age requirements as follows-
- (a) lorry drivers, 18 years instead of the normal 21 years;
- (c) bus drivers carrying passengers on a route which does not exceed 50 km. or not carrying passengers at all, 18 years is substituted for 21 years; and
- (d) all other bus drivers, 20 years is substituted for 21 years.

INSURANCE

SECTION 143 ROAD TRAFFIC ACT 1988

> No person shall use, or cause or permit to be used

> a motor vehicle on a road or other public place

> unless there is in force a policy of insurance or security in respect of third party risks.

Defence

It shall be a defence if a person proves that he was not the owner of the vehicle, nor had he hired the vehicle and it was used in the course of his employment and he did not know or have reason to believe there was no insurance in force.

Exemptions:

The following vehicles are exempt from the requirements of section 143 above:

S 144 RTA 1988

1. owned by a person who has deposited £500,000 with the Supreme Court;
2. owned by a county council or other local authority (for full list see S 144 RTA 1988);
3. owned by a police authority and driven under the owner's control, or a vehicle being driven for police purposes by or under the direction of a constable or person employed by a police authority;
4. being driven for salvage purposes under the Merchant Shipping Act 1995;
5. being driven under the Army Act 1955 or the Air Force Act 1955;
6. owned by a health service body;
7. an ambulance owned by a National Health Service trust;
8. made available by the Secretary of State under the National Health Service Act 1977;
9. made available by the Secretary of State to any local authority, education authority or voluntary organisation in Scotland under the National Health Service (Scotland) Act 1978.

Green Card

Vehicles temporarily in Great Britain for which a Green Card has been issued may use the card the same as insurance. Insurance certificates issued in Community Member States (Austria, Belgium, Czech Republic, Denmark, Estonia, France, Finland, Germany, Greece, Hungary, Iceland, Ireland, Italy, Latvia, Liechtenstein, Lithuania, Luxembourg, Malta, Netherlands, Norway, Poland, Portugal, Cyprus, Slovakia, Slovenia, Spain, Sweden, UK) provide third-party cover throughout all other Member States – there is no need for a Green Card.

S 143 RTA 1988

POWER TO SEIZE VEHICLES DRIVEN WITHOUT LICENCE OR INSURANCE

S 165A ROAD TRAFFIC ACT 1988

If a constable in uniform requires:

1. under S 164, a person to **produce his licence and counterpart** for examination, the person fails to produce them, and the constable has reasonable grounds for believing that a motor vehicle is, or was, being driven by the person without a licence authorising him to drive that vehicle, contrary to S 87(1);
2. under S 165, a person to produce **evidence that the vehicle was not being driven without insurance**, the person fails to produce such evidence, and the constable has reasonable cause to believe that the vehicle was being so driven, contrary to S 143; or
3. under S 163, a person driving a motor vehicle to **stop the vehicle**, the person fails to stop the vehicle, or to stop it long enough, for the constable to make such lawful enquiries as he considers appropriate, and the constable has reasonable grounds for believing that the vehicle is, or was, being driven without a licence or insurance, contrary to S 87(1) or S 143,

the constable may:

    (a) **seize** the vehicle
    (b) **enter**, for the purpose of seizing the vehicle, any premises (other than a private dwelling house), on which he has reasonable grounds for believing the vehicle to be; and
    (c) **use reasonable force**, if necessary, in the exercise of (a) or (b).

Before seizing the vehicle the constable must **warn** the person that he will seize it if the licence and counterpart (or evidence of insurance, as the case may be,) is not produced **immediately**. But a warning need not be given if the circumstances make it impracticable to do so.
If the constable is unable to seize the vehicle immediately, because the person has failed to stop or has driven off, he may seize it at any time within 24 hours.

    Motor vehicle does not include an invalid carriage.

    Private dwelling house does not include any garage or structure occupied with the dwelling house, or any land appurtenant to the dwelling house.

    The **Road Traffic Act 1988 (Retention and Disposal of Seized Motor Vehicles) Regulations 2005** provide for: the retention and safe keeping of motor vehicles (Reg 3), giving of seizure notice (Reg 4), release of vehicles (Reg 5), charges (Reg 6), disposal (Reg 7), and payment of proceeds of sale to the owner (Reg 8).

OPERATORS' LICENCES

GOODS VEHICLES (LICENSING OF OPERATORS) ACT 1995
GOODS VEHICLES (LICENSING OF OPERATORS) REGULATIONS 1995

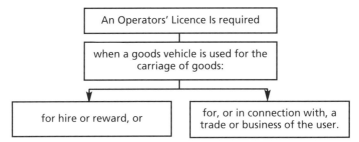

An Operators' Licence Is required

when a goods vehicle is used for the carriage of goods:

| for hire or reward, or | for, or in connection with, a trade or business of the user. |

S2 GV (L OF O) ACT 1995

Vehicles covered

Any vehicle or trailer in the lawful possession of the licence-holder (whether that motor vehicle is specified or not). However a licence may impose maximum weights for motor vehicles and trailers, may prohibit the use of trailers, or may prohibit the use of motor vehicles which are not specified in the licence.

S5 GV (L OF O) ACT 1995

To avoid making application for the authorisation of motor vehicles temporarily in the operator's possession, the original licence may authorise the use of additional vehicles. If such vehicles are acquired, the Licensing Authority must be notified within one month of acquisition of the vehicle.

TYPE   S 3 GOODS VEHICLES (LICENSING OF OPERATORS) ACT 1995

I	**Standard (International)**	For hire or reward or in connection with any trade or business carried on by the holder in both national and international transport.
N	**Standard (National)**	For hire or reward etc in UK.
R	**Restricted**	For carrying goods only in connection with operator's trade or business, other than carrying goods for hire or reward.

S5(6) GV (L OF O) ACT 1995

Displaying operator's disc

All motor vehicles used under a licence must display a disc in a waterproof container on the nearside near the lower edge of the windscreen with the obverse side facing forwards (or, if not fitted with a windscreen, in a conspicuous position on the front or nearside of the vehicle).

REG 23 GV (L OF O) REGULATIONS 1995

OPERATORS' LICENCES – EXEMPTIONS

GOODS VEHICLES (LICENSING OF OPERATORS) ACT 1995
GOODS VEHICLES (LICENSING OF OPERATORS) REGULATIONS 1995

A Goods Vehicle Operators' licence is
not required for the following

---

small goods vehicles:

rigid vehicles not forming part of a combination

1. with relevant **plated** weight of not more than 3.5 tonnes, or

2. if **unplated**, an unladen weight of not more than 1,525 kg;

rigid vehicles forming part of a combination

1. if all the vehicles (except any small trailer with unladen weight not exceeding 1,020 kg) **have relevant plated weights** the aggregate of which does not exceed 3.5 tonnes

2. if any are **not plated**, the aggregate of the unladen weight (excluding and small trailer with unladen weight not exceeding 1,020 kg) does not exceed 1,525 kg;

articulated vehicles

1. if the aggregate of the unladen weight of the tractive unit, together with the **plated weight** of semi-trailer is not more than 3.5 tonnes

2. if semi-trailer unplated, the aggregate unladen weight of tractive unit and semi-trailer is not more than 1,525 kg;

---

goods vehicle used for international carriage

1. a goods vehicle for international carriage by a haulier established in a member State other than the UK and not established in the UK;

2. a goods vehicle for international carriage by a haulier established in Northern Ireland and not established in Great Britain.

3. a foreign vehicle being used temporarily in Great Britain (see following pages).

OPERATORS' LICENCES – EXEMPTIONS cont

GOODS VEHICLES (LICENSING OF OPERATORS) ACT 1995
GOODS VEHICLES (LICENSING OF OPERATORS) REGULATIONS 1995

cont from previous page

A Goods Vehicle Operators' licence is not required for the following

For fuller details consult Sched 3 to the Regulations.

---

agricultural machinery and trailers taxed at the concessionary excise rate and being used for an authorised purpose (SEE PART II, SCHED 3)

civil defence vehicles

dual-purpose vehicles (such as Land Rovers) and trailers

electric vehicles

fire-fighting and rescue vehicles used in mines

hearses and other vehicles used for funerals

local authority vehicles for weights & measures etc. enactments

pre-1977 vehicles not over 1,525 kg unladen, plated between 3.5 tonnes and 3.5 tons

police, fire brigade, ambulance and Serious Organised Crime Agency vehicles

RNLI and Coastguard vehicles

recovery vehicles

road maintenance trailers

road rollers and trailers

showmen's goods vehicles and trailers

snow clearing vehicles and gritters etc

steam-propelled vehicles

tower wagons and trailers carrying only goods used in connection with its work

uncompleted vehicles on test or trial

vehicle allowed to carry out cabotage in the UK under EC Regs

vehicles and their trailers using the roads for less than six miles a week while moving between parts of private premises

vehicles carrying a load for the purposes of the examination of that vehicle

vehicles constructed or adapted primarily for the carriage of passengers and their effects, and trailers drawn thereby

vehicles used by highway authorities for weighing vehicles

vehicles used by or under the control of HM UK Forces

vehicles used solely on aerodromes

vehicles with special fixed equipment (such as road sweepers and feedmobiles)

vehicles with trade plates

visiting Forces' vehicles

water, electricity, gas or telephone vehicles held ready for use in emergencies.

OPERATORS' LICENCES
EXEMPTIONS cont

GOODS VEHICLES (LICENSING OF OPERATORS) ACT 1995
GOODS VEHICLES (LICENSING OF OPERATORS) REGULATIONS 1995

FORGERY (S 38)

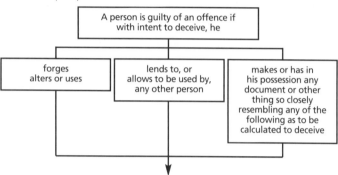

A person is guilty of an offence if with intent to deceive, he

| forges alters or uses | lends to, or allows to be used by, any other person | makes or has in his possession any document or other thing so closely resembling any of the following as to be calculated to deceive |

any operators' licence; any document plate, mark or other thing by which a vehicle is to be identified as being authorised to be used under an operators' licence; any document evidencing the authorisation of any person for the purpose of inspecting maintenance facilities or the seizure or disposal of documents etc.; any certificate of qualification to be engaged in road transport undertakings; or any certificate or diploma of professional competence.

PRODUCTION OF LICENCE (REG 26)

An officer or police constable may require the production of an operator's licence by the holder of such within 14 days at an operating centre or (in the case of the requirement being made by a police officer) at a police station chosen by the licence holder.

Failure to comply is an offence. (REG 32)

POWER TO INSPECT (S 40)

An officer or police constable may, at any reasonable time, enter the premises of an applicant for, or holder of, an operator's licence and inspect any facilities on those premises for maintaining vehicles in a fit and serviceable condition. Any obstruction in the exercise of these powers constitutes an offence.

POWER TO SEIZE DOCUMENTS ETC (S 41)

If an officer or police constable has reason to believe that:
a. a document or article carried on or by the driver of a vehicle, or
b. a document produced to him in pursuance of this Act, is a document or article in relation to which an offence under S 38 (forgery etc) or S 39 (false statement to obtain) relates, he may seize that document or article.

OPERATORS' LICENCES –
FOREIGN VEHICLES TEMPORARILY IN GB

GOODS VEHICLES (LICENSING OF OPERATORS) (TEMPORARY USE IN GREAT BRITAIN)
REGULATIONS 1996 (AS AMENDED BY SI 2004/462)

The requirement to have an operators' licence does not apply to the use of –

1. a foreign goods vehicle carrying specified goods in Great Britain (reg. 4); or

2. a Northern Ireland or foreign goods vehicle used for the carriage of goods between member states of the European Community –
   (a) if it is –
      (i) carrying goods loaded or unloaded not more than 25 km from the GB coast and loaded or unloaded not more than 25 km from the coast of another member state, and the distance (measured in a straight line) between the points of loading and unloading (disregarding any distance over the sea) does not exceed 100 km, or
      (ii) a motor vehicle or trailer drawn by a foreign goods vehicle having a permissible laden weight not over 6 metric tons or a permissible payload not over 3.5 metric tons, or
      (iii) a relief vehicle replacing a broken down vehicle; or
   (b) if it is carrying specified goods; or
   (c) if it is being used on a combined transport operation (see under that heading); or
   (d) if it is carrying goods for or in connection with a trade or business of the undertaking; (reg. 5) or

3. a Northern Ireland or foreign goods vehicle carrying goods for hire or reward under an international licence; (reg. 6)or

4. a foreign goods vehicle with a Community cabotage authorisation or a Northern Ireland goods vehicle carrying goods in GB or between Northern Ireland and GB (reg. 7).

Foreign goods vehicle means a goods vehicle which is –
(a) operated by a person not established in the UK, and is temporarily in GB;
(b) not being used for international carriage by a haulier established in a member state other than the UK;
(c) on a journey, part of which is outside the UK; and
(d) not used to deliver goods in the UK which were loaded in the UK (except under a cabotage agreement). (reg. 3).

Exemptions and modifications

There are specific exemptions and modifications which relate to vehicles from different countries. Where an exemption applies, an operator's licence is not required. The exemptions and modifications concern one or more of the following: specified goods; weight and nature of the vehicle and/or load; and the requirement to carry a permit. These are now discussed on the following pages.

OPERATORS' LICENCES – FOREIGN VEHICLES TEMPORARILY IN GB cont

GOODS VEHICLES (LICENSING OF OPERATORS) (TEMPORARY USE IN GREAT BRITAIN) REGULATIONS 1996

The following table contains the exemptions and modifications which appertain to vehicles from particular countries. Where an exemption or modification applies, an Operator's Licence is not required. The key to specific goods can be found in the list below the table.

Reg.	Country	Exemptions/modifications which apply
8	Albania	May carry any goods
9	Austria	Specified goods: 1,2,4-10,15,17-21,24,26,27 (Sched 2).. But see note 1overleaf.
10	Bulgaria	May carry any goods
11	Channel Islands	May carry any goods
30D	Croatia	May carry any goods
12	Cyprus	Specified goods: 1,2,3,5,9,10,16,22-24. But see note 2 overleaf.
13	Czech Republic	See note 10 overleaf.
15	Estonia	Specified goods: 4,5,9,18,20-24. But see note 3 overleaf.
14	Faroe Islands	May carry any goods
30C	Georgia	Specified goods: 4,5,9,21,29-32. But see note 11 overleaf.
16	Hungary	May carry any goods
20	Isle of Man (Manx)	May carry any goods
17	Jordan	May carry any goods
18	Latvia	May carry any goods
19	Lithuania	May carry any goods.
30A	Macedonia	May carry any goods
30B	Moldova	May carry any goods

Specified Goods (Sched.2): **1** airport luggage, **2** diverted airport luggage, **3** luggage in trailer of passenger vehicle, **4** postal packets, **5** damaged vehicles, **6** animal corpses not for human consumption, **7** bees or fish stock, **8** deceased person, **9** medical or surgical emergency relief goods, **10** household removals, **11** household effects, **12** live animals not for slaughter, **13** spare parts for ocean ships, **14** spare parts and provisions for ships, **15** spare parts and provisions for re-routed ocean ships, **16** spare parts for ocean ships and aircraft, **17** goods carried in guarded security vehicles, **18** works of art, **19** antiques, **20** publicity or educational goods, **21** property, equipment or animals for theatrical, musical, cinema or circus, or sporting events, exhibitions or fairs, or radio or TV broadcasts or films, **22** goods, property or animals for theatrical, musical, film or circus, or sporting events, **23** goods or properties for radio or TV broadcasts or films, **24** goods for fairs and exhibitions, **25** goods for international fairs and exhibitions, **26** refuse, **27** garbage, **28** sewage, **29** refrigerated perishable foodstuffs, **30** broken down vehicles, **31** objects and works of art for exhibitions, **32** samples of objects and materials for publicity or information purposes.

OPERATORS' LICENCES – FOREIGN VEHICLES TEMPORARILY IN GB cont

GOODS VEHICLES (LICENSING OF OPERATORS) (TEMPORARY USE IN GREAT BRITAIN) REGULATIONS 1996

Reg.	Country	Exemptions/modifications which apply
21	Morocco	Specified goods: 2,9,31 But see note 4 overleaf.
22	Northern Ireland	See note 5 overleaf.
23	Poland	May carry any goods
24	Romania	May carry any goods
25	Slovak Republic	May carry any goods
30E	Slovenia	May carry any goods
27	Switzerland	May carry any goods
28	Tunisia	Specified goods: 1-10,13,18,19,21,24,30. But see note 6 overleaf.
29	Turkey	Specified goods: 1-9,17,21,26,27,30. But see note 7 overleaf.
30	Ukraine	Specified goods: 4,5,9,18,20-24. But see note 8 overleaf.
26	USSR (former). Applies to countries not provided for elsewhere	Specified goods: 4,5,8. But also 21-23 if the goods are to be, or are being, returned to the country of origin of the vehicle, or to another country. But see note 9 overleaf.

Specified Goods (Sched.2): **1** airport luggage, **2** diverted airport luggage, **3** luggage in trailer of passenger vehicle, **4** postal packets, **5** damaged vehicles, **6** animal corpses not for human consumption, **7** bees or fish stock, **8** deceased person, **9** medical or surgical emergency relief goods, **10** household removals, **11** household effects, **12** live animals not for slaughter, **13** spare parts for ocean ships, **14** spare parts and provisions for ships, **15** spare parts and provisions for re-routed ocean ships, **16** spare parts for ocean ships and aircraft, **17** goods carried in guarded security vehicles, **18** works of art, **19** antiques, **20** publicity or educational goods, **21** property, equipment or animals for theatrical, musical, cinema or circus, or sporting events, exhibitions or fairs, or radio or TV broadcasts or films, **22** goods, property or animals for theatrical, musical, film or circus, or sporting events, **23** goods or properties for radio or TV broadcasts or films, **24** goods for fairs and exhibitions, **25** goods for international fairs and exhibitions, **26** refuse, **27** garbage, **28** sewage, **29** refrigerated perishable foodstuffs, **30** broken down vehicles, **31** objects and works of art for exhibitions, **32** samples of objects and materials for publicity or information purposes.

OPERATORS' LICENCES – FOREIGN VEHICLES TEMPORARILY IN GB cont

GOODS VEHICLES (LICENSING OF OPERATORS) (TEMPORARY USE IN GREAT BRITAIN) REGULATIONS 1996

Note 1. But doesn't need an operator's licence if the vehicle has a permissible laden weight not exceeding 6 metric tons or a permissible payload not exceeding 3.5 metric tons; or if it is a vehicle used for an abnormal indivisible load or other wide load and Special Types Regs. are complied with; or if it is a relief vehicle for a broken down vehicle (Sched. 3). If carrying goods other than those specified above for or in connection with the user's trade or business, and Sched. 3 does not apply, it doesn't need a licence if it carries a document containing particulars of the user, his trade or business, the goods carried, their loading and unloading points, the vehicle, and the route (Sched. 4). If carrying goods other than those specified above and Scheds. 3, and 4 do not apply, instead of an operator's licence, it may carry a permit from the Secretary of State, authorising the carriage of the goods (Sched. 5).

Note 2. But doesn't need an operator's licence if the vehicle has a permissible laden weight not exceeding 6 metric tons or a permissible payload not exceeding 3.5 metric tons; or if it is a vehicle used for an abnormal indivisible load or other wide load and Special Types Regs. are complied with; or if it is a relief vehicle for a broken down vehicle (Sched. 3). If carrying goods other than those specified above for or in connection with the user's trade or business, and Sched. 3 does not apply, it doesn't need a licence if it carries a document containing particulars of where and when the document was made, the carrier, goods carried, place of loading and unloading, quantity of goods, payload of the vehicle, vehicle index and registration number (or if none, the chassis number), place of entry or exit from UK, and signature of the carrier or his agent (Reg. 12(5)). If carrying goods other than those specified above and Sched. 3, and Reg. 12(5) do not apply, instead of an operator's licence, it may carry a permit from the Secretary of State, authorising the carriage of the goods (Sched. 5).

Note 3. But doesn't need an operator's licence if the vehicle has a permissible laden weight not exceeding 6 metric tons or a permissible payload not exceeding 3.5 metric tons (Sched 3(1)). If carrying goods other than those specified above for or in connection with the user's trade or business, and Sched. 3(1) does not apply, instead of an operator's licence, it may carry a permit from the Secretary of State, authorising the carriage of the goods (Sched. 5).

Note 4. If carrying goods other than those specified above, instead of an operator's licence it may carry a permit from the Secretary of State, authorising the carriage of the goods (Sched. 5).

Note 5. Operator's licence not required if carrying goods for hire or reward and the vehicle is licensed under S17 of the Transport Act (Northern Ireland) 1967. If not carrying goods for hire or reward, it must carry a document containing particulars of the user, his trade or business, the goods carried, their loading and unloading points, the vehicle, and the route (Sched. 4).

Note 6. But doesn't need an operator's licence if the vehicle has a permissible laden weight not exceeding 6 metric tons or a permissible payload not exceeding 3.5 metric tons; or if it is a vehicle used for an abnormal indivisible load or other wide load and Special Types Regs. are complied with; or if it is a relief vehicle for a broken down vehicle (Sched. 3). If carrying goods other than those specified above and Sched.3 does not apply, it may, instead of an operator's licence, carry a permit from the Secretary of State, authorising the carriage of the goods (Sched. 5).

OPERATORS' LICENCES – FOREIGN VEHICLES TEMPORARILY IN GB cont

GOODS VEHICLES (LICENSING OF OPERATORS) (TEMPORARY USE IN GREAT BRITAIN)
REGULATIONS 1996

Note 7. If carrying goods other than those specified above it may, instead of an operator's licence, carry a permit from the Secretary of State, authorising the carriage of the goods (Sched. 5).

Note 8. But doesn't need an operator's licence if the vehicle has a permissible laden weight not exceeding 6 metric tons or a permissible payload not exceeding 3.5 metric tons (Sched 3(1)), or if the goods are carried for or in connection with the trade or business of the carrier. But if none of the preceding exemptions apply, and it is carrying goods other than those specified above, it may, instead of an operator's licence, carry a permit from the Secretary of State, authorising the carriage of the goods (Sched. 5).

Note 9. An operator's licence will not be needed if the vehicle is used for carrying an abnormal indivisible load or other wide load and Special Types Regs. are being complied with, or if it is a relief vehicle for a broken down vehicle. (Sched. 3(2) & (3)). If the preceding exemption does not apply and it is carrying goods other than those which are exempt, it may, instead of an operator's licence, carry a permit from the Secretary of State, authorising the carriage of the goods (Sched. 5). However, all of the aforementioned exemptions are subject to the conditions that (a) the goods are carried under the Convention (as authorised by S.1 of the Carriage of Goods by Road Act 1965) and a consignment note is made out in accordance with that Convention, or (b) if other goods are carried, a document must be carried containing particulars of the date and place the document was made out, name and address of the sender, name and address of the carrier, the date and place of taking over the goods, and their delivery, name and address of the consignee, description of the nature and packing of the goods, the number of packages and their special marks and numbers, the gross weight of the goods, charges relating to the carriage, and instructions for Customs and other formalities. All exemptions are also subject to the carriage on the vehicle of a permit to use the vehicle for the purpose issued by the Secretary of State.

Note 10. Provided it is not at any time during its journey used to carry goods loaded at one place in the UK and delivered to another place in the UK, it will be regarded as a 'foreign goods vehicle' to which Regs. 4, 5, 6 & 7 apply (see earlier) and an Operators' Licence will not be required. Where the vehicle is used to carry goods loaded at one place in the UK and delivered to another place in the UK, it may, instead of an operator's licence, carry a permit from the Secretary of State, authorising the carriage of the goods (Sched. 5).

Note 11. May also carry any goods on the owner's or operator's own account between GB and the Republic of Georgia. But if carrying goods other than those specified above, or carrying any goods to which the aforementioned exemption does not apply, it may, instead of an operator's licence, carry a permit from the Secretary of State, authorising the carriage of the goods (Sched. 5).

EXCISE LICENCES

VEHICLE EXCISE AND REGISTRATION ACT 1994

Excise licences are required by all mechanically propelled vehicles used or kept on a public road maintainable at public expense. Tax rates for goods vehicles depend on the vehicle weight. For HGVs subject to plating and testing this means the maximum weight. For other vehicles it means the weight at which the vehicle can be operated under Construction and Use Regulations. For HGVs the tax rate depends upon not only its weight, but also the number of axles and whether it is rigid or articulated. There are also reduced rates for engines which reduce pollution.

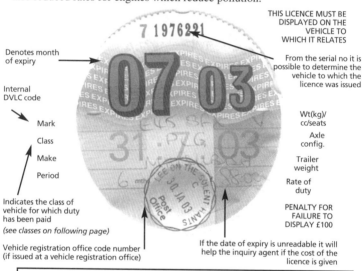

THIS LICENCE MUST BE DISPLAYED ON THE VEHICLE TO WHICH IT RELATES

Denotes month of expiry

From the serial no it is possible to determine the vehicle to which the licence was issued

Internal DVLC code

Mark

Class

Make

Period

Wt(kg)/ cc/seats

Axle config.

Trailer weight

Rate of duty

PENALTY FOR FAILURE TO DISPLAY £100

Indicates the class of vehicle for which duty has been paid
(*see classes on following page*)

Vehicle registration office code number
(if issued at a vehicle registration office)

If the date of expiry is unreadable it will help the inquiry agent if the cost of the licence is given

Exemptions

Electrically assisted pedal cycles

Fire and ambulance vehicles and health service vehicles

Invalid carriages weighing less than 508 kg

Lifeboat haulage vehicles

Mine rescue vehicles

Trams

Vehicles being taken to or from annual test or retest by prior appointment or being driven for the purposes of the test, or being taken to or from a place for relevant work to be carried out on the vehicle following refusal of a certificate.

Old vehicles (more than 25 years old)

Vehicles being imported by members of foreign armed forces, etc.

Vehicles for export

Vehicles carrying disabled persons and registered in name of disabled driver

Veterinary ambulances

Vehicles not constructed, adapted or used to carry any person

Vehicles used for agriculture, horticulture or forestry purposes, passing between different areas of land occupied by the same person and not travelling on public roads (or more than 1.5 km per journey

SECTION 5 AND SCHED 2

EXCISE DUTY CLASSES

SCHED 1 VEHICLES EXCISE AND REGISTRATION ACT 1994

The following details the classes of vehicle as described in the above-mentioned Act and Schedule

Private/light goods
Applies to vehicle not otherwise mentioned in Schedule 1

Motor bicycles and tricycles
The rate of duty is calculated according to the cc of the engine

Buses
The rate of duty is calculated according to the seating capacity. "Bus" means a PSV which is not 'excepted' (less than 9 seats, community bus, or used with educational permit) nor a 'special concessionary vehicle' (see later).

Recovery vehicles.
The rate payable depends on the revenue weight. It is restricted to vehicles constructed or permanently adapted for lifting, towing or transporting a disabled vehicle. It must not be used for any other purpose and may only carry passengers or goods which are being conveyed in the disabled vehicle.

Vehicles used for exceptional loads
These are taxed at the Heavy Tractive Unit rate. An exceptional load is one which by reason of its weight or dimensions cannot be carried in compliance with construction and use regulations and is being carried under special types order.

Haulage vehicles
If a showman's vehicle the rate is the same as the basic goods vehicle, otherwise the general haulage rate applies. A 'haulage vehicle' is one, not being a 'special vehicle', 'special concessionary vehicle', or 'exceptional load', which is constructed and used solely for haulage and not for carrying a load.

Goods vehicles
The rate applicable depends upon revenue weight, the number of axles and whether rigid or articulated. Different scales apply to rigid vehicles over 7,500 kg, tractive units exceeding 7,500 kg, vehicles with reduced plated weights, vehicles for conveying machines, and island goods vehicles.

Special vehicles
The duty applicable is the basic goods vehicle rate. It includes a vehicle over 3,500 kg revenue weight which is not a 'special concessionary vehicle' (see later) and which is a digging machine, mobile crane, works truck, road roller, vehicle not used to carry goods or burden for hire or reward or in connection with a trade or business, and a vehicle designed for use with a semi-trailer but which does not carry goods or burden.

Special concessionary vehicles
The duty payable is 25% of the general rate (private/light goods rate).
Vehicles included in this category are:
(a) Agricultural tractor used for agriculture, horticulture, forestry, or cutting verges/hedges etc
(b) Off road tractor not being an agricultural tractor designed and constructed for use off-roads and not exceeding 25 mph.
(c) Light agricultural vehicle not over 1,000 kg with only 1 seat and used only for agriculture, horticulture or fishery purposes.
(d) Agricultural engine
(e) Mowing machine
(f) Steam powered vehicle
(g) Electrically powered vehicle (not being a motorcycle)
(g) Vehicle used/kept only for snow clearing or salt/grit spreading

Statutory Off-Road Notification
Where a vehicle licence is surrendered, or is not renewed, or the vehicle is kept unlicenced the holder of the licence (or keeper) must declare the address at which the vehicle is being kept. Reg. 26 Road Vehicles (Registration and Licensing) Regulations 2002.

IMMOBILISATION AND REMOVAL OF UNLICENSED VEHICLES

VEHICLE EXCISE DUTY (IMMOBILISATION, REMOVAL AND DISPOSAL OF VEHICLES) REGULATIONS 1997

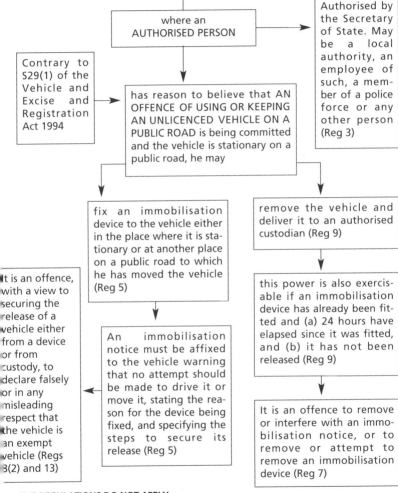

where an AUTHORISED PERSON

Authorised by the Secretary of State. May be a local authority, an employee of such, a member of a police force or any other person (Reg 3)

Contrary to S29(1) of the Vehicle and Excise and Registration Act 1994

has reason to believe that AN OFFENCE OF USING OR KEEPING AN UNLICENCED VEHICLE ON A PUBLIC ROAD is being committed and the vehicle is stationary on a public road, he may

fix an immobilisation device to the vehicle either in the place where it is stationary or at another place on a public road to which he has moved the vehicle (Reg 5)

remove the vehicle and deliver it to an authorised custodian (Reg 9)

It is an offence, with a view to securing the release of a vehicle either from a device or from custody, to declare falsely or in any misleading respect that the vehicle is an exempt vehicle (Regs 3(2) and 13)

An immobilisation notice must be affixed to the vehicle warning that no attempt should be made to drive it or move it, stating the reason for the device being fixed, and specifying the steps to secure its release (Reg 5)

this power is also exercisable if an immobilisation device has already been fitted and (a) 24 hours have elapsed since it was fitted, and (b) it has not been released (Reg 9)

It is an offence to remove or interfere with an immobilisation notice, or to remove or attempt to remove an immobilisation device (Reg 7)

THE REGULATIONS DO NOT APPLY:

(a) if disabled person's badge is displayed (b) exempt vehicle and 'nil' licence displayed, (c) B.M.A. badge is displayed (d) vehicle abandoned, (e) PSV used to carry passengers, (f) construction, maintenance, etc. vehicle (g) Post Office or Royal Mail vehicle delivering or collecting, (h) less than 24 hours since immobilised vehicle was released. (Reg 4)

EXHIBITION OF EXCISE LICENCES

VEHICLE EXCISE AND REGISTRATION ACT 1994
THE ROAD VEHICLES (REGISRATION AND LICENSING) REGULATIONS 2002

> **Excise licences must be fixed to and exhibited on vehicle in a manner prescribed by the regulations**
>
> S 33

Separate offences exist of:

- using or keeping an unlicensed vehicle on a public road   S 29
- contravening terms of trade licence.   S 34
- exhibiting on the vehicle anything which is intended to be mistaken for, or which might reasonably be mistaken for a vehicle licence or a trade licence.   REG. 7

> and must be displayed in a holder to protect it from the weather and must be clearly visible from the nearside of the road.

> no licence need be displayed if the licence has been returned to the secretary of state for the issue of a replacement.

Motor bicycle, tricycle or invalid carriage

Position: nearside of vehicle

Motor bicycle with sidecar attached or drawing a sidecar

Position: nearside of handlebars or nearside of sidecar

Any vehicle fitted with glass windscreen extending to the nearside

Position: on or adjacent to the nearside of the windscreen

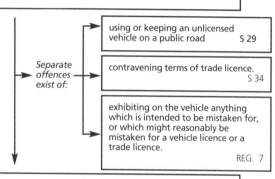

Any other vehicle

- If fitted with cab having nearside window – on that window and not less than 760 mm and not more than 1.8 m above the road surface

REGISTRATION MARKS – FIXING AND LIGHTING
ROAD VEHICLES (DISPLAY OF REGISTRATION MARKS) REGULATIONS 2001

Not fixing registration marks in accordance with these regulations is an offence under S.42 Vehicle Excise and Registration Act 1994.

Exempt Vehicles (Reg.3)
- Invalid carriage not over 254 kg unladen
- Pedestrian controlled vehicle not over 450 kg unladen

Fixing of Plates (Regs. 5–8)
- **Vehicles registered on or after 1.10.38 (or 1.1.48 in Northern Ireland)**
  (Except works trucks, road rollers and agricultural machines)

  Rear
  Must be fixed to the rear of the vehicle or, if towing a trailer, the trailer. If there is more than 1 trailer, must be fixed to the rearmost.
  Unless fixed in accordance with a type approval directive, it must be fixed as follows:
  - Vertically or, where this is not practicable, as near to vertical as possible, and
  - In such position that in normal daylight the characters are easily distinguishable from every part of a square having a diagonal length of:

Width of Characters	Diagonal Length
At least 57 mm	22 m
50 mm	21.5 m
44 mm	18 m

  Front
  Must comply with above vertical and diagonal length requirements. A motor cycle or tricycle which does not have a 4-wheeled vehicle type body **need not** have a front registration plate if first registered before 1.9.01. If after this date, **must not** have one.

- **Vehicles registered before the above dates**
  (Except works trucks, road rollers and agricultural machines)
  Must be fixed on the front of the vehicle. Also on the rear of the vehicle or trailer. If more than 1 trailer, must be fixed to the rearmost trailer.
  Must be vertical or, if not possible, as near to vertical as practicable.
  In normal daylight the characters must be clearly distinguishable from in front and behind the vehicle respectively.
  A motor cycle or tricycle which does not have a 4-wheeled vehicle type body need not have a front registration plate.

- **Works trucks, road rollers and agricultural machines**
  Must be fixed vertically or, where that is not possible, as close to vertical as practicable-
  1. on both sides of the vehicle, characters easily distinguishable from both sides, or
  2. on the rear so as to be easily distinguishable from the behind, or
  3. if a trailer or trailers are being drawn and plates not fixed on the sides of the vehicle, on the trailer or the rearmost if more than one, easily distinguishable from behind.

  If the towing vehicle is an agricultural machine, the plate fixed on the trailer may bear the registration mark of any agricultural machine belonging to the keeper.

Lighting of Rear Plates (Reg. 9)
(Does not apply to works trucks, road rollers, agricultural machines and vehicles first registered before 1.10.38 (or 1.1.48 in Northern Ireland))
Between sunset and sunrise the rear plate, unless lit by light complying with the relevant type approval directive, must be lit so that it is easily distinguishable from every part of a square having a diagonal length of:

Width of Characters	Diagonal Length
44 mm	15 m
Any other case	18 m

REGISTRATION MARKS – SPECIFICATIONS

ROAD VEHICLES (DISPLAY OF REGISTRATION MARKS) REGULATIONS 2001, REG. 10 & SCH. 2

Vehicles registered and new registration plates fitted on or after 1st September 2001

- Must be made of retroreflecting material which complies with BS AU 145d, or
- Any other relevant standard or specification recognised for use in a EEA State and which is of equivalent performance to the BS specification,
  and which in either case is marked with the identification number or mark of that standard or specification.
- The front plate must have black characters and a white background.
- The rear plate must have black characters on a yellow background.

Vehicles registered on or after 1st January 1973 and before 1st September 2001
(Optional – may instead comply with previous section)

- Must be of reflex-reflecting material which complies with BS AU 145a, or
- Any other relevant standard or specification recognised for use in a EEA State and which is of equivalent performance to the BS specification,
  and which in either case is marked with the identification number or mark of that standard or specification.
- The front plate must have black characters and a white background.
- The rear plate must have black characters on a yellow background.

Vehicles registered before 1st January 1973
(Optional – may comply instead with previous 2 sections)

(a) (where the mark may be illuminated from behind by virtue of the translucency of the characters)

- Must be formed of white translucent characters on a black background.
- When illuminated during the hours of darkness the characters must appear white against a black background.

(b) (where the mark is not so constructed)

EITHER:
- Must be made of reflex-reflecting material which complies with BS AU 145.
- Front plate to be black characters on a white background
- Rear plate to be black characters on a yellow background

OR:
- White, silver or grey characters on a black surface
- Characters either indelibly inscribed or attached so that they cannot readily be detached
- May be either
    1. made of cast or pressed metal with raised characters, or
    2. consist of plate to which separate characters are attached, or
    3. consist of a plastic plate having either reverse engraved characters or characters of a foil type, or
    4. consist of an unbroken rectangular area on the surface of the vehicle which is either flat or, if there is no flat area, almost flat.

Other restrictions   (Reg 11)

No reflex-reflecting material may be added, nor must the plate be treated so characters become retroreflective, less easily distinguishable, or less accurately photographed. The plate must not be fixed to the vehicle in a way (e.g. screws or bolts) which changes the appearance of the characters, makes them less distinguishable or prevents or impairs any photographic image. The surface must not comprise or incorporate any design, pattern or texture, or be treated in any way which gives the appearance of such.

REGISTRATION MARKS – LAYOUT
ROAD VEHICLES (DISPLAY OF REGISTRATION MARKS) REGULATIONS 2001
REG. 13 & SCH. 3

A registration mark must be laid out in conformity with one of the diagrams specified below:

Description	Permitted Layouts		
2 letters and 2 numbers followed by a group of 3 letters	**DE51 ABC**	**DE51** **ABC**	–
A single letter and not more than 3 numbers followed by a group of 3 letters	**A123 ABC**	**A123** **ABC**	**A** **123** **ABC**
3 letters followed by a group of not more than 3 numbers and a single letter	**ABC 123A**	**ABC** **123A**	**ABC** **123** **A**
A group of 4 numbers followed by a single letter or a group of 2 letters	**1234 AB**	**12** **34** **AB**	–
A group of not more than 3 numbers followed by a group of not more than 3 letters	**123 AB**	**123** **AB**	–
A group of not more than 3 letters followed by a group of not more than 3 numbers	**AB 123**	**AB** **123**	–
A single letter or group of 2 letters followed by a group of 4 numbers	**AB 1234**	**AB** **12** **34**	–
A group of 3 letters followed by a group of 4 numbers (Northern Ireland)	**ABZ 1234**	**ABZ** **1234**	–
A group of 4 numbers followed by a group of 3 letters (Northern Ireland)	**1234 ABZ**	**1234** **ABZ**	–

Motor cycles may not use a layout in this column

Vehicles first registered or replacement plates fitted (except if vehicle first registered before 1.1.73) on or after 1.9.01 may not use these layouts

REGISTRATION MARKS – SIZE AND SPACING

ROAD VEHICLES (DISPLAY OF REGISTRATION MARKS) REGULATIONS 2001
REG. 14 & SCH. 3

Height

Each character in a registration mark must be **79 mm** high except:

- Vehicle first registered before 1.9.01 – may be **89 mm** high unless:
    1. vehicle was first registered on or after 1.1.73 and fitted with a new registration plate to replace a previous one, or
    2. the vehicle is a motor cycle, motor tricycle, quadricycle, agricultural machine, works truck or road roller.
- Registration mark on a motor cycle, motor tricycle, quadricycle, agricultural machine, works truck or road roller, may be **64 mm** high.

Width of Character

Each character other than the letter "I" and the figure "1" must be:

- If vehicle first registered on or after 1.9.01,
- a new registration plate fitted on or after that date to replace a previous plate (except if vehicle was first registered before 1.1.73),

the width shown in **line 1** of the table below.

In any other case, that shown in **line 2** of the table below.

Width of Stroke forming a Character

Must be that shown in **line 3** of the table below.

Spacing between Characters in a Group

Must be that shown in the table below in **line 4** of the table below except:

1. where the characters are 79 mm or 89 mm high,
2. on a vehicle first registered before 1.9.01,
3. registration mark was fitted to vehicle before 1.9.01, or the vehicle was first registered before 1.1.73, and
4. plate is made of cast or pressed metal with raised characters, then
    - spacing between two characters, one of which is "I" or "1" must be within limits shown in **line 8** of the table below
    - spacing between two characters both of which are "I" or "1" must be within the limits shown in **line 9** of the table below

but where 1 or more characters in a group is "I" or "1" all the characters within that group must be evenly spaced.

Horizontal and Vertical Spacing between Groups of Characters

Must be that shown in **line 5** and **line 6** respectively of the table below.

Width of Margin between Mark and Edge of Plate

Must be that shown in line 7 of the table below.

Imported Vehicles - see Registration Marks - Miscellaneous

DIMENSION	CHARACTER HEIGHT		
	89 mm	**79 mm**	**64 mm**
1. Character width	-	50 mm	44 mm
2. Character width	64 mm	57 mm	44 mm
3. Stroke width	16 mm	14 mm	10 mm
4. Space between characters	13 mm	11 mm	10 mm
5. Horizontal space	38 mm	33 mm	30 mm
6. Vertical space	19 mm	19 mm	13 mm
7. Margin	13 mm	11 mm	11 mm
8. Space between characters	13–37 mm	11–33 mm	–
9. Space between characters	13–60 mm	11–54 mm	–

REGISTRATION MARKS – SYSTEM

The registration mark is made up of seven characters divided into three parts:

| Local memory tag. 1st letter represents the region; 2nd letter relates to a local DVLA office. See list below. In this example 'AV' would be Ipswich. | Age identifier. See list below. In this example '04' would be March 2004. | Three random letters. These make the registration mark unique. |

MEMORY TAGS					
Local Memory Tag	DVLA Office	Local Identifier	Local Memory Tag	DVLA Office	Local Identifier
A	Peterborough	ABCDEFGHJKLMN	M	Manchester	A-Y
A	Norwich	OPRSTU	N	Newcastle	ABCDEFGHJKLMNO
A	Ipswich	VWXY	N	Stockton	RSTUVWXY
B	Birmingham	A-Y	O	Oxford	A-Y
C	Cardiff	ABCDEFGHJKLMNO	P	Preston	ABCDEFGHJ KLMNOPRST
C	Swansea	PRSTUV	P	Carlisle	UVWXY
C	Bangor	WXY	R	Reading	A-Y
D	Chester	ABCDEFGHJK	S	Glasgow	ABCDEFGHJ
D	Shrewsbury	LMNOPRSTUVWXY	S	Edinburgh	KLMNO
E	Chelmsford	A-Y	S	Dundee	PRST
F	Nottingham	ABCDEFGHJKLMNP	S	Aberdeen	UVW
F	Lincoln	PSTVWXY	S	Inverness	XY
G	Maidstone	ABCDEFGHJKLMNO	V	Worcester	A-Y
G	Brighton	PRSTUVWXY	W	Exeter	ABCDEFGHJ
H	Bournemouth	ABCDEFGHJ	W	Truro	KL
H	Portsmouth	KLMNOPRSTUVWXY	W	Bristol	MNOPRSTUVWXY
H		'HW' reserved for the Isle of Wight	Y	Leeds	ABCDEFGHJKL
K	Luton	ABCDEFGHJKL	Y	Sheffield	MNOPRSTUV
K	Northampton	MNOPRSTUVWXY	Y	Beverley	WXY
L	Wimbledon	ABCDEFGHJ			
L	Stanmore	KLMNOPRST			
L	Sidcup	UVWXY			

AGE IDENTIFIERS					
Year	March	Sept	Year	March	Sept
2001	–	51	2005	05	55
2002	02	52	2006	06	56
2003	03	53	2007	07	57
2004	04	54	2008	08	58

REGISTRATION MARKS - MISCELLANEOUS
ROAD VEHICLES (DISPLAY OF REGISTRATION MARKS) REGULATIONS 2001

Style of Characters (Reg. 15)
There are two prescribed fonts and these are described in Schedule 4 of the Regulations, one for characters 79 mm high and another for those being 64 mm high.
A prescribed font must be used
* for vehicles which are first registered on or after 1.9.01
* for new plates fixed to a vehicle on or after 1.9.01 to replace a previous one (except where the vehicle was first registered before 1.1.73).

For all other vehicles, either a prescribed font must be used or a style which is substantially similar so that the characters are easily distinguishable. However, characters must not be formed in any of the following ways:
* italic script
* a font in which the characters are not vertical
* a font in which the curvature or alignment of the lines of the stroke is substantially different from the prescribed font
* using multiple strokes
* using a broken stroke
* in such a way as to make a character appear like a different character

Other Materials on Registration Plate (Reg. 16)
Other than a standards mark (see Reg. 10) and the registration mark, no material may be displayed on a registration plate.
However, **Dual Purpose Plates** which conform to Council Regulation (EC) No. 2411/98 (which recognises distinguishing signs of member states) may display both the registration mark and the international distinguishing sign of the U.K. In this case, no material other that the U.K. sign may be placed in the space provided for that purpose, nor may the sign encroach beyond its margins.
Unless forming part of a dual purpose plate a plate may not be combined with a plate or device containing material which would not be permitted to be displayed on a dual purpose plate.

Culpability (Reg. 19)
The person responsible for complying with these Regulations is the person driving or, where it is not being driven, the person keeping it.

Imported vehicles (Reg. 14A) which do not have European type approval and are constructed in a way which precludes the display of registration marks conforming with Reg. 14 (see previous page), must comply as follows:
Height of characters – 64 mm
Width of characters except 'I' & '1' – 44 mm
Width of stroke of characters – 10 mm
Spacing between any 2 characters in group – 10 mm
Vertical spacing between groups – 5 mm
Width of top and side margins not less than – 5 mm
Space between bottom of mark and bottom of plate not less than – 13 mm
Space between bottom of mark and top of suppler's details not less than – 5 mm

Obscured Registration Mark (S 43 Vehicle Excise and Registration Act 1994)
It is an offence for the person driving (or, where not being driven, the person keeping) to obscure a registration mark, or render or allow it to become not easily distinguishable.

REGISTRATION OFFENCES

VEHICLE EXCISE AND REGISTRATION ACT 1994

INCORRECTLY REGISTERED VEHICLE (S 43C)

A person is guilty of an offence if, on a public road or in a public place, he uses a vehicle which requires an excise licence or a nil licence, when the name and address of the keeper are not recorded on the register, or any of the recorded particulars are incorrect.

FORGERY AND FRAUD (S 44)

A person is guilty of an offence if he forges; or fraudulently alters, uses, lends or allows to be used by another person, any of the following

(a) vehicle licence
(b) trade licence
(c) nil licence
(d) registration mark
(e) registration document; or
(f) trade plate.

PRODUCTION OF REGISTRATION DOCUMENTS (S 28A)

A person using a vehicle in respect of which a registration document has been issued must produce the document for inspection upon being so requested by a constable or authorised person.

The person commits an offence if he fails to comply unless:

(a) he produces the document in person at a police station specified by him, within 7 days of the request, or as soon as reasonably practicable
(b) the vehicle is subject to a lease or hire agreement; the vehicle is not registered in his name, and evidence of the agreement is either produced at the time, or at a police station specified by him within 7 days or as soon as reasonably practicable.

REGISTRATION PLATE SUPPLIERS
VEHICLES (CRIME) ACT 2001
VEHICLES CRIME (REGISTRATION OF REGISTRATION PLATE SUPPLIERS)
REGULATIONS 2008

Registration (S.17 & Reg.3)

Any person who carries on a business as a registration plate supplier in England and Wales must be registered with the Secretary of State. Failure to do so is an offence.

The transfer of possession of a registration plate when the vehicle to which it is fixed is sold or transferred shall not be regarded as an activity of selling registration plates where the seller or transferor is a dealer in vehicles and (a) he has arranged the first registration of the vehicle in the UK on behalf of the intended purchaser or keeper, or (b) the registration plate was not fixed to the vehicle by him or on his behalf.

Keeping of records (S.24 & Reg.7)

For each sale the supplier must keep records on his premises for 3 years. The records must contain details of-
a) information required to be supplied by the purchaser (see below);
b) details of the document used to verify the purchaser's name and address; and
c) details of the document used to verify the connection of the registration mark or the vehicle.

Failure to keep such records is an offence

Provision of information (S.25 & Reg.6)

The supplier must obtain the following details from the purchaser-
a) name and address;
b) where the vehicle is being repaired at the request of an insurance company, the relevant insurance policy number; and
c) the connection of the purchaser with the registration mark or the vehicle to which it is to be attached (unless the vehicle is sold or transferred with the registration plate fixed to it).

Failure to obtain such information is an offence

REGISTRATION PLATE SUPPLIERS cont
VEHICLES (CRIME) ACT 2001
VEHICLES CRIME (REGISTRATION OF REGISTRATION PLATE SUPPLIERS)
REGULATIONS 2008, ROAD SAFETY ACT 2006, S 45

Police powers (S.26)

A constable may at any reasonable time enter and inspect premises which have been registered for the supply of registration plates. He may require production of, and inspect, any registration plates kept on the premises and any records required to be kept, and may take copies. Force may not be used to enter premises unless a warrant has been issued by a justice. Before exercising these powers, the constable must, if required, produce evidence of his identity and authority for entry (if applicable). The above powers are also exercisable by a person authorised by the local authority.

Registration plates (S.28)

A 'registration plate' means a plate or other device which –
(a) displays, in compliance with regulations relating to the manner of display and being easily distinguishable, a registration mark which complies with regulations relating to size, shape and character;

(b) complies with regulations relating to the display of information other than the registration mark; and

(c) is designed to be fixed to a vehicle or trailer in accordance with (i) regulations relating the manner of fixing, and (ii) regulations relating to exempt vehicles, vehicles of the crown, and trailers.

a person who sells a plate or other device

↓

which is not a registration plate because it does not comply with regulations

↓

knowing that it is not, or being reckless as to whether it is, a registration plate

↓

shall be guilty of an offence

In addition, a person commits an offences if he sells a plate or other device which is not a registration plate because it does not comply with regulations relating to (a) size, shape and character, or (b) the manner of display and being easily distinguishable.

Supplying to unregistered persons (S.29)

A person who –
a) supplies a plate, device or other object to an unregistered person (other than an exempt person) who carries on a business of selling registration plates; and
b) knows or reasonably suspects that the plate, etc., will be used for the purposes of that person's business as a registration plate;
shall be guilty of an offence.

TESTING OF VEHICLES OTHER THAN GOODS VEHICLES
SECTION 47 ROAD TRAFFIC ACT 1988
REG. 6 MOTOR VEHICLES (TESTS) REGULATIONS 1981

The offence

A person who uses on a road at any time, or causes or permits to be used, a motor vehicle to which this section applies, and no test certificate has been issued within the preceding 12 months, is guilty of an offence.

Motor vehicles to which this section applies -

(a) those first registered under the Vehicle Excise and Registration Act 1994 (or earlier legislation) not less than **3 years** before (but see below), and

(b) those **manufactured** (see below) not less than 3 years before, which have been **used** (but see below) on roads (in GB or elsewhere) before being so registered, being, in either case, motor vehicles other than goods vehicles which are required to be submitted for a goods vehicle test under S49.

The period of time

In paragraph (a) above, the 3 year period becomes 1 year if the vehicle is-

(a) a motor vehicle used for the carriage of passengers and with more than 8 seats, excluding the drivers',

(b) a taxi, being a vehicle licensed to ply for hire, or

(c) an ambulance (a motor vehicle constructed or adapted, and primarily used, for the carriage of persons to or from medical or dental treatment, and is readily recognisable as such).

The term 'used'

In paragraph (b) above, the use of a vehicle shall be disregarded-

(a) before it is sold or supplied by retail, or

(b) if a dealer authorised under S24 of the Vehicle Excise and Registration Act 1994 has assigned a registration mark to it before it was registered by the Secretary of State.

The term 'manufactured'

In paragraph (b) above the date of manufacture is the last day of the year during which its final assembly is completed.

Exempt vehicles

S47 (requirement for a test certificate) does not apply to the following vehicles:

(i)   heavy locomotive,

(ii)   light locomotive,

(iii)   motor tractor,

TESTING OF VEHICLES OTHER THAN GOODS VEHICLES cont

(iv)   track laying vehicle,

(v)   goods vehicle with design gross weight over 3.5 tonnes,

(vi)   articulated vehicle (not being a bus),

(vii)   vehicle only used in passing between lands occupied by the keeper and not used on public roads for distances exceeding 6 miles in aggregate during that calendar week,

(viii)   works truck,

(ix)   pedestrian controlled vehicle,

(x)   a vehicle (including a mechanically propelled cycle) which is adapted and used, or kept on a road, for invalids, and which (i) does not exceed 306 kg in weight or (ii) does exceed 306 kg but does not exceed 510 kg and is supplied or maintained by or on behalf of the Dept. of Health & Social Security, the Scottish Office or the Welsh Office,

(xi)   vehicle temporarily in GB for less than 12 months and bearing an 'International Circulation' registration mark,

(xii)   vehicle proceeding to a port for export,

(xiii)   vehicle of a visiting force,

(xiv)   vehicle provided for police purposes and maintained in workshops approved by the Secretary of State, or a vehicle provided for purposes of the Serious Organised Crime Agency,

(xv)   an imported vehicle having a date of manufacture not less than three years before, having been used on public roads before being registered, and owned by or in the service of the UK navy, military or air force,

(xvi)   a vehicle registered in Northern Ireland or having a Northern Ireland test certificate,

(xvii)   electronically propelled goods vehicle with design gross weight not over 3500 kg,

(xviii)   hackney carriage or cab licensed to ply for hire,

(xix)   licensed private hire car,

(xx)   agricultural motor vehicle,

(xxi)   motor vehicle constructed and not merely adapted for street cleansing or collection or disposal of refuse or contents of gullies and which is either (i) three wheeled, or (ii) either incapable of exceeding 20 mph. on the level under its own power or has an inside track width of less than 810 mm,

(xxii)   tramcar, and

(xxiii)   trolley vehicle which is not an auxiliary trolley vehicle.

Exempt uses

Vehicles are exempt from the requirement for a test certificate when used for the following purposes:

TESTING OF VEHICLES OTHER THAN GOODS VEHICLES cont

(a)   (i) submitting it by previous arrangement for, or bringing it away from, an examination, or (ii) in the course of an examination, an examiner, Ministry Inspector, designated council inspector, or person acting under their personal direction, taking it to or bringing it from a place where an examination is to be carried out, or (iii) where a test certificate is refused, delivering it by previous arrangement at, or bringing it away from, a place where remedial work has to be done, or (iv) where a test certificate is refused, delivering it, by towing it, to a place where it is to be broken up;

(b)   for any purpose for which use is authorised under S44 (special vehicles not complying with regulations);

(c)   imported into GB whilst being driven from the place of arrival to a place of residence of the owner or driver of the vehicle;

(d)   to lawfully remove it under the Refuse Disposal Amenity Act 1978, the Road Traffic Regulation Act 1967, or an order relating to a parking place;

(e)   detention or seizure by a police constable, for police purposes connected with its detention or seizure;

(f)   any purpose authorised by a Customs and Excise officer after removal, detention or seizure or being condemned as forfeited under the Customs and Excise Management Act 1979;

(g)   testing by a motor trader to whom a trade licence has been issued, during or after repair by the motor trader.

Exempt areas

Vehicles are exempt from the requirement for a test certificate when used on any island in any area mainly surrounded by water from which motor vehicles, unless specially constructed, can not be conveniently driven to a road in any other part of GB by reason of the absence of any bridge, tunnel, ford or other way. However:

(a)   in relation to any vehicle other than a goods vehicle with a design gross weight in excess of 3000 kg but not over 3500 kg, this exemption does not apply to the islands of Isle of Wight, Arran, Bute, Great Cumbrae, Islay, Lewis, Mainland (Orkney), Mainland (Shetland), Mull, North Uist, and Skye; and

(b)   in relation to a goods vehicle with a design gross weight in excess of 3,000 kg but not over 3,500 kg, the exemption does not apply to the islands of Isle of Wight, Lewis, Mainland (Orkney), Mainland (Shetland) and Skye.

PLATING AND TESTING OF GOODS VEHICLES

GOODS VEHICLES (PLATING AND TESTING) REGULATIONS 1988

The following goods vehicles are required to be tested annually, the first examination being not later than the end of the calender month in which falls the first anniversary of the date of registration (or, in the case of a trailer, the date of being sold or supplied by retail).

REG 9

Heavy motor cars and motor cars constructed or adapted for the purpose of forming part of an articulated vehicle

Other motor cars the design gross weight of which exceeds 3,500 kg

Other heavy motor cars semi trailers; converter dollies manufactured or or after 1.1.79

Other trailers, the weight of which, unladen exceeds 1,020 kg

REG 4

- A test certificate is issued and, in the case of a trailer, a test disc is also issued. The disc must be displayed on the trailer in a position where it is conspicuous, readily accessible and clearly visible from the nearside.

Light vehicles

- Goods vehicles under the above weights, private cars and dual-purpose vehicles under 2,040 kg must be submitted for an annual test to an approved garage, starting on the third anniversary of first registration.

- However, certain vehicles have to be tested by the time they are **one year old**: taxis, ambulances, minibuses and other passenger vehicles with more than 8 seats (excluding the driver's).

S 47 ROAD TRAFFIC ACT 1988

PLATING OF GOODS VEHICLES

REGS 66, 70 AND 70A ROAD VEHICLES (CONSTRUCTION AND USE) REGULATIONS 1986
GOODS VEHICLES (PLATING AND TESTING) REGULATIONS 1988

There are two basic types of plate:

Manufacturer's Plate
and Ministry Plate

MANUFACTURER'S PLATE   REG 66 OF THE 1986 REGS

Contains details of maximum permitted weights. Must be fitted to:

(a) heavy motor cars and motor cars first used on or after 1.1.68.

> **Exceptions:** dual-purpose vehicles, agricultural vehicles, works trucks, pedestrian controlled, or passenger vehicles.

(b) buses first used on or after 1.4.82.
(c) wheeled locomotives and motor tractors first used on or after 1.4.73.

> **Exceptions:** agricultural vehicles, industrial tractors, works trucks, engineering plant, or pedestrian controlled vehicles.

(d) wheeled trailers manufactured after 1.1.68 exceeding 1,020 kg UW

> **Exceptions:** those not constructed or adapted to carry a load other than permanent or essentially permanent fixtures – and not exceeding 2,290 kg in total; living van not exceeding 2,040 kg UW; works trailer; trailers for street cleaning or agricultural purposes; broken down vehicle; gritting trailer, trailers manufactured and used initially outside GB.

(e) converter dolly manufactured on or after 1.1.79.

MINISTRY PLATE   REGS 17–22 OF THE 1988

Purpose of examination

Upon submission of the vehicle for its first Goods Vehicle test, the vehicle is also examined for plating. The examination seeks to determine whether:

(a) the vehicle is of a make, model and type to which the standard lists apply. These lists are published by the Goods Vehicle Centre and show, in relation to vehicles of certain constructional particulars, the gross weight, axle weight, and train weight for that type of vehicle;
(b) the constructional particulars relating to that type of vehicle are substantially complied with; and
(c) the weights shown in the standard lists are applicable to the vehicle.

PLATING OF GOODS VEHICLES cont

Production of evidence of conformity

In conjunction with the plating examination, the driver must produce either a certificate of conformity issued by the manufacturer or a Minister's approval certificate as required under the National Type Approval for Goods Vehicles Regulations. This certificate is treated as a plating certificate.

The examination

The examiner ensures that the particulars on the certificate are appropriate for the vehicle; and the vehicle has not been altered. If the examiner is satisfied, that certificate is then deemed to be the plating certificate issued for the purposes of these Regulations. If the examiner is not so satisfied the vehicle must be subject to a full examination and determination of the various weights.

Plating certificate

The plating certificate contains the maximum weights permissible for the vehicle. Once a plating certificate has been issued, a Ministry Plate must be securely affixed, so as to be legible at all times, in a conspicuous and readily accessible position, and in the cab of the vehicle if it has one.

REG 70 C&U REGULATIONS 1986

The certificate is retained by the operator. Following the plating examination, the vehicle may undergo a goods vehicle test. Vehicles submitted for the test are examined by a goods vehicle examiner for compliance with C&U Regulations. Following a successful test, a goods vehicle test certificate is issued in relation to the vehicle.

DIMENSION PLATE

A vehicle which is not a goods vehicle fitted with a Ministry plate in accordance with Reg 70, and which is either (a) a bus or heavy motor car and which was manufactured after 31.5.98, or (b) a trailer used with such a vehicle and manufactured after 31.5.98, must be fitted with a plate in a conspicuous and readily accessible position containing the dimensions of the vehicle. Alternatively, those particulars may be shown in the manufacturer's plate fitted in accordance with Reg 66.

PLATING AND TESTING EXEMPTIONS

SCHED 2 GOODS VEHICLES (PLATING & TESTING) REGULATIONS 1988

> The following are exempt from the requirements of the regulations:

Agricultural motor vehicles and agricultural trailed appliances

Agricultural trailers and agricultural trailed appliances conveyors drawn by an agricultural motor vehicle

breakdown vehicles

converter dollies for agricultural, horticultural or forestry purposes

cranes (mobile)

dual purpose vehicles not constructed or adapted to form part of an articulated vehicle

electrically or steam propelled vehicles

engineering plant (not being moveable plant – being part of motor vehicle or trailer (not constructed to carry load)) designed and constructed for the special purposes of engineering operations

export – vehicles going to a port for export

funeral vehicles used solely for that purpose

heavy motor cars or motor cars constructed or adapted to form part of an articulated vehicle drawing a trailer which is (a) a living van not over 3,500 kg, (b) permanently equipped with medical, dental, veterinary, health, educational, display, clerical or experimental laboratory purposes (but not involving sale hire or loan of goods from the vehicle, or for drain clearing or sewage or refuse collection), or (c) equipped only with automatic over-run brakes. The trailer/vehicle is itself exempt.

heavy motor cars and motor cars forming part of an articulated vehicle drawing a trailer which is being used under "Special Types" authorisation

licenced taxis

lifeboat vehicles

living vans not exceeding 3,500 kg

police and fire vehicles

public service vehicles

road construction vehicles

play buses

snow ploughs and gritters

tower wagons

Vehicles, for street cleansing, refuse collection or disposal, or gully contents collection or disposal, in each case being 3-wheeled vehicles, incapable of exceeding 20 mph, or have inside track width of less than 810 mm

track-laying vehicles

trailers designed for the production of tar-macadam etc

trailers with only over-run brakes

vehicles for servicing, loading, unloading or controlling aircraft, or used on an aerodrome for road cleansing, refuse collection or disposal or gully (or cesspool) contents collection or disposal

motor vehicles first used before 1.1.60 and trailers manufactured before 1.1.60 used unladen

vehicles temporarily in GB for no more than 12 months

vehicles licensed in Northern Ireland and those based on certain specified Scottish Islands

Vehicles and trailers on public roads passing between areas of land in the occupation of the same person and not used for more than 6 miles on public roads in that calendar week

vehicles used for test or trial of new vehicles or equipment

visiting Forces

works trucks and works trailers

MOTORCYCLE PLATES

REG.69 AND SCHED 9 ROAD VEHICLES (CONSTRUCTION AND USE) REGULATIONS

Every motor cycle first used on or after 1.8.77

which is not

a. propelled by an internal combustion engine with a cylinder capacity exceeding:
   i) 150cc if first used before 1.1.82, or
   ii) 125cc if first used on or after 1.1.82, or

b. a mowing machine; or

c. a pedestrian-controlled vehicle

must have a conspicuous and readily accessible plate securely fixed to the vehicle stating whether the machine is a

standard motor cycle

means a motor cycle which is not a moped.

moped

means a motorcycle which has:
(a) maximum design speed not in excess of 30 mph
(b) kerbside weight not exceeding 250 kg
(c) engine not exceeding 50cc (For vehicles first used before 1.8.77 it means a vehicle not over 50cc, with pedals.)

The plate must also include:

- manufacturer's name
- engine capacity
- kerbside weight (mopeds only)
- maximum design speed (mopeds only)
- manufacturer's vehicle identification number
- power to weight ratio (standard motor cycle)
- maximum engine power (standard motor cycle).

TRADE LICENCES
VEHICLE EXCISE AND REGISTRATION ACT 1994
ROAD VEHICLES (REGISTRATION AND LICENSING) REGULATIONS 2002

Trade licences are issued to motor traders, vehicle testers and persons who intend to commence business as such. More than 1 trade licence may be held at a time.

Vehicles covered by the licence (S.11)

1. <u>Motor trader who is a vehicle manufacturer</u> – covers all vehicles temporarily in his possession in the course of his business, all vehicles kept and used by him for research and development, and all vehicles submitted to him by other manufacturers for testing on roads;
2. <u>Any other motor trader</u> – covers all vehicles temporarily in his possession in the course of his business; and
3. <u>Vehicle tester</u> – covers all vehicles submitted to him for testing in the course of his business.

Definition of 'Motor Trader' (S.62)

A person who
   a) manufactures, repairs or deals in, vehicles;
   b) modifies vehicles, whether by the fitting of accessories or otherwise; or
   c) valets vehicles.

Use of vehicles (S.12)
1. Not more than 1 vehicle may be used at a time;
2. May only be used for the purposes described on the following page;
3. May not be kept on a road unless being used on a road;
4. May not carry goods or burden, other than:
     ● A load carried solely for testing the vehicle or its accessories or equipment and which is returned to the place of loading without being unloaded,
     ● Where a vehicle is being delivered or collected, a load consisting of a vehicle to be used for travel to or from the place of delivery or collection,
     ● A load built in as part of the vehicle or permanently attached to it,
     ● Parts, accessories or equipment designed to be fitted to the vehicle, and tools for such fitting,
     ● A trailer other than a disabled vehicle;
5. A vehicle and semi-trailer is regarded as a single vehicle.

TRADE LICENCES cont

Purposes for which a licence may be used (Sched. 6)

1. No person may be carried on the vehicle or any trailer except a person carried in connection with such purposes; and

2. Goods or burden of any description (except specified loads) may not be carried.

A motor trader may use a vehicle (other than a vehicle kept by a vehicle manufacturer solely for research and development) only for the following business purposes:

(a) test or trial or the test or trial of its accessories or equipment;
(b) proceeding to or from a public weighbridge for ascertaining its weight or to or from any place for its registration or inspection;
(c) test or trial for the benefit of a prospective purchaser;
(d) test or trial for the benefit of a person interested in promoting publicity in regard to it;
(e) delivering it to the place where the purchaser intends to keep it;
(f) demonstrating its operation or the operation of its accessories or equipment when it is being handed over to the purchaser;
(g) delivering it to or removing it from one part of the licence holder's premises to another part of his premises, or to those of another manufacturer, repairer or dealer;
(h) proceeding to or returning from a workshop for fitting, painting, valeting or repair;
(i) proceeding to or from the premises of a manufacturer or repairer of or dealer in vehicles to a place from which it is to be transported by train, ship or aircraft;
(j) proceeding to or from any garage, auction room or other place for storage or sale;
(k) proceeding to or from a place of inspection or testing; or
(l) proceeding to a place where it is to be broken up or otherwise dismantled.

Display of Licence (Reg.42)

The trade licence must be exhibited to the front of the vehicle by means of the trade plates issued for the vehicle.

PUBLIC SERVICE VEHICLES

PUBLIC PASSENGER VEHICLES ACT 1981

Definition

A public service vehicle is a motor vehicle (other than a tram car) which is either:

adapted to carry more than eight passengers and used for carrying passengers for hire or reward

not adapted to carry more than eight passengers and used for carrying passengers at separate fares in the course of a business of carrying passengers

However, a small bus (not more than 8 seats) provided for hire with the services of a driver for the purposes of carrying passengers otherwise than at separate fares will not be regarded as a public services vehicle, but may need to be licenced as a private hire vehicle. but this will not apply if the business mainly operates large buses (over 8 seats). (S79A)

See over for fuller explanation

For 'Minibuses', see later this section

PUBLIC SERVICE VEHICLES – DEFINITIONS

PUBLIC PASSENGER VEHICLES ACT 1981

Adapted

There must be sufficient seating for more than eight passengers.

Used

Includes periods when temporarily used without passengers, but its use for such purpose has not been permanently discontinued.

Hire or reward

Would not cover an isolated occasion, nor a social arrangement between friends where contributions are made towards the expenses of the journey. There must be a systematic carrying of passengers beyond the bounds of mere social kindness.

But it would cover the case of payments made by members of an association in respect of a vehicle owned by that association.

Separate fares

Will not be treated as being a PSV (unless adapted to carry more than 8 passengers) if:
(a) the agreement to pay separately must not have been initiated by the driver, owner, person making the vehicle available, or receiving remuneration;
(b) no previous advertisement of separate fares (except under local authority approval);
(c) all passengers going to the same destination;
(d) no differentiation of fares on the basis of distance or time.
Bearing in mind the exceptions already mentioned, it includes the case where a number of passengers are carried and one of them pays the total cost of the journey to the driver and then collects a share from the other passengers.

In the course of a business

Where passengers are carried at separate fares, it shall not be in the course of a business of carrying a passenger if:
● the total fare for the journey does not exceed the running costs of the vehicle for that journey (including depreciation and general wear) and
● the arrangement for the payment of the fares was made before the journey began.

Terminology (PSVs/PCVs)

The change in terminology from PSV to PCV only relates to new issues of driving licences. Old driving licences still refer to a PSV and for other purposes the term PSV remains valid.

Taxis

TRANSPORT ACT 1985

A licensed taxi may carry passengers at separate fares without becoming a PSV if hired in an area where the licensing authority has made a scheme under this section, provided the hiring falls within the terms of the scheme. S 10

Similarly, a licensed taxi or licensed hire car may carry passengers at separate fares without becoming a PSV if all passengers booked their journeys in advance and each consented, when booking, to share the use of the vehicle.

PSVs – LOCAL SERVICES

SECTIONS 3 AND 6 TRANSPORT ACT 1985

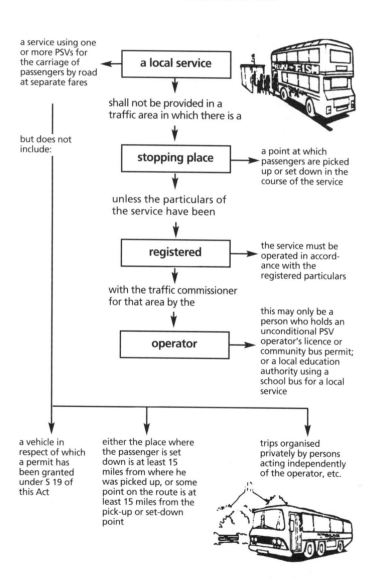

a service using one or more PSVs for the carriage of passengers by road at separate fares ← **a local service**

↓

shall not be provided in a traffic area in which there is a

↓

stopping place → a point at which passengers are picked up or set down in the course of the service

↓

unless the particulars of the service have been

↓

registered → the service must be operated in accordance with the registered particulars

↓

with the traffic commissioner for that area by the

↓

operator → this may only be a person who holds an unconditional PSV operator's licence or community bus permit; or a local education authority using a school bus for a local service

but does not include:

a vehicle in respect of which a permit has been granted under S 19 of this Act

either the place where the passenger is set down is at least 15 miles from where he was picked up, or some point on the route is at least 15 miles from the pick-up or set-down point

trips organised privately by persons acting independently of the operator, etc.

PSV DOCUMENTATION

PUBLIC PASSENGER VEHICLES ACT 1981
PUBLIC SERVICE VEHICLES (OPERATOR'S LICENCE) REGULATIONS 1995

OPERATOR NEEDS:

Registration

In an area where there are stopping places for the services, the holder of an 'unconditional PSV operator's licence' or a 'community bus permit' or an education authority using a free school bus to transport fare-paying passengers, must register particulars of the service with the Traffic Commissioners for that area.

S 6 TRANSPORT ACT 1985

PSV operator's licence   S 12(1)

Permits the operator to run a specified number of vehicles. There are 2 types of licence:
standard authorises the use of any PSV;
restricted authorises the use of
(a) PSVs not adapted to carry more than eight passengers
and
(b) PSVs not adapted to carry more than 16 passengers being operated either
   (i) other than in the course of a business of carrying passengers, or
   (ii) by a person who does not normally operate PSVs adapted to carry more than eight passengers.

S 13(1)

DRIVER NEEDS:

PSV DRIVER'S LICENCE
In addition to an ordinary driving licence, the driver of a PSV requires a PCV Driving Licence. The driver need only be 18 years' old if either:
● he is not carrying passengers and either he or his supervisor holds a PCV Licence, or
● he holds a PCV Licence and is carrying passengers either on a route which is less than 50 km or on a national route but the vehicle is constructed to carry not more than 14 passengers.
A constable may request production within 5 days at an address nominated by the driver.

VEHICLE NEEDS:

CERTIFICATE OF INITIAL FITNESS
A PSV adapted to carry more than 8 passengers requires a certificate indicating that the prescribed conditions as to vehicle fitness are fulfilled.

S 6(1)

Test certificate

All PSVs which are 3 years' old require a test certificate in the same manner as a car.

Operator's disc

Issued in respect of each vehicle run by the holder of an Operators' Licence. It must be exhibited on the vehicle

S 18(1)

The disc and operators licence must be produced within 14 days if so required by a police constable.

REG 1

See also 'Passenger carrying vehicle licences' earlier in this section

MINIBUSES

TRANSPORT ACT 1985

Defined as a motor vehicle adapted to carry more than 8 but not more than 16 seated passengers in addition to the driver. (S19)

Lawful operation depends upon whether the vehicle is being used for hire or reward.
This means for any payment in cash or in kind by, or on behalf of, passengers, giving them the right to be carried.

Not being used for hire or reward.
There is no requirement for an operator's licence or permit. The type of driving licence required depends on when it was issued and the entitlement it contains.

(a) **Car licence held before 1.1.97.** Groups B and D1 (not for hire or reward) (or groups A or B under the old system), will cover the driving of a minibus with a maximum of 17 seats including the driver's, provided the driver is over 21.

(b) **Car licence held since 1.1.97.** May drive a minibus with up to 16 passenger seats provided:
1. driving for a non-commercial body for social purposes;
2. aged 21 or over (if over 70 will have to take a medical);
3. category B licence held for at least 2 years;
4. driving on a voluntary basis;
5. maximum weight not over 3.5 tonnes (plus a 750 kg allowance for equipment for disabled persons;
6. no payment or consideration received (except expenses);
7. no trailer to be drawn; and not outside this country

If used for hire or reward, it will need to be operated on:

(a) Section 19 permit (see following page)
granted to bodies concerned with education, religion, social welfare, or other activities of benefit to the community

(b) Section 22 permit (see later),
this concerns "community bus services", being local services provided by voluntary bodies, or

(c) Full operator's licence (see previous pages)
needed for a profit-making service provided to the general public or for private hire. Drivers are paid.

MINIBUSES – S19 PERMITS

SECTION 19 MINIBUS AND OTHER SECTION 19 PERMIT BUSES REGULATIONS 1987
TRANSPORT ACT 1985 – Ss19 & 20

This provision allows permits to be issued to educational and other bodies.
Exempt from being classified as PSVs, therefore do not need PCV operator's or
driver's licence, if:

- adapted to carry more than eight and not more than 16 passengers
- specified in the permit
- not used for members of the public
- not used for profit
- used only by permit holder
- used in accordance with permit conditions.
- comply with the conditions of fitness:

  a. first used on or after 1.4.88

  REGS 41-43 ROAD VEHICLES (C&U) REGULATIONS 1986

  (locks, doors, seats, fire extinguishers, first aid kit etc.)

  b. before 1.4.88, either as (a) above, or

  REGS 5 -28 MINIBUS (CONDITIONS OF FITNESS, EQUIPMENT AND USE) REGULATIONS 1977

- Permits are granted to bodies concerned with
  - activities for the benefit of the community
  - education
  - recreation
  - religion
  - social welfare.

- Every authorised minibus shall carry a disc and a driver's notice setting out the
conditions which have been imposed.

- Drivers must be over 21. On reaching the age of 70, drivers holding only a 'B'
licence must comply with the medical standards applicable to D1 licences.

MINIBUSES – COMMUNITY BUS SERVICES

COMMUNITY BUS REGULATIONS 1986. TRANSPORT ACT 1985, SS 22 & 23

This allows for "Community bus services" to be granted permits for a local service operated by voluntary bodies. Permits may also be granted for a community bus service and (other than in the course of a local service) which *carries passengers for hire or reward* if this will directly assist by providing financial support for it.

"Community bus service" means a local service provided
(a) by a body concerned with the social and welfare needs of a community;
(b) not profit making either for the body or anyone else
(c) by means of a public service vehicle adapted to carry more than 8 but not more than 16 passengers

Conditions:

(1) Driver receives no payment except expenses
(2) Driver holds either a PCV driver's licence, a PCV Community Licence, a corresponding Northern Ireland PCV licence, or fulfils the following conditions:
    (a) holds a B (other than B1) licence,
    (b) has held the licence for an aggregate of not less than 2 years
    (c) is 21 years of age or over, and
    (d) if 70 years or over is not suffering from any disability which would result in the refusal of a D1 licence
(3) If unable to fulfil 2(a) (b) (c) & (d) above, must comply with the following:
    (a) granted licence before 1.1.97
    (b) holds licence authorising category B other than B1 vehicles, and D1 (not for hire or reward), and
    (c) is 21 years or over

A *permit disc* will be issued and must be affixed inside the vehicle so that it can be read in daylight from outside the vehicle (Reg 4).

A PSV *certificate of initial fitness* is not required provided the vehicle complies with the requirements contained on the following page (S 23(7)).

COMMUNITY BUSES – CONDITIONS OF FITNESS FOR USE

TRANSPORT ACT 1985 S23(7) COMMUNITY BUS REGULATIONS 1986 REG 6 COMMUNITY BUS REGULATIONS 1978 REGS 5-28 ROAD VEHICLES (CONSTRUCTION AND USE) REGULATIONS 1986 REGS 41-43

A Certificate of Initial Fitness is not required for a Community Bus provided it complies with the following conditions.

	First used on or after 1.4.88 (Construction & Use Regs)	First used before 1.4.88 (Community Bus Regs)
FIRE EXTINGUISHERS	Must comply with BS5423 (1977, 1980 or 1987) min. rating 8A or 21B. Readily available, maintained and marked with BS No.	Must comply with BS740/1 1948, 740/2 1952, 138 1948, 1382 1948, 1721 1968, 5423 1977 or 5423 1980. min rating 8A or 21B
FIRST AID	Contents as laid down in the schedule to the relevant regs, in receptacle maintained, suitable, available and prominently marked.	
EXHAUST PIPES	Outlet at rear or offside	Outlet at rear or offside. Not likely to cause fire.
DOORS	One on rearside and one emergency door at rear or offside. No door on offside other than driver's or emergency	If fuel tank behind rear wheels, one on rearside and an emergency door at rear or offside, if not, rear door may be emergency. No door on offside other than driver's or emergency. Unobstructed
EMERGENCY DOORS	Clearly marked as such on inside and outside. Means of operation clearly indicated	
POWER OPERATED DOORS (IF FITTED)	Have windows, operable by driver, operable from inside or outside, soft edges, closing resistance mechanism, not linked to braking system	
LOCKS etc.	Unlockable from inside, prevent accidental operation, open from inside or outside, closing catch, hinged to front, slam locking or warning to driver when opened	
VIEW OF DOORS	Driver to be able to see every door by mirrors, etc	
ACCESS TO DOORS	Unobstructed access from every passenger seat	
GRAB HANDLES	To be fitted to doors to assist passengers entry and exit	
SEATS	Wheelchair anchorages not to be side-facing. No seat to be side facing if immediately in front of rear doors unless protected	
	Not fitted to any door. Securely fixed to vehicle. Not less than 400 mm wide. Fitted with guards to prevent passengers being thrown through doorway	
ELECTRICAL	Current not greater than that for which designed. Cables insulated and protected from damage Fused or circuit breaker fitted. Not exceeding 100 V unless isolating switch fitted	To be guarded against shock or fire. Voltages exceeding 100 V and not earthed must have isolating switch (except HT leads)
FUEL TANKS	No part of fuel system to be in driver or passenger accommodation. Before 1.4.88 must have fuel cut-off and not to carry flammable material unless in suitable packaging.	
STEP LIGHTING	All exits of gangways to be lit	
CONSTRUCTION	To be sound, of suitable materials, properly maintained and designed to withstand stresses	In addition to provisions on left, length not to exceed 7 m and to be single decked.
STABILITY		Able to tilt to 35° without overturning
SUSPENSION		Must prevent excessive body sway
STEERING		No overlock possible
NUTS		All nuts subject to vibration to be locked

HACKNEY CARRIAGES

TRANSPORT ACT 1980

LOCAL AUTHORITY LICENCE

If the vehicle stands or plies for hire in an area to which the Town Police Clauses Act 1847 applies, a local authority licence is required.

PRIVATE HIRE

If the vehicle does not stand or ply for hire a local authority licence is not required, but the vehicle must still display the hackney carriage plate.

TAXI ROOF SIGNS – VEHICLES OTHER THAN TAXIS

Taxis are defined as vehicles which are licensed as such by the local authority.

Any vehicle which is not such a 'taxi' if carrying passengers for hire or reward must **not display** on or above the roof any sign which consists of or includes the word *Taxi* or *Cab* or any word of similar meaning or appearance; or any sign, notice, mark, illumination or other feature which may suggest that the vehicle is a taxi.

S 64

NOTE: (England and Wales only) the 1980 Act does not apply in Scotland

SIGNS ON BUSES CARRYING CHILDREN

REGS 11, 17A AND SCHED 21A ROAD VEHICLES LIGHTING REGULATIONS 1989

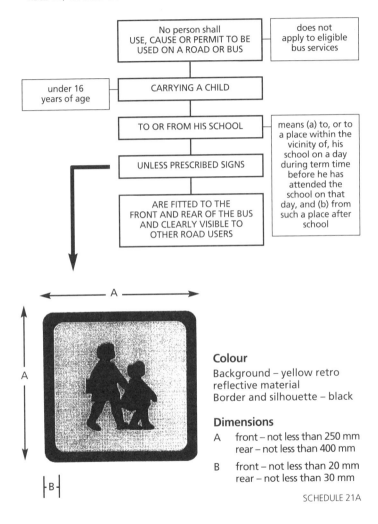

No person shall USE, CAUSE OR PERMIT TO BE USED ON A ROAD OR BUS

does not apply to eligible bus services

CARRYING A CHILD

under 16 years of age

TO OR FROM HIS SCHOOL

means (a) to, or to a place within the vicinity of, his school on a day during term time before he has attended the school on that day, and (b) from such a place after school

UNLESS PRESCRIBED SIGNS

ARE FITTED TO THE FRONT AND REAR OF THE BUS AND CLEARLY VISIBLE TO OTHER ROAD USERS

Colour

Background – yellow retro reflective material
Border and silhouette – black

Dimensions

A   front – not less than 250 mm
     rear – not less than 400 mm

B   front – not less than 20 mm
     rear – not less than 30 mm

SCHEDULE 21A

GOODS VEHICLES – INTERNATIONAL OPERATIONS

> The following list may serve as a guide to the documentation which may be expected to be carried by the driver of a goods vehicle involved in the international carriage of goods

International freight permit

Issued to operators running services from countries with which Britain has entered an agreement.

TIR carnet

Intended to simplify customs procedures and avoid liability to pay customs duty. It is not mandatory but if used the carrying space is sealed by customs and a certificate must be carried in the vehicle. A plate must be displayed on the front and rear showing 'TIR' in white on a blue background. A separate carnet is required for each load carried.

'T' form

Not mandatory. There are two types of certificate. The first is a form T2L which merely establishes the origin of the goods. It is normally used in conjunction with the TIR system to secure lower rates of duty. The second type is an alternative to the TIR system and a form T1 or T2, certified by customs must be carried on the vehicle.

'ATA' carnet

Goods such as samples and display items which are only temporarily imported can receive customs clearance if an 'ATA' carnet is carried.

'ADR' certificate

When dangerous goods are transported, an 'ADR' certificate must be carried to signify that the vehicle and load conform with safety standards. If a tank vehicle or carrying tank containers a Vocational Certificate of Training is needed. A 'Tremcard' should also be carried, together with 'Consignor Declaration'.

Insurance

Although not mandatory, a green card may be carried providing the necessary evidence of cover. In the event of an accident, the police may retain the duplicate page, endorsing the front cover accordingly.
REG 5 MOTOR VEHICLES (INTERNATIONAL MOTOR INSURANCE CARD) REGS 1971

Insurance (cont)

Note that drivers of vehicles from EU Member States will be covered by the insurance issued in that Member State and do not have to produce a green card (see Insurance, earlier).
COUNCIL DIRECTIVE 72/166.

'CMR' consignment note

Operators carrying goods for hire or reward must ensure that a copy of the 'CMR' consignment note is carried on the vehicle, giving all particulars of sender, addressee and load, where goods are carried on the operator's own account (not for hire or reward) only a simple consignment note giving brief particulars is required.
ARTICLE 6, COUNCIL REG 11/1960

Public service vehicles

When used for the international carriage of passengers must carry an authorisation issued by the country of registration.
(ROAD TRANSPORT INTERNATIONAL PASSENGER SERVICES) REGS 1984

PSV Community licences

Council Regulation (EC) No. 11/98 established a community wide licence allowing PSV operators access to the international market for the carriage of passengers. Such carriage between Member States is prohibited without a Community Licence. Current holders of Standard National or International Licences, or Restricted Licences are entitled to be issued with Community Licences.
It is an offence to use, cause or permit a vehicle to be used on a road for UK cabotage operations without a Community licence; or for the driver of the vehicle to fail to produce the licence when requested to do so by an authorised inspecting officer (includes uniformed police officers)
(PUBLIC SERVICE VEHICLES (COMMUNITY LICENCES) REGS 1999
ROAD TRANSPORT (PASSENGER VEHICLES CABOTAGE) REGS 1999

INTERNATIONAL OPERATIONS cont

Registration document

The document (or copy of it) must be carried on the vehicle. If the vehicle is hired, a form VE103 is required.

Driving licence

This may be either an international driving permit or a driving permit issued in the country of origin (domestic driving permit).
ART 2 MOTOR VEHICLES (INTERNATIONAL CIRCULATION) ORDER 1955

Excise Form 115E

This is the authorisation for the vehicle to be in this country. It gives the date by which the vehicle should have returned to its place of origin.

ATP Certificate or Plate

Issued for refrigerated vehicles carrying perishable foodstuffs.

Community Authorisation

For hauliers within the EU. A certified copy must be carried on the vehicle. This is in place of the 'O' licence which is peculiar to the UK.

Letter of Attestation

Where tachograph charts for current week and last day of the previous week are not available due to e.g. holiday, a letter from the employer is needed.

Letter of Authority

Where the driver is not the owner, a letter of authority to drive the vehicle is needed from the owner.

Nationality Sign

The plate appertaining to the country of origin should be affixed to the vehicle.

Tachograph Chart

If vehicle is over 3.5 tonnes.

Passport

Full standard passport is required.

Plating and Testing

Foreign vehicles are exempt from UK requirements for up to 12 months in the UK. However, prohibitions may be issued if defects are discovered following a roadside check.

Operator's Licence

May not be required. See under "Operator's Licence, foreign vehicles temporarily in GB".

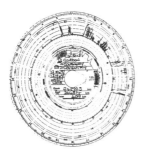

PART 3

LIGHTING
AND MARKING

This section looks at obligatory lights, direction
indicators, reflectors and the use and movement of
lamps. It then moves on to consider the need for fog
lights, reversing lights, warning lights and beacons.
Finally it considers various apsects applicable to
goods vehicles, e.g. marker lamps and reflectors,
and the marking of projecting loads.

OBLIGATORY LAMPS ETC. – DEFINITIONS

REG 18 AND SCHED 1 ROAD VEHICLE LIGHTING REGULATIONS 1989

POSITION LAMP – FRONT OR REAR

A lamp used to indicate the presence and width of a vehicle when viewed from the front or rear.

HEADLAMP

A lamp used to illuminate the road in front of a vehicle and which is not a front fog lamp.

HOURS OF DARKNESS

Means the time between half an hour after sunset and half an hour before sunrise.

MAINTENANCE

REG 23

It is an offence to use, or cause or permit the use of a vehicle

on a road

if the following are not in good working order and, in the case of lamps, clean:

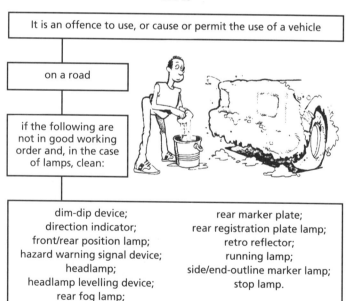

dim-dip device;	rear marker plate;
direction indicator;	rear registration plate lamp;
front/rear position lamp;	retro reflector;
hazard warning signal device;	running lamp;
headlamp;	side/end-outline marker lamp;
headlamp levelling device;	stop lamp.
rear fog lamp;	

OBLIGATORY LAMPS ETC. cont

REG 18 AND SCHED 1 ROAD VEHICLE LIGHTING REGULATIONS 1989

A SOLO MOTOR BICYCLE OR COMBINATION
shall display the following lights unless exempt

Type	Vehicle exemptions
Front position lamp	Solo motor cycle fitted with headlamp
Dipped beam headlamp	First used before 1.1.31
Main beam headlamp	1. Max speed n/e 25 mph. 2. Less than 50cc and first used before 1.1.72 3. First used before 1.1.31. 4. Constructed or adapted for use off roads and can carry only 1 person (If combination, 1 person plus 1 in sidecar)
Direction indicator	1. Max speed n/e 25 mph 2. First used before 1.4.86 3. Constructed or adapted for use off roads and can carry only 1 person. (If combination, 1 person plus 1 in sidecar)
Rear position lamp	None
Stop lamp	1. Max speed n/e 25 mph 2. Less than 50cc and first used before 1.4.86 3. First used before 1.1.36
Rear reg plate lamp	Vehicle not required to have reg plate
Rear retro reflector	None

A PEDAL CYCLE
shall display the following lights unless exempt

Type	exemptions
Front position lamp	None
Rear position lamp	None
Rear retro reflector	None
Pedal retro reflector	Manufactured before 1.10.85

OBLIGATORY LAMPS ETC. cont

REG 18 & SCHED 1 ROAD VEHICLE LIGHTING REGULATIONS 1989

A MOTOR VEHICLE, HAVING 3 OR MORE WHEELS

not being a motor cycle (or combination), pedal cycle, pedestrian-controlled vehicle, horse-drawn vehicle, track-laying vehicle, or trailer drawn by a motor vehicle

shall be fitted with lamps, reflectors, rear markings and devices which are stated below unless exempted:

Exemptions are
– – – – shown in the
following tables

Type	Vehicle exemptions
Front position lamp	none
Dim-dip or running lamp device	1. Max speed n/e 40 mph 2. First used before 1.4.87 3. Home forces' vehicle 4. Vehicles in respect of certain conditions being satisfied re the fitting of lighting and light-signalling devices as per requirements of EEC Directive 76/756 as amended, and alignment of dipped beam headlamps
Dipped beam headlamps	1. Max speed n/e 15 mph 2. Agricultural vehicle or works truck first used before 1.4.86 3. First used before 1.1.31
Main beam headlamp	1. Max speed n/e 25 mph 2. Agricultural vehicle or works truck first used before 1.4.86 3. First used before 1.1.31
Direction indicator	1. Max speed n/e 15 mph 2. Invalid carriage n/e 4 mph 3. Agricultural vehicle, industrial tractor or works truck first used before 1.4.86 4. First used before 1.1.36.
Hazard warning signal device	1. As for 'direction indicators' above 2. First used before 1.4.86
Rear position	None
Rear fog lamp	1. Max speed n/e 25 mph 2. Agricultural vehicle or works truck first used before 1.4.80 3. First used before 1.4.80 4. Width n/e 1,300 mm

OBLIGATORY LAMPS ETC. cont

REG 18 AND SCHED 1 ROAD VEHICLE LIGHTING REGULATIONS 1989

Continued from previous page

Type	Vehicle exemptions cont...
Stop lamp	1. Max speed n/e 25 mph 2. Agricultural vehicle or works truck first used before 1.4.86 3. First used before 1.1.36
Rear registration plate lamp	1. Vehicle not requiring registration plate 2. Works truck
Side retro reflector	1. Max speed n/e 25 mph 2. Goods vehicle: length n/e 6 m and first used on or after 1.4.86; or length n/e 8 m and first used before 1.4.86 3. Passenger vehicle 4. Incomplete vehicle going for completion, storage or display 5. Excavator (special types vehicle) 6. Mobile crane or engineering plant
Rear retro reflector	None
Rear marking	1. Max speed n/e 25 mph 2. UW n/e 3,050 kg and first used before 1.8.82 3. Max gross weight n/e 7,500 kg 4. Passenger vehicle not being articulated bus 5. Articulated tractive unit 6. Incomplete vehicle going for completion, storage or display for sale 7. Agricultural vehicle, works truck or engineering plant first used before 1.4.86 8. First used before 1.1.40 9. Home forces' vehicle 10.Vehicle constructed or adapted for: fire fighting or salvage; or aircraft servicing or controlling; or road maintenance, dispensing tar etc; or transporter for 2 or more vehicles or boats
Side marker lamp	1. Max speed n/e 25 mph 2. Passenger vehicles 3. Incomplete vehicle going for completion, storage or display for sale. 4. Overall length n/e 6 m 5. Vehicle first used before 1.4.91 6. Vehicle first used after 1.4.96 in respect of which certain conditions are satisfied re fitting of lighting and light signalling devices as per EEC Directive 76/756 as amended, and alignment of dipped beam headlamps

OBLIGATORY LAMPS ETC. cont

REG 18 & SCHED 1 ROAD VEHICLE LIGHTING REGULATIONS 1989

TRAILER DRAWN BY A MOTOR VEHICLE

---

shall be fitted with lamps, reflectors, rear
markings and devices which are stated below
unless exempted

Exemptions are
shown in the
following tables

Type	Vehicle exemptions
Front position lamp	1. Trailers for carrying or launching boats 2. Width n/e 1,600 mm 3. Length n/e 2,300 mm and manufactured before 1.10.85
Direction indicator	1. Manufactured before 1.9.65 2. Agricultural vehicle or works trailer manufactured before 1.10.90
Side marker lamp	1. Excluding any drawbar and any fitting, length n/e 6 m or 9.15 m, manufactured before 1.10.90 2 Incomplete trailer going for completion, storage or display for sale 3. Agricultural vehicle or works truck 4. Caravan 5. Trailer for carriage and launching boat 6. Trailer manufactured before 1.10.95 in respect of which certain conditions are satisfied re fitting of lighting and light signalling devices as per EEC Directive 76/756 as amended, and are installed and maintained as per requirements
Rear position lamp	None
Rear fog lamp	1. Manufactured before 1.4.80 2. Width n/e 1,300 mm 3. Agricultural vehicle or works trailer
Stop lamp	Agricultural vehicle or works trailer.

OBLIGATORY LAMPS ETC. cont

REG 18 AND SCHED 1 ROAD VEHICLE LIGHTING REGULATIONS 1989

Continued from previous page

Type	Vehicle exemptions, cont...
End-outline marker lamp	1. Width n/e 2,100 mm 2. Incomplete trailer going for completion, storage or display for sale 3. Agricultural vehicle or works trailer 4. Manufactured before 1.10.90
Rear reg plate lamp	Trailer not required to have a registration plate
Side retro reflector	1. Length n/e 5 m excluding drawbar 2. Incomplete trailer going for completion, storage or display for sale 3. Engineering plant 4. Excavator trailer (Special types vehicle)
Front retro reflector	1. Manufactured before 1.10.90 2. Agricultural vehicle or works trailer
Rear retro reflector	None
Rear marking	1. UW n/e 1,020 kg and manufactured before 1.8.82 2. Max gross weight n/e 3,500 kg 3. Incomplete trailer going for completion storage or display 4. Agricultural vehicle, works trailer or engineering plant 5. Drawn by a bus 6. Home Forces' vehicle 7. Constructed or adapted for fire fighting; aircraft servicing etc. dispensing tar etc. carrying asphalt or macadam, being mixing or drying plant; transporting 2 or more vehicles or boats

LAMPS ETC. – GENERAL EXEMPTIONS

ROAD VEHICLE LIGHTING REGULATIONS 1989

VEHICLES TOWING OR BEING TOWED   REG 6

Type of Vehicle	Exemption
Motor vehicle first used before 1.4.86 and pedal cycle or trailer manufactured before 1.10.85.	Rear position lamp, stop lamp, rear direction indicator, rear fog lamp or rear reflector while a trailer fitted with such is attached to the rear.
Trailer manufactured before 1.10.85.	Front position lamp while being drawn by passenger vehicle.
Trailer manufactured on or after 1.10.85.	Stop lamp, rear fog lamp or rear direction indicator while being drawn by vehicle not requiring them.
Trailer manufactured before 1.10.90.	Stop lamp or direction indicator if towing vehicle is fitted with such and dimensions of trailer allow them to be seen from a point 6 m behind the trailer (does not apply to trailers manufactured on or after 1.10.90). ←6 m →
Vehicle in combination	Rear marking if another vehicle in combination would obscure it.
Broken down vehicle being drawn.	Lamp, reflector or rear marking (except rear position lamps, and rear reflectors between sunset and sunrise).

LAMPS ETC. – GENERAL EXEMPTIONS cont

ROAD VEHICLE LIGHTING REGULATIONS 1989

MASKING, etc.

> A lamp shall not be treated as a lamp if:

1. Painted over or marked, so as not capable of immediate use or of readily being put to use; or
2. No wiring system to electrical source.

REG 4(4)

DURING DAYTIME

> Lamps and reflectors need not be fitted between sunrise and sunset to:

1. Vehicle not fitted with any position lamps
2. Incomplete vehicle going for completion
3. Pedal cycle
4. Pedestrian-controlled vehicle
5. Horse-drawn vehicle
6. Vehicle drawn or propelled by hand, or
7. Combat vehicle.

REG 4 (3)

VEHICLE EXAMINERS

Regulations 11 to 27 do not apply to a vehicle being used by a vehicle examiner appointed under S 66A RTA 1988 in connection with an examination of the vehicle under S 45 of that Act.

USE OF LAMPS

REGS 24 AND 25 ROAD VEHICLE LIGHTING REGULATIONS 1989

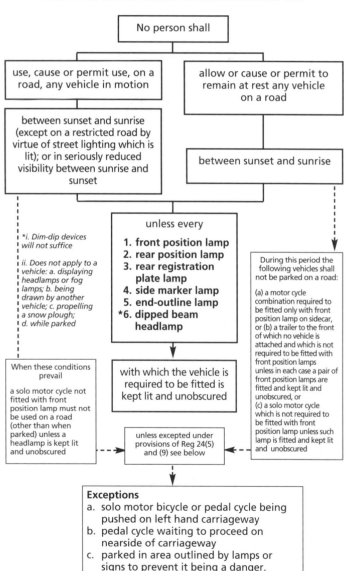

No person shall

use, cause or permit use, on a road, any vehicle in motion

allow or cause or permit to remain at rest any vehicle on a road

between sunset and sunrise (except on a restricted road by virtue of street lighting which is lit); or in seriously reduced visibility between sunrise and sunset

between sunset and sunrise

*i. Dim-dip devices will not suffice

ii. Does not apply to a vehicle: a. displaying headlamps or fog lamps; b. being drawn by another vehicle; c. propelling a snow plough; d. while parked

unless every

1. **front position lamp**
2. **rear position lamp**
3. **rear registration plate lamp**
4. **side marker lamp**
5. **end-outline lamp**
*6. **dipped beam headlamp**

During this period the following vehicles shall not be parked on a road:

(a) a motor cycle combination required to be fitted only with front position lamp on sidecar, or (b) a trailer to the front of which no vehicle is attached and which is not required to be fitted with front position lamps unless in each case a pair of front position lamps are fitted and kept lit and unobscured, or (c) a solo motor cycle which is not required to be fitted with front position lamp unless such lamp is fitted and kept lit and unobscured

When these conditions prevail

a solo motor cycle not fitted with front position lamp must not be used on a road (other than when parked) unless a headlamp is kept lit and unobscured

with which the vehicle is required to be fitted is kept lit and unobscured

unless excepted under provisions of Reg 24(5) and (9) see below

Exceptions
a. solo motor bicycle or pedal cycle being pushed on left hand carriageway
b. pedal cycle waiting to proceed on nearside of carriageway
c. parked in area outlined by lamps or signs to prevent it being a danger.

USE OF LAMPS cont

REG 24(5) ROAD VEHICLE LIGHTING REGULATIONS 1989

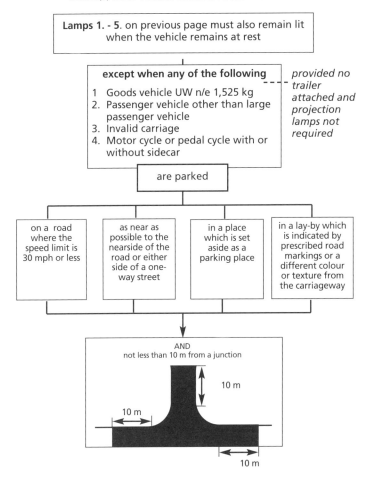

Lamps 1. - 5. on previous page must also remain lit when the vehicle remains at rest

except when any of the following

1. Goods vehicle UW n/e 1,525 kg
2. Passenger vehicle other than large passenger vehicle
3. Invalid carriage
4. Motor cycle or pedal cycle with or without sidecar

provided no trailer attached and projection lamps not required

are parked

| on a road where the speed limit is 30 mph or less | as near as possible to the nearside of the road or either side of a one-way street | in a place which is set aside as a parking place | in a lay-by which is indicated by prescribed road markings or a different colour or texture from the carriageway |

AND
not less than 10 m from a junction

10 m

10 m

10 m

OBSTRUCTION OF LIGHTS   REG 19

At least part of the surface of any obligatory front and rear position lamp, front and rear direction indicator and rear reflector, must be visible when every door, boot or other movable part of the vehicle is in a fixed open position.

MOVEMENT OF LAMPS

ROAD VEHICLE LIGHTING REGULATIONS 1989

| It is an offence to use, cause or permit use, on a road | REG 12 |

a vehicle, load or equipment of which, is fitted with a

lamp , reflector or marking capable of being moved by swivelling, deflecting or otherwise while the vehicle load or equipment of which, is in motion

except:

(a) a headlamp which can be dipped by movement of the headlamp or reflector
(b) a headlamp capable of adjustment to compensate for the effect of its load
(c) a lamp or reflector deflected to the side by the movement of the wheels as it is steered
(d) a headlamp or front fog lamp which can be wholly or partially retracted or concealed
(e) a direction indicator fitted to a motor vehicle first used before 1.4.86
(f) a work lamp
(g) a warning beacon
(h) an amber pedal retro reflector
(i) retro reflective material or retro reflector designed to reflect light to the side of the vehicle and attached to the wheel or tyre of:
    (i) a pedal cycle
    (ii) a trailer drawn by, or a sidecar attached to, a pedal cycle
    (iii) a solo motor bicycle or motor bicycle combination or
    (iv) an invalid carriage
(j) a lamp emitting light to the side, attached to the wheel or tyre of a pedal cycle or, a trailer drawn by, or a sidecar attached to, a pedal cycle or
(k) a lamp attached to a pedal of a pedal cycle.

REG 13

MOVEMENT OF LAMPS cont

ROAD VEHICLE LIGHTING REGULATIONS 1989

It is an offence to use, cause or permit use of

a vehicle fitted with a lamp which automatically emits a

flashing light

except:
(a) a direction indicator
(b) a headlamp fitted to an emergency vehicle
(c) a warning beacon or special warning lamp
(d) a lamp or illuminated signal fitted to a vehicle used for police purposes
(e) a green warning lamp used as an anti-lock brake indicator
(f) lamps forming part of a traffic sign or
(g) a front (or rear) position lamp capable of emitting a flashing light (whether or not it is capable of emitting a steady light), fitted to a pedal cycle or, a trailer drawn by, or a sidecar attached to, a pedal cycle, and which, if it is a lamp required to be fitted by Reg 18, is capable, when emitting a flashing light, of emitting a light to the front (or rear) of an intensity of not less than 4 candelas.

FITTING BEACONS

Other than vehicles mentioned above, it is an offence to fit a warning beacon/special warning light – whether working or not – or a device resembling such.   REG 16

COLOUR OF LIGHT SHOWN BY LAMPS AND RETRO REFLECTORS

REG 11 ROAD VEHICLES LIGHTING REGULATIONS 1989

No vehicle shall be fitted with a lamp or retro reflective material which is capable of showing a red light to the front

except
1. red and white chequered domed lamp or a red and white segmented mast mounted warning beacon fitted to a fire control vehicle*, intended for use at scene of an emergency
2. a side marker lamp or a side retro reflector;
3. retro reflective material or retro reflector designed to reflect light to the side of the vehicle and attached to the wheel or tyre of:
   (i) a pedal cycle
   (ii) a trailer drawn by, or a sidecar attached to a pedal cycle
   (iii) a solo motor bicycle or motor bicycle combination; or
   (iv) an invalid carriage; or a traffic sign.

*For police control vehicle, read blue light and white light from chequered domed lamp fitted to vehicle; and in case of ambulance control vehicle, a green light and white light from chequered domed lamp fitted to vehicle

COLOUR OF LIGHT SHOWN BY LAMPS AND RETRO REFLECTORS cont

REG 11 ROAD VEHICLES LIGHTING REGULATIONS 1989

It is an offence to use, cause or permit use on a road a vehicle readily capable of showing a light other than a red light to the rear:

except

(a) amber light from direction indicator or side marker lamp

(b) white light from reversing lamp

(c) white light from work lamp

(d) vehicle interior illumination lamp

(e) rear registration plate illumination lamp

(f) taxi meter illuminating light

(g) bus route indicator light

(h) blue light & white light from chequered domed lamp on police emergency control vehicle

(i) white light from a red & white chequered domed lamp, or red and white segmented mast-mounted beacon on fire service emergency control vehicle

(j) green light & white light from a chequered domed lamp on ambulance emergency control vehicle

(k) blue warning beacon or rear special warning light on emergency vehicle, or from any police device

(l) amber light from warning beacon fitted to a road clearance vehicle, refuse collection vehicle, breakdown vehicle, vehicle with a maximum speed not over 25 mph or any trailer drawn thereby, wide vehicle (or load) over 2.9 m, vehicle for testing, maintaining, improving, cleansing or watering roads, vehicle for inspecting, cleansing, maintaining, adjusting, renewing or installing any apparatus in, on or under a road, vehicle being used under a S 44 order, escort vehicle, Customs and Excise fuel testing vehicle, survey vehicle, or removal or immobilisation of vehicles under a statutory power

(m) green light from warning beacon used by medical practitioner

(n) yellow light from airport vehicle

(o) any colour light from traffic sign attached to a vehicle

(p) amber light from a pedal cycle pedal lamp

(q) white or amber light from a lamp emitting light to the sides and attached to a wheel of a pedal cycle or a trailer drawn by, or a sidecar attached to, a pedal cycle

(r) reflected light from amber pedal retro reflectors

(s) any colour reflected light from retro reflective material or retro reflector reflecting light to the side and attached to any wheel or tyre of a pedal cycle; a trailer drawn by, or a sidecar attached to, a pedal cycle; a solo motor bicycle or motor bicycle combination; or an invalid carriage

(t) reflected light from amber retro reflective material on a road clearance vehicle

(u) reflected light from yellow retro reflective registration plates

(v) reflected light from yellow retro reflective material in a prescribed rear marking fitted to - a motor vehicle not over 7500 kg gross weight, a motor vehicle first used before 1.8.82 with unladen weight over 3000 kg, a trailer with a maximum gross weight over 3500 kg, a trailer manufactured before 1.8.82 with unladen weight over 1000 kg, a trailer forming part of a combination of vehicles one of which is a type mentioned in a previous item, or a load carried by any vehicle

(w) reflected light from orange retro reflective material in a sign fitted to the rear of a vehicle carrying a dangerous substance

(x) reflected light from yellow retro reflective material in a sign fitted to the rear of a bus; or

(y) reflected light from yellow reflective material in a sign fitted to the rear of a school bus.

HEADLAMPS

REG 18 AND SCHEDS 1, 4 AND 5 ROAD VEHICLES LIGHTING REGULATIONS 1989

For exemptions see under 'Lights, obligatory' and 'Lights, exemptions'

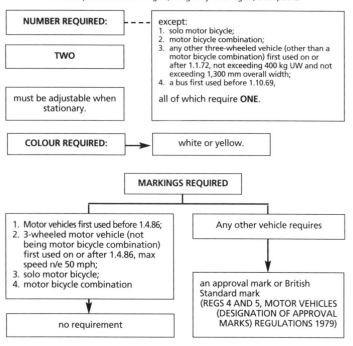

NUMBER REQUIRED:

TWO

must be adjustable when stationary.

except:
1. solo motor bicycle;
2. motor bicycle combination;
3. any other three-wheeled vehicle (other than a motor bicycle combination) first used on or after 1.1.72, not exceeding 400 kg UW and not exceeding 1,300 mm overall width;
4. a bus first used before 1.10.69,

all of which require **ONE**.

COLOUR REQUIRED: → white or yellow.

MARKINGS REQUIRED

1. Motor vehicles first used before 1.4.86;
2. 3-wheeled motor vehicle (not being motor bicycle combination) first used on or after 1.4.86, max speed n/e 50 mph;
3. solo motor bicycle;
4. motor bicycle combination

Any other vehicle requires

an approval mark or British Standard mark
(REGS 4 AND 5, MOTOR VEHICLES (DESIGNATION OF APPROVAL MARKS) REGULATIONS 1979)

no requirement

WATTAGE REQUIRED

Motor vehicle	Minimum wattage	
	Dipped	Main
four or more wheels		
1. first used on or after 1.4.86	NR*	NR*
2. first used before 1.4.86	30	30
three wheels (not combination)		
1. first used on or after 1.4.86		
a. max 50 mph	15	NR*
b. over 50 mph	NR*	NR*
2. first used before 1.4.86	24	30
solo motor bicycle (incl combination)		
a. n/e 250cc and n/e 25 mph	10	15
b. n/e 250cc over 25 mph	15	15
c. over 250cc	24	30

Must be capable of being dipped, and motor vehicles first used on or after 1.4.86 must be fitted with a circuit-closed tell-tale.

Must not cause undue dazzle or discomfort, or be lit while parked
REG 27

Must be kept clean and in good working order
REG 23

HEADLAMPS cont

REG 18 AND SCHEDS 1, 4 AND 5 ROAD VEHICLES LIGHTING REGULATIONS 1989
For exemptions see under 'Lights, obligatory' and 'Lights, exemptions'

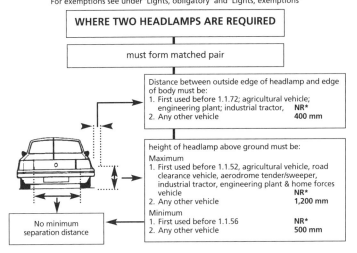

WHERE TWO HEADLAMPS ARE REQUIRED

must form matched pair

Distance between outside edge of headlamp and edge of body must be:
1. First used before 1.1.72; agricultural vehicle; engineering plant; industrial tractor, **NR***
2. Any other vehicle **400 mm**

height of headlamp above ground must be:

Maximum
1. First used before 1.1.52, agricultural vehicle, road clearance vehicle, aerodrome tender/sweeper, industrial tractor, engineering plant & home forces vehicle **NR***
2. Any other vehicle **1,200 mm**

Minimum
1. First used before 1.1.56 **NR***
2. Any other vehicle **500 mm**

No minimum separation distance

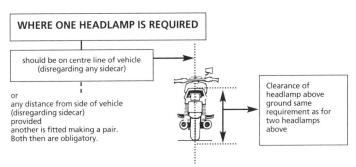

WHERE ONE HEADLAMP IS REQUIRED

should be on centre line of vehicle (disregarding any sidecar)

or
any distance from side of vehicle (disregarding sidecar)
provided
another is fitted making a pair.
Both then are obligatory.

Clearance of headlamp above ground same requirement as for two headlamps above

NOTE * *NR – no requirement*

OPTIONAL LAMPS

● Any number may be fitted but must comply with vertical fitting and colour requirements.

If first used after 1.4.91 only one pair of dipped headlamps may be shown at a time. Two pairs may be fitted only if one pair is for driving in other countries on the right of the road.

FRONT POSITION LAMPS

REG 18 AND SCHEDS 1 AND 2 ROAD VEHICLES LIGHTING REGULATIONS 1989

For exemptions see under 'Lights, obligatory' and 'Lights, exemptions'

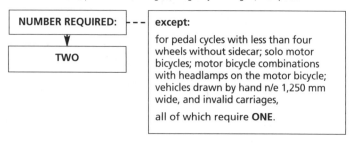

NUMBER REQUIRED:	except:
TWO	for pedal cycles with less than four wheels without sidecar; solo motor bicycles; motor bicycle combinations with headlamps on the motor bicycle; vehicles drawn by hand n/e 1,250 mm wide, and invalid carriages, all of which require **ONE**.

COLOUR REQUIRED: WHITE

unless incorporated in headlamp which is yellow.

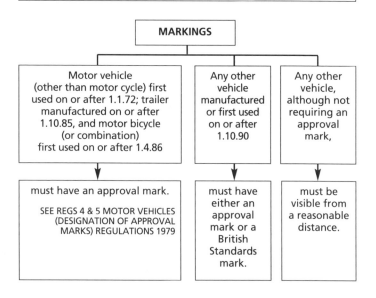

MARKINGS

Motor vehicle (other than motor cycle) first used on or after 1.1.72; trailer manufactured on or after 1.10.85, and motor bicycle (or combination) first used on or after 1.4.86	Any other vehicle manufactured or first used on or after 1.10.90	Any other vehicle, although not requiring an approval mark,
must have an approval mark. SEE REGS 4 & 5 MOTOR VEHICLES (DESIGNATION OF APPROVAL MARKS) REGULATIONS 1979	must have either an approval mark or a British Standards mark.	must be visible from a reasonable distance.

Must be kept clean and in good working order.   REG 23

Optional Lamps

Any number may be fitted – apart from for solo motor bicycles first used after 1.4.91, which can have a maximum of two.   SCHED. 2.

FRONT POSITION LAMPS cont

REG 18 AND SCHEDS 1 AND 2 ROAD VEHICLES LIGHTING REGULATIONS 1989

For exemptions see under 'Lights, obligatory' and 'Lights, exemptions'

WHERE 2 LAMPS ARE REQUIRED TO BE FITTED

must form matched pair

Distance between outside edge of front position lamp and edge of body must be:
1. First used on or after 1.4.86, **400 mm**
2. Trailer manufactured on or after 1.10.85, **150 mm**
3. Any other vehicle manufactured on or after 1.10.85, **400 mm**
4. Motor vehicle first used before 1.4.86 and any other vehicle manufactured before 1.10.85, **510 mm**

Height of front position lamp above ground must be:
Minimum, no requirement
Maximum
1. First used before 1.4.86 and trailer manufactured before 1.10.85, **2,300 mm**
2. Motor vehicle first used on or after 1.4.86 maximum speed n/e 25 mph, **2,100 mm**
3. Bus and road clearance vehicle, **NR***
4. Any other vehicle, **1,500 mm**, unless structure makes it impracticable, then **2,100 mm**

No minimum separation distance

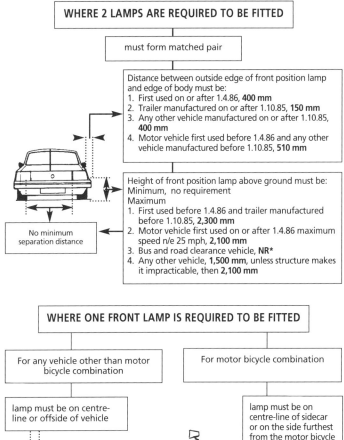

WHERE ONE FRONT LAMP IS REQUIRED TO BE FITTED

For any vehicle other than motor bicycle combination

For motor bicycle combination

lamp must be on centre-line or offside of vehicle

lamp must be on centre-line of sidecar or on the side furthest from the motor bicycle

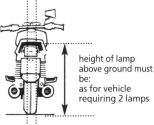

height of lamp above ground must be:
as for vehicle requiring 2 lamps

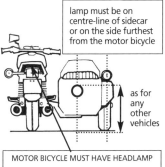

as for any other vehicles

MOTOR BICYCLE MUST HAVE HEADLAMP

REAR POSITION LAMPS

REG 18 AND SCHEDS 1 AND 10 ROAD VEHICLES LIGHTING REGULATIONS 1989
For exemptions see under 'Lights, obligatory' and 'Lights, exemptions'

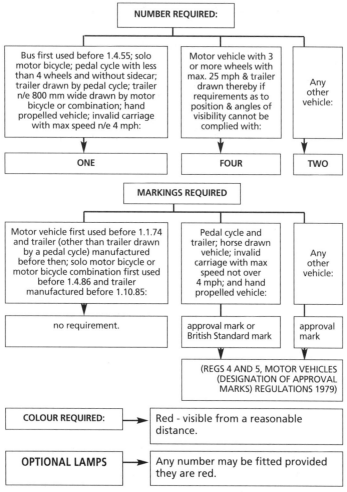

NUMBER REQUIRED:

Bus first used before 1.4.55; solo motor bicycle; pedal cycle with less than 4 wheels and without sidecar; trailer drawn by pedal cycle; trailer n/e 800 mm wide drawn by motor bicycle or combination; hand propelled vehicle; invalid carriage with max speed n/e 4 mph:	Motor vehicle with 3 or more wheels with max. 25 mph & trailer drawn thereby if requirements as to position & angles of visibility cannot be complied with:	Any other vehicle:
ONE	**FOUR**	**TWO**

MARKINGS REQUIRED

Motor vehicle first used before 1.1.74 and trailer (other than trailer drawn by a pedal cycle) manufactured before then; solo motor bicycle or motor bicycle combination first used before 1.4.86 and trailer manufactured before 1.10.85:	Pedal cycle and trailer; horse drawn vehicle; invalid carriage with max speed not over 4 mph; and hand propelled vehicle:	Any other vehicle:
no requirement.	approval mark or British Standard mark	approval mark
	(REGS 4 AND 5, MOTOR VEHICLES (DESIGNATION OF APPROVAL MARKS) REGULATIONS 1979)	

COLOUR REQUIRED: → Red - visible from a reasonable distance.

OPTIONAL LAMPS → Any number may be fitted provided they are red.

Pedal cycles

A flashing rear light fitted to a pedal cycle, a trailer drawn by, or sidecar attached to, a pedal cycle, must flash at between 60 and 240 per minute. (Sched. 10)

● Must be kept clean and in good working order   REG 23

REAR POSITION LAMPS cont

REG 18 AND SCHEDS 1 AND 10 ROAD VEHICLES LIGHTING REGULATIONS 1989
For exemptions see under 'Lights, obligatory' and 'Lights, exemptions'

WHERE TWO REAR POSITION LAMPS ARE REQUIRED TO BE FITTED

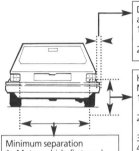

Distance between outside edge of rear position lamp and edge of body must be:
1. Motor vehicle first used before 1.4.86 and any other vehicle manufactured before 1.10.85, **800 mm**
2. Any other vehicle, **400 mm**

Height of rear position lamp above ground must be:
Maximum
1. Large passenger vehicle first used before 1.4.86, **NR***
2. Motor vehicle first used before 1.4.86 not being large passenger vehicle, **2,100 mm**
3. Trailer manufactured before 1.10.85, **2,100 mm**
4. Agricultural vehicle, horse drawn vehicle, industrial tractor and engineering plant, **2,100 mm**
5. Any other vehicle, **1,500 mm** (unless impracticable), then, **2,100 mm**
Minimum
1. Motor vehicle first used before 1.4.86 and any other vehicle manufactured before 1.10.85, **NR***
2. Any other vehicle, **350 mm**

Minimum separation
1. Motor vehicle first used before 1.4.86 and any other vehicle manufactured before 1.10.85, **NR***
2. Any other vehicle, width n/e 1,400 mm, **400 mm**
2. Any other vehicle, **500 mm**

WHERE ONE REAR POSITION LAMP IS REQUIRED TO BE FITTED

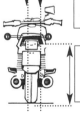

must be positioned on centre line or off-side

height above ground as for vehicles requiring 2 lamps (above)

WHERE FOUR REAR POSITION LAMPS ARE REQUIRED TO BE FITTED

Height above ground for the second pair, **NR***

Max distance from side of vehicle

for one pair, as for vehicles requiring two lamps

Minimum separation

One pair must satisfy the requirements above for 2 lamps, the other pair, **NR***

*NR = not required

REAR RETRO REFLECTORS

REG 18 AND SCHEDS 1 AND 18 ROAD VEHICLES LIGHTING REGULATIONS 1989

For exemptions see under 'Lights, obligatory' and 'Lights, exemptions'

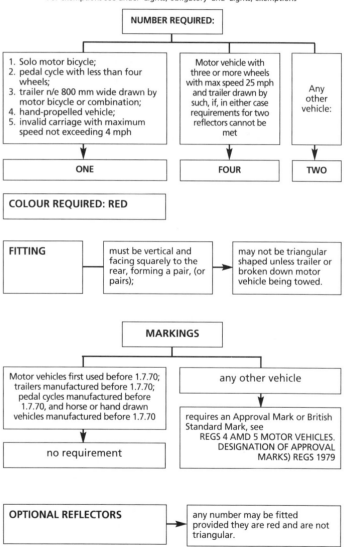

NUMBER REQUIRED:

1. Solo motor bicycle; 2. pedal cycle with less than four wheels; 3. trailer n/e 800 mm wide drawn by motor bicycle or combination; 4. hand-propelled vehicle; 5. invalid carriage with maximum speed not exceeding 4 mph	Motor vehicle with three or more wheels with max speed 25 mph and trailer drawn by such, if, in either case requirements for two reflectors cannot be met	Any other vehicle:
ONE	**FOUR**	**TWO**

COLOUR REQUIRED: RED

FITTING	must be vertical and facing squarely to the rear, forming a pair, (or pairs);	may not be triangular shaped unless trailer or broken down motor vehicle being towed.

MARKINGS

Motor vehicles first used before 1.7.70; trailers manufactured before 1.7.70; pedal cycles manufactured before 1.7.70, and horse or hand drawn vehicles manufactured before 1.7.70	any other vehicle
no requirement	requires an Approval Mark or British Standard Mark, see REGS 4 AMD 5 MOTOR VEHICLES. DESIGNATION OF APPROVAL MARKS) REGS 1979

OPTIONAL REFLECTORS	any number may be fitted provided they are red and are not triangular.

● Must be kept clean and in good working order   REG 23

REAR RETRO REFLECTORS cont

REG 18 AND SCHEDS 1 AND 18 ROAD VEHICLES LIGHTING REGULATIONS 1989

For exemptions see under 'Lights, obligatory' and 'Lights, exemptions'

WHERE TWO RETRO REFLECTORS ARE REQUIRED TO BE FITTED

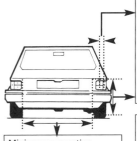

Distance between outside edge of retro reflectors and edge of body must be:
1. Bus first used before 1.10.54 and horse-drawn vehicle manufactured before 1.10.85, **NR***
2. Vehicle constructed or adapted to carry round timber, **765 mm**
3. Any other motor vehicle first used before 1.4.86 and any other vehicle manufactured before 1.10.85, **610 mm**

Any other vehicle, **400 mm**

Height of retro reflectors above ground must be:
Maximum
1. Motor vehicle first used before 1.4.86 and any other vehicle manufactured before 1.10.85, **1,525 mm**
2. Any other vehicle, **900 mm**, (unless impracticable), then **1,200 mm**

Minimum
1. Motor vehicle first used before 1.4.86 and any other vehicle manufactured before 1.10.85, **NR***
2. Any other vehicle, **350 mm**

Minimum separation
1. Motor vehicle first used before 1.4.86 and any other vehicle manufactured before 1.10.85, **NR***
2. Any other vehicle n/e 1,300mm wide, **400 mm**
3. Any other vehicle, **600 mm**

***NR** = no requirement*

WHERE ONE REAR RETRO REFLECTOR IS REQUIRED TO BE FITTED

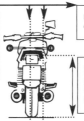

must be positioned on centre line or off-side

height above ground as for vehicles requiring two (above)

WHERE FOUR REAR RETRO REFLECTORS ARE REQUIRED TO BE FITTED

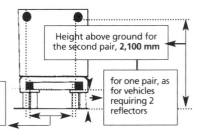

Height above ground for the second pair, **2,100 mm**

for one pair, as for vehicles requiring 2 reflectors

Minimum separation: one pair as per vehicle requiring two, the other pair, no requirement.

FRONT RETRO REFLECTORS

REG 18 AND SCHEDS 1 AND 21 ROAD VEHICLES LIGHTING REGULATIONS 1989

For exemptions see under 'Lights, obligatory' and 'Lights, exemptions'

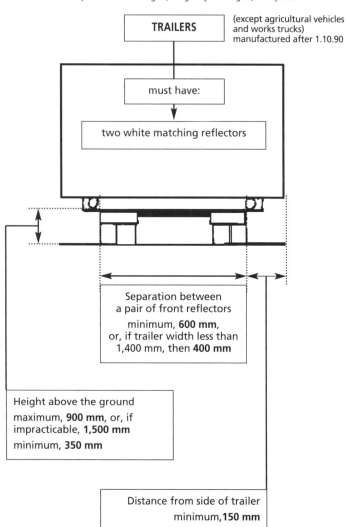

TRAILERS (except agricultural vehicles and works trucks) manufactured after 1.10.90

must have:

two white matching reflectors

Separation between a pair of front reflectors

minimum, **600 mm**, or, if trailer width less than 1,400 mm, then **400 mm**

Height above the ground

maximum, **900 mm**, or, if impracticable, **1,500 mm**

minimum, **350 mm**

Distance from side of trailer

minimum, **150 mm**

SIDE RETRO REFLECTORS

REG 18 AND SCHEDS 1 AND 17 ROAD VEHICLES LIGHTING REGULATIONS 1989
For exemptions see under 'Lights, obligatory' and 'Lights, exemptions'

NUMBER REQUIRED:

Motor vehicle first used on or after 1.4.86 and trailer manufactured on or after 1.10.85:

two on each side and as many more as required.

any other vehicle:

two on each side.

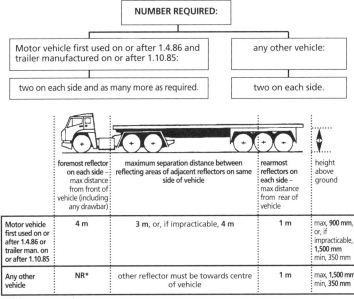

	foremost reflector on each side – max distance from front of vehicle (including any drawbar)	maximum separation distance between reflecting areas of adjacent reflectors on same side of vehicle	rearmost reflectors on each side – max distance from rear of vehicle	height above ground
Motor vehicle first used on or after 1.4.86 or trailer man. on or after 1.10.85	4 m	3 m, or, if impracticable, 4 m	1 m	max, **900 mm**, or, if impracticable, **1,500 mm** min, 350 mm
Any other vehicle	NR*	other reflector must be towards centre of vehicle	1 m	max, **1,500 mm** min, 350 mm

NR* = no requirement

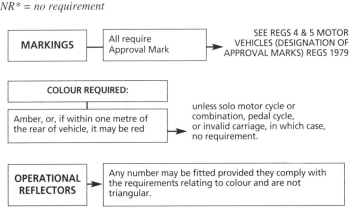

| **MARKINGS** | All require Approval Mark | SEE REGS 4 & 5 MOTOR VEHICLES (DESIGNATION OF APPROVAL MARKS) REGS 1979 |

COLOUR REQUIRED:

Amber, or, if within one metre of the rear of vehicle, it may be red

unless solo motor cycle or combination, pedal cycle, or invalid carriage, in which case, no requirement.

| **OPERATIONAL REFLECTORS** | Any number may be fitted provided they comply with the requirements relating to colour and are not triangular. |

- Must be kept clean and in good working order.
- Must be vertical and facing squarely to the side.
- May not be triangular.

REG 23

DIRECTION INDICATORS

REG 18 AND SCHEDS 1 AND 7 ROAD VEHICLES LIGHTING REGULATIONS 1989

For exemptions see under 'Lights, obligatory' and 'Lights, exemptions'

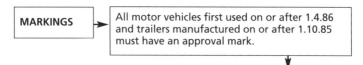

MARKINGS →	All motor vehicles first used on or after 1.4.86 and trailers manufactured on or after 1.10.85 must have an approval mark.

SEE REGS 4 AND 5 MOTOR VEHICLES (DESIGNATION OF APPROVAL MARKS) REGS 1979

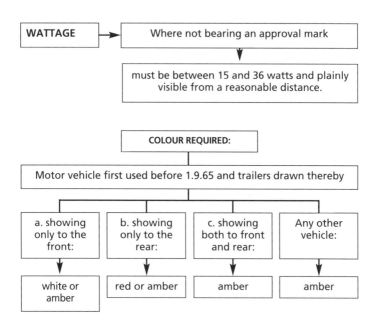

WATTAGE →	Where not bearing an approval mark

must be between 15 and 36 watts and plainly visible from a reasonable distance.

COLOUR REQUIRED:

Motor vehicle first used before 1.9.65 and trailers drawn thereby

a. showing only to the front:	b. showing only to the rear:	c. showing both to front and rear:	Any other vehicle:
white or amber	red or amber	amber	amber

FITTING

- All indicators on one side should be operated by one switch, and shall flash in phase (except motor cycles and pedal cycles which may flash alternately).

- Must be an operational tell-tale unless the driver can see the indicators from the driving position.

- Must flash between 60 and 120 flashes per minute. Must form a pair (or if more than 2 – 2 pairs).

DIRECTION INDICATORS cont

REG 18 AND SCHEDS 1 AND 7 ROAD VEHICLES LIGHTING REGULATIONS 1989

For exemptions see under 'Lights, obligatory' and 'Lights, exemptions'

Minimum separation distance between indicators on opposite sides of vehicle

A motor vehicle (other than solo motor bicycle or motor bicycle combination or invalid carriage having maximum speed not exceeding 8 mph) first used on or after 1.4.86; a trailer manufactured on or after 1.10.85; a horse-drawn vehicle, pedestrian controlled vehicle and vehicle drawn or propelled by hand, **500 mmsss**

or, if the overall width of vehicle is less than 1,400 mm, **400 mm**

Before above date, **NR***

Height above ground

Maximum
motor vehicle first used before 1.4.86 & trailer manufactured before 1.10.85, NR* maximum speed n/e 25 mph , NR* any other vehicle, **1,500 mm** unless impracticable, then, **2,300 mm**

Minimum, **350 mm**

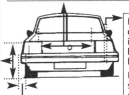

Minimum separation distance between front indicator and any headlamp or front fog lamp

Motor vehicle not being solo motor bicycle or motor bicycle combination first used on or after 1.4.95
CAT 1 indicator, **40 mm**;
CAT 1a indicator, **20 mm**;
CAT 1b indicator, **NR***

Before above date, **NR***

Maximum distance from side of vehicle

Motor vehicle first used before 1.4.86; trailer manufactured before 1.10.85;
solo motor bicycle, pedal cycle, horse-drawn vehicle or vehicle drawn by hand, **NR***

Before the above dates, **NR***

Any other vehicle, **400 mm**

Minimum separation distance between front indicator and headlamp or foglamp

for solo motor bicycles or motor bicycle combination first used on or after 1.4.86 (includes combinations), **100 mm**

before above date, **NR***

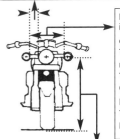

Minimum separation distance between indicators on opposite sides of vehicle

over 50cc and first used on or after 1.4.86:
front, **300 mm**; rear, **240 mm**; side, **NR***

n/e 50 cc and first used on or after 1.4.86 and pedal cycle:
front, **240 mm**; rear, **180 mm**; side, **NR***

Combination first used on or after 1.4.86, **400 mm**

Invalid carriage maximum speed n/e 8 mph:
front, **240 mm**; rear, **300 mm**

Before the above dates – **NR***

Height above ground as shown for above

* NR = no requirement

● Must be kept clean and in good working order.   REG 23

STOP LAMPS

REG 18 AND SCHEDS 1 AND 12 ROAD VEHICLES LIGHTING REGULATIONS 1989

For exemptions see under 'Lights, obligatory' and 'Lights, exemptions'

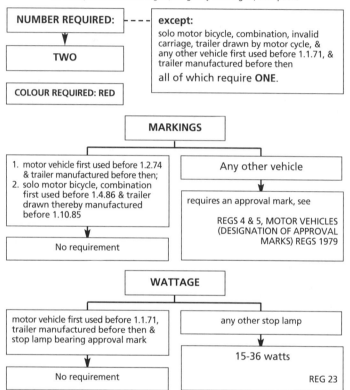

NUMBER REQUIRED:	except:
↓	solo motor bicycle, combination, invalid carriage, trailer drawn by motor cycle, & any other vehicle first used before 1.1.71, & trailer manufactured before then
TWO	all of which require **ONE**.

COLOUR REQUIRED: RED

MARKINGS

1. motor vehicle first used before 1.2.74 & trailer manufactured before then; 2. solo motor bicycle, combination first used before 1.4.86 & trailer drawn thereby manufactured before 1.10.85	Any other vehicle
	requires an approval mark, see REGS 4 & 5, MOTOR VEHICLES (DESIGNATION OF APPROVAL MARKS) REGS 1979
No requirement	

WATTAGE

motor vehicle first used before 1.1.71, trailer manufactured before then & stop lamp bearing approval mark	any other stop lamp
	15-36 watts REG 23
No requirement	

ELECTRICAL CONNECTIONS

A motor bicycle (including combination) first used on or after 1.4.86 must be capable of operating the stop lamp by both front and back brakes.
Every other vehicle and trailer must operate the stop lamp by the braking system.

OPTIONAL LAMPS

Any number may be fitted but they must comply with all other requirements relating to obligatory stop lamps except minimum separation distance between 2 stop lamps.

● Must be kept clean & in good working order   Reg 23

STOP LAMPS cont

REG 18 AND SCHEDS 1 AND 12 ROAD VEHICLES LIGHTING REGULATIONS 1989

For exemptions see under 'Lights, obligatory' and 'Lights, exemptions'

WHERE TWO STOP LAMPS ARE FITTED

↓

must be at least one on each side
must form matched pairs

If also fitted in rear window of vehicle first used after 1.4.91, must be between 20 and 60 candelas

↓

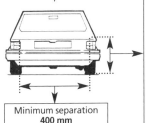

Minimum separation
400 mm

Clearance of headlamp above ground must be:

maximum:
motor vehicle first used before 1.1.71, trailer manufactured before then & motor vehicle with max speed n/e 25 mph, **NR ***;

any other vehicle, **1,500 mm** and (unless impracticable) **2,100 mm**;

minimum
motor vehicle first used before 1.1.71. & trailer manufactured before then, **NR***;

any other vehicle, **350 mm**

WHERE ONE IS FITTED

↓

to be fitted on centre line or offside
(disregarding the combination).

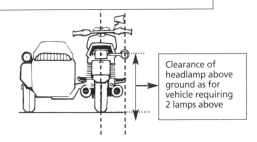

Clearance of headlamp above ground as for vehicle requiring 2 lamps above

---

* NR - no requirement

REAR FOG LAMPS

REG 18 SCHEDS 1 AND 11
ROAD VEHICLES LIGHTING REGULATIONS 1989

For exemptions see under 'Lights, obligatory' and 'Lights, exemptions'

NUMBER REQUIRED:

↓

ONE

COLOUR REQUIRED: RED

MARKINGS

↓

must have an approval mark, see

REGS 4 & 5, MOTOR VEHICLES (DESIGNATION OF APPROVAL MARKS) REGS 1979

ELECTRICAL CONNECTIONS

Must not be capable of being operated by braking systems. A circuit-closed tell-tale must be fitted.

OPTIONAL LAMPS

motor vehicle first used before 1.4.80 and any other vehicle manufactured before 1.10.79:	any other vehicle

↓ ↓

any number may be fitted provided they comply with requirements relating to separation distance between fog & stop lamps, & colour. They must not be capable of being operated by the braking system.	not more than 2 may be fitted (in addition to obligatory lamps) and they must comply with all other requirements of obligatory rear fog lamps.

Must not cause undue dazzle or discomfort, be lit when parked, nor be used except in seriously reduced visibility.

REG 27

REAR FOG LAMPS cont

REG 18 SCHEDS 1 AND 11
ROAD VEHICLES LIGHTING REGULATIONS 1989

For exemptions see under 'Lights, obligatory' and 'Lights, exemptions'

WHERE TWO REAR FOG LAMPS ARE FITTED

Laterally there is no fitting requirement, but

must form a matching pair if vehicle first used on or after 1.4.86, or trailer manufactured on or after 1.10.85.

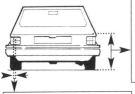

Height of fog lamp above ground must be:

maximum
1. agricultural vehicle, engineering plant and motor tractor, **2,100 mm**;
2. any other vehicle, **1,000 mm**;

minimum, **250 mm**.

Minimum separation distance between fog lamp and stop lamp, **100 mm**

WHERE ONE REAR FOG LAMP IS FITTED

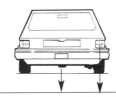

Fitted on centre line or offside of the vehicle (disregarding any sidecar forming part of motor bicycle combination)

● Must be kept clean, in good working order and maintained so as not to cause undue dazzle or inconvenience

REG 23

FRONT FOG LAMPS

REG 20 AND SCHED 6
ROAD VEHICLES LIGHTING REGULATIONS 1989
For exemptions see under 'Lights, obligatory' and 'Lights, exemptions'

> **These lamps are not obligatory, but must comply with the following:**

NUMBER:

motor vehicles (other than motor bicycle or motor bicycle combination) first used on or after 1.4.91 – not more than two.

Any other vehicle, no requirement

COLOUR: white or yellow

MARKINGS:

first used before 1.4.86, no requirement

any other vehicle needs an approval mark, see:
REGS 4 & 5, MOTOR VEHICLES (DESIGNATION OF APPROVAL MARKS) REGULATIONS 1979

When used as a pair in seriously reduced visibility in place of obligatory head lights, **400 mm**

Any other case, **no requirement**

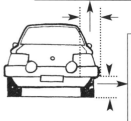

Maximum height above the ground:
1. agricultural vehicle, road clearance vehicle aerodrome fire tender or runway sweeper, industrial tractor, engineering plant & home forces vehicle, **no requirement**
2. any other vehicle, **1,200 mm**

Minimum height above the ground, **no requirement**

● Must not cause undue dazzle or discomfort, be lit when parked, nor be used except in seriously reduced visibility

REG 27

● Must be kept clean, in good working order and maintained so as not to cause undue dazzle or inconvenience

REG 23

REVERSING LIGHTS

REG 20 AND SCHED 14
ROAD VEHICLES LIGHTING REGULATIONS 1989
For exemptions see under 'Lights, obligatory' and 'Lights, exemptions'

> **These lamps are not obligatory, but must comply with the following:**

NUMBER: not more than two

COLOUR: white

POSITION: no requirement

MARKINGS

Motor vehicle first used on or after 1.4.86 and trailer manufactured on or after 1.10.85 requires an approval mark. See
REGS 4 AND 5 OF THE MOTOR VEHICLES (DESIGNATION OF APPROVAL MARKS) REGS 1979

Any other vehicle, no requirement

WATTAGE

Lamp bearing approval mark, no requirement

All other lamps n/e 24 watts each.

TELL-TALE

Motor vehicle first used on or after 1.7.54 with automatic switching of lamp upon selection of reverse gear, no requirement

A motor vehicle first used before 1.7.54, no requirement

Any other motor vehicle first used on or after 1.7.54 requires a circuit-closed tell-tale.

A vehicle which is not a motor vehicle, no requirement

● Must be kept clean, in good working order and maintained so as not to cause undue dazzle or inconvenience

REG 23

● Must only be lit for reversing.

REG 27

HAZARD WARNING

REG 18 AND SCHEDS 1 AND 8 ROAD VEHICLES LIGHTING REGULATIONS 1989

For exemptions see under 'Lights, obligatory' and 'Lights, exemptions'

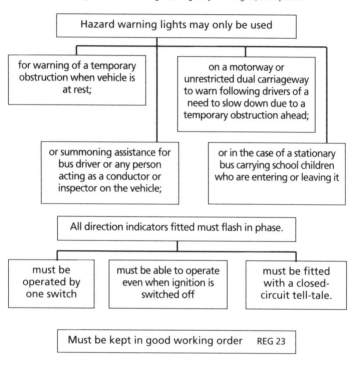

Hazard warning lights may only be used

for warning of a temporary obstruction when vehicle is at rest;

on a motorway or unrestricted dual carriageway to warn following drivers of a need to slow down due to a temporary obstruction ahead;

or summoning assistance for bus driver or any person acting as a conductor or inspector on the vehicle;

or in the case of a stationary bus carrying school children who are entering or leaving it

All direction indicators fitted must flash in phase.

must be operated by one switch

must be able to operate even when ignition is switched off

must be fitted with a closed-circuit tell-tale.

Must be kept in good working order   REG 23

REAR REGISTRATION PLATE LAMP

REG 18 AND SCHED 1 ROAD VEHICLES LIGHTING REGULATIONS 1989

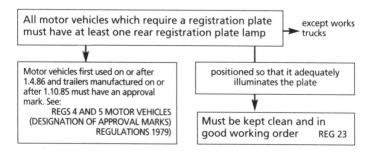

All motor vehicles which require a registration plate must have at least one rear registration plate lamp

except works trucks

Motor vehicles first used on or after 1.4.86 and trailers manufactured on or after 1.10.85 must have an approval mark. See:
REGS 4 AND 5 MOTOR VEHICLES (DESIGNATION OF APPROVAL MARKS) REGULATIONS 1979)

positioned so that it adequately illuminates the plate

Must be kept clean and in good working order   REG 23

WARNING BEACONS

ROAD VEHICLES LIGHTING REGULATIONS 1989

For exemptions see under 'Lights, obligatory' and 'Lights, exemptions'

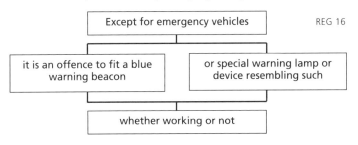

| Except for emergency vehicles | REG 16 |

| it is an offence to fit a blue warning beacon | or special warning lamp or device resembling such |

| whether working or not |

- *For improper use of beacons see Reg 27*
- *See also Reg 11 (colour of light)*

| Must be visible from any point a reasonable distance from the vehicle. |

| May be blue, amber green or yellow | IN ACCORDANCE WITH REG 11. |

| Light to be displayed between 60 and 240 equal times per minute at constant intervals. |

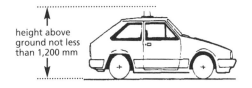

height above ground not less than 1,200 mm

| It is an offence to use on an unrestricted dual carriageway, on which it is lawful to travel at 50 mph or more | REG 17 |

| a motor vehicle with four or more wheels, having max. speed not exceeding 25 mph | → | unless it has at least one amber warning beacon. |

| But this does not apply to a vehicle first used before 1.1.47 or to a vehicle or trailer only quickly crossing the carriageway |

SIDE MARKER LAMPS

REGS 18, 20, 22 AND SCHEDS 1 AND 9 ROAD VEHICLES LIGHTING REGS 1989

For exemptions see under 'Lights, obligatory' and 'Lights, exemptions'

It is an offence to use, cause or permit to be used, on a road

during the hours of darkness
or in seriously reduced visibility in the daytime

| any vehicle | or combination of vehicles |

unless fitted with side marker lamps as detailed in the following diagrams

OPTIONAL LAMPS: ----> Any number may be fitted provided they comply with colour requirements.

1. Vehicle or combination overall length (including load) exceeding 18.3 m

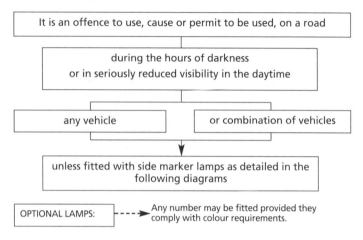

One side marker lamp in this area **9.15 m max**

Lamps needed in this area so that distance between lamps **does not exceed 3.05 m**

One lamp in this area **3.05 m max**

Max 2,300 mm
Min NR*

2. Combination of vehicles overall length (including load) exceeding 12.2 m but not exceeding 18.3 m and carrying a load supported by any two of the vehicles but not including a load carried by an articulated vehicle.

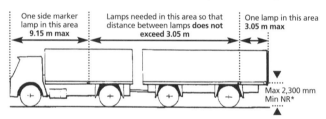

One side marker lamp within 1,530 mm of rear of towing vehicle.

1,530 mm

1,530 mm max

Max. 2,300 mm
Min. NR*

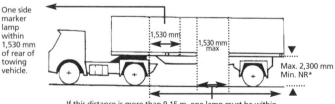

If this distance is more than 9.15 m, one lamp must be within 1,530 mm behind centre point of overall length of load. This also applies to any other trailer.

* NR = no requirement

SIDE MARKER LAMPS cont

REGS 18, 20, 22 AND SCHEDS 1 AND 9 ROAD VEHICLES LIGHTING REGS 1989

For exemptions see under 'Lights, obligatory' and 'Lights, exemptions'

IN ADDITION
to **1.** and **2.** on previous page

3. **Motor vehicles first used after 1.4.91 and trailers manufactured after 1.10.90 must also comply with the following:**

Lamps must be amber,

OR

a. may be red
if within 1 m of rear

b. may be red to rear and white to front
if on a trailer manufactured before 1.10.90.

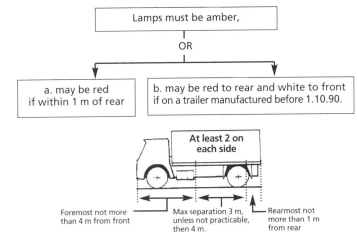

At least 2 on each side

Foremost not more than 4 m from front — Max separation 3 m, unless not practicable, then 4 m. — Rearmost not more than 1 m from rear

Exceptions:

1. agricultural or works trailers;
2. caravan;
3. length n/e 6 m and first used before 1.4.91 (but if trailer manufactured before 1.10.90 n/e 9.15 m);
4. max speed n/e 25 mph;
5. passenger vehicle;
6. proceeding for completion or sale;
7. vehicle for carrying or launching boat.

END-OUTLINE MARKER LAMPS

REGS 18, 20, AND SCHEDS 13 ROAD VEHICLES LIGHTING REGULATIONS 1989

For exemptions see under 'Lights, obligatory' and 'Lights, exemptions'

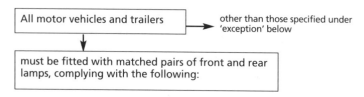

All motor vehicles and trailers	other than those specified under 'exception' below

must be fitted with matched pairs of front and rear lamps, complying with the following:

Distance between end-outline marker and side of vehicle not more than **400 mm**

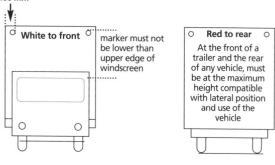

White to front — marker must not be lower than upper edge of windscreen

Red to rear — At the front of a trailer and the rear of any vehicle, must be at the maximum height compatible with lateral position and use of the vehicle

The white front and rear red lamps may be combined to form a single lamp.

OPTIONAL LAMPS: — Any number of optional lamps may be fitted but must comply with colour requirements.

Exceptions

Motor vehicles
1. First used before 1.4.91.
2. Incomplete vehicle going for completion, storage or display for sale.
3. Maximum speed n/e 25 mph
4. Overall width n/e 2,100 mm.

Trailers
1. Agricultural vehicle.
2. Incomplete trailer going for completion, storage or display for sale.
3. Manufactured before 1.10.90.
4. Overall width n/e 2,100 mm.
5. Works trailer.

REAR REFLECTIVE MARKERS – REQUIREMENTS

REGS 18, 20, AND SCHED 19 ROAD VEHICLES LIGHTING REGULATIONS 1989

For exemptions see under 'Lights, obligatory' and 'Lights, exemptions'

The following vehicles are required to be fitted with the type of reflector indicated (and illustrated on the following pages).

TYPE	Motor vehicles first used before 1.4.96 and trailers manufactured before 1.10.95	Any motor vehicles regardless of date of first use, and any trailer regardless of date of manufacture
	TYPE	
 13 m long	1, 2 or 3 motor vehicle not over	A, B, C or D
	4 or 5 motor vehicle over 13 m long	E, F, G or H
 combination of vehicles not over 11 m overall length	1, 2 or 3 trailer forming part of a	A, B, C or D
 trailer forming part of a combination of vehicles over 11 m but not over 13 m overall length	1, 2, 3, 4 or 5	Any of types A - H
 trailer forming part of a combination of vehicles over 13 m overall length	4 or 5	E, F, G or H

REAR REFLECTIVE MARKERS – TYPES

1

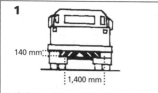

140 mm

1,400 mm

Vertical centre-line of marker fitted on the vertical centre-line of vehicle.
Not protruding beyond either side of vehicle

2

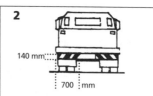

140 mm

700 mm

Of equal size and shape
Fitted as near as possible to outer edge of vehicle but not protruding beyond.

For 1 and 2: angle of bars, **46 °**
width and distance apart of bar, **140 mm**

3

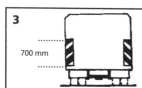

700 mm

Equal size and shape
Fitted as near as possible to outer edge of vehicle but not protruding beyond.

4

225 mm

1,265 mm

Vertical centre-line of marker fitted on the vertical centre-line of vehicle.
Not protruding beyond either side of vehicle.

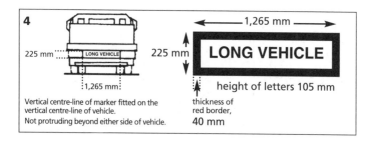

1,265 mm

225 mm

LONG VEHICLE

height of letters 105 mm

thickness of
red border,
40 mm

REAR REFLECTIVE MARKERS – TYPES cont

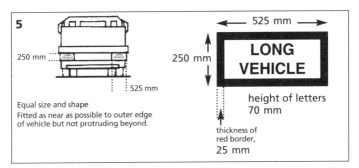

5

250 mm

525 mm

Equal size and shape
Fitted as near as possible to outer edge
of vehicle but not protruding beyond.

525 mm

250 mm

LONG VEHICLE

height of letters
70 mm

thickness of
red border,
25 mm

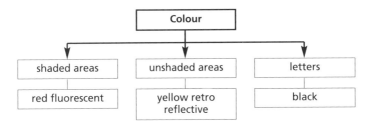

Colour

shaded areas	unshaded areas	letters
red fluorescent	yellow retro reflective	black

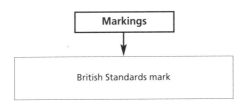

Markings

British Standards mark

REAR REFLECTIVE MARKERS –
TYPES cont

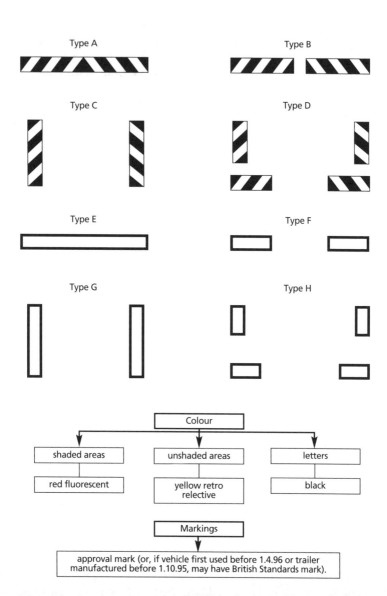

Type A

Type B

Type C

Type D

Type E

Type F

Type G

Type H

Colour		
shaded areas	unshaded areas	letters
red fluorescent	yellow retro relective	black

Markings
approval mark (or, if vehicle first used before 1.4.96 or trailer manufactured before 1.10.95, may have British Standards mark).

LAMPS ON PROJECTING LOADS

REG 21 ROAD VEHICLE LIGHTING REGULATIONS 1989

It is an offence to use, cause or permit use of vehicle during hours of darkness or in seriously reduced visibility unless it complies with the following:

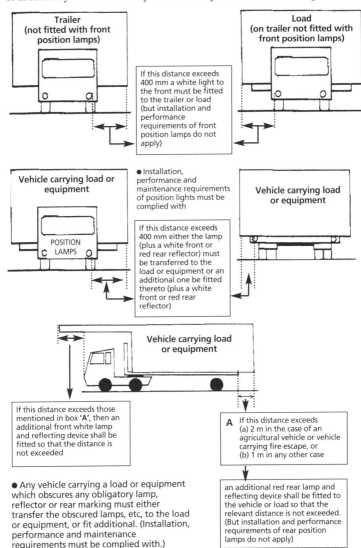

Trailer (not fitted with front position lamps)

If this distance exceeds 400 mm a white light to the front must be fitted to the trailer or load (but installation and performance requirements of front position lamps do not apply)

Load (on trailer not fitted with front position lamps)

Vehicle carrying load or equipment

POSITION LAMPS

● Installation, performance and maintenance requirements of position lights must be complied with

If this distance exceeds 400 mm either the lamp (plus a white front or red rear reflector) must be transferred to the load or equipment or an additional one be fitted thereto (plus a white front or red rear reflector)

Vehicle carrying load or equipment

Vehicle carrying load or equipment

If this distance exceeds those mentioned in box 'A', then an additional front white lamp and reflecting device shall be fitted so that the distance is not exceeded

A If this distance exceeds (a) 2 m in the case of an agricultural vehicle or vehicle carrying fire escape, or (b) 1 m in any other case

● Any vehicle carrying a load or equipment which obscures any obligatory lamp, reflector or rear marking must either transfer the obscured lamps, etc, to the load or equipment, or fit additional. (Installation, performance and maintenance requirements must be complied with.)

an additional red rear lamp and reflecting device shall be fitted to the vehicle or load so that the relevant distance is not exceeded. (But installation and performance requirements of rear position lamps do not apply)

PROJECTION MARKERS

SCHED 12 ROAD VEHICLES (CONSTRUCTION AND USE) REGULATIONS 1986

Projection	Requirement
Forward or rearward projection exceeding 1.83 m	End markers unless rear marking is in accordance with the Lighting Regs
Forward projection exceeds 2 m or rearward exceeds 3 m	One side marker on each side
Forward projection exceeds 4.5 m that or rearward exceeds 5 m	Extra side markers on each side so that horizontal distance between marker and end of projection or between adjacent markers on the same side, does not exceed: forward projection - 2.5 m rearward projection - 3.5 m

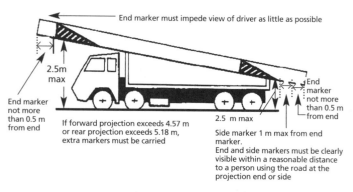

End marker must impede view of driver as little as possible

2.5m max

End marker not more than 0.5 m from end

If forward projection exceeds 4.57 m or rear projection exceeds 5.18 m, extra markers must be carried

2.5 m max

End marker not more than 0.5 m from end

Side marker 1 m max from end marker.
End and side markers must be clearly visible within a reasonable distance to a person using the road at the projection end or side

Markers must have alternating red and white stripes 100 mm wide, with 50 mm wide red border. Each not less than 610 mm high

not less than 1,520 mm

side marker

front or rear end marker

- Must be kept illuminated between sunset and sunrise.
- End projection markers are not required if reflective rear markings are carried on the load.

TRAILER PLATES – REAR REFLECTORS

REG 18 AND SCHEDS 1 AND 18 ROAD VEHICLES LIGHTING REGULATIONS 1989

REG 3 EEC DIRECTIVE 76/757

A trailer (other than a broken down motor vehicle) manufactured on or after 1.7.70 must have a pair of reflex reflectors of one of the following types:

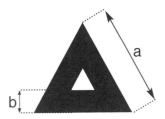 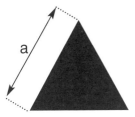

a must be 150 mm or over but must not exceed 200 mm

b must be at least $\dfrac{9}{5}$ (ie greater than or equal to)

c must not exceed 15 mm (ie less than or equal to)

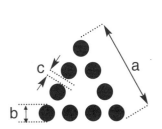 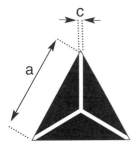

RESTRICTIONS ON USE OF LAMPS

REG 27 ROAD VEHICLES LIGHTING REGULATIONS 1989

This regulation applies to lamps other than those to which Reg 24 applies (requirements regarding the use of front and rear position lights, rear registration plate lamps, side marker lamps and end-outline marker lamps).

No person shall use, cause or permit to be used on a road any vehicle on which any lamp, device or beacon specified in the table below is used in a manner specified in the table.

Type of lamp, etc.	Manner of use prohibited
Headlamp	(a) Causing undue dazzle or discomfort to other persons using the road, or (b) lit when parked.
Front fog lamp	(a) Causing undue dazzle or discomfort to other persons using the road, (b) lit other than in seriously reduced visibility, or (c) lit when parked.
Rear fog lamp	(a) Causing undue dazzle or discomfort to the driver of a following vehicle, (b) lit other than in seriously reduced visibility, or (c) except in emergency, lit when parked.
Reversing lamp	Lit except for the purpose of reversing.
Hazard warning device	Other than - (a) to warn of a temporary obstruction when the vehicle is at rest, (b) on a motorway or unrestricted dual carriageway to warn following drivers of a need to slow down due to a temporary obstruction ahead, (c) to summon assistance for a driver, conductor or inspector of a bus, or (d) a school bus when stationary and children under 16 are entering or leaving.
Blue warning beacon and special warning lamp	Lit except - (a) at the scene of an emergency, or (b) to indicate to persons using the road the urgency of the purpose, or to warn of the presence of the vehicle or hazard.
Amber warning beacon	Lit except - (a) at the scene of an emergency, or (b) to warn persons of the presence of the vehicle, (c) a breakdown vehicle at the scene of a breakdown, accident, or drawing a broken-down vehicle, (d) escort vehicle, where abnormal load is (i) over 2.9 m wide (ii) over 18.65 m long, or (iii) authorised by Secretary of State under S 44, or (e) escort vehicle other than for an abnormal load and travelling at not more than 25 mph.
Green warning beacon	Lit except while occupied by a medical practitioner in an emergency.
Yellow warning beacon	Lit on a road.
Work lamp	(a) Causing undue dazzle or discomfort to the driver of a vehicle, or (b) lit except to illuminate a working area, accident, breakdown or works in the vicinity of the vehicle.
Any other lamp	Causing undue dazzle or discomfort to other persons using the road.

PART 4

DRIVER'S HOURS

AND RECORDS

Here we discuss the need to comply with
driver's hours and the keeping of records.
The use of the tachograph and possible
malpractices are then considered.
Both community and domestic rules
are explained.

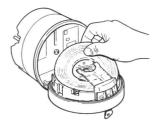

DRIVERS' HOURS AND RECORDS – APPLICATION

REGULATIONS (EC) 561/2006, 3821/1985 & THE COMMUNITY DRIVERS' HOURS AND RECORDING EQUIPMENT REGULATIONS 2007 (S.I. 1819/2007)

Before deciding whether a driver has to comply with either community or domestic rules relating to duty limits and records, it is necessary to consider the type of vehicle and the purpose for which it is being used.

Community rules

Regulations 561/2006 and 3821/1985 (community rules) deal with hours of work and recording equipment respectively. Reg. 561/2006 defines the vehicles and purposes to which **both** sets of regulations apply. It also lays down rules on driving times, breaks and rest periods for drivers engaged in the carriage of goods and passengers by road.

The regulations apply to:

(a)   the carriage by road of goods where the permissible mass of the vehicle, including any trailer, or semi-trailer, exceeds 3.5 tonnes, or

(b)   the carriage by road of passengers by vehicles which are constructed or permanently adapted for carrying more than nine persons including the driver, and are intended for that purpose.

It applies, irrespective of the country of registration of the vehicle, to carriage by road undertaken:

(a)   exclusively within the community; or

(b)   between the community, Switzerland and the countries party to the Agreement on the European Economic Area.

Where operations are undertaken outside these areas, then if the vehicle is registered in the community or in a country which is a contracting party to the European Agreement concerning the Work of Crews of Vehicles engaged in International Road Transport (AETR) then AETR rules apply to the whole of the journey. These rules are aligned to the provisions of these regulations. If the vehicle is registered in a third country which is not a contracting party to AETR, then AETR rules apply only to that part of the journey within the community or within the territory of the country which is a contracting party (Art. 2).

The regulations do not apply to carriage by road by:

(a)   vehicles used for the carriage of passengers on regular services where the route covered does not exceed 50 km;

(b)   vehicles with a maximum authorised speed not exceeding 40 kph;

(c)   vehicles owned or hired without a driver by the armed services, civil defence services, fire services, and forces responsible for maintaining public order when the carriage is undertaken as a consequence of the tasks assigned to these services and is under their control;

DRIVERS' HOURS AND RECORDS – APPLICATION cont

(d) vehicles, including vehicles used in the non-commercial transport of humanitarian aid, used in emergencies or rescue operations;

(e) specialised vehicles used for medical purposes;

(f) specialised breakdown vehicles operating within a 1000 km radius of their base;

(g) vehicles undergoing road tests for technical development, repair or maintenance purposes, and new or rebuilt vehicles which have not yet been put into service;

(h) vehicles or combinations of vehicles with a maximum permissible mass not exceeding 7.5 tonnes used for the non-commercial carriage of goods;

(i) commercial vehicles, which have a historic status according to the legislation in the Member State in which they are being driven (S.I. 1819/2007 defines this as being manufactured more than 25 years before the date on which it is being driven) and which are used for the non-commercial carriage of passengers or goods (Art. 3).

Further exemptions from the Community Drivers' Hours Regulation (561/2006)

Articles 13(1) and 14(1) of 561/2006 allow member states to allow other exemptions to cater for individual conditions or exceptional circumstances. Accordingly, S.I. 1819/2007 granted exemptions from Art. 6 (daily driving time, weekly driving time, accumulated driving time during two consecutive weeks, and the requirement to record 'other work'); Art. 7 (requirement to take a break after 4 ½ hours driving); Art. 8 (daily and weekly rest periods); and Art. 9 (provisions relating to the vehicle being transported by ferry or train).

These exemptions apply to:

1. Any vehicle which is owned or hired without a driver by a public authority to undertake carriage by road otherwise than in competition with private transport undertakings, such vehicle being:

   (a) used for the provision of ambulance services by a relevant NHS body, or in pursuance of arrangements made by such a body or with the relevant minister;

   (b) used for the transport of organs, blood, equipment, medical supplies or personnel by a relevant NHS body, or in pursuance of arrangements made by such a body or with the relevant minister;

DRIVERS' HOURS AND RECORDS – APPLICATION cont

(c) used by a local authority to provide social service functions for old persons or welfare arrangements for physically or mentally handicapped persons;

(d) used by Her Majesty's Coastguard, a general lighthouse authority or a local lighthouse authority;

(e) used for the purpose of maintaining railways by the British Railways Board, the holder of a network licence, Transport for London or a subsidiary, a Passenger Transport Executive, or a local authority;

(f) used by the British Waterways Board for the purpose of maintaining navigable waterways.

2. Any vehicle which is being used or hired without a driver by an agricultural, horticultural, forestry, farming or fishery (but only to carry live fish or a catch of fish for processing) undertaking for carrying goods as part of its own entrepreneurial activity within a 100 km radius of its base.

3. Any tractor which is used for agricultural or forestry work within 100 km radius of its base.

4. Any vehicle which has a maximum permissible mass not exceeding 7.5 tonnes being used for carrying materials, equipment or machinery for the driver's use in connection with his work. But the vehicle must be used within a 50 km radius from its base, or the driving of the vehicle must constitute the driver's main activity.

5. Any vehicle which operates exclusively on an island which does not exceed 2300 sq kms and is not linked to the rest of GB by a bridge, ford or tunnel open for use by motor vehicles.

6. Any vehicle which is used by an undertaking for the carriage of goods within a 50 km radius from its base, propelled by natural or liquefied gas or electricity and has a maximum permissible mass, including that of any trailer or semi-trailer, not exceeding 7.5 tonnes.

7. Any vehicle which is being used for driving instruction and examination with a view to obtaining a driving licence or certificate of professional competence. But not if the vehicle, trailer or semi-trailer is being used for the commercial carriage of goods or passengers.

8. Any vehicle which is being used in connection with-

(a) sewerage, flood protection, water, gas or electricity maintenance services;

(b) road maintenance or control;

DRIVERS' HOURS AND RECORDS –
APPLICATION cont

(c) door-to-door household refuse collection or disposal;

(d) telegraph or telephone services;

(e) radio or television broadcasting; or

(f) the detection of radio or television transmitters or receivers.

9. Any vehicle with not more than 17 seats, including the driver's seat, used exclusively for the non-commercial carriage of passengers.

10. Any specialised vehicle which is being used for transporting circus or funfair equipment.

11. Any mobile project vehicle the primary purpose of which is use as an educational facility when stationary, and which is specially fitted for that purpose.

12. Any vehicle which is being used for the collection of milk from farms or for the return to farms of milk containers or milk products intended for animal feed.

13. Any vehicle which is being used to carry animal waste or carcasses which are not intended for human consumption.

14. Any vehicle which is used exclusively on roads inside hub facilities, eg ports, interports and railway terminals.

15. Any vehicle which is being used to carry live animals from a farm to a market, or from a market to a slaughterhouse, where, in either case the distance does not exceed 50 kms.

16. Any vehicle which has a maximum permissible mass not exceeding 7.5 tonnes; is being used to deliver items as part of a universal service by a universal service provider (community postal services); being used within 50 km radius of its base; and the driving of which does not constitute the driver's main activity.

17. Any vehicle which is being used by the Royal National Lifeboat Institution for the purpose of hauling lifeboats.

18. Any vehicle which was manufactured before 1st January 1947.

19. Any vehicle which is propelled by steam.

Further exemptions from the Community Recording Equipment Regulation (3821/1985)

Similarly, S.I. 1819/2007 granted exemptions from the recording equipment Regulations (3821/1985). The exemptions apply to vehicles included above (except item 16) plus any vehicle being used for collecting sea coal.

DRIVERS' HOURS AND RECORDS – APPLICATION cont

Domestic Rules

Although all of the above activities are exempt from **community rules**, any vehicle or driver in the following list will have to comply with the **domestic rules** relating to **drivers' hours** (Transport Act 1968). There are numerous exemptions.

1. **Vehicles** (S 95)
   (a) **Passenger vehicles:**
      (i) public service vehicles; and
      (ii) motor vehicles (other than public service vehicles) constructed or adapted to carry more than 12 passengers.
   (b) **Goods vehicles:**
      (i) heavy locomotives, light locomotives, motor tractors and any motor vehicle so constructed that a trailer may, by partial superimposition, be attached to the vehicle in such a manner as to cause a substantial part of the weight of the trailer to be borne by the vehicle; and
      (ii) motor vehicles (except those mentioned in (a) above) constructed or adapted to carry goods other than the effects of passengers.
   (c) **Other vehicles:** (motor vehicle, tractor, trailer and semi-trailer) not falling within (a) or (b) above, whether laden or not, used for the carriage of passengers or goods within the community, which are not listed in the 'general exemption' to community rules listed in Art. 3 of 561/2006 above. The effect of this is to include a vehicle not otherwise required to have a tachograph whilst drawing a trailer for the purpose of carrying goods.
2. **Drivers** (S 95) A person who drives a vehicle subject to domestic rules in the course of his employment; and a person who drives such a vehicle for the purposes of trade or business carried on by him (an owner-driver).
3. **Crown service** (S 102). Vehicles and persons in the public service of the Crown, except for motor vehicles owned by the Secretary of State for Defence and used for naval, military or air force purposes or in the case of vehicles so used while being driven by persons subject to the orders of a member of the armed forces of the Crown.

Exemptions from domestic rules

1. **Tramcars** (S 102A). Tramcars and trolley vehicles operated under statutory powers.
2. **Police and Fire** (S 102). Motor vehicles while being used for police or fire brigade purposes.

DRIVERS' HOURS AND RECORDS – APPLICATION cont

Driving for both community and domestic purposes

The domestic code does not apply to any community driving or work.

Where during any working day, a driver spends time both on community driving or work and on domestic driving or work:

  (a) any time spent on community driving or work shall be regarded for the purposes of periods of driving, the length of the working day, or calculating periods of driving where the driver does not drive for more than 4 hours, as time spent on domestic driving or work; and

  (b) any time spent on community driving or work shall not be regarded an interval of rest for the purposes of the domestic code.

DRIVERS' HOURS (HARMONISATION WITH COMMUNITY RULES) REGULATIONS 1986.

DRIVERS' HOURS – COMMUNITY RULES

REGULATION (EC) 561/2006

Minimum ages (Art. 5)
The minimum age for conductors is 18 years. The minimum age for drivers' mates is 18 years but this may be reduced to 16 if the carriage is within one member state within 50 km radius of base; the reduction is for the purpose of vocational training; and there is compliance with limits regarding employment matters.

Daily driving (Art.6)
Not to exceed nine hours. May be extended to at most 10 hours not more than twice a week.

Weekly driving (Art.6)
Not to exceed 56 hours. Shall not result in the maximum weekly working time being exceeded (See later).

Two consecutive weeks (Art. 6)
Total accumulated driving time not to exceed 90 hours.

Other work (Art. 6)
All activities except driving, including work for the same or another employer, within or without the transport sector must be recorded either manually on a record sheet, a print-out or by manual input facilities on recording equipment. This also includes driving time in commercial operations not covered by this regulation, and any periods of availability since the last daily or weekly rest period.

Breaks (Art. 7)
After four and a half hours driving the driver must take an uninterrupted break of not less than 45 minutes, unless he takes a rest period. This break may be replaced by a break of at least 15 minutes followed by a break of at least 30 minutes each distributed over the period so as to comply with the break requirement.

Daily rest (Art. 8)
Within each period of 24 hours after the end of the previous daily rest period or weekly rest period a driver shall have taken a new daily rest period of at least 11 hours. A daily rest period may be extended to make a regular weekly rest period or a reduced weekly rest period.

DRIVERS' HOURS – COMMUNITY RULES – cont
REGULATION (EC) 561/2006

By way of derogation, within 30 hours of the end of a daily or weekly rest period, a driver engaged in multi-manning must have taken a new daily rest period of at least nine hours.

Regular daily rest period (Art. 4)
This means a period of rest of at least 11 hours. Alternatively, this may be taken in two periods, the first of which must be an uninterrupted period of at least three hours and the second an uninterrupted period of at least nine hours.

Reduced daily rest (Art. 8)
If the proportion of the daily rest which falls within that 24-hour period is at least nine hours but less than 11 hours, the daily rest period will be regarded as a reduced daily rest period. At most three reduced daily rest periods may be taken between any two weekly rest periods.

Regular weekly rest period (Art. 4)
Any period of rest of at least 45 hours.

Reduced weekly rest (Art. 4)
Any period of rest of less than 45 hours, which may, subject to the conditions laid down in Art. 8, be shortened to a minimum of 24 consecutive hours.

Rest period in two consecutive weeks (Art. 8)
In any two consecutive weeks a driver shall take at least:
– two regular weekly rest periods, or
– one regular weekly rest period and one reduced weekly rest period of at least 24 hours. However, the reduction shall be compensated by an equivalent period of rest taken en bloc before the end of the third week following the week in question.

A weekly rest period shall start no later than at the end of six 24-hour periods from the end of the previous weekly rest period.

Any rest taken as compensation for a reduced weekly rest period shall be attached to another rest period of at least nine hours.

Daily rest periods and reduced weekly rest periods away from base may be taken in a vehicle, as long as it has suitable sleeping facilities for each driver, and the vehicle is stationary.

A weekly rest period that falls in two weeks may be counted in either week, but not in both.

DRIVERS' HOURS – COMMUNITY RULES – cont

REGULATION (EC) 561/2006

Vehicles transported by ferry or train (Art. 9)

Where a driver accompanies a vehicle which is transported by ferry or train, and takes a regular daily rest period, that period may be interrupted not more than twice by other activities not exceeding one hour in total. During that regular daily rest period the driver shall have access to a bunk or couchette.

Travelling time (Art. 9)

Any time spent travelling to a location to take charge of a vehicle falling within the scope of this regulation, or to return from that location, when the vehicle is neither at the driver's home nor at the employer's operational centre where the driver is normally based, shall not be counted as a rest or break unless the driver is on a ferry or train and has access to a bunk or couchette.

Driving other vehicles (Art. 9)

Any time spent by a driver driving a vehicle which falls outside the scope of this regulation to or from a vehicle which falls within the scope of this regulation, which is not at the driver's home or at the employer's operational centre where the driver is normally based, shall count as other work.

DRIVERS' HOURS – COMMUNITY RULES – cont
REGULATION (EC) 561/2006

Departure from the rules on grounds of safety (Art. 12)
Provided that road safety is not thereby jeopardised and to enable the vehicle to reach a suitable stopping place, the driver may depart from Articles 6 to 9 to the extent necessary to ensure the safety of persons, the vehicle or its load. The driver shall indicate the reason for such departure manually on the record sheet of the recording equipment or on a printout from the recording equipment or in the duty roster, at the latest on arrival at the suitable stopping place.

Definitions
'Carriage by road' means any journey made entirely or in part on roads open to the public by a vehicle, whether laden or not, used for the carriage of passengers or goods.
'Driver' means any person who drives the vehicle even for a short period, or who is carried in a vehicle as part of his duties to be available for driving if necessary.
'Rest' means any uninterrupted period during which a driver may freely dispose of his time.
'Week' means the period of time between 00.00 on Monday and 24.00 on Sunday.
'Daily driving time' means the total accumulated driving time between the end of one daily rest period and the beginning of the following daily rest period or between a daily rest period and a weekly rest period.
'Weekly driving time' means the total accumulated driving time during a week.
'Multi-manning' means during each period of driving between any two consecutive daily rest periods, or between a daily rest period and a weekly rest period, there are at least two drivers in the vehicle to do the driving. For the first hour of the multi-manning the presence of another driver or drivers is optional but for the remainder of the period it is compulsory.

DRIVERS' HOURS – COMMUNITY RULES – cont

REGULATION (EC) 561/2006

'Driving period' means the accumulated driving time from when a driver commences driving following a rest period or a break until he takes a rest period or break. The driving period may be continuous or broken.

DRIVERS' HOURS – DOMESTIC RULES

TRANSPORT ACT 1968, S 96

Daily driving

Limited to periods amounting in aggregate to **10 hours** maximum on any working day. No account is taken of any time spent driving elsewhere than on a road for the purposes of agriculture or forestry. See also the exceptions later regarding driving for less than 4 hours per day, and emergencies.

Breaks

After a period of, or periods in aggregate of, **5 and a half hours**, a break of not less than half an hour must be taken unless such a break was taken during the period(s). This provision will not apply to any day when the driver does not drive a vehicle to which the regulations apply. See also the exceptions later regarding driving for less than 4 hours per day, goods vehicles generally and light goods vehicles.

Working day

Must not exceed **11 hours** unless:

(a) during that day the driver is off duty for a period(s) of not less than the difference between his working day and **11 hours**, in which case the working day must not exceed **12 and a half hours**; or

(b) during that day all of his driving time is spent driving one or more express or contract carriages, and he is able to take a break of not less than **4 hours**, in which case his working day must not exceed **14 hours**.

(c) where the driver of a goods vehicle engaged in the collection and transport of milk, in order to either (i) meet the special needs occasioned by an outbreak of foot-and-mouth disease in GB, or (ii) to deal with the effects of such an outbreak, the working day is increased to **13 hours** (S.I. 2007/2370).

This provision will not apply to any day when the driver does not drive a vehicle to which the regulations apply. See also the exceptions later regarding driving for less than 4 hours per day, emergencies, goods vehicles generally and light goods vehicles.

Daily rest

Between any two successive working days there must be a rest period of not less than **11 hours**, unless all or the greater part of his driving time is spent driving one or more passenger vehicles, in which case on one occasion in each working week the rest period may be not less than **9 and a half hours**. Where

DRIVERS' HOURS – DOMESTIC RULES cont

TRANSPORT ACT 1968, S 96

an employee-driver is on call during a rest period, this will still count as being a rest period.

See the exceptions (later in the chapter) regarding driving for less than 4 hours per day and goods vehicles generally.

DRIVERS' HOURS – DOMESTIC RULES
cont

TRANSPORT ACT 1968, S 96

Working week

A driver must not be on duty in any working week for periods amounting in aggregate to more than **60 hours**. On any day when the driver does not drive a vehicle to which the regulations apply, the period(s) of duty for that day shall, if amounting to more than 11 hours, be treated as amounting to 11 hours only. See also the exceptions later regarding driving for less than 4 hours per day and goods vehicles generally.

Weekly rest

For each working week a driver must be off duty for a period of not less than **24 hours**, either falling wholly in that week or beginning in that week and ending in the next week. However, where the rest period ends in the next week, no part of that period (except after the expiry of that 24 hours) may count towards the next week's rest period.

The requirement to take 24 hours rest will not apply if the driver, on each working day falling wholly or partly in that week, drives one or more stage carriages and that week is immediately preceded by a week when he *did* take the 24 hour rest period (or when he was not at any time on duty).

See the exceptions regarding driving for less than 4 hours per day and goods vehicles generally.

Exemptions
Driving periods of not more than 4 hours

None of the above-mentioned requirements will apply if in each of the periods of 24 hours (beginning at midnight) in a working week the driver does not drive for a period, or aggregate of periods, of more than **4 hours**. No account is taken of any time spent driving elsewhere than on a road for the purposes of agriculture or forestry. However, in relation to the requirements relating to **daily driving, breaks after 5 and a half hours, and the working day**, those provisions will still have effect in relation to the whole of any working day falling partly in that week and partly in a week where the requirement is not satisfied. See also the modification relating to goods vehicles generally and passenger vehicles (below).

Emergencies

A driver who during the working day spends all or the greater part of the time driving **goods vehicles** and who spends time on duty during that working day

DRIVERS' HOURS – DOMESTIC RULES cont

TRANSPORT ACT 1968, S 96

dealing with any of the types of **emergency** mentioned below is exempted from the requirements relating to the **10 hour limit on daily driving and the 11 hour limit to the working day**, subject to the condition that he does not spend time on such duty (otherwise than dealing with the emergency) for a period(s) of more than **11 hours**. The types of emergency are:

1. events which cause or are likely to cause such:
    (a) danger to life or health of one or more individuals or animals; or
    (b) a serious interruption in the maintenance of public services for the supply of water, gas, electricity or drainage or of telecommunication or postal services; or
    (c) a serious interruption in the use of roads, railways, ports or airports as to necessitate the taking of immediate action to prevent the occurrence or continuance of such danger or interruption, and
2. events which are likely to cause such serious damage to property as to necessitate the taking of immediate action to prevent the occurrence of such damage.

DRIVERS' HOURS (GOODS VEHICLES) (EXEMPTIONS) REGS 1986.

Goods vehicles generally

Where during any **working day** a driver spends all or the greater part of the time driving **goods vehicles**, he is subject to the following:

(a) he need not take half an hour break after 5 and a half hours
(b) the exemption relating to extending his working day to 12 and a half hours in a case where he is off duty during that day for a period(s) not less than the time by which his working day exceeds 11 hours, does not apply
(c) the provisions relating to daily rest, the length of the working week, and weekly rest do not apply
(d) the exemption which exists on any day when the driver does not drive a vehicle to which the regulations apply (breaks after 5 and a half hours and working day provisions) is modified so that he is only exempt from the 11 hour working day
(e) the exemption relating to driving for not more than 4 hours (see above) is modified so that only the provisions relating to the **10 hour daily driving limit and the 11 hour working day** will continue to apply in relation to the whole of any working day falling partly in that week and partly in a week where the requirement is not satisfied, and

DRIVERS' HOURS – DOMESTIC RULES cont

TRANSPORT ACT 1968, S 96

(f)   the definition of 'working day' (see later) is modified to mean (i) any working period when he is on duty which is not aggregated with any other such period, and (ii) where a working period is followed by one or more such periods beginning within 24 hours after the beginning of that period, the aggregate of such periods and the portion of the other period which falls into those 24 hours.

DRIVERS' HOURS (GOODS VEHICLES) (MODIFICATIONS) ORDER 1986, ART 2

Light goods vehicles

Where during any **working week** a driver spends all of the time driving **light goods vehicles** (see definition below):

(a) solely in connection with the profession of medical practitioner, nurse, midwife, dentist or veterinary surgeon
(b) wholly or mainly in connection with any service of inspection, cleaning, maintenance, repair, installation or fitting
(c) solely while acting as a commercial traveller and only carrying goods for soliciting orders
(d) solely while acting in the course of employment by the AA, RAC or RSAC; or
(e) solely in connection with the business of cinematography or of radio or television broadcasting,

the requirements are modified not only as per goods vehicles (above) but also the working day restriction of 11 hours does not apply, nor does the requirement to take breaks after 5 and a half hours.

DRIVERS' HOURS (GOODS VEHICLES) (MODIFICATIONS) ORDER 1986, ART 3

Passenger vehicles

Where a driver spends all or the greater part of his time driving one or more passenger vehicles the following modifications apply:

(a)   **Breaks**. After a period of, or periods in aggregate of, 5 and a half hours, a break of not less than half an hour must be taken unless such a break was taken during the period(s). However, this will not apply if, within a continuous period of 8 and a half hours the driver drives for periods in aggregate of not more than 7 hours and 45 minutes and he has taken a period (or aggregate of periods) of not less than 45 minutes rest from driving.

(b)   **Working day**. Not to exceed **16 hours**.

DRIVERS' HOURS – DOMESTIC RULES cont

TRANSPORT ACT 1968, S 96

(c) **Daily rest**. Not to be less than **10 hours** except that on not more than 3 occasions in any working week it may be reduced to not less than 8 and a half hours.

(d) **Working week**. No maximum.

(e) **Weekly rest**. In every 2 consecutive working weeks there must be a period of at least **24 hours** off duty, either falling wholly in those weeks or beginning in the second of those weeks and ending in the first of the next 2 weeks (but in this latter case no part may be taken to satisfy the requirement of the next 2 weeks except anything over 24 hours).

(f) **Less than 4 hours driving**. If he drives for a period (or aggregate of periods) of not more than 4 hours in more than 2 of the 24 hours beginning at midnight which make up the working week, then none of the above (a) to (e) apply.

(g) **Working day**. Means (a) any period during which a driver is on duty and is not aggregated with any other period; and (b) where any period during which he is on duty is not followed by a period of rest of not less than 10 hours (or 8 and a half hours where permitted), the aggregate of that period and each successive such period until there is such an interval between aggregated periods.

DRIVERS' HOURS (PASSENGER AND GOODS VEHICLES) (MODIFICATIONS) ORDER 1971.

Definitions
Light goods vehicle
Means a goods vehicle with permissible maximum weight not over 3.5 tonnes; or a dual purpose vehicle (see definition under Con & Use Regs).

Working day
Means (a) any period during which a driver is on duty and is not aggregated with any other period; and (b) where any period during which he is on duty is not followed by a period of rest of not less than 11 hours (or 9 and a half hours where permitted), the aggregate of that period and each successive such period until there is such an interval between aggregated periods. (But see the modification to this definition for 'goods vehicles generally' and 'passenger vehicles' above).

Working week
Means a week beginning at midnight between Sunday and Monday (unless modified by the traffic commissioner for an area). S 103 Transport Act 1968.

DRIVERS' RECORDS – APPLICATION

REGULATIONS (EC) 561/2006 & 3821/85, THE COMMUNITY DRIVERS' HOURS AND RECORDING EQUIPMENT REGULATIONS 2007 (S.I. 1819/2007) & DRIVERS' HOURS (GOODS VEHICLES) (KEEPING OF RECORDS) REGULATIONS 1987 (S.I. 1987/1421)

Community rules

Under Art 3 of Reg. 3821/85 recording equipment shall be installed and used in vehicles registered in a member state which are used for the carriage of passengers or goods by road, except the vehicles referred to in Art. 3 of Reg. (EC) 561/2006 and those exempt by S.I. 1819/2007 (for both exemptions see earlier under 'Drivers' Hours and Records – Application').

Domestic rules

Reg. 4 of S.I. 1987/1421 requires the drivers of goods vehicles and their employers to comply with domestic rules governing the keeping of record books.

'Goods vehicle' means-

    (a)   heavy locomotives, light locomotives, motor tractors and any motor vehicle so constructed that a trailer may by partial superimposition be attached to the vehicle in such a manner as to cause a substantial part of the weight of the trailer to be borne by the vehicle; and

    (b)   motor vehicles (except those mentioned in (a) above) constructed or adapted to carry goods other than the effects of passengers (S.95 Transport Act 1968).

Exemptions (Regs. 4 & 12)

The domestic rules do not apply-

1. to a journey made or work done where the community rules apply;
2. where a driver does not during any working day drive any goods vehicle other than one which is exempt from the requirement to have an operators' licence (including one in the public service of the Crown;
3. where in any working day the driver does not drive a goods vehicle for more than four hours (no account being taken of off-road driving for the purpose of agriculture, forestry or quarrying) and does not drive any such vehicle outside a radius of 50 km from its operating centre;
4. where during any working day a driver does not spend all or the greater part of his driving time in driving goods vehicles.

DRIVERS' RECORDS – APPLICATION – cont

Driving both goods and passenger vehicles (Reg. 13)

The requirement to keep record books will, however, apply to a driver who in any working week drives goods and passenger vehicles as it applies to drivers who only drive goods vehicles, and the entries in the record book will apply to the driving of both vehicles.

If a driver of both goods and passenger vehicles has a different employer for each, his 'employer' shall, for the purpose of issuing record books, be his employer in relation to the goods vehicle(s) regardless of which employed him first.

'Passenger vehicle' means-

    (a)   public service vehicles; and

    (b)   motor vehicles (other than PSVs) constructed or adapted to carry more than 12 passengers (S.95 Transport Act 1968).

RECORD BOOKS

DRIVER'S HOURS (GOODS VEHICLES) (KEEPING OF RECORDS)
REGULATIONS 1987

RECORD BOOKS

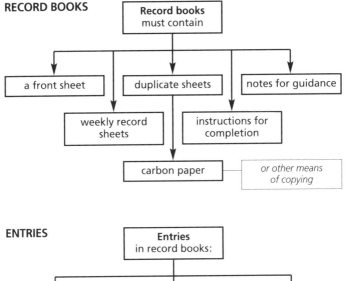

Record books
must contain

a front sheet

duplicate sheets

notes for guidance

weekly record
sheets

instructions for
completion

carbon paper

*or other means
of copying*

ENTRIES

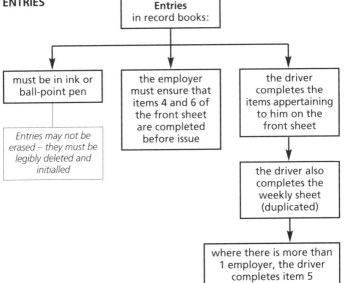

Entries
in record books:

must be in ink or
ball-point pen

*Entries may not be
erased – they must be
legibly deleted and
initialled*

the employer
must ensure that
items 4 and 6 of
the front sheet
are completed
before issue

the driver
completes the
items appertaining
to him on the
front sheet

the driver also
completes the
weekly sheet
(duplicated)

where there is more than
1 employer, the driver
completes item 5

RECORD BOOKS cont

DRIVER'S HOURS (GOODS VEHICLES) (KEEPING OF RECORDS)
REGULATIONS 1987

Model For Driver's Record Book
a. Front sheet

RECORD BOOK FOR DRIVERS IN ROAD TRANSPORT

1. Date book first used ....

2. Date book last used ....

3. Surname, first name(s), and address of holder of book ....
....
....

4. Name, address, telephone number and stamp (if any) of
employer/under-taking ....
....
....

5. Name, address, telephone number and stamp (if any) of any other
employer(s) ....
....
....

6. Operator's Licence No. (Nos) ....

---

b. Weekly sheet

WEEKLY SHEET							
1. DRIVER'S NAME			2. PERIOD COVERED BY SHEET WEEK COMMENCING (DATE)............................ TO WEEK ENDING (DATE)................................				
DAY ON WHICH DUTY	*REGISTRATION NO OF VEHICLE(S)*	*PLACE WHERE VEHICLE(S) BASED*	*TIME OF GOING ON DUTY*	*TIME OF GOING OFF DUTY*	*TIME SPENT DRIVING*	*TIME SPENT ON DUTY*	*SIGNA-TURE OF DRIVER*
MONDAY							
TUESDAY							
WEDNESDAY							
THURSDAY							
FRIDAY							
SATURDAY							
SUNDAY							
10. CERTIFICATION BY EMPLOYER		I HAVE EXAMINED THE ENTRIES IN THIS SHEET SIGNATURE..					

RECORDING EQUIPMENT
TRANSPORT ACT 1968
COUNCIL REGULATION 3821/85 (AS AMENDED BY COUNCIL REGULATIONS
3314/90, 3688/92, 2479/95, 1056/97, 2135/98, 1360/02, 1882/03, 432/04 561/06
AND THE PASSENGER AND GOODS VEHICLES
(COMMUNITY RECORDING EQUIPMENT REGULATION) REGULATIONS 2006)

The equipment used to record drivers' periods of duty is called a 'tacho-graph'. The early models are called 'analogue' tachographs and consist of a speedometer and mileage counter fitted with a clock and recording mechanism. A waxed circular disc is inserted into the equipment and this is rotated by the clock mechanism. Three styli record vehicle speed, movement and distance travelled. For chart analysis see following page.

However, these are vulnerable to tampering and damage. In addition the charts used are not always interchangeable between units. An increase in security has been achieved with the introduction of electronic modular units which still use charts but have a remote speedometer fitted and an encrypted sender unit signal.

RECORDING EQUIPMENT cont

In order to increase security further, the 'digital' tachograph has recently been introduced. The Vehicle Unit (VU) is located within the cab. It interchanges signals with the speedometer and vehicle gearbox. The VU is able to hold data on drivers of the vehicle and their periods of driving and duty for approximately 12 months. It also holds data relating to faults, attempts to tamper, over speeding, calibration details, and when data was accessed. The VU records all times in Universal Time Co-ordinated (UTC) – also known as Greenwich Mean Time (GMT), so the **stored** data will be 1 hour behind in British Summer Time. The visual display on the VU may be set to local time but this will not affect the stored internal data.

To use the VU or to gain access to its stored data, a 'smart card' must be inserted. It takes the place of the tachograph sheet (known as the disc or chart) which is used in analogue equipment. The cards are issued to drivers, companies, workshops and enforcement officers according to their specific needs.

RECORDING EQUIPMENT cont

There are 4 cards used by the digital tachograph system

Driver Card
Used by drivers to allow the recording of drivers' hours. Before the commencement of a journey the card is inserted into the first or second man slot on the VU. When double manned and changing from driver to co-driver the card is swapped between slots. The driver and vehicle details are recorded automatically, as are details of faults, interference, errors and over speeding. Different activities are recorded by changing the mode switch. Periods working away from the vehicle are recorded manually. This information is stored for 28 days on the driver card, and for at least a year on the VU.

Company Card
For use by the operator to protect and download the data

Workshop Card
Available only to approved calibration centres

Control Card
Available only to VOSA and Police for carrying out enforcement

RECORDING EQUIPMENT – CHART ANALYSIS

1. Hours divisions 2. Speed trace 3. Driver mode: When the stylus is in the drive position and the vehicle is moving, the trace is broader than when the vehicle is stationary 4. Distance trace: Each complete zig-zag represents 10 km 5. Chart centre 6. End of duty/driving 7. Delay on route 8. Delivery 9. Work other than driving 10.Rest period 11.Start of duty/driving 12.Name of driver 13.Start place 14.Finish place 15. Start date 16.Finish date 17. Vehicle registration number 18. Finish odometer reading 19. Start odometer reading 20.Total distance travelled (km)

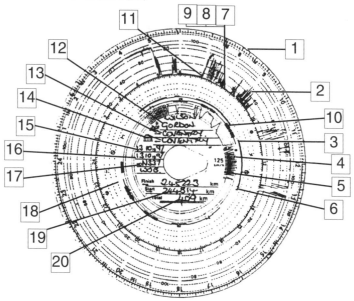

Distance Travelled

This is recorded by the innermost stylus. Every 10 km the stylus oscillates once, so that by counting the peaks, the journey length is measured.

Vehicle Movement

The middle stylus indicates when the vehicle is moving and hence records the hours at the wheel. By turning a knob, the driver can also record how the rest of his time has been apportioned between other work, eg loading and rest periods.

Speed

This is indicated by the outermost stylus and a jagged – as opposed to a smooth – trace indicates heavy use of the break and accelerator. A warning light goes on when a pre-selected speed is exceeded.

RECORDING EQUIPMENT cont

COUNCIL REGULATION 3821/85
TRANSPORT ACT 1968

Definitions

Recording equipment. The total equipment intended for installation in road vehicles to show, record and store automatically or semi automatically details of the movement of such vehicles and of certain work periods of their drivers (Annex 1 & 1A). In essence, this means either an ordinary (analogue) tachograph, or suitable recording equipment for a driver card with memory – a digital tachograph.

Record sheet. A sheet designed to accept and retain recorded data, to be placed in the recording equipment and on which the marking devices inscribe a continuous record (Annex 1).

Company card. A tachograph card issued to the company owning or holding the vehicle. It allows the display, printing and down-loading of data stored in the locked recording equipment.

Driver card. A tachograph card issued to the driver. It identifies the driver and allows for storage of driver activity data.

Requirement

Unless exempt, recording equipment must be installed and used in vehicles registered in a member state (Art 3). A digital tachograph is one which complies with Annex 1B of Council Regulation 3821/85. A vehicle put into service for the first time before 1st May 2006 must comply with either Annex 1 (analogue tachograph) or Annex 1B (digital). A vehicle put into service for the first time on or after that date must comply with Annex 1B (digital). (Art.27 Council Reg. 561/2006 and S.I. 1117/2006). It is an offence (S 97) to use, cause or permit to be used a vehicle (see earlier for vehicles subject to the requirement) unless equipment has been installed (or repaired) in accordance with the regulations and is being used in accordance with Arts 13–15 (see later). Defences:

(a) that he did not know, nor ought to have known, that it was not installed (or repaired) in accordance with the regulations;
(b) the vehicle was proceeding to a place for such equipment to be installed;
(c) it was not reasonably practicable for the equipment to be repaired by an approved fitter or workshop and the driver has complied with Art 16 by marking the sheet with the required particulars (see later);
(d) in the case of a seal being broken, that such breakage could not be avoided, it was not reasonable for it to be replaced by an approved fitter or workshop, and in all other respects Arts 13–15 were being complied with (see later); and

268 The Traffic Officer's Companion

RECORDING EQUIPMENT cont
COUNCIL REGULATION 3821/85
TRANSPORT ACT 1968

(e) in the case of a driver card not being used, that the card was damaged, malfunctioning, lost or stolen; the driver has complied with Art. 16 by marking the sheet with the required particulars and reporting the incident; and in all other respects Arts 13–15 were being complied with (see later).

Type approval

A member state may grant type approval for any type of recording equipment and to any model record sheet or memory card (Art. 5). In such cases, an EEC type approval mark is issued.

Installation and inspection

Recording equipment may be installed or repaired only by approved fitters or workshops, and a special mark must be placed on the seal which is affixed. An installation plaque must be fitted to certify that it has been fitted in accordance with regulations. In addition, in relation to digital tachographs, the electronic security data for carrying out authentication checks must be entered (Art. 12).

Use of Equipment

(a) **Responsibility**. The employer and drivers must ensure the correct functioning and proper use of, the recording equipment and the driver card (where a digital tachograph is fitted) (Art. 13).

(b) **Issue of sheets**. The employer must issue sufficient approved record sheets to drivers of vehicles fitted with tachographs (bearing in mind the length of period of service, the possibility of damage, or that they may be taken by an authorised officer) (Art. 14).

(c) **Printing**. Where the vehicle is fitted with a digital tachograph, the employer and driver must ensure that such printing as requested may be carried out correctly (Art. 14).

(d) **Retention and production**. The undertaking shall keep record sheets and printouts, whenever printouts have been made to comply with Art 15(1), in chronological order and in a legible form for at least a year after their use and shall give copies to the drivers concerned who request then. The undertaking shall also give copies of downloaded data from the driver cards to the drivers concerned who request them and the printed papers of these copies. The record sheets, printouts and downloaded data shall be produced or handed over at the request of any authorised inspecting officer. (Art. 14).

RECORDING EQUIPMENT cont
COUNCIL REGULATION 3821/85
TRANSPORT ACT 1968

Driver cards/sheets

(a) **Description**. Driver cards are issued by the member state where the driver normally resides and is valid for up to 5 years. They are issued only to drivers to whom Reg 3820/85 (driver's hours) applies. A driver may only have one driver card and he may use only his own personal card. A driver card which is defective or expired may not be used. It is personal to him and may not be suspended or withdrawn unless it has been falsified, or the driver is using a card which is not his, or it has been fraudulently obtained (Art. 14).

(b) **Use and renewal**. Drivers must not use a dirty or damaged record sheet or driver's card, and it must be adequately protected. A driver card may be renewed not later than 15 days before the expiry date. If a sheet is damaged it must be attached to the replacement sheet. If a driver card is damaged, malfunctions or is lost or stolen, the driver must apply within 7 calendar days for a replacement. If the card is damaged, malfunctions, or is not in the possession of the driver, the driver shall at the start of the journey print out the details of the vehicle and enter onto it the driver's details, including his signature and the periods of driving, etc. At the end of the journey he must print out the periods of time recorded by the recording equipment and mark it with the driver's details, including his signature. Drivers must use record sheets or driver cards every day on which they are driving, starting from the moment they take over the vehicle. The record sheet or driver card may not be withdrawn before the end of the daily working period unless otherwise authorised. No record sheet or driver card may be used to cover a period longer than that for which it was intended (Art. 15).

(c) **Operation and completion of record sheets**. If the driver is away from the vehicle and is unable to use the equipment, the times shall (a) if the vehicle is fitted with an analogue tachograph (annex 1), be entered on the record sheet, either manually, by automatic recording or other means, legibly and without dirtying the sheet; or (b) if the vehicle is fitted with digital recording equipment (annex 1B), be entered onto the driver card using the manual entry facility provided. Where there is more than one driver and the vehicle is fitted with a digital recording equipment, each driver shall ensure that his driver card is inserted into the correct slot on the tachograph. The record sheet must be amended as necessary should there be more than one driver so the information is recorded on the sheet of the driver who is actually driving. Drivers must ensure that times recorded on the sheet

RECORDING EQUIPMENT cont
PASSENGER AND GOODS VEHICLES (RECORDING EQUIPMENT)
(TACHOGRAPH CARD) REGULATIONS 2006 COUNCIL REGULATION
3821/85 TRANSPORT ACT 1968
EC REG. 561/2006, & PASSENGER AND GOODS VEHICLES (RECORDING
EQUIPMENT) (DOWNLOADING AND RETENTION OF DATA)
REGULATIONS 2008

agrees with the official time in the country of registration of the vehicle; operate switch mechanisms to record periods of time driving, doing other work, periods of availability (waiting at their post, sitting beside the driver whilst the vehicle is in motion, or on a bunk whilst the vehicle is in motion) and breaks. Each crew member must enter on his record sheet his surname and first name, date and place where the use of the sheet begins and ends, registration number of each vehicle to which he is assigned, the odometer reading at the start of the first journey on the sheet, the end of the last journey, and, in the event of a change of vehicle, readings on both vehicles, and the time of any change of vehicle (Art. 15).

(d) **Country symbols**. The driver must enter in the digital tachograph the symbols of the countries in which he begins and ends his daily work period (and more specific geographical information if required). This may be done manually or automatically if linked to a satellite tracking system (Art. 15).

(e) **Design**. Analogue tachographs must be so designed that it is possible for an authorised officer, after opening the equipment, to read the recordings for the 9 hours preceding the time of the check without permanently deforming, damaging or soiling the sheet. It must also be designed so that, without opening it, it is possible to verify that recordings are being made (Art. 15).

(f) **Production of sheets/data to inspecting officer**. The driver of a vehicle fitted with an **analogue tachograph**, must be able to produce to an inspecting officer: (a) the record sheets for the current week and those used by the driver for the previous 28 days, (b) the driver card if he holds one, and (c) any manual record and printout made during the current week and the previous 28 days as required under this Regulation and Reg. 561/2006. The driver of a vehicle fitted with a **digital tachograph** must be able to produce to an inspecting officer: (a) his driver card, (b) any manual record and printout made during the current week and the previous 28 days as required under this Regulation and Reg. 561/2006, and (c) the record sheets corresponding to the same period during which he drove a vehicle fitted with an analogue tachograph conforming with Annex 1. (Art. 15).

Offences relating to record sheets, recorded data and seals

(a) **Delivery of record sheets and other documents.** Any (a) record sheets or (b) manual records or printouts made in accordance with the Community Recording Equipment Regulation, relating to the driver of

RECORDING EQUIPMENT cont

PASSENGER AND GOODS VEHICLES (RECORDING EQUIPMENT)
(TACHOGRAPH CARD) REGULATIONS 2006 COUNCIL REGULATION
3821/85 TRANSPORT ACT 1968

a vehicle to which S97 applies, must be delivered within the delivery period (42 days starting on the day after the latest date to which the document relates) to the undertaking to whose orders he was subject in driving the vehicle. Failure to do so is an offence. If the transport undertaking fails to ensure that the driver complies, it also commits an offence. Where the driver is subject to the orders of two or more transport undertakings, the document must be delivered to the undertaking to whose orders he was first subject during the period. (S 97C)

(b) **Vehicle Units: downloading data.** Art. 10 of EC Reg. 561/2006 requires a transport undertaking using vehicles fitted with digital tachographs to ensure that all data are downloaded from the vehicle unit and driver card and kept for at least 12 months. Such data must be accessible, either directly or remotely, from the premises of the undertaking should an inspecting officer request it.

Under S 97D, data must be downloaded from a **vehicle unit** within the downloading period which is:

Case	Period begins	Period ends
Undertaking has not previously downloaded data	The first day on which the vehicle is controlled by the undertaking	On the earlier of (a) the expiry of 56 days starting on the first day of the download period; (b) any downloading of data before the expiry of that period
The undertaking uses the vehicle during the period of 56 days starting on the day after the last downloading	On the day after the last downloading	
The undertaking does not use the vehicle during the period of 56 days starting on the day after the last downloading	On the first day of the use of the vehicle after the last downloading	

RECORDING EQUIPMENT cont

PASSENGER AND GOODS VEHICLES (RECORDING EQUIPMENT)
(TACHOGRAPH CARD) REGULATIONS 2006 COUNCIL REGULATION
3821/85 TRANSPORT ACT 1968

Under S 97E data must be downloaded from a **driver card** within the downloading period which is:

Case	Period begins	Period ends
Undertaking has not previously downloaded data	The first day on which the driver drives for the undertaking	On the earlier of (a) the expiry of 28 days starting on the first day of the download period; (b) any downloading of data before the expiry of that period
The undertaking has previously downloaded data	On the first day on which the driver drives after the last downloading	
The undertaking does not use the vehicle during the period of 56 days starting on the day after the last downloading	On the first day of the use of the vehicle after the last downloading	

An undertaking commits an offence if it fails to download in accordance with Ss 97D and 97E above, or fails to download data and permit inspection and copying of the data when required by an inspecting officer. (S 97F).

(c) **Falsifying, etc. of sheets/data**. It is an offence to falsify, suppress or destroy data recorded on the record sheet, stored in the recording equipment or on the driver card, or print-outs from the recording equipment for a digital tachograph. It is also an offence to manipulate the recording equipment, record sheet or driver card which may result in data and/or printed information being falsified, suppressed or destroyed. No device which could be used to this effect may be present on the vehicle. (Art. 15)

(d) **Forgery, etc. of seals**. A person who, with intent to deceive, forges, alters or uses any seal, commits an offence. (S 97AA)

RECORDING EQUIPMENT cont

PASSENGER AND GOODS VEHICLES (RECORDING EQUIPMENT)
(TACHOGRAPH CARD) REGULATIONS 2006 COUNCIL REGULATION
3821/85 TRANSPORT ACT 1968

Offences relating tachograph cards.

(a) **Driver cards.** A person commits an offence if: (i) he uses, attempts to use or is in possession of more than one driver card on which he is identified as the holder (except a card which is time-expired or will become time-expired within 1 month); (ii) he uses or attempts to use a driver card on which he is not identified as the holder; (iii) with intent to deceive, he makes a false statement or forges or alters a document for the purpose of obtaining a driver card; (iv) he uses or is in possession of a driver card issued in consequence of an application which included, with intent to deceive, a false statement or forged or altered document; (v) he uses or is in possession of a driver card which has been forged or altered; (vi) he causes or permits any use or possession of a driver card in any of the above circumstances;   or
(vii) causes or permits the making of any false statement or forgery or alteration of a document in any of the above circumstances. (Reg 3)

(b) **Workshop cards.** A person commits an offence if: (i) he uses, attempts to use or is in possession of more than one workshop card on which he is identified as the holder (except a card which is time-expired or will become time-expired within 1 month) or more than one PIN in respect of the same place of work; (ii) he uses or attempts to use a workshop card or PIN of which he is not the identified holder; (iii) he uses or attempts to use a workshop card or PIN in circumstances unconnected with the place of work for which that card or PIN was issued; (iv) with intent to deceive, he makes a false statement or forges or alters a document for the purpose of obtaining a workshop card or PIN; (v) he uses or is in possession of a workshop card or PIN issued in consequence of an application which included, with intent to deceive, a false statement or forged or altered document; (vi) uses or is in possession of a workshop card which has been forged or altered; (vii) he divulges to another person, or permits another person to use, the PIN used in connection with a workshop card of which he is identified as the holder; (viii) he causes or permits any use or possession of a workshop card or PIN in any of the above circumstances;   or
(vii) causes or permits the making of any false statement or forgery or alteration of a document in any of the above circumstances. (Reg 4)

(c) **Lost, stolen, damaged or malfunctioning cards.** (i) If a card is lost or stolen the person to whom the card was issued shall notify the Secretary of State in writing. (ii) If it is damaged or malfunctions, the person to whom it was issued shall return it to the

RECORDING EQUIPMENT cont

PASSENGER AND GOODS VEHICLES (RECORDING EQUIPMENT)
(TACHOGRAPH CARD) REGULATIONS 2006 COUNCIL REGULATION
3821/85 TRANSPORT ACT 1968

Secretary of State. Failure to comply with either requirement is an offence. (Reg 5)

(d) **Card particulars.** When the details of the holder of any tachograph card cease to be correct, the holder must notify the Secretary of State of the details which require correction and must surrender the card when required to do so.Where a card is issued in error, or with an error or omission, the holder may be required to surrender the card. Failure to comply with any such requirement is an offence. (Reg 6)

(e) **Unauthorised cards.** A tachograph card must be surrendered by the person possessing it if it is a card: (i) on which the person using the card is not identified as the holder; (ii) which has been falsified; or (iii) which has been issued in consequence of an application which included a false statement or forged or altered document. Failure to surrender such a card is an offence. A constable or vehicle examiner appointed under S66A of the Road Traffic Act 1988 may remove and retain any such card which has not been surrendered. (Reg 7)

Malfunctioning equipment

In the event of a breakdown or faulty operation of the equipment, the employer shall have it repaired by an approved fitter or workshop as soon as circumstances permit. If the vehicle is unable to return to the premises within 1 week, the repair shall be carried out en route. Failure to comply may result in a prohibition. While the recording equipment is unserviceable or malfunctioning, drivers shall mark on the record sheet, or on a temporary sheet to be attached to the record sheet or driver card, his driver card number and/or name and/or driving licence number, his signature and all information relating to the periods which are no longer being recorded or printed. If a driver card is damaged, malfunctions or is lost or stolen, the driver shall, at the end of his journey, print out the information which has been recorded, and mark on that document his driver card number and/or name and/or driving licence number, and sign it. If a driver card is damaged or it malfunctions, it must be returned to the issuing authority.

Inspection of records, etc. relating to recording equipment

An officer may require any person to produce and permit him to inspect, remove, retain and copy: (a) if the person is the owner of the vehicle, any document for the purpose of ascertaining whether provisions have been complied with; (b) any record sheet or hard copy of electronically stored data which is required by the regulations to be retained or

RECORDING EQUIPMENT cont
PASSENGER AND GOODS VEHICLES (RECORDING EQUIPMENT)
(TACHOGRAPH CARD) REGULATIONS 2006 COUNCIL REGULATION
3821/85 TRANSPORT ACT 1968

produced; (c) any book, register or other document required by community rules or which may reasonably be required to ascertain whether community rules have been complied with. He may also require any person to: (a) produce and permit him to inspect any driver card which that person is required to produce; and (b) permit the officer to copy the data stored on the driver card (and to remove temporarily the card to do so) and to remove and retain the copy. (S 99ZA)

Power of entry, inspection, etc. of vehicles

An officer may at any time enter any vehicle to which S 97 of the Act applies in order to inspect that vehicle and any recording equipment in or on it. Where he enters he may:

(i)   inspect, remove, retain and copy any record sheet on which a record has been produced by means of analogue recording equipment or on which an entry has been made

(ii)   inspect, remove, retain and copy any hard copy of data which was stored on digital recording equipment or driver card

(iii) inspect, remove, retain and copy any other document which he may reasonably require to ascertain whether the community rules have been complied with

(iv)   inspect any driver card, copy the data stored on it (using any digital recording equipment in or on the vehicle or temporarily removing the driver card for the purpose of copying data) and remove and retain the copy

(v)   copy data stored on any digital recording equipment in or on the vehicle and remove and retain that copy

(vi)   inspect any recording equipment that is in or on the vehicle and, if necessary for the purposes of the inspection, remove it from the vehicle

(vii) retain the recording equipment as evidence if he finds that it has been interfered with

(viii) inspect the vehicle for any device which is capable of interfering with the proper operation of any recording equipment in or on the vehicle

(ix)   inspect anything in or on the vehicle which he suspects of being such a device and, if necessary for inspecting it, remove it from the vehicle, and retain it as evidence if he finds that it is capable of interfering with the equipment. (S 99ZB)

If the officer has reason to believe that any recording equipment in or on the vehicle has been interfered with so as to affect its proper operation, or

RECORDING EQUIPMENT cont

PASSENGER AND GOODS VEHICLES (RECORDING EQUIPMENT)
(TACHOGRAPH CARD) REGULATIONS 2006 COUNCIL REGULATION
3821/85 TRANSPORT ACT 1968

there is in or on the vehicle any device capable of doing so, he may require the driver or operator to take the vehicle to a specified address for the purpose of inspection of the vehicle, equipment or device. (S 99ZB)

Power to enter premises

An officer may, at any reasonable time, enter any premises on which he has reason to believe that a relevant vehicle is kept; any document mentioned in S 99ZA above is to be found; any driver card or copy of data previously stored on a driver card or recording equipment is to be found; or any digital recording equipment is to be found.

Inspection of vehicle, documents, etc. on premises

Where an officer so enters any such premises, he may inspect any relevant vehicle he finds there; inspect, remove, retain and copy any S 99ZA document he finds there; make a copy of any data; inspect any driver card he finds there and copy the data stored on it, and remove and retain the copy; copy data stored on any digital recording equipment, and remove and retain the copy; inspect any recording equipment he finds there and remove it from the premises for inspection; retain any such recording equipment as evidence if he finds it has been interfered with; inspect anything which he believes is a device capable of interfering with the equipment and remove it from the premises for inspection; retain any such device as evidence if he finds that it is capable of such interference. An officer may detain any vehicle during such time as is required for the exercise of his powers (S 99ZB). Where an officer takes hard copy as mentioned above he may require a person to sign it to confirm it is a true and complete record of his activities. (S 99ZC)

Offences relating to inspections and recordings

(a) **Obstructing an officer**. It is an offence to fail, without reasonable excuse, to comply with any requirement under S 99ZA to 99ZC above; or to obstruct an officer under S 99ZB or S 99ZF. (S 99ZD)

(b) **False records and data**. A person commits an offence if:

    (i)   he makes, causes or permits to be made, a relevant record or entry (one required under the Community Recording Equipment Regulations or S 97 of the 1968 Act, or an entry in a book, register or document required by the community rules) which he knows to be false

    (ii)   with intent to deceive, he alters, or causes or permits to be altered, a relevant record or entry

RECORDING EQUIPMENT cont
PASSENGER AND GOODS VEHICLES (RECORDING EQUIPMENT)
(TACHOGRAPH CARD) REGULATIONS 2006 COUNCIL REGULATION
3821/85 TRANSPORT ACT 1968

(iii)   he destroys or suppresses, or causes or permits to be destroyed or suppressed, a relevant record or entry

(iv)   he fails without reasonable cause to make a relevant record or entry, or causes or permits such a failure

(v)   he records or causes or permits to be recorded any data which he knows to be false on any recording equipment or driver card, or on any hard copy of data previously stored thereon

(vi)   with intent to deceive, he alters, or causes or permits to be altered, any data stored on recording equipment or on a driver card, or appearing on any copy of data previously stored

(vii)   with intent to deceive, he produces anything falsely purporting to be a hard copy of data stored on recording equipment or driver card

(viii)   he destroys or suppresses, or causes or permits to be destroyed or suppressed, any data stored in compliance with the community rules on recording equipment or driver card

(ix)   he fails without reasonable excuse to record any data on recording equipment or driver card, or causes or permits such failure

(x)   he produces, supplies or installs any device that is designed to interfere with the proper operation of the recording equipment, or that is designed to enable the falsification, alteration, destruction or suppression of data stored in compliance with the community rules on recording equipment or driver card; or

(xi)   without reasonable excuse he provides information which would assist other persons in producing such a device. (S 99ZE)

Power to seize documents

If an officer has reason to believe that an offence under S 99ZE has been committed in respect of any document inspected by him under S 99ZA or S 99ZB above, he may seize that document. (S 99ZF)

Power to prohibit driving of vehicle. If:

(a)   the driver of a UK vehicle (for foreign vehicles see following pages) obstructs an **authorised person** in the exercise of his powers under S 99(2) (entry and inspection), S 99(3) (detention of vehicle), or S 99ZB (see above), or fails to comply with a requirement made by an authorised person under S 99(1) (production and inspection), or S 99ZA to S 99ZC (see above), or

(b)   there appears to have been a contravention of any of the provisions of (i) S 96 (permitted driving time and periods of duty),

RECORDING EQUIPMENT cont
PASSENGER AND GOODS VEHICLES (RECORDING EQUIPMENT) (TACHOGRAPH CARD) REGULATIONS 2006 COUNCIL REGULATION 3821/85 TRANSPORT ACT 1968

S 97 (installation and use of recording equipment) or S 98 (written records), and any orders or regulations under those sections, or (ii) the applicable community rules; or there will be such a contravention if the vehicle is driven on a road, or

(c)   it appears that an offence under S99(5) (making a record or entry which is false, or altered with intent to deceive) or S 99ZE (see above) has been committed in respect of a UK vehicle or its driver,

the authorised person may prohibit the driving of the vehicle on a road either for a specified period or for a limited time. In such cases he may also direct the driver to remove the vehicle to such a place and subject to such conditions as are specified. The prohibition will not apply to such a direction. A written notice must be given to the driver. (S 99A)

'Authorised person' includes a constable authorised by the chief officer of police. (S 99A)

Failure to comply with prohibition

Any person who drives a vehicle on a road in contravention of a prohibition, causes or permits such a contravention, or refuses or fails to comply within a reasonable time with a direction given with the prohibition, commits an offence. (S 99C)

PROHIBITION OF DRIVING FOREIGN VEHICLES

ROAD TRAFFIC (FOREIGN VEHICLES) ACT 1972

This power applies to any foreign (meaning not registered in the UK) goods vehicle or foreign public service vehicle, and may be exercised by (a) an **examiner** (includes a constable authorised for the purpose by the chief officer of police), or (b) an **authorised person** (means a person authorised to weigh vehicles under S 78).

Where an **examiner** exercises any of the functions in Table A below and the driver obstructs him, or refuses, neglects or otherwise fails to comply with any such requirement,

OR

if it appears to the **examiner** that there has been a contravention of any of the requirements listed in Table B below, or that there will be such a contravention if the vehicle is driven on a road

then the **examiner** may prohibit the driving of the vehicle on a road absolutely or for a specified purpose, and/or for a specified period or without limitation of time (S1).

A prohibition imposed by an **examiner** because of a contravention of S 40A RTA 1988 (dangerous condition), or Regs under S 41 of that Act (construction, weight, etc.) may contain a direction that it is irremovable unless the vehicle has been inspected at an official testing station.

TABLE A	
Provision	**Function**
S 99 Transport Act 1968	To inspect and copy record sheets, books, registers and other documents required to be carried on goods vehicles and public service vehicles, to inspect driver cards and recording equipment and to copy data recorded on such cards or equipment or to inspect and copy record sheets on which records have been produced by such equipment or entries have been made.
S 67 Road Traffic Act 1988	To test the condition of motor vehicles on roads.
S 68 Road Traffic Act 1988	To inspect vehicles to secure proper maintenance.
Reg 16 Road Transport (International Passenger Services) Regulations 1984	To require the production of, and to inspect, copy and mark, documents required to be kept or carried on certain passenger vehicles.

PROHIBITION OF DRIVING FOREIGN VEHICLES cont

ROAD TRAFFIC (FOREIGN VEHICLES) ACT 1972

TABLE A – cont

Provision	Function
Art. 3a(3) Council Reg 684/92	To require the production of a certain document which is required to be kept on board certain passenger vehicles.
Art 5(4) Council Reg 881/92	To require the production of a certified copy of a community authorisation which is required to be kept on board certain goods vehicles.
Reg 7 Road Transport (Passenger Vehicle Cabotage) Regs. 1999	To require the production of certain documents which are required to be kept on board certain passenger vehicles.

TABLE B

Provision	Effect
S 2 Goods Vehicles (Licensing of Operators) Act 1995	User to have operators' licence.
Regulations under S 57(2)(d) of the above Act	Goods vehicles to be identified by plates, marks, etc.
S 96–98 Transport Act 1968 and Regs and Orders made thereunder, and the applicable Community rules	Limits of driving time and periods of duty of drivers of goods vehicles and PSVs; installation of recording equipment and keeping of records.
Orders under S 100 Transport Act 1968	International agreements.
S 40A Road Traffic Act 1988	Motor vehicle or trailer in dangerous condition, etc.
Regs Under S 41 Road Traffic Act 1988	Regulation of the construction, weight, equipment and use of motor vehicles and trailers.
Reg 4 Passenger and Goods Vehicles (Recording Equipment) Regs 1977	Retention of records produced by recording equipment.
Reg 16 Road Transport (International Passenger Services) Regs 1980	Production, inspection, copying and marking of documents required to be carried.
Reg 19 of the above Regs and Reg 19 Road Transport (International Passenger Services) Regs 1984	Contravention of community instruments and other requirements relating to international passenger services.
Regs 3 & 7 Goods Vehicles (Community Authorisations) Regs 1992	Contravention of requirements relating to goods vehicles.

PROHIBITION OF DRIVING FOREIGN VEHICLES cont
ROAD TRAFFIC (FOREIGN VEHICLES) ACT 1972

TABLE B – cont

Provision	Effect
Regs 3 & 7 Public Service Vehicles (Community Licences) Regs. 1999	Contravention of certain requirements relating to international passenger services.
Regs 3, 4 & 7 Road Transport (Passenger Vehicles Cabotage) Regs 1999	Contravention of certain requirements relating to national passenger services by a carrier registered in a foreign member state.

Where a driver obstructs an **authorised person** in the exercise of his functions under Ss 78 and 79, or refuses, neglects or otherwise fails to comply with any requirement made thereunder, or it appears to the authorised person that any weight limit has been exceeded, or will be exceeded if driven on a road, the authorised person may prohibit the driving of the vehicle on a road, either absolutely or for a specified purpose. The prohibition may be against driving until the weight has been reduced and official notification has been given that it is permitted to proceed.

Where an **examiner or authorised person** imposes a prohibition he may also direct the driver to remove the vehicle to such a place and subject to such conditions as are specified. The prohibition will not apply to such a direction. A written notice must be given to the driver.

Enforcement
Any person who drives, or causes or permits the driving of, a vehicle in contravention of a prohibition, or who refuses, neglects or otherwise fails to comply with a direction to remove the vehicle, commits an offence. Where a constable in uniform suspects a driver to have committed such an offence, he may detain the vehicle and direct it to be removed by an appropriate person.

WORKING TIME
ROAD TRANSPORT (WORKING TIME) REGULATIONS 2005
ROAD TRANSPORT (WORKING TIME) (AMENDMENT) REGULATIONS 2007

These regulations prescribe the maximum weekly working time and maximum average weekly working time of mobile workers who, in the course of their work, drive or travel in goods or passenger vehicles which are covered by the Community Driver's Hours (Reg. (EC) 561/2006). The regulations are enforced and prosecuted by inspectors appointed by the Secretary of State.

Working time must not exceed 60 hours per week and must not exceed an average of 48 hours in a reference period (approximately 17 weeks).

Breaks of not less than 15 minutes must be taken after not more than 6 hours work. For working time between 6 and 9 hours, the break must be not less than 30 minutes, and for over 9 hours, the break must be at least 45 minutes. Breaks may be taken in separate periods of not less than 15 minutes each.

Rest periods are the same as for drivers under the Community Driver's Hours Regulations.

Night work shall not exceed 10 hours in any period of 24 hours (extendable by agreement).

Records must be kept by the employer for at least 2 years.

PART 5

MISCELLANEOUS

This section is intended as a 'catch-all' to
cater for those aspects of traffic law which
do not readily fall within other parts
of the book. The major aspects include
vehicle testing, drink driving, speed
limits and the carriage of
dangerous goods.

TESTING ON ROADS

ROAD TRAFFIC ACT 1988, SS. 67, AND SCHED 2

If not authorised, no power to detain unless too defective to allow to proceed, or following an accident

A constable authorised in writing by the chief constable

The following persons also have powers to test motor vehicles under Section 67:

1. Vehicles Examiners appointed under Section 66A of the Road Traffic Act, 1988.

may test **motor vehicles on a road**

2. Persons appointed to examine and inspect public carriages under Metropolitan Public Carriage Act, 1869.

3. Persons appointed to act under Section 67 by the Secretary of State.

4. Persons appointed by a police authority to act for Chief Officer of police area for purposes of Section 67 of the Road Traffic Act, 1988.

for brakes, silencers, steering gear, tyres, noise, smoke, fumes or vapour, lights and reflectors or condition which would involve danger of injury to any person

where any construction and use defect is found the examiner may give a written notice requiring

See next page if the driver elects for the test to be deferred.

a **declaration** that the vehicle has been sold or disposed of, or not intended to be used on a road

or

a **certificate** from a testing station stating that the defect has been rectified

TESTING ON ROADS cont

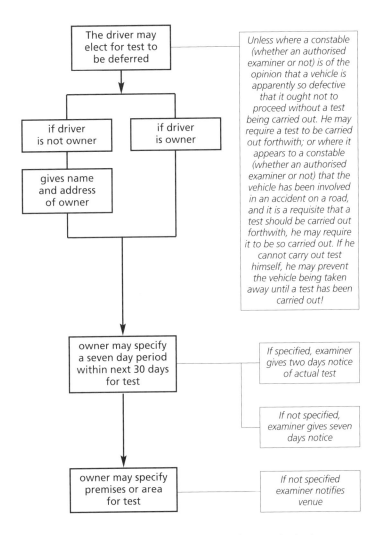

The driver may elect for test to be deferred

Unless where a constable (whether an authorised examiner or not) is of the opinion that a vehicle is apparently so defective that it ought not to proceed without a test being carried out. He may require a test to be carried out forthwith; or where it appears to a constable (whether an authorised examiner or not) that the vehicle has been involved in an accident on a road, and it is a requisite that a test should be carried out forthwith, he may require it to be so carried out. If he cannot carry out test himself, he may prevent the vehicle being taken away until a test has been carried out!

if driver is not owner

if driver is owner

gives name and address of owner

owner may specify a seven day period within next 30 days for test

If specified, examiner gives two days notice of actual test

If not specified, examiner gives seven days notice

owner may specify premises or area for test

If not specified examiner notifies venue

It is an offence to obstruct an authorised constable, (or authorised examiners) or to fail to comply with a lawful requirement.

TESTING ON PREMISES

ROAD VEHICLES (CONSTRUCTION AND USE) REGULATIONS 1986, REG 74
ROAD VEHICLES LIGHTING REGULATIONS 1989, REG 28

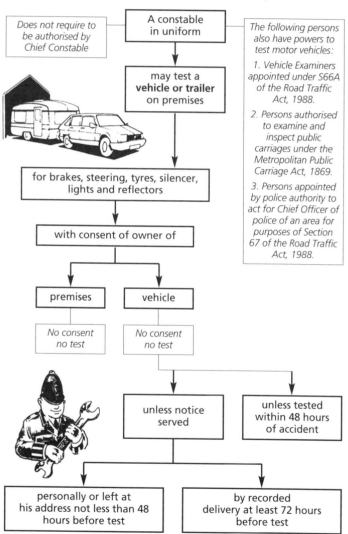

*Does not require to
be authorised by
Chief Constable*

A constable
in uniform

*The following persons
also have powers to
test motor vehicles:*

*1. Vehicle Examiners
appointed under S66A
of the Road Traffic
Act, 1988.*

may test a
vehicle or trailer
on premises

*2. Persons authorised
to examine and
inspect public
carriages under the
Metropolitan Public
Carriage Act, 1869.*

for brakes, steering, tyres, silencer,
lights and reflectors

*3. Persons appointed
by police authority to
act for Chief Officer of
police of an area for
purposes of Section
67 of the Road Traffic
Act, 1988.*

with consent of owner of

premises

vehicle

*No consent
no test*

*No consent
no test*

unless notice
served

unless tested
within 48 hours
of accident

personally or left at
his address not less than 48
hours before test

by recorded
delivery at least 72 hours
before test

REMOVAL OF VEHICLES

REMOVAL AND DISPOSAL OF VEHICLES REGULATIONS 1986, REGS 3 AND 4
ROAD TRAFFIC OFFENDERS ACT 1988, S. 91

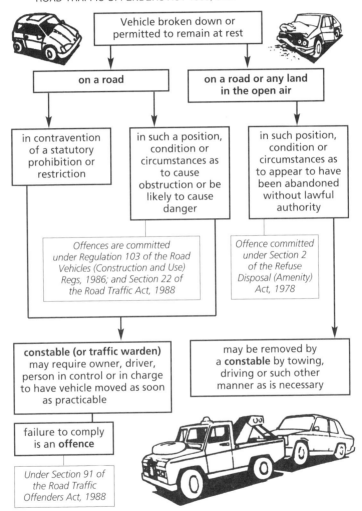

Vehicle broken down or
permitted to remain at rest

on a road

**on a road or any land
in the open air**

in contravention
of a statutory
prohibition or
restriction

in such a position,
condition or
circumstances as
to cause
obstruction or be
likely to cause
danger

in such position,
condition or
circumstances as
to appear to have
been abandoned
without lawful
authority

*Offences are committed
under Regulation 103 of the Road
Vehicles (Construction and Use)
Regs, 1986; and Section 22 of
the Road Traffic Act, 1988*

*Offence committed
under Section 2
of the Refuse
Disposal (Amenity)
Act, 1978*

constable (or traffic warden)
may require owner, driver,
person in control or in charge
to have vehicle moved as soon
as practicable

may be removed by
a **constable** by towing,
driving or such other
manner as is necessary

failure to comply
is an **offence**

*Under Section 91 of
the Road Traffic
Offenders Act, 1988*

*Note: Reference to traffic wardens having power under reg 3 (above) to require
vehicle to be removed only applies in England and Wales.*

MOTOR SALVAGE OPERATORS
VEHICLES (CRIME) ACT 2001

A motor salvage operator is a person who carries on a business which consists-

1. wholly or partly in recovery for re-use or sale of salvageable parts from motor vehicles and the subsequent sale or other disposal for scrap of the remainder of the vehicles;
2. wholly or mainly in the purchase of written-off vehicles and their subsequent repair and resale;
3. wholly or mainly in the sale or purchase of motor vehicles which are to be the subject of any of the above activities;
4. wholly or mainly in activities which fall within 2 or 3 above. (S 1)

A person who carries out the business of a motor salvage operator must **register** with the local authority. It is an offence to make false statements in an application for registration. (S 1 & 10)

Entry and Inspection of Premises

A constable may at any reasonable time enter and inspect **registered** premises which are occupied by an operator as a motor salvage yard. (Force may not be used in executing any warrant to enter) (S 9)

Requirement to keep Records

Records (electronic or manual) must be kept at the premises of details relating to the vehicle, the supplier or person receiving (including proof of identity), condition of vehicle, date of transaction and date details were entered on the record. (S 7)

Inspection of Records

A constable may at any reasonable time-

1. require production of, and inspect, any motor vehicles or salvageable parts kept on **registered** premises; and
2. require production of, inspect and take copies of or extracts from any records which the operator is required to keep. (S 9)

Warrant to Enter Premises

In order to secure compliance with regulations, or to ascertain whether provisions are being complied with, a Justice of the Peace may issue a warrant authorising a constable to enter and inspect specified premises. (Other than as mentioned above, reasonable force may be used to execute a warrant). If required by the owner or occupier of the premises, the constable shall produce evidence of his identity and his authority for entering, before doing so. (S 9)

Giving False Particulars

A person who sells a motor vehicle to a motor salvage operator commits an offence if he gives him a false name or address. (S 12)

Note: The parts of the Vehicles (Crime) Act 2001 detailed on this page do not apply to Scotland.

TAKING A CONVEYANCE WITHOUT AUTHORITY

THEFT ACT 1968

Without having the consent of the owner or other lawful authority, taking a conveyance for his own or another's use, or knowing that a conveyance has been taken without the consent of the owner or other lawful authority, drives it or allows himself to be carried in or on it.

The conveyance must be moved, however short the distance may be, merely trying to start an engine will not suffice. Also, it must be taken for use as a conveyance, merely pushing it around the corner for a prank will not satisfy this offence. *S 12(1)*

Conveyance

Constructed or adapted for the carriage of a person by land, water or air.

A similar offence exists in relation to pedal cycles but it is not an arrestable offence.
S 12(5)

AGGRAVATED VEHICLE-TAKING ACT 1992
adds S 12A TO THE THEFT ACT 1968.

Provides for obligatory disqualification and endorsement where the above offence under S 12(1) has been committed and, before the vehicle was recovered, the vehicle was driven dangerously or was damaged or was driven in a way which led to personal injury or damage to other property.

Note: These offences only apply in England and Wales (as Theft Act 1968 does not apply to Scotland) – Scots officers should consult Section 178 of the Road Traffic Act 1988; Re: Taking of Motor Vehicles without Consent etc.

VEHICLE INTERFERENCE

S 9 CRIMINAL ATTEMPTS ACT 1981

A person is guilty of this offence if he interferes with

a motor vehicle or trailer

anything carried in or on a motor vehicle or trailer

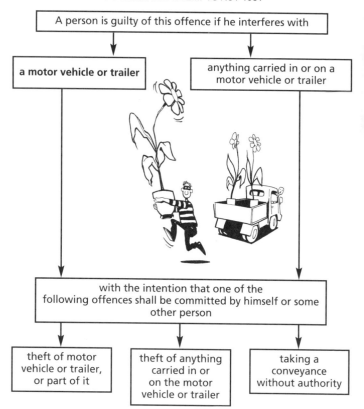

with the intention that one of the following offences shall be committed by himself or some other person

theft of motor vehicle or trailer, or part of it

theft of anything carried in or on the motor vehicle or trailer

taking a conveyance without authority

Any arrest must be in accordance with the Police and Criminal Evidence Act 1984

Note:

1. The above legislation is only applicable to England and Wales.

2. A person may still be guilty of an offence under S 25 of the Road Traffic Act 1988, if, while a motor vehicle is on a road or local authority parking place, he gets onto the vehicle or tampers with the brakes or other parts of its mechanism.

DRINK/DRIVING

ROAD TRAFFIC ACT 1988, S.4 AND 5

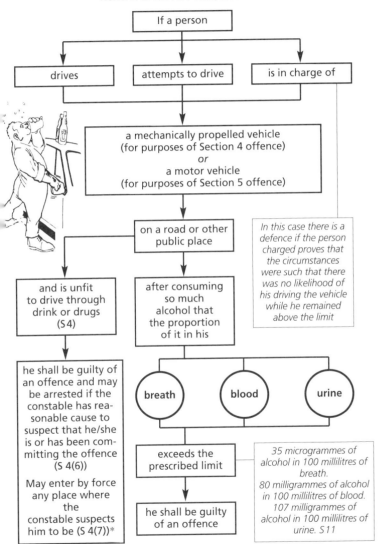

If a person

drives → attempts to drive → is in charge of

a mechanically propelled vehicle
(for purposes of Section 4 offence)
or
a motor vehicle
(for purposes of Section 5 offence)

on a road or other public place

In this case there is a defence if the person charged proves that the circumstances were such that there was no likelihood of his driving the vehicle while he remained above the limit

and is unfit to drive through drink or drugs (S 4)

after consuming so much alcohol that the proportion of it in his

he shall be guilty of an offence and may be arrested if the constable has reasonable cause to suspect that he/she is or has been committing the offence (S 4(6))

May enter by force any place where the constable suspects him to be (S 4(7))*

breath   blood   urine

exceeds the prescribed limit

35 microgrammes of alcohol in 100 millilitres of breath. 80 milligrammes of alcohol in 100 millilitres of blood. 107 milligrammes of alcohol in 100 millilitres of urine. S 11

he shall be guilty of an offence

*Section 4 (7) does not extend to Scotland and nothing in that subsection affects any rule of law in Scotland concerning the right of a concerning the right of a constable to enter any premises for any purpose.

BREATH TESTS

ROAD TRAFFIC ACT 1988 (AS AMENDED BY THE SERIOUS ORGANISED CRIME AND POLICE ACT 2005, AND THE RAILWAYS AND TRANSPORT SAFETY ACT 2003)

POWER TO ADMINISTER PRELIMINARY TESTS (S 6)

If a constable reasonably suspects that a person:

1) is driving, is attempting to drive or is in charge of a motor vehicle on a road or other public place, AND has alcohol or a drug in his body or is under the influence of a drug (S 6(2))
2) has been driving, attempting to drive or in charge of a motor vehicle on a road or other public place while having alcohol or a drug in his body or while unfit to drive because of a drug AND still has alcohol or a drug in his body or is still under the influence of a drug (S 6(3))
3) is or has been driving, attempting to drive or in charge of a motor vehicle on a road or other public place AND has committed a traffic offence while the vehicle was in motion (S 6(4))
4) was driving, attempting to drive or in charge of a motor vehicle at the time an accident occurred owing to the presence of the motor vehicle on a road or other public place (S 6(5))

then the person commits an offence if without reasonable excuse he fails to co-operate with a **preliminary test** required by the constable (who must be in uniform if the requirement is made under S 6(2) to (4) above).

'**Preliminary test**' means a 'preliminary breath test', 'preliminary impairment test' or 'preliminary drug test'. (See later).

Traffic offence means an offence under:
(a) Part 2 of the Public Passenger Vehicles Act 1981 (fitness of PSVs, operators' licences, and regulation and conduct of drivers, inspectors, conductors and passengers)
(b) The Road Traffic Regulation Act 1984 (traffic regulation provisions, crossings and playgrounds, parking places, traffic signs, speed limits, etc.)
(c) The Road Traffic Offenders Act 1988 (other than part 3 – fixed penalties), or
(d) The Road Traffic Act 1988 (other than part 5 – driving instruction).

BREATH TESTS cont
ROAD TRAFFIC ACT 1988 (AS AMENDED BY THE SERIOUS ORGANISED CRIME AND POLICE ACT 2005, AND THE RAILWAYS AND TRANSPORT SAFETY ACT 2003)

PRELIMINARY BREATH TESTS (S 6A)

A specimen of breath is provided to obtain, by means of a device, an indication as to whether the proportion of alcohol in the person's breath or blood is likely to exceed the prescribed limit. Breath tests required under S 6(2) to (4) (see earlier) may be administered only at or near the place where the requirement is imposed. If required under S 6(5) they may be administered either:

(a) at or near the place where the requirement is imposed, or
(b) if the constable thinks it expedient, at a police station specified by the officer.

PRELIMINARY IMPAIRMENT TESTS (S 6B)

This is a procedure whereby the constable administering the test:

(a) observes the person in his performance of tasks specified by the constable, and
(b) makes such other observations of the person's physical state as the constable thinks expedient.

The test may be administered:
(a) at or near the place where the requirement is imposed, or
(b) if the constable thinks it expedient, at a police station specified by the officer.

The constable may administer a test only if he is authorised by the Chief Officer of Police, and he must have regard to the code of practice, which aims to ensure that the test indicates:

(a) whether a person is unfit to drive, and
(b) if he is, whether or not his unfitness is likely to be due to drink or drugs.

It also contains provisions about the giving of approval to carry out tests, and the kind of training and qualification required before authorisation is given.

PRELIMINARY DRUG TESTS (S 6C)

In this procedure a specimen of sweat or saliva is obtained and used, by means of a device, to indicate whether a person has a drug in his body.

BREATH TESTS cont

ROAD TRAFFIC ACT 1988 (AS AMENDED BY THE SERIOUS ORGANISED CRIME AND POLICE ACT 2005, AND THE RAILWAYS AND TRANSPORT SAFETY ACT 2003)

The test may be administered:

(a) at or near the place where the requirement is imposed, or
(b) if the constable thinks it expedient, at a police station specified by the officer.

ARREST (S 6D)

A constable may arrest a person without warrant if, as a result of a preliminary breath test, the constable reasonably suspects that the proportion of alcohol in the person's breath or blood exceeds the prescribed limit (Subs 1).

If specimens of breath have been provided under S 7 this does not prevent the above power of arrest if the constable has reasonable cause to believe that the device used to analyse the specimens has not produced a reliable indication of the proportion of alcohol in the breath of the person. (Subs 1A).

A constable may arrest a person without warrant if:

(a) the person fails to co-operate with a preliminary test under S 6, and
(b) the constable reasonably suspects that the person has alcohol or a drug in his body, or is under the influence of a drug. (Subs 2).

A person arrested under this section may, instead of being taken to a police station, be detained at or near the place where the preliminary test was, or would have been administered, with a view to imposing on him there a requirement under S 7 (Subs 2A).

A person may not be arrested under this section whilst at a hospital as a patient (Subs 3).

Note: Subsections 1A and 2A of section 6D, which were introduced by section 154 of the Serious Organised Crime and Police Act 2005, do not apply to Scotland.

POWER OF ENTRY (S 6E)

A constable may enter any place (using reasonable force if necessary) for the purpose of:

(a) imposing a requirement under S 6(5) following an accident in a case where the constable reasonably suspects that the accident involved the injury of any person, or
(b) arresting a person under S 6D following such an accident.

This section does not extend to Scotland and does not prejudice any rule or enactment about the right of a constable in Scotland to enter any place.

PROVISION OF SPECIMENS FOR ANALYSIS

ROAD TRAFFIC ACT 1988 S 7 (AS AMENDED BY THE SERIOUS ORGANISED
CRIME AND POLICE ACT 2005, AND THE RAILWAYS AND TRANSPORT SAFETY
ACT 2003)

*Due to the fact that the provisions of section 154 of the Serious Organised
Crime and Police Act 2005 have made substantial ammendments to section 7
of the Road Traffic Act 1988, which do not apply to Scotland, the law under
section 7 as it operates in Scotland is provided in the Scottish supplement on
page 337. As a result, the information on pages 276 and 277 is not relevant to
Scots officers.*

When specimens may be required

(1) If investigating one of the following offences under the Road Traffic Act
1988:

(a) causing death by careless driving when under the influence of drink or
drugs (S 3A),

(b) driving or being in charge when under the influence of drink or drugs
(S 4), or

(c) driving or being in charge with alcohol above the limit (S 5),

a constable may require a person to provide:

(a) two specimens of breath for analysis by a device (Subs 1(a)), or

(b) a specimen of blood or urine for laboratory test (Subs 1(b)).

Where specimens may be required

(2)   A requirement to provide specimens of breath can only be made:

    (a)   at a police station

    (b)   at a hospital, or

    (c)   at or near a place where a breath has been administered to obtain
an indication as to whether the amount of alcohol in his breath or
blood is likely to exceed the limit (or would have been administered but for a failure to co-operate).

(2B)   But the constable must be in uniform or requiring a test under S 6(5)
(accident).

(2D)   Where a requirement is made under subsection 1(a) above at a place
other than a police station, such a requirement may subsequently be
made at a police station if:

    (a)   a testing device was not available at that place or it was for any
other reason not practicable to use a device there, or

    (b)   the constable who made the previous requirement has reasonable
cause to believe that the device used has not produced a reliable
indication of the proportion of alcohol in the breath of the person
concerned.

PROVISION OF SPECIMENS FOR ANALYSIS cont

ROAD TRAFFIC ACT 1988 S 7 (AS AMENDED BY THE SERIOUS ORGAN-ISED CRIME AND POLICE ACT 2005, AND THE RAILWAYS AND TRANS-PORT SAFETY ACT 2003)

Circumstances in which blood or urine specimens may be taken

(3) A requirement to provide a specimen of **blood or urine** under sub-section 1(b) above can only be made at a police station or a hospital; and it cannot be made at a police station unless:

(a) the constable has reasonable cause to believe that for medical reasons a specimen of **breath** cannot be provided, or

(b) specimens of breath have not been provided elsewhere and at the time the requirement is made, a breath test device is not available at the police station or it is for any other reason not practicable to use such a device there, or

(c) a breath test device has been used (at the police station or else-where) but the constable has reasonable cause to believe that it has not produced a reliable indication of the proportion of alcohol in the breath of the person, or

(d) as a result of a preliminary drug test, the constable has reason-able cause to believe that the person required to provide a specimen of blood or urine has a drug in his body; or

(e) the offence is one under S 3A (death by careless driving) or S 4 (driving or in charge under the influence) and the constable has been advised by a medical practitioner that the condition of the person might be due to some drug;

but may then be made even though the person has already provided, or been required to provide, two specimens of breath.

Blood or urine?

(4) Where a specimen of blood or urine is to be taken, the question whether it is to be blood or urine is decided by the constable, unless a medical practitioner is of the opinion that for medical rea-sons blood should not be taken, in which case it will be urine.

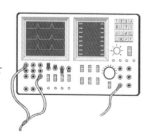

Provision of urine specimen

(5) A specimen of urine shall be provided within 1 hour of the require-ment following the provision of a previous specimen.

PROVISION OF SPECIMENS FOR ANALYSIS cont

ROAD TRAFFIC ACT 1988 S 7 (AS AMENDED BY THE SERIOUS ORGAN-
ISED CRIME AND POLICE ACT 2005, AND THE RAILWAYS AND TRANS-
PORT SAFETY ACT 2003)

Failure to provide specimen

(6) A person who, without reasonable excuse, fails to provide a specimen when required to do so is guilty of an offence.

(7) When requiring a specimen, the constable must warn the person that a failure to provide it may render him liable to prosecution. (S 7)

Specimens of blood taken from persons incapable of consenting (S 7A)

(1) A constable may make a request to a medical practitioner for him to take a specimen of blood from a person irrespective of whether that person consents if:

    (a) the constable would, but for any incapacity of the person to give consent or for any objection under S 9, be entitled under S 7 to require the provision of a specimen for laboratory test;

    (b) it appears to the constable that the person has been involved in an accident that is under investigation, or the circumstances of such an accident;

    (c) it appears to the constable that the person is or may be incapable of giving a valid consent to the taking of a specimen of blood; and

    (d) it appears to the constable that the incapacity is attributable to medical reasons.

(2) A request shall not be made to a medical practitioner:

    (a) who for the time being has any responsibility for the clinical care of the person; or

    (b) other than a police medical practitioner unless:

        (i) it is not reasonably practicable for the request to be made to a police medical practitioner; or

        (ii) it is not reasonably practicable for a police medical practitioner to take the specimen.

(3) A medical practitioner to whom a request is made, if he thinks fit:

    (a) may take a specimen of blood irrespective of the consent of the person; and

    (b) provide the sample to the constable.

(4) Such a specimen shall not be subject to laboratory test unless the person from whom it was taken:

    (a) has been informed that it was taken; and

PROVISION OF SPECIMENS FOR ANALYSIS cont

ROAD TRAFFIC ACT 1988 S 7 (AS AMENDED BY THE SERIOUS ORGAN-
ISED CRIME AND POLICE ACT 2005, AND THE RAILWAYS AND TRANS-
PORT SAFETY ACT 2003)

- (b) has been required by a constable to give his permission for a laboratory test of the specimen; and
- (c) has given his permission.
(5) On requiring a person to give his permission the constable must warn that person that a failure to give the permission may render him liable to prosecution.
(6) A person who, without reasonable excuse, fails to give his permission for a laboratory test of such a specimen is guilty of an offence.

Police medical practitioner means one who is engaged under any agreement to provide medical services for purposes connected with the activities of the police force.

Choice of Specimens of Breath (S 8)

Of any two specimens of breath provided under S 7, that with the lower proportion of alcohol in the breath shall be used and the other shall be disregarded.

If the specimen with the lower proportion of alcohol contains no more than 50 microgrammes of alcohol in 100 millilitres of breath, the person who provided it may claim that it should be replaced by a specimen of blood or urine under S 7(4) (see earlier), in which case, neither specimen of breath shall be used.

If the person who makes the claim was required to provide specimens of breath under S 7 at or near a place mentioned in S 7(2)(c) (see earlier), a constable may arrest him without warrant.*

Hospital Patients (S 9)

(1) While a person is at hospital as a patient he shall not be required to co-operate with a preliminary test or to provide a specimen under S 7 unless the medical practitioner in immediate charge of his case has been notified of the proposal to make the requirement, and:
- (a) if the requirement is then made, it shall be for co-operation with a test administered, or for the provision of a specimen, at the hospital but,
- (b) if the medical practitioner objects on the ground specified in subs (2) below, the requirement shall not be made.

As section 7(2)(c) is not applicable to Scotland, the power of arrest mentioned in the aforementioned paragraph does not extend to Scotland.

PROVISION OF SPECIMENS FOR ANALYSIS cont

ROAD TRAFFIC ACT 1988 S 7 (AS AMENDED BY THE SERIOUS ORGAN-
ISED CRIME AND POLICE ACT 2005, AND THE RAILWAYS AND TRANS-
PORT SAFETY ACT 2003)

(1A)   While a person is in hospital as a patient, no specimen of blood shall be taken from him under S 7A and he shall not be required to give his permission for a laboratory test of a specimen taken under that section unless the medical practitioner in immediate charge of his case:
  (a)   has been notified of the proposal to take the specimen or to make the requirement; and
  (b)   has not objected on the ground specified in subs (2).

(2)   The ground on which the medical practitioner may object is:
  (a)   in a case falling within subs (1), that the requirement or the provision of the specimen or (if one is required) the warning required by S 7(A) would be prejudicial to the proper care and treatment of the patient; and
  (b)   in the case falling within subs (1A), that the taking of the specimen, the requirement or the warning required by S 7A(5) would be so prejudicial.

Detention of Persons (S 10)

(1)   A person required under S 7 or 7A to provide a specimen of breath, blood or urine may afterwards be detained at a police station (or, if the specimen was provided otherwise than at a police station, arrested and taken to and detained at a police station*) if a constable has reasonable grounds for believing that, were that person then driving or attempting to drive, he would commit an offence under S 4 or 5.

(2)   Subs 1 above does not apply if it ought reasonably to appear to the constable that there is no likelihood of his driving or attempting to drive whilst his ability is impaired or the proportion of alcohol exceeds the limit.

(2A)   A person who is at hospital as a patient shall not be arrested and taken from there to a police station if it would be prejudicial to his proper care and treatment. *This paragraph does not apply in Scotland.*

(3)   Where drugs are involved, the question of impairment must be subject to advice from a medical practitioner.

*Information contained within brackets does not apply to Scotland. See Supplement for Scotland.

SPEED LIMITS

ROAD TRAFFIC REGULATION ACT 1984

The maximum speed at which a vehicle can travel depends upon the road concerned and the type of vehicle

Road
If street lights are provided and are placed not more than 200 yards apart, speed is restricted to 30 mph
S 82

Vehicle
Section 86 makes it an offence to drive in excess of the speed specified on the following pages in relation to a vehicle of that class

In this case, evidence of the absence of derestriction signs shall be evidence that it was a restricted road
S 85(5)

In Scotland, if there is a system of carriageway lighting where lamps are placed not more than 185 m apart, and road is of a class or type specified in regulations by Secretary of State, then speed is restricted to 30 mph

Evidence
Evidence of the opinion of one witness is not enough to secure a conviction
S 89(2)

If there is no system of street lighting not more than 200 yards (185 m in Scotland) apart then there must be traffic signs

Employers
An employer may be guilty of procuring or inciting an employee to commit an offence if he publishes or issues a time-table or schedule or gives directions to complete a journey within such a time as cannot be achieved without exceeding the speed limit. S 89(4)

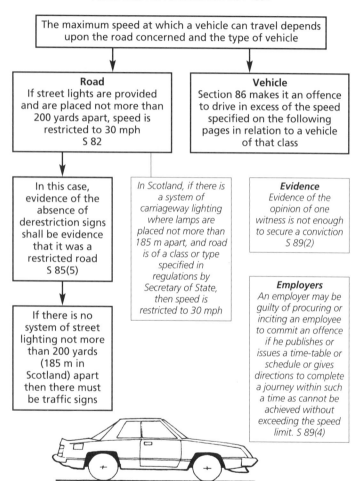

Exemptions
No statutory speed limit applies to any vehicle being used for fire brigade, ambulance or police purposes if observance would be likely to hinder the use of the vehicle for the purpose it was being used on that occasion. The exemption also applies to vehicles being used for Serious Organised Crime Agency purposes while being driven by a person who is trained to drive the vehicle at high speeds (or is being trained to do so).

SPEED LIMITS cont

ROAD TRAFFIC REGULATION ACT 1984 S 86 AND SCHED. 6

motorway   *dual carriageway*   *other road*

Cars, small vans and dual-purpose vehicles

This limit was set by the 70 mph, 60 mph and 50 mph (Temporary Speed Limit) Order 1977, which was continued indefinitely by SI 1978 No 1548. The limit refers to all vehicles unless a lesser one applies.

(70) (70) (60)

Passenger vehicle, motor caravan or dual purpose vehicle without trailer

uw over 3.05 tonnes or adapted to carry more than 8 passengers.
a) Overall length n/e 12 m

(70) (60) (50)

b) Overall length over 12 m
Note: Coaches which could exceed the motorway limit must be fitted with a governor.

(60) (60) (50)

Invalid carriage

(N/A) (20) (20)

Passenger vehicle, motor caravan, car-derived van or dual purpose vehicle drawing one trailer

(60) (60) (50)

(A 'car-derived van' is a goods vehicle derivative of a passenger vehicle and which has a maximum laden weight not over 2000 kg.)

As above, drawing more than one trailer

(40) (20) (20)

SPEED LIMITS cont

ROAD TRAFFIC REGULATION ACT 1984 S 86 AND SCHED. 6

Goods vehicle

With max laden weight n/e 7.5 tonnes but which is not an articulated vehicle, or is not drawing a trailer, or is not a car-derived van.

(A 'car-derived van' is a goods vehicle derivative of a passenger vehicle and which has a maximum laden weight not over 2000 kg.)

Drawing 1 trailer (other than a car-derived van) – aggregate max. laden weight of both n/e 7.5 tonnes.

Goods vehicle other than a car-derived van drawing more than 1 trailer.

Goods vehicle max. laden weight over 7.5 tonnes not drawing trailer

Goods vehicle drawing 1 trailer with aggregate max. laden weight of vehicle and trailer over 7.5 tonnes.

Articulated goods vehicle

Max laden weight n/e 7.5 tonnes.

Max laden weight over 7.5 tonnes

SPEED LIMITS cont

ROAD TRAFFIC REGULATION ACT 1984 S 86 AND SCHED. 6

Motor tractor

Light or heavy locomotive with required springs and wings (other than industrial tractor).

(40) (30) (30)

As above drawing 1 trailer also complying with springs and wings.

(40) (30) (30)

Vehicle and/or trailer as above not complying with springs and wings.

(20) (20) (20)

Vehicle (and trailer if drawn) where at least one wheel has a resilient tyre and all other (if any) have pneumatic tyres.

(20) (20) (20)

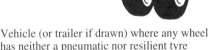

Vehicle (or trailer if drawn) where any wheel has neither a pneumatic nor resilient tyre *(does not apply if track-laying)*.

(5) (5) (5)

Works truck

(18) (18) (18)

Industrial tractor

(N/A) (18) (18)

Agricultural motor vehicle

(40) (40) (40)

Vehicle displaying 'Low Platform Trailer' plate (LL). *REG 100A RV (CON & USE) REGS 1986*

(40) (40) (40)

Vehicle displaying 'Restricted Speed Vehicle' plate (50). *REG 100A RV (CON & USE) REGS 1986*

(50) (50) (50)

SPEED LIMITERS – BUSES

THE ROAD VEHICLES (CONSTRUCTION AND USE) REGULATIONS 1986
REGS. 36A & 70A

A speed limiter is a device designed to limit the maximum speed of a motor vehicle by controlling the power output of the engine. They must be fitted to buses in the following circumstances:

Date of first use	Weight (tonnes)	Maximum Speed Exceeding (km/h)	Speed calibrated to (km/h)	Effective from
On or after 1.4.74 and before 1.1.88	N/A	112.65	112.65	Currently applies
On or after 1.1.88	Over 7.5	100	100	Currently applies
Before 1.1.05	Over 10	100	100	1.1.05
Before 1.10.01	Over 7.5 but not over 10	100	100	1.1.05
On or after 1.1.05	Over 5 but not over 10	100	100	1.1.05
On or after 1.1.05	Not over 5	100	100	If used solely for national transport operations, 1.1.08, otherwise, 1.1.05
On or after 1.10.01 and before 1.1.05	Complies with 88/77/EEC & not over 10	100	100	If used for both national and international transport operations, 1.1.06. If used only for national operations, 1.1.07

Requirements:
1. the limiter must be sealed by an authorised sealer to prevent improper interference or adjustment and against any interruption of its power supply
2. maintained in good and efficient working order
3. must be calibrated to the set speed as above
4. must comply with the appropriate British Standard, Community Directive or equivalent standard.

Exemptions. This regulation does not apply to a vehicle:
1. being taken for a limiter to be installed, calibrated, repaired or replaced
2. completing a journey during which the limiter has accidentally ceased to function.
3. owned by the Secretary of State for Defence and used for naval, military or air force purposes
4. used for naval, military or air force purposes while being driven by a erson subject to the orders of a member of the armed forces, or
5. used for fire and rescue authority purposes or in the exercise of any function of a relevant authority for ambulance or police purposes.

Plates. A plate must be fitted in a conspicuous position in the driving compartment of the vehicle, clearly and indelibly marked with the speed at which the limiter has been set.
International means outside the UK.
National means within the UK.
Transport operations means transport of passengers in a vehicle designed for such purpose.

SPEED LIMITERS – GOODS VEHICLES
THE ROAD VEHICLES (CONSTRUCTION AND USE) REGULATIONS 1986
REGS 36B & 70A

A speed limiter is a device designed to limit the maximum speed of a motor vehicle by controlling the power output of the engine. They must be fitted to goods vehicles in the following circumstances:

Date of first use	Weight (tonnes)	Maximum Speed Exceeding	Speed calibrated to	Effective from
On or after 1.8.92 and before 1.1.05	Over 7.5 but not over 12	60 mph	60 mph	Currently applies
On or after 1.1.88	Over 12	90 km/h	90 km/h	Currently applies
On or after 1.1.05	Over 3.5 but not over 12	90 km/h	90km/h	If maximum weight does not exceed 7.5 tonnes and used solely for national transport operations, 1.1.08, otherwise 1.1.05.
On or after 1.10.01 and before 1.1.05, but is not a vehicle included in the top row of this table.	Complies with 88/77/EEC and is over 3.5 but not over 12	90 km/h	90 km/h	If used for both national and international transport operations, 1.1.06, but if used solely for national operations, 1.1.07.

Requirements: See previous page.

Exemptions. This regulation does not apply to a vehicle:
1. being taken for a limiter to be installed, calibrated, repaired or replaced; or
2. completing a journey during which the limiter has accidentally ceased to function;
3. owned by Secretary of State and used for naval, military or air force purposes;
4. driven for naval, military or air force purposes by a person under their orders;
5. being used for fire, ambulance or police purposes; or
6. used only in passing between lands occupied by the keeper of the vehicle for not more than 6 miles per week.

Plates. A plate must be fitted in a conspicuous position in the driving compartment of the vehicle, clearly and indelibly marked with the speed at which the limiter has been set.

International means outside the UK.

National means within the UK.

Transport operations means transport of goods in a vehicle designed for such purpose.

CARRIAGE OF DANGEROUS GOODS
CARRIAGE OF DANGEROUS GOODS AND USE OF TRANSPORTABLE PRESSURE EQUIPMENT
REGULATIONS 2007 AND THE EUROPEAN AGREEMENT CONCERNING INTERNATIONAL
CARRIAGE OF DANGEROUS GOODS BY ROAD 2007 (ADR 2007)

Introduction
Explosives, corrosives, flammables and dangerous goods such as these pose risks
to people and the environment when transported. In an attempt to reduce such
risks, and to effectively and safely deal with accidents or incidents, both GB and
international legislation has been introduced.

The 2007 regulations impose requirements and prohibitions relating to the carriage
of dangerous goods, and the use of transportable pressure equipment. They imple-
ment EC Council Directives and the European Agreement concerning International
Carriage of Dangerous Goods by Road 2007 (ADR 2007). Clearly, the quantity of
information contained in ADR can not be reflected here. However, wherever possible the reader is referred to the particular section of ADR. In the references below,
ADR 1.2.1 for example, refers to Part 1, Chapter 2, Section 1 of ADR.

Dangerous Goods (ADR 1.2.1). These are defined as substances and articles
the carriage of which is prohibited by ADR, or authorised only under the conditions prescribed therein.

Classes (ADR 2.1.1.1). Goods are divided according to their properties into 9
classes which are:
1. Explosives;
2. Gases: compressed liquefied or dissolved under pressure;
3. Flammable liquids;
4. 1. Flammable solids;
   2. Substances liable to spontaneous combustion;
   3. Substances which, in contact with water, emit flammable gases;
5. 1. Oxidising substances;
   2. Organic peroxides;
6. 1. Toxic substances;
   2. Infectious substances;
7. Radioactive material;
8. Corrosive substances;
9. Miscellaneous dangerous substances and articles.

Classification of Goods (Reg. 47 & ADR 2.1–2.3). Before consigning goods
the consignor must:
- classify the goods in accordance with the general requirements of ADR 2.1;
- assign the appropriate UN number, state their name and description and the
  packing group in accordance with the Dangerous Goods List (DGL) (see below);
- comply with any specific provision as indicated in the DGL relating to the
  goods; and
- classify the goods in accordance with the relevant test methods set out in
  ADR 2.2 & 2.3.

The Dangerous Goods List (Reg. 49 & ADR 3.2). ADR 3.2 Table A is the
Dangerous Goods List (DGL) which lists all dangerous goods in UN number
order. It also contains, in relation to each entry, the name, class, classification
code, packing group, labelling requirements, any special provisions, and quantity
limitations.

CARRIAGE OF DANGEROUS GOODS – EXEMPTIONS

CARRIAGE OF DANGEROUS GOODS AND USE OF TRANSPORTABLE PRESSURE EQUIPMENT REGULATIONS 2007 AND ADR 2007

Exemptions (ADR 1.1.3, 1.1.4). There are a number of exemptions from the Regulations and ADR. These can range from total exemption to partial or conditional. They can be conveniently grouped as follows:

Nature of the Transport Operation (ADR 1.1.3.1). Subject to certain conditions, ADR does not apply to:

- carriage by private individuals where goods are packaged for retail sale and intended for their personal or domestic use, or for leisure or sporting activities provided that measures have been taken to prevent any leakage of contents. Dangerous goods in IBCs (Intermediate Bulk Containers), large packagings or tanks are not considered to be packaged for retail sale.
- machinery or equipment not specifically listed in the Dangerous Goods List (ADR Part 3) and which contain dangerous goods; provided that measures have been taken to prevent any leakage of contents
- carriage of up to 450 litres per packing, and providing measure have been taken to prevent leakage (except class 7 goods) by enterprises ancillary to their main activity;
- carriage by, or under supervision of, the emergency services, in particular breakdown vehicles carrying other vehicles carrying dangerous goods; and
- emergency transport to save human lives or protect the environment.
- uncleaned empty static storage vessels (subject to conditions).

Gases (ADR 1.1.3.2). The following gases are exempt from ADR:

- in the tanks of a vehicle, for its propulsion or operation of its equipment;
- in the tanks of a vehicle being transported;
- groups O & A (ADR 2.2.2.1);
- in equipment used for the operation of the vehicle, eg fire extinguishers;
- in special equipment of the vehicle, eg cooling systems
- in foodstuffs or beverages.

Liquid Fuels (ADR 1.1.3.3). ADR does not apply to the carriage of liquid fuels:

- in the tanks of a vehicle, for its propulsion or operation of its equipment, provided the total quantity does not exceed 1500 litres in fixed tanks and 60 litres in portable containers, per transport unit;
- in the tanks of vehicles or other conveyance (eg a boat) and being carried as a load.

Special Provisions and Limited Quantities (ADR 1.1.3.4).

- Part 3 of ADR lists all dangerous articles and substances packed in limited quantities (The Dangerous Goods List). When a special provision appears in the list against the entry for a particular article or substance, a partial or total exemption will apply in accordance with that provision (ADR 3.2 & 3.3);
- Certain dangerous goods packed in limited quantities may be exempt if certain conditions are met (ADR 3.4).

Empty Uncleaned Packagings (ADR 1.1.3.5). Such packagings which have contained substances of classes 2, 3, 4.1, 5.1, 6.1, 8 & 9 are not subject to ADR if adequate measures have been taken to nullify the hazard.

CARRIAGE OF DANGEROUS GOODS – EXEMPTIONS cont

CARRIAGE OF DANGEROUS GOODS AND USE OF TRANSPORTABLE PRESSURE EQUIPMENT REGULATIONS 2007 AND ADR 2007

Quantities Carried per Transport Unit (ADR 1.1.3.6) In Chapter 3.2 of ADR dangerous goods are assigned to transport categories 0, 1, 2, 3 or 4. The maximum quantity (not counting those exempted by 1.1.3.2 – 1.1.3.5 above) of goods per transport unit must not exceed the limits in the table on the following page.

Transport Category	Substances or Articles	Max. Total Quantity per Transport Unit*
0	Class 1: 1.1A/1.1L/1.2L/1.3L/1.4L and UN No.0190 Class 3: UN No. 3343 Class 4.2: Substances belonging to packing group 1 Class 4.3: UN Nos. 1183, 1242, 1295, 1340, 1390, 1403, 1928, 2813, 2965, 2968, 2988, 3129, 3130, 3131, 3134, 3148, 3396, 3398 and 3399 Class 5.1: UN No. 2426 Class 6.1: UN Nos. 1051, 1600, 1613, 1614, 2312, 3250 and 3294 Class 6.2: UN Nos. 2814 and 2900 Class 7: UN Nos. 2912 to 2919, 2977, 2978 and 3321 to 3333 Class 8: UN No. 2215 (MALEIC ANHYDRIDE, MOLTEN) Class 9 UN Nos. 2315, 3151, 3152 and 3432 and apparatus containing such substances or mixtures Empty uncleaned packagings, except those classified under UN No. 2908, having contained substances classified in this transport category	0
1	Substances and articles belonging to packing group I and not classified in transport category 0 Substances and articles of the following classes: Class 1: 1.1B to 1.1J[a]/ 1.2B to 1.2J/1.3C/1.3G/1.3H/1.3J1.5D[a] Class 2: groups T, TC[a], TO, TF, TOC and TFC aerosols: groups C, CO, FC, T, TF, TC, TO, TFC and TOC Class 4.1: UN Nos. 3221 to 3224 and 3231 to 3240 Class 5.2: UN Nos. 3101 to 3104 and 3111 to 3120	20

CARRIAGE OF DANGEROUS GOODS – EXEMPTIONS cont

CARRIAGE OF DANGEROUS GOODS AND USE OF TRANSPORTABLE PRESSURE EQUIPMENT REGULATIONS 2007 AND ADR 2007

Transport Category	Substances or Articles	Max. Total Quantity per Transport Unit*
2	Substances or articles belonging to packing group II and not classified in transport categories 0, 1 or 4 Substances of the following classes: Class 1: 1.4B to 1.4G and 1.6N Class 2: group F, aerosols: group F Class 4.1: UN Nos. 3225 to 3230 Class 5.2: UN Nos. 3105 to 3110 Class 6.1: substances and articles belonging to packing group III Class 9: UN No. 3245	333
3	Substances or articles belonging to packing group III and not classified in transport categories 0, 2 or 4 Substances and articles of the following classes: Class 2: groups A and O, aerosols: groups A and O Class 3: UN No. 3473 Class 8: UN Nos. 2794, 2795, 2800 and 3028 Class 9: UN Nos. 2990 and 3072	1000
4	Class 1: 1.4S Class 4.1: UN Nos. 1331, 1345, 1944, 1945, 2254 and 2623 Class 4.2: UN Nos. 1361 and 1362 packing group III Class 7: UN Nos. 2908 to 2911 Class 9: UN No. 3268 Empty uncleaned packagings, having contained dangerous goods, except for those classified in transport category 0	**Unlimited**

[a]For UN Nos. 0081, 0082, 0084, 0241, 0331, 0332, 0482, 1005 and 1017, the total maximum quantity per transport unit shall be 50 kg.

CARRIAGE OF DANGEROUS GOODS – EXEMPTIONS cont

CARRIAGE OF DANGEROUS GOODS AND USE OF TRANSPORTABLE PRESSURE EQUIPMENT REGULATIONS 2007 AND ADR 2007

* This means:

for articles, gross mass in kilograms;

for solids, liquefied gases, refrigerated liquefied gases and dissolved gases, net mass in kilograms;

for liquids and compressed gases, nominal capacity of receptacles in litres.

Where dangerous goods of different transport categories are carried in the same transport unit, the sum of-
- the quantity of substances and articles of transport category 1 multiplied by '50';
- the quantity of substances and articles of transport category 1 referred to in note ª above, multiplied by '20';
- the quantity of substances and articles of transport category 2 multiplied by '3'; and
- the quantity of substances and articles of transport category 3;

shall not exceed "1000".

Dangerous goods exempted in accordance with 1.1.3.2 to 1.1.3.5 (see earlier) shall not be taken into account

Where the quantity of dangerous goods does not exceed the above values, the following provisions of ADR will not apply:

Provision	Covering
1.10	Security measures or precautions to minimise theft or misuse of dangerous goods that may cause danger
5.3	Placarding and marking of containers etc.
5.4.3	Documentation – instructions in writing
7.2, except V5 & V8 of 7.2.4	Carriage in packages
CV1 of 7.5.11	Prohibitions on loading and unloading in public places
Part 8 except 8.1.2.1(a). 8.1.4.2 – 8.1.4.5, 8.2.3, 8.3.3, 8.3.4, 8.3.5, 8.4, & S1(3), S1(6), S2(1), S4, S14–S21 of 8.5	Vehicle crews, equipment, operation and documentation and approval of vehicles
Part 9	

Transport Chain (ADR 1.1.4.2). Goods which do not entirely meet the requirements of ADR but conform with the requirements of the International Maritime Dangerous Goods Code (IMDG), may be accepted for carriage in a transport chain including maritime or air carriage provided they comply with the requirements of IMDG.

CARRIAGE OF DANGEROUS GOODS – EXEMPTIONS cont.

CARRIAGE OF DANGEROUS GOODS AND USE OF TRANSPORTABLE PRESSURE EQUIPMENT
REGULATIONS 2007 AND ADR 2007

The 2007 Regulations give further exemptions. These include-

1. **Special authorisations.** Where carriage takes place wholly within GB written authority may be issued by the Secretary of State (for all classes of dangerous goods) or the Health and Safety Executive (only for class 1 goods) to carry for a limited time dangerous goods contrary to the prohibitions or requirements arising out of these regulations. The authorisation will set out the carriage which is authorised, the reason for the authorisation being issued, and the period of validity. (Reg. 9).

2. **Armed Forces.** Where certain class 6.2 goods or certain class 9 goods are carried in an armed forces vehicle or train they are exempt from the requirements of Part 2 of these regulations (ADR) and the additional requirements of Part 5. Similarly there is exemption from a number of requirements where the goods are carried on a vehicle used in connection with training on a special occasion which has been notified to the police and fire and rescue authority (Reg. 10).

3. **The Channel Tunnel.** The requirements of Part 2 of these regulations (ADR) and the additional requirements of Part 5 do not apply to the carriage of dangerous goods on any part of the Channel Tunnel system (Reg. 11).

4. **Certain Vehicles.** The requirements of Part 2 of these regulations (ADR) and the additional requirements of Part 5 do not apply to the carriage of dangerous goods on a vehicle which is not: a trailer; not a motor vehicle (complete or incomplete); or which is a vehicle which runs on rails; is an agricultural or forestry tractor; or is mobile machinery; or a trailer being towed by any such vehicle (Reg. 12).

5. **Enclosed Areas.** The requirements of Part 2 of these regulations (ADR) and the additional requirements of Part 5 do not apply to the carriage of dangerous goods if the carriage is wholly within the perimeter of an enclosed area (Reg. 13).

6. **Crossing Public Roads.** The requirements of Part 2 of these regulations (ADR) and the additional requirements of Part 5 do not apply to the carriage of classes 2 to 6, 8 or 9 goods being delivered between private premises and a vehicle in the immediate vicinity of the premises; or passing between one part of private premises and another part of private premises, situated in the immediate vicinity of those premises, where both parts are occupied by the same person, even if those parts are separated by a road. Where class 1 or 7 goods are being carried, some provisions will still apply (Reg. 14).

7. **Old Tanks.** Regs. 52 (use of tanks) and 60 (testing) will not apply to tanks, pressure receptacles for a battery-vehicle, or pressure receptacles for a multiple element gas container (MEGC) constructed on or before 9/5/04 and used wholly within GB (Reg. 15).

CARRIAGE OF DANGEROUS GOODS – EXEMPTIONS cont.

CARRIAGE OF DANGEROUS GOODS AND USE OF TRANSPORTABLE PRESSURE EQUIPMENT REGULATIONS 2007 AND ADR 2007

8. **Old Pressure Receptacles.** These are cylinders, tubes and cryogenic receptacles constructed before 30/06/03; and other pressure receptacles constructed before 9/5/04 and intended to be used wholly within GB Regs 51 & 55 (use and testing) do not apply (Reg. 16).

9. **Liquefied Gas.** Regs 51, 52 & 60 (use and testing) do not apply but other standards set up by the GB competent authority may have to be met (Reg. 17).

10. **Commercial Products containing Radioactive Material.** The requirements of Part 2 of these regulations (ADR) and the additional requirements of Part 5 do not apply to the carriage in a vehicle of not more than (a) 500 smoke detectors for domestic use each with activity not exceeding 40 kBq; or (b) five gaseous tritium light devices each with activity not exceeding 10 GBq (Reg. 18).

11. **Class 1 Goods.** The load threshold table (see earlier) is amended so that the quantities of Class 1 goods which may be carried are (Reg. 19):

1A	Class 1: 1.1B to 1.1J/1.2B to 1.2J/1.3G/1.3H/1.3J/1.5D	50
2A	Class 1: 1.4B to 1.4G and 1.6N	500

12. **UN0335 Fireworks.** Special provisions do not apply if the net explosive mass per transport unit does not exceed 4000 kg provided the net explosive mass per vehicle does not exceed 3000 kg (Reg. 20).

CARRIAGE OF DANGEROUS GOODS – EXEMPTIONS cont.

CARRIAGE OF DANGEROUS GOODS AND USE OF TRANSPORTABLE PRESSURE EQUIPMENT
REGULATIONS 2007 AND ADR 2007

However, where class 1 goods are being carried by individuals for private use, the regulations will not apply provided the net mass of explosives on a transport unit does not exceed (a) in the case of fireworks, 50 kg; and (b) in any other case, 30 kg, and the individual has taken all precautions to prevent risk, and there is no unauthorised access to the goods. If the vehicle is being used to carry passengers for hire or reward the net mass of explosives carried by a passenger may not exceed 2 kg provided they are kept with that person and kept properly packed (Regs. 86 & 89).

13. **Metal Drums and Metal Intermediate Bulk Containers (IBCs).** Reg. 39 (approval for carriage and markings) does not apply to a drum or IBC exceeding 50 litres in capacity and which was manufactured (a) less than 15 years before consignment; and (b) before 1/7/95 (Reg. 21).

14. **Alcohol in Wooden Casks.** Regs. 39 (safety obligations), 51 (use of packaging) and 53 (marking and labelling) do not apply to wooden casks of not more than 1000 litres capacity; carried in a closed vehicle; no other goods are being carried on the transport unit; and the transport unit complies with Reg. 91 and Part 1 of Sched. 7 (placards, marks and plates) (Reg. 22).

15. **Alternative to Orange-coloured Plates for Class 7 Goods** (Reg. 23). Where
    (a) class 7 goods are carried by road;
    (b) the packages being carried only contain class 7 goods that are (i) fissile excepted; (ii) not fissile; or (iii) a combination of (i) and (ii);
    (c) the transport unit has a maximum permissible mass which does not exceed 3.5 tonnes;
    (d) the number of packages does not exceed 10; and
    (e) the sum of the transport indexes of the packages does not exceed three,

a notice complying with the below conditions may be displayed instead of the orange-coloured plate markings which would otherwise be required by ADR 5.3.2.

The conditions are-
    (a) the notice shall include the words (in capital letters as indicated)-
        (i) 'This vehicle is carrying RADIOACTIVE MATERIAL'; and
        (ii) 'In the case of accident get in touch at once with THE POLICE';
    (b) the capital letters in the word 'RADIOACTIVE' shall be not less than 12 mm high and all other capital letters in the notice shall be not less than 5 mm high;

CARRIAGE OF DANGEROUS GOODS – EXEMPTIONS cont.

CARRIAGE OF DANGEROUS GOODS AND USE OF TRANSPORTABLE PRESSURE EQUIPMENT REGULATIONS 2007 AND ADR 2007

(c) the notice shall state the name, address and telephone number of a person capable of providing advice that would be of assistance in an emergency;

(d) all lettering on the notice shall be black, bold and legible;

(e) all lettering on the notice shall be embossed or stamped; and

(f) the notice shall be-

   (i) not less than 12 cm square;

   (ii) fireproof to the extent that the words on the notice shall remain legible after exposure to a fire involving the vehicle;

   (iii) securely posted in the vehicle in a position where it is plainly visible to the driver, but does not obstruct his view of the road;

   (iv) displayed only when the vehicle is carrying radioactive material.

16. **International Transport Operations.** This means the carriage of goods, including by more than one mode of transport, from consignor to consignee where that carriage takes place in more than one state. In such cases, the derogations from these regulations contained in Regulations 14 to 34 (miscellaneous exceptions) and 91 (plating and marking for carriage within GB) do not apply. But the following regulations will apply if delivering goods for onward carriage to, or carrying goods following arrival from, an airport or harbour, provided the operation takes place entirely within GB: Reg. 19 (Load threshold for class 1 goods), Reg. 20 (UN 0335 Fireworks), Reg. 23 (Alternative to orange-coloured plates for class 7 goods), Reg. 29 (Quantities of class 1 explosives), Reg. 31 (Exemption from fire equipment for certain class 7 goods), Reg. 33 (Supervision of vehicles carrying class 1 goods), and Reg. 34 (Construction requirements of vehicles constructed before 1.1.97) (Reg 35).

17. **Packages in Limited Quantities.** Where (a) goods are carried in packages in limited quantities (as per the Dangerous Goods List), (b) the quantities do not exceed (i) 30 kgs or litres per type, colour, strength or inner package size, and (ii) a total of 333 kgs or litres per transport unit, and (c) the goods have been removed from their outer packaging for delivery to a retailer or end-user, then Regs. 53 and 54 do not apply in respect of the requirement for markings to be affixed.

CARRIAGE OF DANGEROUS GOODS – EXEMPTIONS cont.

CARRIAGE OF DANGEROUS GOODS AND USE OF TRANSPORTABLE PRESSURE EQUIPMENT REGULATIONS 2007 AND ADR 2007

However, this exemption does not apply to goods in class 1 (explosives), 4.2 (spontaneous combustion substances), 6.2 (infectious substances) or 7 (radioactive material) (Reg. 26).

CARRIAGE OF DANGEROUS GOODS – GENERAL REQUIREMENTS

CARRIAGE OF DANGEROUS GOODS AND USE OF TRANSPORTABLE PRESSURE EQUIPMENT
REGULATIONS 2007 AND ADR 2007

Training (Reg. 38). Any person involved in the carriage of dangerous goods must ensure that he and his employees responsible for such carriage eg loaders, unloaders and freight forwarders, receive the required training (but not drivers who have received training under Reg. 64). Such training must be documented in accordance with regulations.

Driver Training (Reg. 64 & ADR 8.2.1 & 8.5). The carrier must ensure that drivers of vehicles over 3.5 tonnes carrying dangerous goods, drivers of tank vehicles, and drivers of vehicles carrying class 1 dangerous goods (explosives) or certain class 7 material, has received training in accordance with ADR and holds a vocational training certificate stating that he has attended such training and has passed an examination.

Safety (Reg. 39 & ADR 1.4). The carrier must comply with all general safety measures and those particular safety measures which apply to him. Also, anyone involved in the carriage of dangerous goods, such as loaders, unloaders, packers, fillers and tank container operators, must take any necessary action to avoid the consequences of foreseeable danger and notify the emergency services where there is an immediate risk.

Safety Advisers (Reg. 43 & ADR 1.8.3.1, & 1.8.3.3 – 1.8.3.9). Any carrier, filler or loader involved in the carriage of dangerous goods must comply with the provisions relating to the appointment and duties of safety advisers, whose duty it is to ensure that all activities are conducted in accordance with safety requirements. But a person whose main or secondary activity does not relate to the carriage of dangerous goods, does not need to appoint a safety adviser. Nor does one need to be appointed if the carriage of goods is in quantities less than specified amounts.

Accidents or Incidents (Reg. 44 & ADR 1.8.5.1 & 1.8.5.3). Where a serious accident or incident takes place during the carriage of dangerous goods, the carrier must report it to the Department for Transport and comply with specified reporting procedures.

Prohibition of Certain Dangerous Goods (Reg. 48 & ADR 2.2). Carriers must not accept any goods for carriage if they are prohibited by ADR, eg Class 3 substances which form peroxides easily, nor must they carry such goods in a manner contrary to any requirement.

Packaging (Reg. 51 & ADR 4.1). The packer or consignor must ensure that the goods are packed in accordance with the specified packing provisions. Goods must be packed in packings strong enough to withstand the shocks and loadings encountered during carriage.

CARRIAGE OF DANGEROUS GOODS – GENERAL REQUIREMENTS cont

CARRIAGE OF DANGEROUS GOODS AND USE OF TRANSPORTABLE PRESSURE EQUIPMENT
REGULATIONS 2007 AND ADR 2007

Marking and Labelling (Reg. 53 & ADR 5.1, 5.2, & 5.5). The packer or consignor must ensure that the goods are marked and labelled in accordance with requirements of ADR, and that the corresponding placards, marks, plates and hazard identification numbers are displayed on the vehicle. The appropriate documentation must be carried on the vehicle. These are discussed in detail on the following pages.

Construction and Testing (Regs. 54–57). All packaging must be manufactured, reconditioned, tested and marked in accordance with requirements. Similar provisions apply to pressure receptacles, aerosol dispensers, gas cartridges, tanks, battery-vehicles, battery wagons, multiple-element gas containers, infectious substances, and radioactive material.

Carriage, Loading, Unloading and Handling (Reg. 62). The carrier or loader of goods carried in large containers, portable tanks, tank-containers or packages, must ensure that the requirements of ADR in relation to carriage, loading, unloading and handling are met. The carrier or filler of a vehicle, wagon, container or tank must ensure that such carriage is authorised by ADR and all requirements are met.

Construction and Approval of Vehicles (Reg. 65). The carrier must ensure that any vehicle carrying dangerous goods complies with the requirements of ADR relating to the construction, equipment and approval of vehicles applicable to the type of vehicle, carriage and goods in question.

Transportable Pressure Equipment (Regs. 72–80). This means a pressure receptacle, battery-vehicle, battery-wagon, multiple element gas container or tank intended to be used to carry class 2 goods (see above), stabilised hydrogen cyanide, anhydrous fluoride or hydrofluoric acid. All transportable pressure equipment (including valves if fitted) must bear a conformity marking, the number of the assessing body and the required markings. They must be periodically inspected and suitably so marked.

Class 1 Goods – Attendants and Security (Regs. 81, 83 & 85–87). When carrying class 1 goods (explosives) in a transport unit the driver must be accompanied by an attendant to ensure the security of the goods when the vehicle is not parked. The attendant must have received suitable training and have written security instructions. Such goods must be segregated from any persons carried on the vehicle, in a separate compartment. Where passengers are being carried for hire or reward a person may only carry a maximum of 2 kg net mass of the weaker types e.g. cartridges and fireworks.

CARRIAGE OF DANGEROUS GOODS – GENERAL REQUIREMENTS cont

CARRIAGE OF DANGEROUS GOODS AND USE OF TRANSPORTABLE PRESSURE EQUIPMENT REGULATIONS 2007 AND ADR 2007

Keeping of Information (Reg. 90). Where regulations require that a transport document accompanies the goods (see later), the carrier must keep these records for at least 3 months after the completion of the journey.

Trailers (ADR 8.1.1). Transport units loaded with dangerous goods may not draw more than one trailer (or semi-trailer).

Fire-fighting equipment (ADR 8.1.4 & 8.3.2). Every transport unit carrying dangerous goods must carry at least one portable fire extinguisher with a capacity of at least 2 kg suitable for engine or cab fires and additional portable extinguishers as follows:
(a) max. permitted mass over 7.5 tonnes – 1 or more with a minimum capacity of 12 kg of which at least 1 has a minimum capacity of 6 kg;
(b) between 3.5 and 7.5 tonnes – 1 or more with a minimum capacity of 8 kg of which at least 1 has a minimum capacity of 6 kg;
(c) up to 3.5 tonnes – 1 or more with a minimum capacity of 4 kg
The crew must be aware of how to use the equipment.

Miscellaneous Equipment (ADR 8.1.5). When carrying dangerous goods, transport units must carry the following equipment:
(a) at least 1 chock suitable for the weight and wheel size, 2 self-standing warning signs, suitable warning vest or clothing for each crew member, and a pocket lamp for each crew member;
(b) a respiratory protective device;
(c) personal protection and equipment necessary to carry out the written emergency action.

Passengers (ADR 8.3.1). No passengers may be carried apart from members of the crew.

Supervision of Vehicles (ADR 8.4). Vehicles carrying dangerous goods over specified amounts must be supervised or parked unsupervised in a secure depot or factory premises. If such facilities are not available, the vehicle may be parked in an isolated position as follows:
(a) a vehicle park supervised by an attendant who has been notified of the load and the whereabouts of the driver;
(b) alternatively, but only if such a place is not available, in a public or private vehicle park where the vehicle is not likely to suffer damage from other vehicles;
(c) alternatively, but only if neither of the above are available, in a suitable open space separated from the public highway and from dwellings, where the public does not normally pass or assemble.

CARRIAGE OF DANGEROUS GOODS – MARKING, LABELLING & PLACARDING

CARRIAGE OF DANGEROUS GOODS AND USE OF TRANSPORTABLE PRESSURE EQUIPMENT REGULATIONS 2007 AND ADR 2007

Marking of Packages (Reg. 53 & ADR 5.2). Each package must be clearly and durably marked with the appropriate UN number. If unpackaged, the marking must be displayed on the article, on its cradle, or on its storage, handling or launching device. All markings must be readily visible and legible and able to withstand open weather exposure. In addition:

- Class 1 packages must bear the proper shipping name;
- Class 2 packages must bear the proper shipping name. For compressed gases, either the maximum filling mass and the tare of the receptacle, or the gross mass, and the date of the next periodic inspection; and
- Class 7 packages must be marked with: the identification of the consignor or consignee; the proper shipping name; if gross mass is over 50 kg, the gross mass; the package type; and, for type B(U), B(M) or C packages, a trefoil.

Labelling of Packages (Reg. 53 & ADR 5.2.2). Each article or substance listed in the Dangerous Goods List (DGL) must have affixed the label(s) indicated in the list for that item. Alternatively, prescribed indelible danger marks may be affixed. Special provisions apply to self-reacting substances, organic peroxides, infectious substances, and radioactive material. Labels must conform with the colour, symbols and general format as shown on the following pages. They must be able to withstand open weather exposure without substantial reduction in effectiveness.

Marking and Placarding of Vehicles etc. (Reg. 53 & ADR 5.3).
Placarding. When required, placards must be affixed to the exterior surface of containers, multiple-element gas containers (MEGCs), tank containers, portable tanks and vehicles. The Dangerous Goods List (DGL) indicates the type of label for the specific goods carried. Except for Class 7 goods (radioactive) they must conform to the colour, symbols and general format as shown in the following pages, dimensions 250 mm × 250 mm, and display the prescribed numbers for the goods in question in characters 25 mm high. For radioactive goods the placard is as shown alongside, but for tanks with capacity not more than 3 m^3, and for small packages, they may, instead display the label shown on the following pages. For classes 1 & 7, if the surface area is insufficient, the size may be reduced to 100 mm × 100 mm.

CARRIAGE OF DANGEROUS GOODS – MARKING, LABELLING & PLACARDING cont

CARRIAGE OF DANGEROUS GOODS AND USE OF TRANSPORTABLE PRESSURE EQUIPMENT REGULATIONS 2007 AND ADR 2007

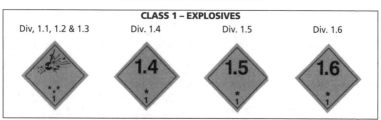

CLASS 1 – EXPLOSIVES

Div, 1.1, 1.2 & 1.3   Div. 1.4   Div. 1.5   Div. 1.6

CLASS 2 – GLASS

Flammable   Non-flammable, non toxic   Toxic

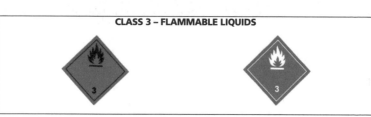

CLASS 3 – FLAMMABLE LIQUIDS

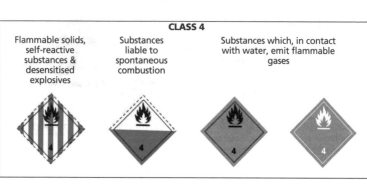

CLASS 4

Flammable solids, self-reactive substances & desensitised explosives

Substances liable to spontaneous combustion

Substances which, in contact with water, emit flammable gases

CARRIAGE OF DANGEROUS GOODS –
MARKING, LABELLING & PLACARDING cont

CARRIAGE OF DANGEROUS GOODS AND USE OF TRANSPORTABLE PRESSURE EQUIPMENT
REGULATIONS 2007 AND ADR 2007

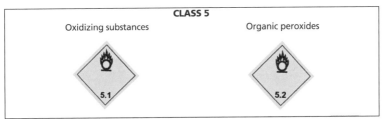

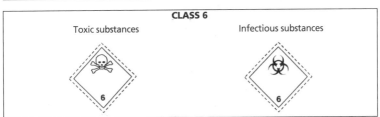

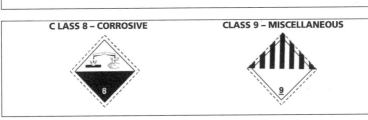

CARRIAGE OF DANGEROUS GOODS – MARKING, LABELLING & PLACARDING
cont

CARRIAGE OF DANGEROUS GOODS AND USE OF TRANSPORTABLE PRESSURE
EQUIPMENT REGULATIONS 2007 AND ADR 2007

Orange Coloured Plate Marking (ADR 5.3.2.1.1). Transport units carrying dangerous goods must display two vertical rectangular reflectorized orange plates, one on the front and one on the rear, perpendicular to the longitudinal axis of the vehicle. The plates are similar to that shown below except that they are not divided into two halves and the numbers do not appear.

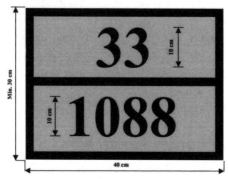

But if there is insufficient area, the size may be reduced to 30 cm base, 12 cm high and 10 mm border.

Plates which do not relate to the goods carried (or residues thereof) must be removed or covered.

Hazard Identification Numbers (HIN) (ADR 5.3.2.1.2). Where a HIN appears alongside the goods in the DGL, two additional plates, as shown above, must be displayed, one on each side of the transport unit, tank, tank-compartment or container. These plates have a horizontal black line in the centre, displaying the HIN in the top half and the UN number in the bottom half. In certain circumstances, eg tanks containing aviation fuel, transport units only carrying one substance, or solid substances in bulk for tank-containers, it will be sufficient only to display the front and rear plates provided they bear the HIN and UN number. But see below for the requirement to display the EAC (Emergency Action Code) instead of the HIN.

CARRIAGE OF DANGEROUS GOODS – MARKING, LABELLING & PLACARDING cont

CARRIAGE OF DANGEROUS GOODS AND USE OF TRANSPORTABLE PRESSURE EQUIPMENT REGULATIONS 2007 AND ADR 2007

Mark for Elevated Temperature Substances (ADR 5.3.3). Where the DGL requires the container of a substance to bear such a mark, it shall be displayed on both sides and at the rear for vehicles, and on both sides and at both ends for containers, tank-containers and portable tanks. The form of the mark is shown below, with sides of at least 250 mm.

Meaning of Hazard Identification Numbers. The HIN is the number displayed in the top half of the orange plate shown on the opposite page. The UN number is shown in the bottom half. The number consists of 2 or 3 figures which indicate the hazard described in the first table on the following page.

Doubling of a figure indicates an intensification of the hazard. Where the hazard can be identified by a single figure, this is followed by a zero. Numbers prefixed with the letter 'X' indicate that the substance will react dangerously with water, and water may only be used with the approval of experts.

It should be noted that certain numbers have a special meaning, as shown in the second table on the following page.

CARRIAGE OF DANGEROUS GOODS – MARKING, LABELLING & PLACARDING cont

CARRIAGE OF DANGEROUS GOODS AND USE OF TRANSPORTABLE PRESSURE
EQUIPMENT REGULATIONS 2007 AND ADR 2007

Hazard Identification Numbers (ADR 5.3.2.3.1)

Figure	Hazard
2	Emission of gas due to pressure or to chemical reaction
3	Flammability of liquids (vapours) and gases or self-heating liquid
4	Flammability of solids or self-heating solid
5	Oxidising (fire-intensifying) effect
6	Toxicity or risk of infection
7	Radioactivity
8	Corrosivity
9	Risk of spontaneous violent reaction

Combinations of Numbers having a Special Meaning

Number	Special Meaning
22	Refrigerated liquefied gas (asphyxiant)
323	Flammable liquid which reacts with water, emitting flammable gases
333	Pyrophoric liquid
362	Flammable liquid, toxic, which reacts with water, emitting flammable gases
382	Flammable liquid, corrosive, which reacts with water, emitting flammable gases
423	Solid which reacts with water, emitting flammable gases
44	Flammable solid, in the molten state at an elevated temperature
446	Flammable solid, toxic, in the molten state, at an elevated temperature
462	Toxic solid which reacts with water, emitting flammable gases
482	Corrosive solid which reacts with water, emitting flammable gases
539	Flammable organic peroxide
606	Infectious substance
623	Toxic liquid, which reacts with water, emitting flammable gases
642	Toxic solid which reacts with water, emitting flammable gases
823	Corrosive liquid which reacts with water, emitting flammable gases
842	Corrosive solid which reacts with water, emitting flammable gases
90	Environmentally hazardous substance; miscellaneous dangerous substances
99	Miscellaneous dangerous substance carried at an elevated temperature

CARRIAGE OF DANGEROUS GOODS – MARKING, LABELLING & PLACARDING FOR CARRIAGE WITHIN GB

CARRIAGE OF DANGEROUS GOODS AND USE OF TRANSPORTABLE PRESSURE EQUIPMENT REGULATIONS 2007

Placards, Marks and Plates for Carriage within GB (Reg. 91).
Where dangerous goods (other than class 7 goods) are being carried in tanks or in bulk, and by a transport unit registered in G.B. and the whole of the carriage operation takes place in G.B. then the following conditions, in addition to the ADR requirements regarding marking, labelling and placarding mentioned in the previous pages will apply:

HIN (Sched. 7 (1)). If orange coloured plates bearing the HIN are required, then the HIN is to be replaced by the Emergency Action Code (EAC) (See following page).

Emergency Action Codes (EACs). These are also known as Hazchem codes and are for the use of the emergency services in conjunction with EAC cards. They indicate the action which may be necessary during an incident. In brief, where goods are transported by tank or in bulk on internal transport operations in GB, vehicles registered in GB and on domestic journeys must display the EAC. All other vehicles must display the HIN. The EAC, together with the appropriate danger label is displayed on the Hazard Warning Panel as shown below.

Orange-coloured plate where only one type of dangerous good is carried.
(Sched. 7(2)).
If the goods are being carried in a battery-vehicle, tank-vehicle or transport unit or in a container in bulk-

    (a)   the orange-coloured plates bearing a hazard identification number shall be displayed on the sides of the vehicle, etc.; and

    (b)   an identical plate shall be affixed to the rear in place of the plain orange plate.

Orange-coloured plate where more than one type of dangerous good is carried (Sched. 7(3)).
If the goods are being carried in a tank or in bulk in a transport unit or a battery-vehicle or a tank-vehicle with more than one tank, element or container-

    (a)   the orange-coloured plates bearing a hazard identification number shall be displayed on the sides of the vehicle, etc., except that (i) only one on each side of the transport unit, etc. shall bear the emergency action code; and (ii) the remaining plates shall bear only the UN number and shall be 150mm in height; and

    (b)   an identical orange-coloured plate shall be affixed to the rear of the vehicle, etc., except that it shall display the emergency action code only in the top half of the plate.

But if more than one type of dangerous good is being carried in a transport unit or a tank vehicle with more than one tank and those goods are (a) UN 1202

CARRIAGE OF DANGEROUS GOODS – MARKING, LABELLING & PLACARDING FOR CARRIAGE WITHIN GB cont

CARRIAGE OF DANGEROUS GOODS AND USE OF TRANSPORTABLE PRESSURE EQUIPMENT REGULATIONS 2007

Diesel fuel or gas oil or heating oil, light; (b) UN 1203 Petrol or motor spirit or gasoline; or (c) UN 1223 kerosene, then the requirements of Sched. 7(2) shall be met, except that the orange-coloured plates need only bear the emergency action code and UN number for the most hazardous of the goods being carried."

Emergency Contacts (Sched. 7(4)). Where dangerous goods are being carried in tanks, a telephone number where specialist advice may be obtained, must be displayed on the rear of the transport unit and on both sides of the tank, tank frame or transport unit in the immediate vicinity of the orange plate displaying the EAC. The sign must be in black digits not less than 30 mm in height against an orange background. The telephone number may be substituted by the phrase "consult local depot" or "contact local depot" if (a) the name of the carrier appears on the transport unit or tank, (b) the chief fire officer for each area through which it passes has been notified of the address and telephone number of the depot, and (c) each fire officer has indicated that he is satisfied with the arrangements.

Hazard Warning Panels (Sched. 7(5)). Instead of placards and orange plates, hazard warning panels may be displayed provided the following conditions are complied with:

(a) they must be displayed in accordance with the above as if they were orange plates;

(b) orange-coloured except the part containing the placard (200 mm × 200 mm) which must be white;

(c) if more than one placard, must be horizontally adjacent;

(d) clearly visible and conforming to the diagram below.

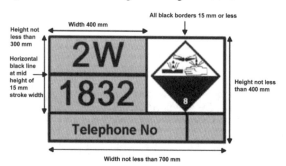

If dangerous goods are carried in a tank constructed on or after 1/01/05, the orange-coloured plate shall be indelible and remain legible after it has been engulfed in fire for 15 minutes.

EMERGENCY ACTION CODE (HAZCHEM) – INTERPRETATION

The first character of the EAC refers to the firefighting extinguishing media as follows:

1   coarse water spray
2   fine water spray
3   normal foam
4   dry agent

The second character has the following meaning (NB there may be more than one meaning):

S, T, Y or Z means normal firefighting clothing is appropriate.

P, R, W or X means special protective clothing is required.

P, S, W or Y means there is a danger that the substance can be violently or explosively reactive.

W, X, Y or Z means spillages, contaminated fire and decontamination run-off should be prevented from entering drains, etc.

P, R, S or T means that where there is an immediate threat to people, spillages and contaminated run-off may be washed to drains with large quantities of water.

E following the first two characters indicates that there may be a public safety hazard outside the immediate area of the incident. In consultation with the Fire and Rescue incident commander and a product expert the following actions should be considered:

EMERGENCY ACTION CODE (HAZCHEM) – INTERPRETATION cont

People warned to stay indoors with all doors and windows closed, preferable in rooms upstairs and facing away from the incident. Ignition sources should be eliminated and any ventilation stopped. All non-essential personnel to move at least 250 metres away from the incident.

Numerical and Alphabetical List of Dangerous Goods
The Dangerous Goods Emergency Action Code List 2007 contains the following information regarding dangerous goods:
1   United Nations (UN) number
2   Substance
3   Emergency Action Code
4   Advice on Additional Personal Protection
5   Hazards
6   Hazard Identification Number

CARRIAGE OF DANGEROUS GOODS – DOCUMENTATION

CARRIAGE OF DANGEROUS GOODS AND USE OF TRANSPORTABLE PRESSURE EQUIPMENT
REGULATIONS 2007

ADR 8.1.2. requires that, in addition to the documents required by other regulations, when dangerous goods are carried they must be accompanied by the following documents:

Dangerous Goods Transport Document (ADR 5.4.1). This document contains the UN number, the proper shipping name, the classification code, the packing group, the number and description of packages, the total quantity of each different item, names and addresses of the consignor and consignee, and any declaration as required by any special agreement.

Container Packing Certificate (ADR 5.4.2). If the carriage of dangerous goods in a large container precedes a voyage by sea, a container packing certificate must be provided with the transport document.

Instructions in Writing (ADR 5.4.3). As a precaution against any accident or emergency which might occur, the driver must be given instructions in writing specifying precisely for each group of goods the nature of the danger inherent in the goods and the action to be taken. The instructions must be kept in a readily identifiable form in the driver's cab. The carrier must ensure that the driver understands the instructions and is capable of carrying them out properly. Instructions not applicable to the goods on board must be kept separate from the pertinent documents to avoid confusion.

Identification (ADR 1.10.1.4). Each member of a vehicle crew shall carry with them means of identification, which includes their photograph during the carriage of dangerous goods.

Certificate of Approval (ADR 9.1.3). Eertain vehicles (types EX/11 or EX/111 (explosives), FL (low flashpoint liquids, etc.), OX (hydrogen peroxide, etc.) and AT (other tank containers, etc.)) are subject to an annual technical inspection in their country of origin to ensure that they conform with the relevant provisions of ADR. All vehicles, regardless of the type must undergo an annual inspection to ensure they conform to the general safety regulations in that country. The certificate of approval must be carried.

Driver's Training Certificate (ADR 8.2.1). Drivers of:

(a) vehicles carrying dangerous goods;

(b) vehicles carrying dangerous goods in tanks with a capacity of more than 1 m³ (a specialist training course must be attended);

(c) battery vehicles with a capacity of more than 1 m³ (a specialist training course must be attended);

(d) vehicles carrying dangerous goods in tank containers, portable tanks or MEGCs with an individual capacity exceeding 3 m³ (a specialist training course must be attended);

(e) vehicles carrying class 1 goods (explosives) or certain class 7 goods (radioactive); shall carry a certificate stating that they have participated in

CARRIAGE OF DANGEROUS GOODS – DOCUMENTATION cont

CARRIAGE OF DANGEROUS GOODS AND USE OF TRANSPORTABLE PRESSURE EQUIPMENT REGULATIONS 2007

training and have passed an examination on the particular requirements that have to be met when carrying dangerous goods (a specialist training course must be attended).

Competent Authority Approval (ADR 8.1.2.2(c)). Certain types of explosives, organic peroxides and self reacting substances must have the approval of the competent authority. A copy of the permit must be carried on the vehicle.

Exemptions from the Need to Carry Transport Documents. Where goods of class 2 to 6, 8 & 9 are being carried in quantities not exceeding those listed for that transport category (see table earlier), the 'Dangerous Goods Transport Document' (ADR 5.4.1), and the 'Container Packing Certificate' (ADR 5.4.2) need not be carried. Where class 1 goods are being carried and are of a type listed in Schedule 4 to the regulations (there are over 30 listed items), the above-mentioned documents need not be carried provided the net mass of materials carried does not exceed the maximum laid down. (Reg. 30).

ANIMALS IN TRANSIT
ANIMAL HEALTH ACT 1981, WELFARE OF ANIMALS (TRANSPORT) (ENGLAND) ORDER 2006, & REGULATION (EC) 1/2005

Enforcement
Article 21 of the 2006 order places responsibility for enforcement of that order with local authorities. However, S 60 of the 1981 Act requires the police to execute and enforce the 1981 Act and orders made under it by the Minister. The 2006 order was made under the 1981 Act.

Duties and authorities of constables (S 60)
Where a person is seen or found committing, or is reasonably suspected of being engaged in committing, an offence against the Act (including EC Regulation 1/2005), a constable may, without warrant, stop and detain him. The constable may, whether or not so stopping or detaining the person, stop, detain and examine any animal, vehicle, boat or thing to which the offence or suspected offence relates, and require it forthwith to be taken back to or into any place or district from which it was unlawfully removed, and execute and enforce that requisition.

Offences under Council Regulation 1/2005
Article 5 of the order states that a person who fails to comply with any of the below-mentioned provisions of Council Regulation (EC) 1/2005 is guilty of an offence against the Act. The provisions of 1/2005 relevant to the police are:

Art. 3 (general conditions for the transport of animals);
Art. 4(1) (transport documentation);
Art. 6(1) & 6(5) (transporters); and
Certain parts of Chapter 3, Annex 1 (transport practices).

Each of these is covered in more detail below. For the purpose of the EC provisions 'animal' means live vertebrate animals.

General conditions for the transport of animals (Art. 3)
No person shall transport animals or cause animals to be transported in a way likely to cause injury or undue suffering to them. In addition the following conditions shall be complied with:

(a)   arrangements must be made to minimise the length of the journey and to meet the animals' needs during the journey;

(b)   the animals must be fit for the journey;

(c)   the means of transport must be designed, constructed, maintained and operated so as to avoid injury and suffering and ensure the safety of the animals;

(d)   the loading and unloading facilities must be adequately designed, constructed, maintained and operated so as to avoid injury and suffering and ensure the safety of the animals;

ANIMALS IN TRANSIT cont
ANIMAL HEALTH ACT 1981, WELFARE OF ANIMALS (TRANSPORT) (ENGLAND) ORDER
2006, & REGULATION (EC) 1/2005

(e)   personnel handling the animals must be trained or competent and must not use violence or any method likely to cause unnecessary fear, injury or suffering;

(f)   transport must be carried out without delay and welfare conditions regularly checked and appropriately maintained;

(g)   sufficient floor area and height must be provided, appropriate to the size of the animal and the intended journey; and

(h)   water, feed and rest must be offered at suitable intervals, appropriate in quality and quantity to the size and species of the animal.

Transport documentation. (Art. 4(1))
No person shall transport animals without carrying documents in the transport stating:

(a)   their origin and ownership;

(b)   their place of departure;

(c)   the date and time of departure;

(d)   their intended place of destination; and

(e)   the expected duration of the intended journey.

Such documents shall be kept for six months after the completion of the journey (Art. 5 of the 2006 Order).

Transporters (Arts. 6(1) & (5))
No person shall act as transporter unless he holds an authorisation issued by a competent authority for either a normal journey or a long journey (over 8 hours). A copy shall be made available to the competent authority when transported.

No person shall drive or act as attendant on a road vehicle transporting domestic equidae or domestic bovine, ovine, caprine or porcine species or poultry unless he holds a certificate of competence, which shall be made available to the competent authority when the animals are transported.

Transport practices. (Chapter 3, Annex 1)
It shall be prohibited to:

(a)   strike or kick the animals;

(b)   apply pressure to any particular sensitive part of the body in such a way as to cause them unnecessary pain or suffering;

(c)   suspend the animals themselves by mechanical means;

(d)   lift or drag the animals by head, ears, horns, legs, tail or fleece, or handle them in such a way as to cause unnecessary pain or suffering;

(e)   use prods or other implements with pointed ends; or

(f)   knowingly obstruct any animal which is being driven or led through any part where animals are handled.

ANIMALS IN TRANSIT cont
ANIMAL HEALTH ACT 1981, WELFARE OF ANIMALS (TRANSPORT) (ENGLAND) ORDER
2006, & REGULATION (EC) 1/2005

The use of instruments which administer electric shocks shall be avoided as far as possible. In any case these instruments shall only be used for adult bovine animals and adult pigs which refuse to move and only when they have room ahead of them in which to move. The shocks shall last no longer than one second, be adequately spaced and shall only be applied to the muscles of the hindquarters. Shocks shall not be used repeatedly if the animal fails to respond. Animals shall not be tied by the horns, antlers or nose rings, nor the legs tied together. Calves shall not be muzzled. Domestic equidae older than eight months shall wear halters during transport except for unbroken horses.

When animals need to be tied, the ropes, tethers or other means used shall be:

    (a)   strong enough not to break during normal transport conditions;

    (b)   such as to allow the animals, if necessary, to lie down and to eat and drink; and

    (c)   designed in such a way as to eliminate any danger of strangulation or injury, and so as to allow the animals to be quickly released.

Offences under the Welfare of Animals (Transport) Order 2006
The definition of 'animals' under S 87 of the 1981 Act means cattle, sheep, goats and all other ruminating animals and swine. Article 3 of the 2006 Order extended this to include all vertebrate animals and cold-blooded invertebrate animals.

General provisions on the protection of animals during transport (Art.4)
    (1)   It is an offence to transport any animal in a way which causes, or is likely to cause, injury or unnecessary suffering to that animal.

    (2)   It is an offence to transport any animal except in such receptacles or means of transport, under conditions (in particular with regard to space, ventilation, temperature and security) and with such supply of liquid and oxygen, as are appropriate for the species concerned.

    (3)   This article applies to the transport of cold-blooded invertebrate animals.

    (4)   It also applies to vertebrate animals except those for which provision has already been made in Council Reg. 1/2005.

Transport (Art. 5)
A person who fails to comply with any of the following provisions of Council Regulation (EC) 1/2005 (see above) commits an offence against the Act-

    (a)   article 3 (general transport conditions);

    (b)   article 4(1) (transport documentation);

    (c)   article 6(1) & (5)(transporters);

    (d)   chapter III annex 1 (prohibited transport practices mentioned above).

REPORTING OF ACCIDENTS
ROAD TRAFFIC ACT 1988, S. 170 AS AMENDED BY S.I.2000/726

IF, OWING TO THE PRESENCE OF A

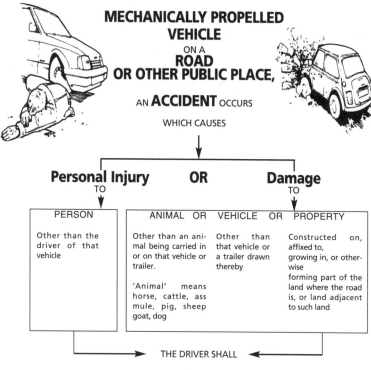

MECHANICALLY PROPELLED VEHICLE
ON A
ROAD
OR OTHER PUBLIC PLACE,

AN **ACCIDENT** OCCURS

WHICH CAUSES

Personal Injury   OR   Damage
TO   TO

PERSON	ANIMAL OR	VEHICLE OR	PROPERTY
Other than the driver of that vehicle	Other than an animal being carried in or on that vehicle or trailer. 'Animal' means horse, cattle, ass mule, pig, sheep goat, dog	Other than that vehicle or a trailer drawn thereby	Constructed on, affixed to, growing in, or otherwise forming part of the land where the road is, or land adjacent to such land

THE DRIVER SHALL

STOP

and if requested to do so give his name and address and the name and address of the owner of the vehicle and particulars of the vehicle to any person having grounds for requiring   S
170(2)

If he doesn't give his name and address he must as soon as practicable and in any case within 24 hours

report to the police

S 170(3) AND (6)

If the accident involves personal injury he must also

produce insurance

At the time of the accident or, if he fails to do so, to the police as soon as reasonably practicable and, in any case, within 24 hours (But he will not be guilty of the offence of failing to produce the insurance if he does so within 7 days).

DUTY TO GIVE INFORMATION AS TO DRIVER

S.172 Road Traffic Act, 1988

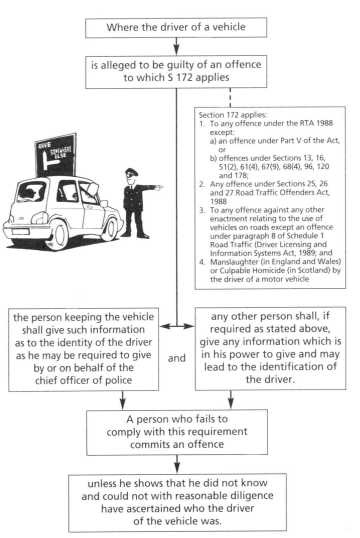

Where the driver of a vehicle

↓

is alleged to be guilty of an offence to which S 172 applies

Section 172 applies:
1. To any offence under the RTA 1988 except:
   a) an offence under Part V of the Act, or
   b) offences under Sections 13, 16, 51(2), 61(4), 67(9), 68(4), 96, 120 and 178;
2. Any offence under Sections 25, 26 and 27 Road Traffic Offenders Act, 1988
3. To any offence against any other enactment relating to the use of vehicles on roads except an offence under paragraph 8 of Schedule 1 Road Traffic (Driver Licensing and Information Systems Act, 1989; and
4. Manslaughter (in England and Wales) or Culpable Homicide (in Scotland) by the driver of a motor vehicle

the person keeping the vehicle shall give such information as to the identity of the driver as he may be required to give by or on behalf of the chief officer of police

and

any other person shall, if required as stated above, give any information which is in his power to give and may lead to the identification of the driver.

↓

A person who fails to comply with this requirement commits an offence

↓

unless he shows that he did not know and could not with reasonable diligence have ascertained who the driver of the vehicle was.

POWERS OF ARREST WITHOUT WARRANT
POLICE AND CRIMINAL EVIDENCE ACT 1984 (AS AMENDED BY THE
SERIOUS ORGANISED CRIME AND POLICE ACT 2005)

Constables (S 24)

1. **A constable** may arrest without warrant:
   - (a) anyone who is **about to commit** an offence
   - (b) anyone who is **in the act of committing** an offence
   - (c) anyone whom he has **reasonable grounds** for suspecting to be **about to commit** an offence
   - (d) anyone whom he has **reasonable grounds** for suspecting to be **committing** an offence.
2. If a constable has **reasonable grounds for suspecting that an offence has been committed**, he may arrest without a warrant anyone whom he has **reasonable grounds to suspect of being guilty** of it.
3. If an offence **has been committed**, a constable may arrest without a warrant
   - (a) anyone who **is guilty** of the offence
   - (b) anyone whom he has **reasonable grounds for suspecting to be guilty** of it.

Grounds for exercising the powers

The powers of arrest are only exercisable if the constable has reasonable grounds for believing that it is necessary to arrest the person for any of the following reasons-

- (a) to enable the name of the person in question to be ascertained (in the case where the constable does not know, and cannot readily ascertain, the person's name, or has reasonable grounds for doubting whether a name given by the person as his name is his real name)
- (b) correspondingly as regards the person's address
- (c) to prevent the person in question:
  - (i) causing physical injury to himself or any other person
  - (ii) suffering physical injury
  - (iii) causing loss of or damage to property
  - (iv) committing an offence against public decency (but this only applies where members of the public going about their normal business cannot reasonably be expected to avoid the person in question)
  - (v) causing an unlawful obstruction of the highway.
- (d) to protect a child or other vulnerable person from the person in question
- (e) to allow the prompt and effective investigation of the offence or of the conduct of the person in question
- (f) to prevent any prosecution for the offence from being hindered by the disappearance of the person in question.

These powers have effect in relation to any offence, whenever committed

The 'General Arrest Conditions' and the definition of 'Serious Arrestable Offence' cease to have effect. (SOCAP S 110)

Note: Legislation not applicable in Scotland.

POWERS OF ARREST WITHOUT WARRANT cont

POLICE AND CRIMINAL EVIDENCE ACT 1984 (AS AMENDED BY THE
SERIOUS ORGANISED CRIME AND POLICE ACT 2005)

Other persons (S 24A)

A person other than a constable may arrest without a warrant:
- (a) anyone who is **in the act of committing** an indictable offence
- (b) anyone whom he has **reasonable grounds for suspecting to be committing** an indictable offence.

Where an indictable offence has been committed, a person other than a constable may arrest without a warrant:
- (c) anyone who **is guilty** of the offence
- (d) anyone whom he has **reasonable grounds for suspecting to be guilty** of it.

Grounds for exercising the powers

The powers of arrest are only exercisable if:
- (a) the person making the arrest has reasonable grounds for believing that it is necessary to arrest the person in question for any of the following reasons:
  - (i) causing physical injury to himself or any other person
  - (ii) suffering physical injury
  - (iii) causing loss of or damage to property; or
  - (iv) making off before a constable can assume responsibility for him; and
- (b) it appears to the person making the arrest that it is not reasonably practicable for a constable to make it instead.

These powers have effect in relation to any offence, whenever committed

The 'General Arrest Conditions' and the definition of 'Serious Arrestable Offence' cease to have effect. (SOCAP S 110)

Note: Legislation not applicable in Scotland.

MODE OF ARREST

POLICE AND CRIMINAL EVIDENCE ACT 1984, SS 28 AND 30

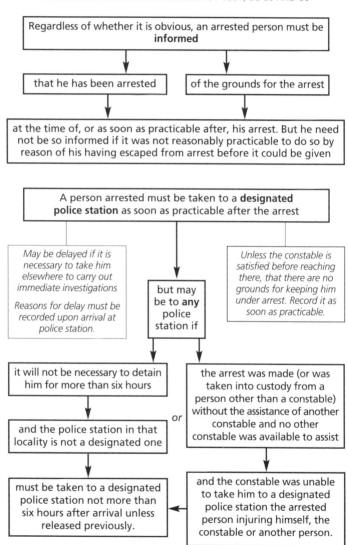

Regardless of whether it is obvious, an arrested person must be **informed**

that he has been arrested

of the grounds for the arrest

at the time of, or as soon as practicable after, his arrest. But he need not be so informed if it was not reasonably practicable to do so by reason of his having escaped from arrest before it could be given

A person arrested must be taken to a **designated police station** as soon as practicable after the arrest

May be delayed if it is necessary to take him elsewhere to carry out immediate investigations

Reasons for delay must be recorded upon arrival at police station.

but may be to **any** police station if

Unless the constable is satisfied before reaching there, that there are no grounds for keeping him under arrest. Record it as soon as practicable.

it will not be necessary to detain him for more than six hours

and the police station in that locality is not a designated one

or

the arrest was made (or was taken into custody from a person other than a constable) without the assistance of another constable and no other constable was available to assist

must be taken to a designated police station not more than six hours after arrival unless released previously.

and the constable was unable to take him to a designated police station the arrested person injuring himself, the constable or another person.

Not applicable to Scotland.

ROAD CHECKS

POLICE AND CRIMINAL EVIDENCE ACT 1984, S 4

Under certain circumstances, a police constable needs authority to carry out a road check

What is a road check?

The exercise in a locality of the power conferred by S 163 of the Road Traffic Act 1988, to stop either all vehicles or vehicles selected by any criterion.

What type of check needs to be authorised?

Where it is necessary to ascertain whether a vehicle is carrying:

- a person who has committed an indictable offence (other than a traffic or excise offence) and may be in the locality
- a person who is a witness to an indictable offence
- a person who intends to commit an indictable offence and may be in the locality
- a person who is unlawfully at large and may be in the locality

Who can authorise it?

Normally a superintendent must authorise it in writing. But may be authorised by an officer below that rank as a matter of urgency, in which case, as soon as practicable, he must make a written record of the time he gives it and cause a superintendent to be informed.

The locality at which the check is to be carried out must be specified.

How long may it last?

The superintendent or above (not below) must specify a period, not exceeding seven days, during which it may take place (may be renewed in writing). He may direct whether it shall be continuous or conducted at specified times.

Not applicable to Scotland.

STOP AND SEARCH

Serious Violence

Where a superintendent or above (or inspector if incident is imminent) reasonably believes that incidents involving serious violence may take place in his area and it is expedient to prevent their occurrence he may authorise (in writing) stopping and searching of persons and vehicles in that locality for a period not exceeding 24 hours for offensive weapons or dangerous instruments. Constable in uniform may stop any person or vehicle and make any search he thinks fit whether or not he has any grounds for suspecting that weapons or articles of that kind are present.

S 60 CRIMINAL JUSTICE AND PUBLIC ORDER ACT 1994

Not applicable in Scotland.

Prevention of Terrorism

Where it appears to an officer of the rank of commander/assistant chief constable that it is expedient in order to prevent acts of terrorism (connected with Northern Ireland or of any description but not connected solely with the affairs of the UK) he may authorise the stopping and searching of person or vehicles (including ships and aircraft) for up to 28 days in a specified locality. In the exercise of these powers a constable may stop any vehicle or person and make any search he thinks fit whether or not he has any grounds for suspecting that articles of terrorism are being carried.

S 81 CRIMINAL JUSTICE AND PUBLIC ORDER ACT 1994

Raves – stopping persons from attending

If a constable in uniform reasonably believes that a person is on his way to a gathering to which S 63, Criminal Justice and Public Order Act 1994 applies, and in respect of which a direction is in force, he may stop that person and direct him not to proceed in the direction of that gathering. This power may be exercised within five miles of the boundary of the site of the gathering. Failure to comply is an offence.

S 65 CRIMINAL JUSTICE AND PUBLIC ORDER ACT 1994

POWER TO STOP VEHICLES
S. 163 ROAD TRAFFIC ACT 1988

A person driving a
mechanically propelled vehicle

or riding a cycle

on a road must

STOP

the vehicle (or cycle) on being
required to do so by a
constable in uniform.

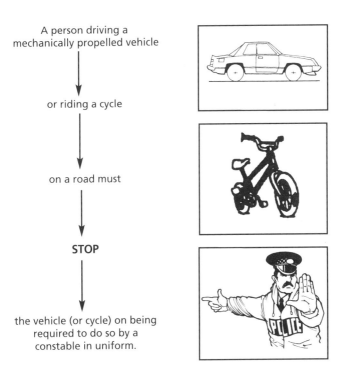

FAILURE TO COMPLY IS AN OFFENCE.

SEIZURE OF VEHICLES
POLICE REFORM ACT 2002, S 59
POLICE (RETENTION AND DISPOSAL OF MOTOR VEHICLES) REGULATIONS 2002

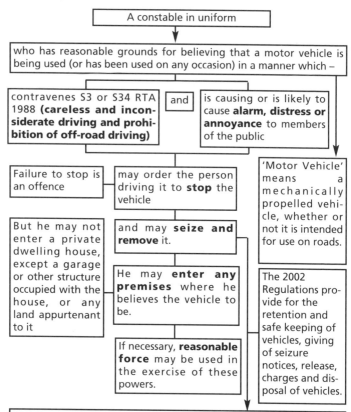

A constable in uniform

who has reasonable grounds for believing that a motor vehicle is being used (or has been used on any occasion) in a manner which –

contravenes S3 or S34 RTA 1988 **(careless and inconsiderate driving and prohibition of off-road driving)**

and

is causing or is likely to cause **alarm, distress or annoyance** to members of the public

Failure to stop is an offence

may order the person driving it to **stop** the vehicle

'Motor Vehicle' means a mechanically propelled vehicle, whether or not it is intended for use on roads.

But he may not enter a private dwelling house, except a garage or other structure occupied with the house, or any land appurtenant to it

and may **seize and remove** it.

He may **enter any premises** where he believes the vehicle to be.

The 2002 Regulations provide for the retention and safe keeping of vehicles, giving of seizure notices, release, charges and disposal of vehicles.

If necessary, **reasonable force** may be used in the exercise of these powers.

But he must first warn him that he will seize it if such use continues or is repeated; and the use has continued or been repeated after the warning. But a warning need not be given if (a) it is impracticable for him to give the warning; (b) he has already given a warning on that occasion in respect of the use of that vehicle or another vehicle by that or another person; (c) he believes that such a warning has been given on that occasion by someone else; or (d) the person has already been warned by him or someone else within the previous 12 months whether or not it was in respect of the same vehicle or the same or similar use.

TAXI TOUTS

S 167 CRIMINAL JUSTICE AND PUBLIC ORDER ACT 1994

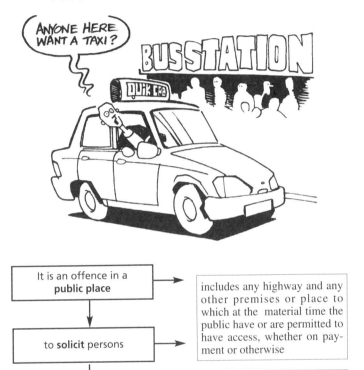

It is an offence in a **public place**	includes any highway and any other premises or place to which at the material time the public have or are permitted to have access, whether on payment or otherwise
to **solicit** persons	
to hire vehicles to carry them as passengers	*mere display of a sign on a vehicle that it is for hire is not soliciting*

Does not include soliciting persons to hire licensed taxis or public service vehicles on behalf of a holder of a PSV operator's licence with his authority.

Note: Legislation not applicable in Scotland.

BUILDERS' SKIPS

HIGHWAYS ACT 1980

Offences   S 139

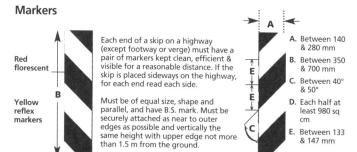

- Depositing a skip without the written permission of the highway authority
- Failing to comply with any conditions contained in the authorisation
- Not having skip properly lighted at night
- Not having it removed as soon as reasonably practicable after it has been filled
- Not having name and address or telephone number of owner clearly and indelibly marked on the skip.

'Skip'

A container designed to be carried on a vehicle and deposited on a road for the collection and removal of rubble etc.

Markers

Red florescent

Yellow reflex markers

Each end of a skip on a highway (except footway or verge) must have a pair of markers kept clean, efficient & visible for a reasonable distance. If the skip is placed sideways on the highway, for each end read each side.

Must be of equal size, shape and parallel, and have B.S. mark. Must be securely attached as near to outer edges as possible and vertically the same height with upper edge not more than 1.5 m from the ground.

A. Between 140 & 280 mm

B. Between 350 & 700 mm

C. Between 40° & 50°

D. Each half at least 980 sq cm

E. Between 133 & 147 mm

BUILDERS' SKIPS (MARKINGS) REGULATIONS 1984

Proceedings

may be taken against the owner * and/or any person whose act resulted in the offence

* If hired for more than a month or subject of an HP agreement, hirer becomes the owner. An owner hiring out his skip must ensure hirers are aware of their duties.

Defence

That the offence was a result of an act or default of another and reasonable precautions had been taken to avoid any contravention

Police powers

A constable in uniform may require the owner to remove or re-position the skip as soon as possible. The constable has power to remove or re-position it himself and any expenses incurred may be recovered from the owners.   S 140(2)

Not applicable to Scotland – See Scots provisions re Builder's Skips in Roads (Scotland) Act 1984.

NOTICE OF INTENDED PROSECUTION

ROAD TRAFFIC OFFENDERS ACT 1988, SS. 1 AND 2

> In relation to certain offences, a person will not be convicted *unless:*

	or		or	
At the time of the offence he was warned that the question of prosecuting him would be considered		within 14 days of the offence a summons was served on him		within 14 days of the offence a notice of intended prosecution was sent to the driver or rider (or in the case of motor vehicles, the registered keeper)

By delivering it to him; by addressing it to him and leaving it at his last known address; or by sending it by registered post, recorded delivery service or first class post addressed to him at his last known address

But the above requirement will not apply if, at the time of the offence or immediately thereafter, an accident occurs owing to the presence on a road of a vehicle in respect of which the offence was committed.

Offences involved include   *(SCHED 1)*

● Dangerous driving ● Careless and inconsiderate driving ● Leaving a vehicle in dangerous position ● Dangerous cycling ● Careless and inconsiderate cycling ● Failing to comply with traffic directions ● Failing to comply with traffic signs (see below) ● Exceeding a speed limit or restriction under S14 and S16 (temporary restrictions), S17 (Special Roads), S88 (temporary minimum speed limits) or S89 (speeding generally) of The Road Traffic Regulation Act 1984.

Signs

The offence concerns only the following signs which are contained in Reg 10 of The Traffic Signs Regulations 2002. Contravention of others should be dealt with under the relevant order.

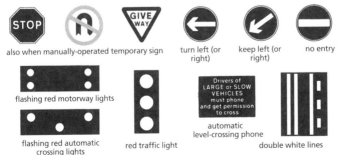

STOP also when manually-operated temporary sign

turn left (or right)

keep left (or right)

no entry

flashing red motorway lights

flashing red automatic crossing lights

red traffic light

Drivers of LARGE or SLOW VEHICLES must phone and get permission to cross — automatic level-crossing phone

double white lines

Also: ● weak bridge weight limit contravention ● height limit contravention ● route for use by buses, tram cars, pedal cycles only ● give way to traffic from right at roundabout ● manually operated stop sign at roadworks ● hatch markings on road ● give way at double broken lines ● hatched box at junction or level crossing ● tramcar prohibition sign ● green arrow traffic light.

CRASH HELMETS

S16 ROAD TRAFFIC ACT 1988. MOTOR CYCLES (PROTECTIVE HELMENTS) REGULATIONS 1998 AS AMENDED BY S.I. 2000/1488

Protective Headgear

Every person driving or riding on a motor bicycle (other than as a passenger in a sidecar) on a road.

- must wear protective headgear.

- must be securely fastened to the head of the wearer by means of straps or other fastening provided for that purpose.

- must bear a mark indication compliance with the British Standard or be of a type which, by virtue of its shape, material and construction could reasonable be expected to afford protection similar to, or greater than, a helmet which conforms to the British Standard, an accepted EEA Standard or of ECE Regulations.

A person who drives or rides a motorcycle in contravention of the aforementioned commits an offence. Note that provided the person committing the offence is 16 years or over no other person can be charged with aiding and abetting or causing or permitting the offence.

S16(4) RTA 1988

The regulations do not apply to

- mowing machine

- vehicle being propelled by a person on foot

- follower of Sikh religion while wearing a turban

ROAD TRAFFIC ACT 1988, S 16

'Motor bicycle'

means a two-wheeled motor cycle with or without a sidecar. If the distance between any two wheels is less than 460mm they shall be regarded as one wheel

REG 4

MOTOR CYCLE EYE PROTECTORS
ROAD TRAFFIC ACT 1988, S.18
MOTOR CYCLE (EYE PROTECTORS) REGULATIONS 1999

It is not an offence NOT to use such an appliance

If a person driving or riding on a motor cycle on a road

otherwise than in a sidecar

uses an appliance of any description

Designed or adapted for use
1. with any headgear, or
2. by being attached to or placed on the head.
(e.g. eye protectors or headphones)

Must conform with
1. BS 4110:1979 (Grade X, XA, YA or ZA);
2. a standard accepted by an EEA state;
3. ECE Reg. 22.05; or
4. Council Directive 89/686/EEC
and must bear the mark of conformity with the relevant standard.

which is not of a type prescribed

or is used in contravention of regulations

he will be guilty of an offence.

Any person who sells, or offers for sale, any appliance which is not of a prescribed type, will be guilty of an offence.

Will also be deemed to comply if first used before 1.4.89, designed to correct defective sight, transmits 50% or more of the light, and doesn't fragment if fractured.

Does not apply to mowing machines; vehicles propelled by a person on foot; vehicles temporarily in GB for not more than 1 year; or armed forces personnel on duty, wearing service eye protectors.

MOTORWAYS

MOTORWAYS TRAFFIC (ENGLAND AND WALES) REGULATIONS 1982
(as amended). MOTORWAYS TRAFFIC (SCOTLAND) REGULATIONS 1995.
The following details apply under respective regulations to both sides of the border. The
numbers of the Scottish Regulations are shown in brackets.

Driving

Must not drive on any part of the motorway other than the carriageway.

REG 5 (REG 4)

Must drive with the central reservation on the right or offside unless directed otherwise. *REG 6 (REG 5)*

Stopping

Must not stop or remain at rest on a carriageway or verge unless broken down (includes mechanical defect, lack of fuel, water or oil), involved in an accident, illness, emergency, to recover or remove an object on the motorway, or to give help to a person in such circumstances.

If stoppage is necessary on the carriageway the vehicle must be moved onto the verge as soon as practicable. If stopped on the verge, must not cause obstruction or danger to vehicles on the carriageway, and shall not remain at rest longer than is necessary in the circumstances. *REG 7 (REG 6)*

Reversing

A vehicle shall not be reversed unless it is necessary to enable it to move forward or to be connected to another vehicle. *REG 8 (REG 7)*

L Drivers

Persons who have not passed a test to drive must not use the motorway. (Does not apply to large goods vehicles or passenger-carrying vehicle (over 16 passengers, or over 8 and for hire or reward)). *REG 11 (REG 10)*

Lanes (three-lane motorways)

The following vehicles may not use the right hand lane of a 3 lane (or more) carriageway: Goods vehicle max laden weight over 7.5 tonnes; a goods vehicle with maximum weight exceeding 3.5 tonnes but not exceeding 7.5 tonnes, and which requires a speed limiter to be fitted under Reg 36B of RV Construction & Use Regs 1986; passenger vehicle constructed or adapted to carry more than 8 seated passengers in addition to the driver, with maximum laden weight over 7.5 tonnes; a passenger vehicle constructed or adapted to carry more than 8 seated passengers in addition to the driver, the maximum weight of which does not exceed 7.5 tonnes; and which requires a speed limiter to be fitted under Reg 36A of RV Construction & Use Regs 1986; motor vehicle drawing a trailer; motor tractor, light locomotive or heavy locomotive; except when necessary to pass an exceptionally wide load. *REG 12 (For Scots regulation see page 340)*

Pedestrians

Prohibited from using any part of the motorway except when necessary to do so as a result of accident, emergency or vehicle at rest on motorway as a result of circumstances specified in Regulation 7 (above), or with permission of constable to investigate accident, or he is performing his duty as constable, member of fire brigade, or ambulance service, or where necessary to carry out maintenance, repairs cleaning, etc, of motorway or structures on, under, over motorway, or to remove vehicles from motorway, or carry out surveys, in spections, etc, under authority of Secretary of State.

REG 15 (REG 13 – note REG 7 (above) for Scots is REG 6)

Animals

Not to be allowed to leave the vehicle, but if this is necessary, must not be allowed on the carriageway and must be on a lead or kept under proper control.

REG 14 (REG 12)

 # EYESIGHT

S.96 ROAD TRAFFIC ACT 1988
MOTOR VEHICLES (DRIVING LICENCES) REGULATIONS 1999

If a driver's eyesight is such (whether through a defect which cannot be corrected or which is not for the time being corrected) that he cannot comply with the following requirements, he commits an offence:

Category of licence	Size of character	From a distance of
A,B,B+E,F,G,H,K,L,P & the former cat.N. Also C1, C1+E (8.25 tonnes), D1 & D1+E if in force before 1.1.97 or granted on the expiry of such a licence, coming into force not later than 31.12.97	79 mm high & 57 mm wide	12.3 m for cat. K 20.5 m in any other case
	79 mm high & 50 mm wide	12 m for cat. K 20 m in any other case
Any other category	79.4 mm high	20.5 m

(S.96 & Regs. 70 & 72)

A constable who suspects that a driver may be guilty of this offence may require him to submit to a test using no other means of correction than he used at the time of driving. It is an offence to refuse to submit to the test. (*Reg. 96*)

PHYSICAL HEALTH

- An applicant for a driving licence must declare whether or not he/she is suffering from or has suffered from a relevant or prospective disability – making a false declaration is an offence. (*S.92*)
- A licence holder who becomes aware that he is suffering from a relevant or prospective disability (which will last for longer than three months) must inform the Secretary of State who may then serve notice on the licence holder, revoking the licence. Failure to notify such disabilities is an offence. (*S.94*)
- The following disabilities are prescribed by Reg 71:
  - epilepsy
  - severe mental handicap
  - liability to sudden attacks of giddiness or fainting for whatever reason, and regardless of whether a heart regulator etc. has been implanted to prevent it
  - persistent use of drugs or alcohol
  - and any other disability likely to cause driving to be a danger to the public.

STOPPING DISTANCES

Highway Code

Speed (mph)	20	30	40	50	60	70
Distance (feet)	40	75	120	175	240	315

DRIVING INSTRUCTION
ROAD TRAFFIC ACT 1988, Ss 123, 135 & 137
MOTOR CARS (DRIVING INSTRUCTION) REGULATIONS 2005
MOTOR CARS (DRIVING INSTRUCTION) (AMENDMENT)
REGULATIONS 2008

A driving instructor and his employer, if any, (does not apply to police or Serious Organised Crime Agency) will be guilty of an offence if paid instruction in the driving of a motor car is given unless he

is **registered** and he exhibits his certificate on the vehicle

FRONT OF CERTIFICATE	REAR OF CERTIFICATE

or has a trainee's licence and he exhibits his licence on the vehicle

FRONT OF LICENCE	REAR OF LICENCE
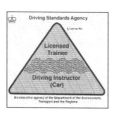	

Fitted behind the nearside edge of the windscreen so that the front can be seen from the outside the vehicle and the back can be seen from the nearside seat. Must be produced if required to a police constable or other authorised peson within 7 days or as soon as reasonably practicable.

It is an offence for an unregistered person to —
  a) take or use a prescribed title;
  b) wear or display a prescribed badge or certificate; or
  c) use any title, etc., implying that he is registered.
A badge is issued which resembles the front of the certificate/licence.

PEDESTRIAN CROSSINGS

ZEBRA, PELICAN AND PUFFIN PEDESTRIAN CROSSINGS REGULATIONS AND GENERAL
DIRECTIONS 1997 (THE 1997 REGS.)
TRAFFIC SIGNS REGULATIONS 2002 (THE 2002 REGS.)

Zebra, Pelican and Puffin are dealt with by the 1997 Regs., Equestrian, Toucan and Pedestrian Controlled are contained in the 2002 Regs. Light sequences are as follows.

Zebra – Yellow globe mounted to a post at each end of the crossing

Pelican – Light signals in the sequence steady green, steady amber, steady red, flashing amber (the latter indicating that a pedestrian still has precedence otherwise the vehicle may proceed).

Puffin
Equestrian
Toucan } Light signals in the sequence red, red and amber together, green, amber.
Pedestrian-
Controlled

Each type has a controlled area indicated by road markings on each side of the crossing.

Offences

(1) Vehicle or any part of it **stopping within the limits of the crossing** unless prevented by circumstances beyond driver's control or to avoid injury or damage. (Zebra, Pelican and Puffin only. Reg. 18 1997 Regs.)

(2) **Pedestrian remaining on crossing** longer than necessary to cross. (Zebra, Pelican and Puffin only. Reg. 19 1997 Regs.)

(3) Vehicle **stopping within a controlled area** (Reg. 20 1997 Regs., Reg. 27 2002 Regs.) except:

    (a) to give precedence to a pedestrian on the crossing

    (b) prevented by circumstances beyond driver's control or to avoid injury or damage

    (c) for police, Serious Organised Crime Agency, fire or ambulance purposes

    (d) for purposes of a building operation, demolition or excavation; removal of obstruction; maintenance, etc., of the road; or gas, water, electricity or telecommunications. (But in relation to any of these operations only for so long as is necessary to complete the operation and if the vehicle cannot be stopped elsewhere)

    (e) P.S.V. providing a local service, or carrying passengers at separate fares (but may not stop on the crossing itself)

    (f) vehicle stopping to make a left or right turn

(4) **Contravening red light** at crossing (Reg. 23 1997 Regs., Reg. 36 2002 Regs.)

(5) **Overtaking** within the controlled area on the approach to the crossing (Reg. 24 1997 Regs., Reg. 28 2002 Regs.)

(6) **Failing to give precedence to a pedestrian** on a Zebra crossing (Reg. 25 1997 Regs.)

(7) **Failing to give precedence to a pedestrian** on a Pelican crossing when amber signal is flashing (Reg. 26 1997 Regs.)

MISCELLANEOUS DRIVING OFFENCES
ROAD TRAFFIC ACT 1988 (AS AMENDED BY THE ROAD SAFETY ACT 2006)

Causing death by dangerous driving
(RTA S 1)

A person who causes the death of another person by driving a mechanically propelled vehicle dangerously on a road or other public place is guilty of an offence.

Dangerous driving
(RTA S 2)

A person who drives a mechanically propelled vehicle dangerously on a road or other public place is guilty of an offence.

Definition of 'dangerously'
(RTA S 2A)

A person drives dangerously if

- the way he drives falls far below what would be expected of a competent driver, and
- it would be obvious to a competent and careful driver that driving in that way would be dangerous.
- it is obvious to a competent and careful driver that driving the vehicle in its current state would be dangerous.

Causing death by careless, or inconsiderate, driving (RTA S 2B (inserted by the Road Safety Act 2006))

A person who causes the death of another person by driving a mechanically propelled vehicle on a road or other public place without due care and attention, or without reasonable consideration for other persons using the road or place, is guilty of an offence.

Causing death by driving: unlicensed, disqualified or uninsured drivers (RTA S 3ZB (inserted by the Road Safety Act 2006))

A person is guilty of an offence if he causes the death of another person by driving a motor vehicle on a road and, at the time when he is driving, he is committing an offence under S 87(1) (no licence), S 103(1)(b) (disqualified), or S 143 (uninsured).

Careless or inconsiderate driving
(RTA S 3)

A person who drives a mechanically propelled vehicle on a road or other public place without due care and attention or without reasonable consideration for other persons using the road is guilty of an offence.

Meaning of careless, or inconsiderate, driving (RTA S 3ZA)

The following meanings apply to Ss 2B and 3 above and S3A below:

A person is to be regarded as **driving without due care and attention** if (and only if) the way he drives falls below what would be expected of a competent and careful driver. In determining what would be expected of a competent and careful driver regard shall be had not only to the circumstances of which he could be expected to be aware but also to any circumstances shown to have been within the knowledge of the accused.

A person shall be regarded as **driving without reasonable consideration** for other persons only if those other persons are inconvenienced by his driving.

Causing death by careless driving when under influence of drink or drugs. (RTA S 3A)

If a person causes the death of another person by driving a mechanically propelled vehicle on a road or other public place without due care and attention, or without reasonable consideration for other persons using the road or place, and-

(a) he is, at the time when he is driving, unfit to drive through drink or drugs, or

(b) he has consumed so much alcohol that the proportion of it in his breath, blood or urine at that time exceeds the prescribed limit, or

(c) he is, within 18 hours after that time, required to provide a specimen in pursuance of S 7 of this Act, but without reasonable excuse fails to provide it, or

(d) he is required by a constable to give his permission for a laboratory test of a specimen of blood taken from him under S 7A of this Act, but without reasonable excuse fails to do so,

he is guilty of an offence.

A person shall be taken to be **unfit to drive** at any time when his ability to drive properly is impaired.

Subsections (b), (c) and (c) above shall not apply to a person driving a mechanically propelled vehicle other than a motor vehicle.

Dangerous or careless cycling (RTA Ss 28 AND 29)

A person who rides a cycle on a road dangerously, without due care and attention or without reasonable consideration for other persons using the road is guilty of an offence.

Causing danger to road users (RTA S 22A)

A person who, intentionally and without lawful authority or reasonable cause,

- causes anything to be on or over a road, or
- interferes with a motor vehicle, trailer or cycle, or
- interferes directly or indirectly with traffic equipment, (traffic signs, barriers, etc)

in such circumstances that it would be obvious to a reasonable person that to do so would be dangerous, is guilty of an offence.

PARKING

ROAD TRAFFIC REGULATION ACT 1984, S 99, REMOVAL AND DISPOSAL
OF VEHICLES REGULATIONS 1986

Removal of vehicles illegally, obstructively or dangerously parked or abandoned or broken down

Regulations may be made (see below) to permit the removal of vehicles at rest on a road in contravention of any statutory prohibition or restriction or in such a position or in such condition or in such circumstances as to cause obstruction to persons using the road or as to cause danger to such persons. Reg. 4 of the Regulations empowers a constable to remove a vehicle which he could require to be removed or which has been abandoned on a road or on land in the open air.

Emergency removal   ROAD TRAFFIC REGULATION ACT 1984, S 49(4), (4A).

A vehicle left in an authorised parking place may be removed in an emergency where the authority which designated the parking place has so empowered the chief officer of police. A constable acting under the instruction of the chief officer of police may suspend a designated parking place for up to seven days to mitigate congestion or obstruction of traffic or in exceptional circumstances.

Disabled Persons   ROAD TRAFFIC REGULATION ACT 1984 S 117.

DISABLED PERSONS (BADGES FOR MOTOR VEHICLES) (ENGLAND) REGULATIONS 2000 and LOCAL AUTHORITIES TRAFFIC ORDERS (EXEMPTIONS FOR DISABLED PERSONS)(ENGLAND) REGULATIONS 2000. Similar provisions have been introduced for Wales and Scotland.

Restriction of parking orders under Ss 1, 6, 9, 35, 45, or 46 of the Road Traffic Regulation Act 1984 shall provide for an exemption for a disabled person's vehicle displaying in the relevant position a disabled person's badge and, where the period of prohibition is more than 3 hours, an parking disk with the time at which parking began marked. Wrongful use of a disabled person's badge is an offence.

PART 6

SUPPLEMENT
FOR SCOTLAND

A NOTE TO OFFICERS SERVING IN SCOTTISH POLICE FORCES

The original intention of the *Traffic Officer's Companion* was to provide operational officers serving in English and Welsh police forces with a handy guide book on Road Traffic legislation.

The book has been very successful and has proved itself to be a valuable asset to operational police officers in England and Wales. In discussions with Jane's Police Review. I was invited to adapt Gordon Wilson's works in order that officers in Scottish forces could benefit from his skills.

As a result I have prepared the enclosed supplement for officers in the Scottish police forces. This supplement deals not only with Traffic legislation which is only applicable to Scotland but also contains additional legislation common in Scotland.

In keeping with Gordon Wilson's works, the relevant legislation has been subjected to practical interpretation. It should not, therefore be regarded as a definitive work of reference and specific technical details may require further research. On no account should it be used for study purposes by candidates sitting the Police (Scotland) Promotion Examinations.

Unless stated otherwise the text in the main part of this book is applicable to Scotland.

John Pilkington LLB BA
Former Inspector Strathclyde Police

MEANING OF THE TERM 'ROAD'
SECTION 151, ROADS (SCOTLAND) ACT 1984

Definition of 'road'

Any way (other than a waterway) over which there is a public right of passage (by whatever means and whether subject to a toll or not) and includes the road's verge and any bridge (whether permanent or temporary) over which, or tunnel through which, the road passes, and any reference to a road includes a part thereof.

Unless stated otherwise, officers in Scotland should use the above definition of a road as they work through this book.

The term 'public road' as defined for the Vehicle Excise and Registration Act 1994 has the same meaning as is applied by the Roads (Scotland) Act 1984, and means a road which a Roads Authority has a duty to maintain.

CONTROL OF BUILDERS' SKIPS ON ROADS

SECTION 85 ROADS (SCOTLAND) ACT 1984

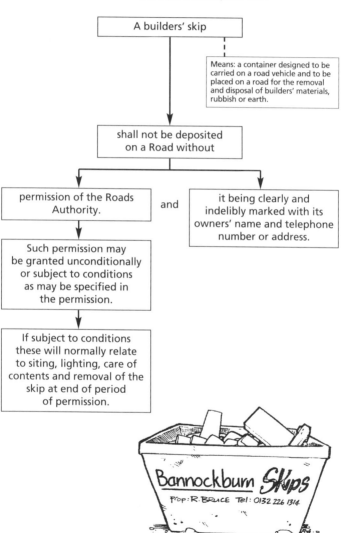

A builders' skip

Means: a container designed to be carried on a road vehicle and to be placed on a road for the removal and disposal of builders' materials, rubbish or earth.

shall not be deposited on a Road without

permission of the Roads Authority.

and

it being clearly and indelibly marked with its owners' name and telephone number or address.

Such permission may be granted unconditionally or subject to conditions as may be specified in the permission.

If subject to conditions these will normally relate to siting, lighting, care of contents and removal of the skip at end of period of permission.

Bannockburn *Skips*

Prop: R. Bruce Tel: 0132 226 1314

Offence S 85(3)

For the owner of the skip who uses it, or causes or permits it to be used on a road in contravention of Section 85.

Defence S 85(4)

It is a defence, (except in relation to the offence of not having owner's name etc, on the skip), to prove another person undertook the responsibility of complying with the permission/condition contravened, and that the offence was committed without the consent or connivance of the owner; and that other person may be charged with and convicted of the contravention as if he were the owner.

REMOVAL OF SKIP etc.
SECTION 86

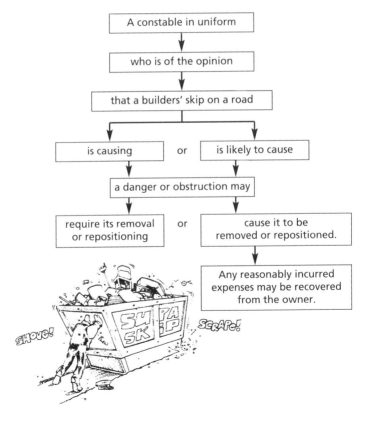

A constable in uniform

↓

who is of the opinion

↓

that a builders' skip on a road

↓

is causing or is likely to cause

↓

a danger or obstruction may

require its removal or repositioning or cause it to be removed or repositioned.

↓

Any reasonably incurred expenses may be recovered from the owner.

CONTROL OF OBSTRUCTIONS ON ROADS

SECTION 59 ROADS (SCOTLAND) ACT 1984

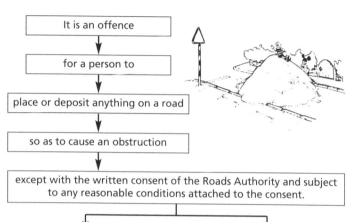

It is an offence

↓

for a person to

↓

place or deposit anything on a road

↓

so as to cause an obstruction

↓

except with the written consent of the Roads Authority and subject to any reasonable conditions attached to the consent.

A person who contravenes Section 59 may be required by the Roads Authority or a constable in uniform to remove the obstruction forthwith.

↓

Failure to comply with this requirement is an offence.

↓

Where:

1. a person does not comply with the above requirement;

2. the person who caused the obstruction cannot be traced; or

3. in a case of emergency, the Roads Authority or a constable may remove the obstruction or cause it to be removed and recover reasonably incurred expenses from the person responsible for the obstruction

The provisions of Section 59 do not apply in respect of:

1. the deposit of building materials under provisions of Section 58 of the Act; or

2. deposit of Builders' Skips under Section 85 of the Act;

3. unauthorised abandonment of motor vehicles, etc (which is covered by the provisions of the Refuse Disposal (Amenity) Act 1978; or

4. to works covered by Part IV of the New Roads and Street Works Act 1991.

RESTRICTION ON PLACING BRIDGES, ETC. OVER ROADS

SECTION 90 ROADS (SCOTLAND) ACT, 1984

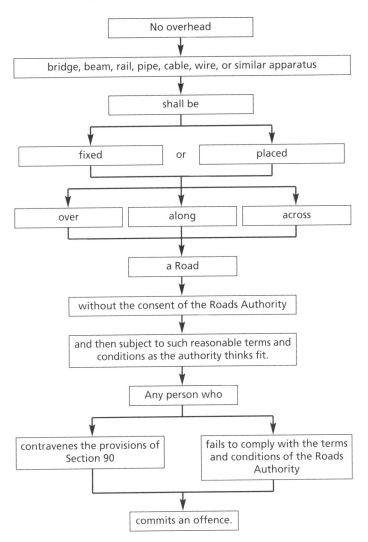

No overhead

bridge, beam, rail, pipe, cable, wire, or similar apparatus

shall be

fixed   or   placed

over   along   across

a Road

without the consent of the Roads Authority

and then subject to such reasonable terms and conditions as the authority thinks fit.

Any person who

contravenes the provisions of Section 90

fails to comply with the terms and conditions of the Roads Authority

commits an offence.

DEPOSIT OF MUD ETC. ON ROAD
SECTION 95 ROADS (SCOTLAND) ACT, 1984

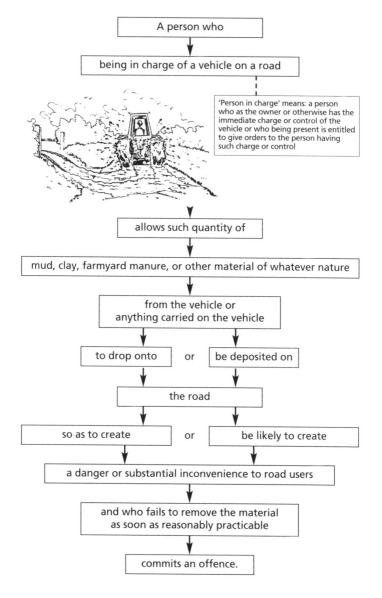

A person who

↓

being in charge of a vehicle on a road

'Person in charge' means: a person who as the owner or otherwise has the immediate charge or control of the vehicle or who being present is entitled to give orders to the person having such charge or control

↓

allows such quantity of

↓

mud, clay, farmyard manure, or other material of whatever nature

↓

from the vehicle or anything carried on the vehicle

↓

to drop onto　or　be deposited on

↓

the road

↓

so as to create　or　be likely to create

↓

a danger or substantial inconvenience to road users

↓

and who fails to remove the material as soon as reasonably practicable

↓

commits an offence.

DAMAGE TO ROADS
SECTION 100 ROADS (SCOTLAND) ACT, 1984

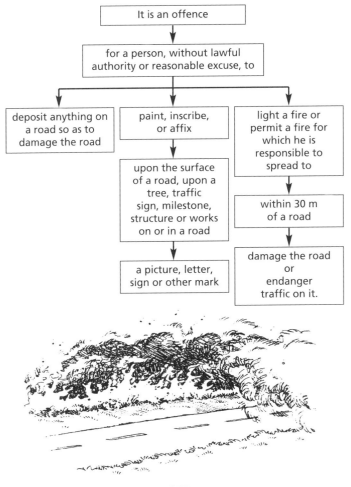

It is an offence

for a person, without lawful authority or reasonable excuse, to

deposit anything on a road so as to damage the road	paint, inscribe, or affix	light a fire or permit a fire for which he is responsible to spread to

upon the surface of a road, upon a tree, traffic sign, milestone, structure or works on or in a road

within 30 m of a road

a picture, letter, sign or other mark

damage the road or endanger traffic on it.

NOTE

A farmer who culpably and recklessly endangered the public, by neglecting to ensure that no danger was caused to persons on a public road from a fire – he had set to straw in his field, which spread to vegetation at the side of the road and smoke obscured visibility, causing a collision – was found guilty of the common law crime of Culpable and Reckless Fire-Raising.

PLACING ROPES ETC. IN ROAD
SECTION 101 ROADS (SCOTLAND) ACT, 1984

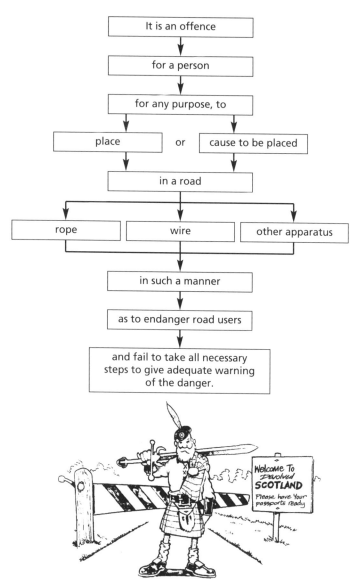

It is an offence

for a person

for any purpose, to

place — or — cause to be placed

in a road

rope | wire | other apparatus

in such a manner

as to endanger road users

and fail to take all necessary steps to give adequate warning of the danger.

AIDING AND ABETTING – ROAD TRAFFIC OFFENCES IN SCOTLAND

In order to charge a person with aiding and abetting the commission of an offence, it is necessary to prove that he knew of the circumstances constituting the offence and helped in its commission.

Section 119 Road Traffic Regulation Act, 1984 contains provisions relating to aiding and abetting certain Traffic offences in Scotland and provides that 'a person who aids, abets, counsels, procures or incites any other person to commit an offence against the provisions of the Road Traffic Regulation Act, 1984 and any regulations made under that Act, shall be guilty of an offence and shall be liable, on conviction, to the same punishment as might be imposed on conviction of the first mentioned offence.

Care has to be taken when dealing with other Traffic offences outwith the scope of the Road Traffic Regulation Act, 1984. Where such offences employ the words **use**, **cause** or **permit**, then an accessory to the offence should be prosecuted for **causing and permitting** the offence rather than **aiding and abetting**. If, however, there is a clear case of a person having aided and abetted a Traffic offence not covered by the Road Traffic Regulation Act 1984, the offender should be charged with a contravention of Section 293 Criminal Procedure (Scotland) Act 1995 and shall be liable to the same penalties as the original offender.

DON'T WORRY, YOU'LL GET A L'CENCE WHEN YOU'RE OLD ENOUGH TO PASS THE TEST!

TAKING MOTOR VEHICLES WITHOUT AUTHORITY (STATUTORY CLANDESTINE POSSESSION)

SECTION 178 ROAD TRAFFIC ACT, 1988

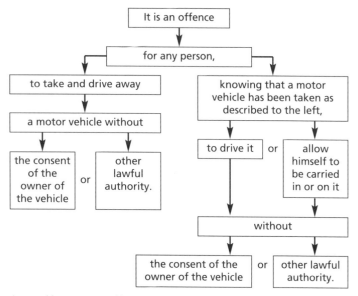

A constable may arrest without warrant any person he reasonably suspects of having committed or having attempted to commit this offence.

An offence under Section 178 may only be committed in respect of motor vehicles (ie, mechanically propelled vehicles intended or adapted for use on the roads). A person who takes and drives away a mechanically propelled vehicle (not intended or adopted for use on the roads) without the consent of owner, etc would commit theft or clandestine possession.

Note 1: An accused who proves he acted in the reasonable belief that he had lawful authority or that the owner of the motor vehicle would, in the circumstances, have given consent if he had been asked for it, shall not be convicted.

Note 2: Section 178 is generally intended to deal with cases where motor vehicles are taken, driven away and then abandoned. If, however, the vehicle were abandoned in a place where it is unlikely to be found, the offender may be held to have committed theft, rather than a contravention of Section 178.

Note 3: Where the police trace the vehicle, while still in the possession of the person(s) who took and drove it away without authority, it is normal to charge the offender(s) with theft, rather than a contravention of Section 178. However, the final decision as to the charge rests with the Procurator Fiscal.

CARELESS DRIVING – CASE LAW
USE OF TELEPHONES IN VEHICLES

As a result of telephones being fitted to vehicles, a body of Scots Case Law has grown up relating to the use of telephones in moving vehicles and the offence of careless driving under Section 3 of the Road Traffic Act, 1988.

There are three main cases to consider:

1. *McPhail v Haddow 1990 S.C.C.R 339*

   In this case, the accused was charged with careless driving for using a portable telephone while driving. The court held that, in the absence of any lack of control over the vehicle or any danger to others, there was no evidence of careless driving.

2. *Rae v Friel 1992 S.C.C.R 688*

   In this case the accused was charged with careless driving for travelling in excess of 70 mph on a motorway while holding a telephone in one hand and overtaking five other vehicles in two overtaking manoeuvres. He had only one hand on the steering wheel during these manoeuvres.

   The court held the important feature was that the accused overtook five vehicles, and that if any of them had happened suddenly to move out into the overtaking lane an emergency would have been created to which the accused would not have been able to react appropriately – as a result the accused was convicted of careless driving.

3. *Stock v Carmichael 1993 S.C.C.R 136*

   In this case, there was no overtaking manoeuvre, but evidence was led that the driver was not aware of a police vehicle alongside him and that the use of the telephone, except in an emergency, was a breach of the Highway Code.

   The court held the driver was guilty of careless driving in this case but stressed that each case depends on its own facts and circumstances.

POWER OF ARREST IN SCOTLAND FOR DANGEROUS OR CARELESS DRIVING OR CYCLING

S 167 ROAD TRAFFIC ACT, 1988

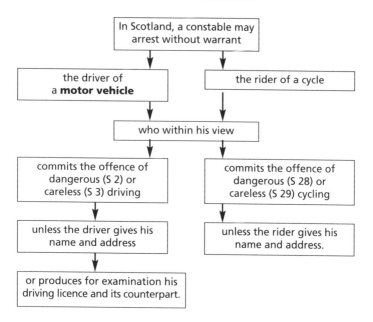

NOTE

Although Section 2 and 3 offences may be committed in any mechanically propelled vehicle, the powers provided under Section 167 in respect of Sections 2 and 3 can only be used against the driver of a **motor vehicle** (ie a mechanically propelled vehicle intended or adapted for use on the roads).

Refusal to provide name and address etc

Section 169 Road Traffic Act 1988 provides that if the driver of a mechanically propelled vehicle, who is alleged to have committed an offence under Section 2 or 3 RTA 1988, or the rider of a cycle who is alleged to have committed an offence under Section 28 or 29 RTA 1988, refuses – on being required by **any person** having reasonable grounds for so requiring – to give his name or address, or gives a false name or address is guilty of an offence.

NOTE: Section 169 applies throughout Great Britain

PEDAL CYCLES

1. Dangerous cycling
S28 ROAD TRAFFIC ACT 1988

It is an offence for a person to ride a cycle dangerously on a road.

A person is to be regarded as riding a cycle dangerously if (and only if):
a) the way he rides falls far below what would be expected of a competent and careful cyclist; and
b) it would be obvious to a competent and careful cyclist that riding in that way would be dangerous.

The term 'dangerous' refers to danger either of injury to any person or of serious damage to property.

2. Careless and inconsiderate cycling
SECTION 29 ROAD TRAFFIC ACT 1988

It is an offence for a person to ride a cycle on a road without due care and attention, or without reasonable consideration for other persons using the road.

PEDAL CYCLES cont

3. Cycling when under the influence of drink or drugs

Section 30 Road Traffic Act, 1988

It is an offence

↓

for a person

↓

to ride a cycle on a road or other public place

↓

when unfit to ride through drink or drugs –

↓

that is to say – is under the influence of drink or a drug to such an extent as to be incapable of having proper control of the cycle.

↓

A constable may arrest without warrant a person found committing this offence.

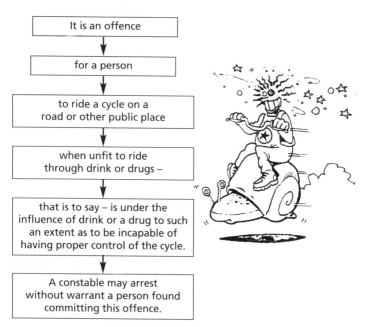

NOTE

Under the provisions of Section 294 Criminal Procedure (Scotland) Act, 1995 any person who **attempts** to ride a cycle on a road or other public place when unfit to ride through drink or drugs also commits an offence under Section 30 of the Road Traffic Act, 1988.

The police have no power to require a cyclist suspected of contravening Section 30 to provide specimens of breath, blood or urine. However, the cyclist may be requested to provide such specimens and/or undergo a medical examination and tests provided he is informed that he is entitled to refuse and, that if he agrees, the results may be used in evidence.

DRINK, DRUGS & DRIVING – PROVISION OF SPECIMENS FOR ANALYSIS IN SCOTLAND

SECTION 7, AS AMENDED BY ROAD TRAFFIC ACT 1991, THE CRIMINAL PROCEDURE AND INVESTIGATIONS ACT 1996 AND THE RAILWAYS AND TRANSPORT SAFETY ACT 2003

When specimens may be required

(1) If investigating one of the following offences under the Road Traffic Act 1988:

  i) causing death by careless driving when under the influence of drink or drugs (S 3A),

  ii) driving or being in charge when under the influence of drink or drugs (S 4), or

  iii) driving or being in charge with alcohol above the limit (S 5),

a constable may require a person to provide:

  (a) two specimens of breath for analysis by means of a device of a type approved by the Secretary of State; or

  (b) to provide a specimen of blood or urine for a laboratory test.

Where specimens may be required

(2) A requirement under this section to provide specimens of breath can only be made at a police station.

Circumstances in which blood or urine specimens may be taken

(3) A requirement under this section to provide a specimen of blood or urine can only be made at a police station or at a hospital; and it cannot be made at a police station unless:

  (a) the constable making the requirement has reasonable cause to believe that for medical reasons a specimen of breath cannot be provided or should not be required; or

  (b) at the time the requirement is made a device or a reliable device of the type mentioned in subsection (1)(a) above is not available at the police station or it is then for any other reason not practicable to use such a device there; or

  (c) a device of the type mentioned in subsection (1)(a) above has been used at the police station but the constable who required the specimens of breath has reasonable cause to believe that the device has not produced a reliable indication of the proportion of alcohol in the breath of the person concerned, or

DRINK, DRUGS & DRIVING – PROVISION OF SPECIMENS FOR ANALYSIS IN SCOTLAND cont

SECTION 7, AS AMENDED BY ROAD TRAFFIC ACT 1991, THE CRIMINAL PROCEDURE AND INVESTIGATIONS ACT 1996 AND THE RAILWAYS AND TRANSPORT SAFETY ACT 2003

    (d) as a result of the administration of a preliminary drug test, the constable making the requirement has reasonable cause to believe that the person required to provide a specimen of blood or urine has a drug in his body, or

    (e) the suspected offence is one under section 3A or 4 of this Act and the constable making the requirement has been advised by a medical practitioner that the condition of the person required to provide the specimen might be due to some drug;

but may then be made notwithstanding that the person required to provide the specimen has already provided or been required to provide two specimens of breath.

Blood or urine?

(4)   If the provision of a specimen other than a specimen of breath may be required in pursuance of this section the question of whether it is to be a specimen of blood or a specimen of urine shall be decided by the constable making the requirement, but if a medical practitioner is of the opinion for medical reasons a specimen of blood cannot or should not be taken, the specimen shall be a specimen of urine.

Provision of urine specimen

(5)   A specimen of urine shall be provided within one hour of the requirement for its provision being made and after the provision of a previous specimen of urine.

Failure to provide specimen

(6)   A person who, without reasonable excuse, fails to provide a specimen when required to do so in pursuance of this section is guilty of an offence.

(7)   A constable must, on requiring any person to provide a specimen in pursuance of this section, warn him that a failure to provide it may render him liable to prosecution.

RESTRICTIONS ON USE OF RIGHT-HAND LANE ON SCOTS MOTORWAYS
REGULATION 11 MOTORWAYS TRAFFIC (SCOTLAND) REGULATIONS 1995

(1)   Subject to the provisions of paragraphs (2) and (3) below
- a goods vehicle having a maximum laden weight exceeding 7.5 tonnes;
- or a passenger vehicle which is constructed or adapted to carry more than eight seated passengers in addition to the driver, the maximum laden weight of which exceeds 7.5 tonnes; or
- a motor vehicle drawing a trailer; and
- a vehicle which is a motor tractor, a light locomotive or a heavy locomotive.

shall not be driven, or moved, or stopped, or remain at rest on the right-hand lane of a length of carriageway which has three or more traffic lanes at any place where all the lanes are open for use by traffic proceeding in the same direction.

(2)   The prohibition does not apply to a vehicle
- while it is being driven on any right-hand lane such as is mentioned in paragraph (1) insofar as it is necessary for the vehicle to be driven to enable it to pass another vehicle which is carrying or drawing a load of exceptional width; or
- so as to prevent that vehicle joining or leaving the motorway by means of a road giving access to or from that motorway on the right hand side of the carriageway.

(3)   Nothing in this regulation shall have effect so as to require a vehicle to change lane during a period when it would not be reasonably practicable for it to do so without involving danger or injury to any person or inconvenience to other traffic.

CONVERSION TABLES

LENGTH

1 Millimetre	= 0.03937 Inch	1 Inch	= 25.4 Millimetres
1 Centimetre	= 0.3937 Inch	1 Inch	= 2.54 Centimetres
1 Metre	= 39.37 Inches	1 Foot	= 0.3048 Metre
1 Metre	= 3.2808 Feet	1 Yard	= 0.9144 Metre
1 Metre	= 1.0936 Yards	1 Mile	= 1.609 Kilometres

WEIGHT

1 Gramme	= 15.432 Grains	1 Ounce	= 28.35 Grammes
1 Gramme	= 0.03527 Ounce	1 Pound	= 453.6 Grammes
1 Kilogramme	= 2.2046 Pounds	1 Ton	= 1.016 Tonnes
1 Tonne	= 0.9842 Ton		

LIQUID MEASURE

$\frac{1}{2}$ Litre	= 0.880 Pints	1 Pint	= 20 Fluid Ounces
1 Litre	= 1.760 Pints	1 Pint	= 0.568 Litres
1 Litre	= 0.220 Gallons	1 Quart	= 1.136 Litres
10 Litres	= 2 Galls 1$\frac{1}{2}$ Pts (approx)	1 Gallon	= 4.546 Litres

SQUARE MEASURE

1 Sq. Millimetre	= 0.00155 Sq.in.	1 Sq. Kilometre	= 0.3861 Sq. Miles
1 Sq. Centimetre	= 0.155 Sq.inch	1 Sq. Inch	= 6.452 Sq. Cms
1 Sq. Metre	= 10.764 Sq.Feet	1 Sq. Foot	= 0.0929 Sq.Metres
1 Sq. Metre	= 1.196 Sq.Yards	1 Sq. Yard	= 0.836 Sq. Metres
1 Are	= 0.0247 Acres	1 Acre	= 0.4047 Hectare
1 Hectare	= 2.471 Acres	1 Sq.Mile	= 2.5899 Sq. Kms
1 Acre	= 4840 Sq. Yards	1 Sq. Mile	= 640 Acres

VELOCITY

1 M.P.H.	= 0.44704 Metre/Sec.	1 Km./Hr.	= 0.911 Ft./Sec.
1 M.P.H.	= 1.60934 Km./Hr.	1 Km./Hr.	= 0.6214 M.P.H.

INCHES		MILLIMETRES	FEET		METRES
0.039	1	25.4	3.281	1	0.305
0.079	2	50.8	6.562	2	0.610
0.118	3	76.2	9.843	3	0.914
0.157	4	101.6	13.123	4	1.219
0.197	5	127.0	16.404	5	1.524
0.236	6	152.4	19.685	6	1.829
0.276	7	177.8	22.966	7	2.134
0.315	8	203.2	26.247	8	2.438
0.354	9	228.6	29.528	9	2.743
0.394	10	254.0	32.81	10	3.048

YARDS		METRES	SQ. FT.		SQ. METRES
1.094	1	0.914	10.764	1	0.093
2.187	2	1.829	21.528	2	0.186
3.281	3	2.743	32.292	3	0.279
4.375	4	3.658	43.056	4	0.372
5.468	5	4.572	58.819	5	0.456
6.562	6	5.486	64.583	6	0.557
7.655	7	6.401	75.347	7	0.650
8.749	8	7.315	86.111	8	0.743
9.842	9	8.223	96.875	9	0.836
10. 936	10	9.114	107.640	10	0.929

OUNCES		GRAMMES	POUNDS		KILOGRAMMES
0.035	1	28.350	2.205	1	0.454
0.071	2	56.699	4.409	2	0.9072
0.106	3	85.049	6.614	3	1.361
0.141	4	113.398	8.819	4	1.814
0.176	5	141.748	11.023	5	2.268
0.212	6	170.097	13.228	6	2.722
0.247	7	198.447	15.432	7	3.175
0.282	8	226.796	17.637	8	3.629
0.317	9	255.146	19.842	9	4.082
0.353	10	283.500	22.046	10	4.536

PINTS		LITRES	GALLONS		LITRES
1.761	1	0.568	0.22	1	4.55
3.521	2	1.136	0.44	2	9.09
5.282	3	1.704	0.66	3	13.64
7.043	4	2.272	0.88	4	18.18
8.804	5	2.840	1.10	5	22.73
10.564	6	3.408	1.32	6	27.28
12.325	7	3.976	1.54	7	31.82
14.086	8	4.544	1.76	8	36.37
15.847	9	5.112	1.98	9	40.91
17.600	10	5.680	2.20	10	45.46

MILES		KILOMETRES	MILES		KILOMETRES
0.31	$^1/_2$	0.8	3.42	$5^1/_2$	8.8
0.62	1	1.6	3.73	6	9.7
0.93	$1^1/_2$	2.4	4.04	$6^1/_2$	10.5
1.24	2	3.2	4.35	7	11.3
1.55	$2^1/_2$	4.0	4.66	$7^1/_2$	12.0
1.86	3	4.8	4.97	8	12.9
2.17	$3^1/_2$	5.6	5.28	$8^1/_2$	13.7
2.49	4	6.4	5.59	9	14.5
2.80	$4^1/_2$	7.2	5.90	$9^1/_2$	15.3
3.11	5	8.0	6.21	10	16.1

TABLE OF LEGISLATION

Legislation	Page
70 mph, 60 mph and 50 mph (Temporary Speed Limit) Order 1977	301
Animal Health Act 1981	331
Aggravated Vehicle-Taking Act 1992	289
Carriage of Dangerous Goods and Use of Transportable Pressure Equipment Regulations 2007	
Regs. 9–16	311–312
Regs. 17–22	312–313
Reg. 38–39	316
Reg. 43–44	316
Reg. 47	306
Reg. 48	316
Reg. 49	306
Reg. 51	316
Reg. 53	317
Regs 54–57	317
Reg. 62	317
Reg. 64	316
Reg. 65	317
Regs. 72–80	317
Reg. 81	317
Reg. 83	317
Regs. 85–87	317
Reg. 86	313
Reg. 89	313
Reg. 90	318
Reg. 91	325
Sched. 7	325
Community Bus Regulations 1978	189
Community Bus Regulations 1986	188, 189
Community Directive 70/156	6
Community Directive 2003/97	71
Community Directive 2005/27	71
Community Drivers' Hours and Recording Equipment Regulations 2007	242
Council Regulation 561/2006	267, 242

Legislation	Page
Council Regulation 3821/85	
Art. 3	267
Art. 5	268
Arts. 12–14	268
Art. 15	269, 270
Annex 1	267
Annex 1A	267
Council Regulation 1/2005	331
Criminal Attempts Act 1981	290
Criminal Justice and Public Order Act 1994	340, 343
Criminal Procedure (Scotland) Act 1995	365, 370
Disabled persons (Badges for Motor Vehicles) (England) Regulations 2000	354
Drivers' Hours (Goods Vehicles) (Exemptions) Regs. 1986	256
The Drivers' Hours (Goods Vehicles) (Keeping of Records) Regulations 1987	259, 261, 262
Drivers' Hours (Goods Vehicles) (Modifications) Order 1986	257
Drivers' Hours (Harmonisation with Community Rules) Regulations 1986	247
Driving Licence (Community Driving Licence) Regulations 1996	140, 143
Driving Licences (Exchangeable Licences) Order 2007	140
EEC Directive 76/757	239
Goods Vehicles (Ascertainment of Maximum Gross Weights) Regulations 1976	31
Goods Vehicles (Licensing of Operators) Act 1995	
S2	149
S3	149
S5	149
S38	152
S40	152
S41	152
Goods Vehicles (Licensing of Operators) Regulations 1995	
Reg 23	149
Reg 26	152
Reg 32	152
Sched. 3	151
Goods Vehicles (Licensing of Operators) (Temporary Use in Great Britain) Regulations 1996	153–157

Legislation	Page
Goods Vehicles (Plating and Testing) Regulations 1988	
Reg 4	175
Reg 9	175
Regs 17–22	176
Sched. 2	178
Highways Act 1980	
S139, 140	344
Local Authorities Traffic Orders (Exemptions for Disabled Persons) (England) Regulations 2000	354
Motor Cars (Driving Instruction) Regulations 2005	350
Motor Cars (Driving Instruction) (Amendment) Regulations 2008	350
Motor Cycle Noise Act 1987	45
Motor Cycle (Eye Protectors) Regulations 1999	347
Motor Cycles (Protective Helmets) Regulations 1998	346
Motor Cycle Silencer and Exhaust System Regulations 1995	
Regs 3, 4 & 5	45
Motor Vehicles (Tests) Regulations 1981	172
Motor Vehicles (Driving Licences) Regulations 1999	
Reg 4	122
Reg 5	121
Reg 6	128
Reg 8	129
Reg 9	135
Reg 11	132
Reg 16	130
Reg 19	126
Reg 20	139
Reg 40	122
Reg 43	126
Reg 44A	126
Reg 50	125
Reg 51	107
Reg 54	133
Regs 70, 72	349
Reg 76	124
Reg 80	140
Reg 83	139
Reg 96	349
Sched. 2	122, 126, 128
Motor Vehicles (International Circulation) Order 1975	140
Motor Vehicle Tyres (Safety) Regulations 1994	51

Legislation	Page
Motor Vehicles (Wearing of Seat Belts) Regulations 1993	64, 66, 67
Motor Vehicles (Wearing of Seat Belts by Children in Front Seats) Regulations 1993	65
Motorways Traffic (England and Wales) Regulations 1982	348
Motorways Traffic (Scotland) Regulations 1995	348, 373
Passenger and Goods Vehicles (Recording Equipment) (Downloading and Retention of Data) Regulations 2008	270
Passenger and Goods Vehicles (Recording Equipment) (Tachograph Card) Regulations 2006	271, 272, 273
Police and Criminal Evidence Act 1984	
S4	291
S24	336
S28, 30	338
Police Reform Act 2002	342
Police (Retention and Disposal of Motor Vehicles) Regulations 2002	342
Public Passenger Vehicles Act 1981	
S12	185
S13	185
S79A	182
Public Service Vehicles (Operator's Licence) Regulations 1995	
Reg 1	185
Refuse Disposal (Amenity) Act 1978	360
Removal and Disposal of Vehicles Regulations 1986	287
Road Safety Act 2006	
S 26	113
S 45	175
Road Traffic Act 1988	
S1, 2, 2A	352
S3	352, 367
S3A	353
S3ZA	352
S4	291
S5	291
S6	292
S6A, 6B, 6C	293
S6D, 6E	294
S7	295, 296
S7A	297

Legislation	Page
S8, 9, 10	298–299
S15	65–68
S15B	63
S16	346
S18	347
S22	287
S22A	353
S28, 29	353, 368, 369
S30	370
S40A	44
S47	168
S67	284
S70	19
S71	19
S78	19
S87	136
S88	136
S92	349
S94	349
S96	349
S101	135
S108	4
S121	5
S123	350
S135	350
S137	350
S143	147
S144	147
S163	341
S164, 165	139
S165A	148
S167	368
S169	368
S170	334
S172	335
S178	366
S185	3
S187	4
Sched. 2	284
Road Traffic (Foreign Vehicles) Act 1972	279–281
Road Traffic (New Drivers) Act 1995	134

Legislation	Page
Road Traffic Offenders Act 1988	
S1, 2	345
S28	137, 138
S91	287
Sched. 1	345
Road Traffic Regulation Act 1984	
S82	300
S85	300
S86	301–303
S89	300
S99	354
S119	365
Sched. 6	301–303
Road Transport (Working Time) Regulations 2005	282
Roads (Scotland) Act 1984	
S59	360
S85	358
S90	361
S95	362
S100	363
S101	364
S151	357
Road Vehicles (Authorisation of Special Types) (General) Order 2003	
Arts 12–15	102
Arts. 16–18	103
Arts. 19–23	90
Arts. 24–28	91
Art. 29	93
Arts. 30, 31	91
Arts. 32, 33	92
Arts. 38, 39	94
Art. 40	95
Art. 42–44, 46, 47	96
Art. 49	97
Art. 50, 51	98
Art. 52	99
Arts. 53, 54, 55	100, 101
Sched. 1:	
Paras 2, 3, 4, 7–12, 13, 15	76
Paras 16–25	77
Paras 26–29	78
Para 30	79

Legislation	Page
Para 31	79, 80
Para 32	80
Para 35	81
Sched. 2	82–84
Sched. 3	85–87
Sched. 4	88, 89
Sched. 5	104
Sched. 6	104
Sched. 7	104
Sched. 8	105, 106
Sched. 10	92
Sched. 11	95
Sched. 12	101
Road Vehicles (Authorised Weight) Regulations 1998	32
Road Vehicles (Construction and Use) Regulations 1986	
Reg 3	2, 3, 4, 5, 12, 16
Reg 7	8–11
Reg 8	15
Reg 9	17
Reg 10	35
Reg 10A	36
Reg 10B	36
Reg 11	12
Reg 12	14
Reg 13	13
Reg 13A	13
Reg 13B	13
Reg 13C	13
Reg 15	27
Reg 16	27
Reg 24	48
Reg 26	48–50
Reg 27	48–50
Reg 30	74
Reg 32	74
Reg 33	69–73
Reg 34	74
Reg 35	56
Reg 36	56
Reg 36A	304
Reg 36B	305
Reg 37	54, 55
Reg 38	110

Legislation	Page
Regs 41–43	189
Reg 46	57, 58
Reg 47	59, 60
Reg 48	61
Reg 48A	62
Reg 49	108
Reg 51	107
Reg 53	110
Reg 54	45
Reg 57A	45
Reg 57B	45
Reg 60	110
Reg 61	46, 47
Reg 61A	46, 47
Reg 64	109
Reg 65	109
Reg 66	176
Reg 69	179
Reg 70	176, 177
Reg 70A	304, 305
Reg 74	286
Reg 75	20, 22–25, 27
Reg 76	21, 28
Reg 77	25, 26, 28
Reg 78	20, 29
Reg 79	30
Reg 81	11, 16
Reg 83	38, 39, 42
Reg 84	40
Reg 86A	43
Reg 87	27, 41
Reg 89	41
Reg 90	42
Reg 92	43
Reg 93	43
Reg 97	45, 111
Reg 98	110
Reg 100	44
Regs 101–102	111
Reg 103	111, 287
Reg 104	112
Regs 105–107, 109	112
Reg 110	113

Legislation	Page
Sched. 9	179
Sched. 11	25
Sched. 11A	28
Sched. 12	238
Road Vehicles (Display of Registration Marks)	
Regulations 2001	
Regs. 3, 5–9	163
Regs. 10, 11	163, 164
Reg 13	165
Reg 14	166
Reg 14A	168
Reg 15	168
Reg 16	168
Reg 19	168
Sched. 2	160–164
Sched. 3	161, 162–165
Road Vehicles Lighting Regulations 1989	
Reg 4	203
Reg 6	202
Reg 11	191, 208–209, 229
Reg 12	206
Reg 13	206
Reg 16	207
Reg 17A	191
Reg 18	210–225
Reg 19	205
Reg 20	226–227, 230–233
Reg 21	237
Reg 22	230–231
Reg 23	210, 212, 214, 216, 219, 221–222, 225–228
Reg 24	204, 205
Reg 25	204
Reg 27	210, 224, 226, 227, 240
Reg 28	286
Sched. 1	196–201, 210–223, 225, 228, 230, 231, 239

Legislation	Page
Sched. 2	212, 213
Sched. 4	210, 211
Sched. 5	210, 211
Sched. 6	226
Sched. 7	220, 221
Sched. 8	228
Sched. 9	230, 231
Sched. 10	214, 215
Sched. 11	224, 225
Sched. 12	222, 223
Sched. 13	232
Sched. 14	227
Sched. 17	219
Sched. 18	216, 217
Sched. 21	218
Sched. 21A	191
Road Vehicles (Registration and Licensing) Regulations 2002	
Reg 7	162
Reg 26	160
Reg 42	181
Section 19 Minibus and other Section 19 Permit Buses Regulations 1987	187
Serious Organised Crime and Police Act 2005	336, 337
Theft Act 1968	
S12, 12A	289
Traffic Signs Regulations 2002	351
Transport Act 1968	
S95	246
S96	253–258
S97	267, 274, 276, 277
S99C	278
S99ZB	275
S99ZC	276
S99ZD	276
S99ZE	277
S99ZF	277
S102	246
S102A	246
S103	258

Legislation	Page
Transport Act 1980	190
Transport Act 1985	
S3	184
S6	184, 185
S10	183
S19	186, 187
S22, 23	188, 189
Vehicles (Crime) Act 2001	
S1, 7, 9, 10, 12	288
S17, 24, 25	170
S26, 28, 29	171
Vehicles Crime (Registration of Registration plate Suppliers) Regulation 2008	
Regs 3, 6, 7	170
Vehicle Drivers (Certificates of Professional Competence) Regulations 2007	
Reg 3	144
Reg 8	145
Reg 9	145
Reg 10	145
Reg 11	146
Reg 13	146
Reg 14	146
Reg 15	146
Vehicles Excise and Registration Act 1994	
S5	158
S11	180
S12	180
S28A	169
S29	162
S33	162
S34	162
S43C	169
S44	169
S62	180
Sched. 2	158
Sched. 6	181
Vehicles Excise Duty (Immobilisation, Removal and Disposal of Vehicles) Regulations 1997	161

Legislation	Page
Welfare of Animals (Transport) (England) Order 2006	331–333
Zebra, Pelican and Puffin Pedestrian Crossings Regulations and General Directions, 1997	351

INDEX

A

Abnormal loads	76–81
weight	75–81
Accident	
duty to report	334
ADR certificate	192
ADR Requirements	306
Age, driving for	131, 135
Aggravated vehicle taking	289
Agricultural vehicle	
projections	90
wide	91
Alarms, vehicle	54
Anchorage points	57, 58
Animals, transport of	331–333
Arrest	
mode of	338
powers of	336–337
Articulated vehicle	268
definition	4
length	8
matching	26
weight	25, 26
ATA carnet	192
Axle weights	29–30, 34

B

Beacons, warning	229
Blood specimens	295
Breath tests	292–294
specimens	295–297
specimens (Scotland)	371
Builders' skips	344
Bus	
definition	5, 17
maximum height	17
maximum weight	20

C

Caravan, passenger	39
Careless	
cycling	368, 382
driving	352, 368
Careless driving, causing death	352
Careless driving, meaning	352
Carriage by road definition	251
Categories of vehicles	122, 123
Causing death	352
Certificate of Professional	
Competence	144–146
Chemicals	
conveyance of	289–307
Child, definition	68
CMR consignment note	192

Closely spaced axle	
definition	30
Control of vehicle	110
Conversion tables	375
CPC	144–146
Crash helmets	346

D

Danger to road users	44
Dangerous	
cycling	345, 368
driving	345, 368
Dangerous substances	
conveyance	289–307
documentation	306
hazchem	327
hazchem code	327
Dangerous vehicles	44
Date of birth	
requirement to give	140
Definitions	2–5
Direction indicators	220–221
Disabled driver	
parking	354
speed limits	300
Disqualified, causing death	
whilst driving	352
Disqualified, driving whilst	136
Documentation	
definitions	115–117
driving licences	117–140
HGV	154
producing	139
Doors, opening	112
Downloading data, recording	
equipment	271
Drink/driving	281, 285
breath tests	284, 291
causing death	352
penalties	370
specimens	294–297
Drink/drugs (Scotland)	370–371
Driver	
control	112
newly qualified	134
Drivers' hours and records	242
application	259
breaks	248–250
community rules	248–252
daily driving	253
daily rest	253
departure from provisions	251
domestic rules	253–258
driving periods	255
emergencies	255
ferries and trains	248
general exemption from EC	243–247
goods vehicles	256

light goods vehicles	257
passenger vehicles	257
public authority	243
rest periods	243
weekly rest	249
working day	253
working week	253
Driving	
carelessly	352
dangerously	352
Driving instruction	350
Driving whilst disqualified	136
Driving licence, causing	
death whilst driving without	352
Driving licences	
endorsement offence codes	137–138
foreigners	140–141
full	124
groups	126
HGV classes	133
HGV types	133
instructor	350
LGV/PCV exemptions	125
LGV licences	133
minimum ages	135
motor cycles	131
newly qualified	134
ordinary, classes	141
PCV licences	117
production	139, 149
provisional	130, 132
renewal	136
trainee	133
Driving, inconsiderate	352
Driving, inconsiderate, causing death	352
Driving under age	136
Dual purpose vehicle definition	4
Duty to give information as to driver	335

E

Emergency Action Code	325
Emergency removal of vehicle	354
End-outline marker lamps	232
Endorsement offence codes	137
Engine stopping	110
Engineering plant	85–87
European Community Countries	140
Eyesight	
power to test	349
requirements	349
Excavators	92–94
Excessive noise	
avoidance	45, 111
Excise duty	
classes	159–160
Excise licence	158
exhibition	162
Exhaust system	45
Experimental vehicles	94–95

F

Flashing lights,	
use	220–221
Fog lamps	
front	226
rear	224–225
Foreign vehicles	
documentation	192–193
driving licence	140–141
excise forms	193
registration document	193

G

General arrest	
conditions	336–337
Glass	74
Goods vehicle	
definition	3
international operation	192, 193
maximum height	35
operators' licences	149–157
plating	175–178
tests	175, 178
Grass cutting machines	75
Ground clearance	14

H

Hackney carriages	190
roof signs	190
Hazard Identification Number	324
Hazard lights	228
Hazard warning	
labels	319
panels	319
signs (diamonds)	320, 321
Hazchem, interpretation	327
Headlamps	210–211
definition	196
Heavy locomotive	
definition	3
Heavy motor car definition	3
Height	
maximum	17, 37
travelling	35
HGV	
documentation list	116
Horn	54
Hours of darkness	
definition	192

I

Inconsiderate driving	352
Inconsiderate driving, meaning	352
Indicators, direction	220–221
Insecure load	44

Instruction, driving 350
Insurance, causing death whilst
 driving without 352
Insurance, driving without 147
Insurance 147
 European Community
  vehicles 192
 foreign vehicles 192
International catagories 6–7
International freight permit 192
Invalid carriage definition 5
 registration mark 163
 speed limits 300–303

L

Lamps, see Lights 202–205
Large bus, definition 68
Large child, definition 68
Large Goods Vehicles
 definition 5
 licence 125, 133
Legislation, table of 377–388
Length, calculation 11
Light goods vehicle, definition 68
Light locomotive definition 3
Lights
 bicycle 197
 cleanliness 196
 colour 208
 daytime 203
 direction indicators 220–221
 end-outline marker 232
 exceptions 204
 exemptions 198–199
 flashing 216–217
 fog, front 226
 fog, rear 224–225
 front 212–213
 hazard 228
 headlamps 210–211
 maintenance 196
 motor cycle 197
 movement 206
 obligatory 196–201
 obligatory, use 205–206
 obstruction of 205
 offences 192
 position 196–198
 projecting loads 237
 rear 214–215
 reflectors 216–217
 registration plate 228
 restriction on use of 240
 reversing 227
 side marker 230–231
 stop 222–223
 using 204–205
 warning beacons 229

Living van 42
Load
 abnormal 75–81
 insecure 44
 projecting, lights 237

M

Manufacturer's plate 18, 176
Marker lamps
 end-outline 232
 side 230–231
Markers
 projection 238
 reflective, rear 233–236
 side 230–231
Mascots 110
Medium-sized goods
 vehicle, definition 4
Minibuses, PSV, as 184
Ministry plate 18, 184
Mirrors
 fitting 70
 requirement 69
 use 69–73
Mobile telephones 113
Moped
 definition 5
 plates 179
Motor car, definition 2
Motorcycle
 crash helmets 346
 definition 5
 driving licence 122, 131
 footrests 111
 lamps 197
 noise 111
 plates 179
 registration mark 168
 sidestands 110
 silencer 45
 trailer 40
 training certificate 133
Motor tractor
 definition 3
Motor vehicle
 categories 122–123
 definition 2
 ground clearance 14
 length 9
Motorways 348
 speed limits 300–303

N

Noise
 excessive 45, 111
Notice of intended
 prosecution 345
Notional gross weight 31

O

Obligatory lights 196–201
  exemptions 202–203
Obstruction 111
Offences 196, 352
Offence codes 137
Opening doors 112
Operator's licence 149–157
  exemptions 150–151
  foreign vehicles 153–157
  types 149
Overhang 12

P

Parking
  darkness in 112
  disabled person 354
  emergency removal 354
  lights 192
  removal of vehicle 346
Passenger carrying vehicle
  definition 5
  licence 135
Passenger, danger – causing 44
Pedal cycles, lamps 197
Pedal cycles
  (Scotland) 369
Pedestrian crossings 351
Penalty Points 137
Physical health 349
Plates
  exemptions 178
  goods vehicles 172
  hackney carriages 190
  mopeds 179
  motor cycles 179
  trade 180
  trailer 175
Plating
  goods vehicles 175
Position lamp
  definition 196
Position lamp, rear 196
Powers of arrest (Scotland)
  careless driving 368
  careless cycling 368–369
  dangerous cycling 368–369
  dangerous driving 368
Powers of arrest 336–338
Power to sieze vehicle 148
Production of
  documents 334
Projecting load
  lights 237
Projection markers 105–106, 238
Prohibition of driving foreign
  vehicles 279–281
Provisional driving licence 117, 127, 129, 130, 132
  certificate of fitness 189
  definitions 183
  documentation 185
  local services 184
  minibuses 186–188
  operator's disc 185
  test certificate 185

Q

Qualified driver, definition 119

R

Radio–suppression 110
Rearguards 108
Recording equipment 263
  chart equipment 266
  definition 267
  downloading data 271
  drivers cards/sheets 269
  failure to comply 278
  inspection 275–276
  installation and inspection 268
  malfunctioning equipment 274
  offences 276
  requirement 267
  type approval 268
Record books 261–262
Reflective markers
  rear 223–236
Reflectors
  front 218
  rear 216–217, 223–236, 239
  side 219
  trailer 239
Registration marks 163–168
  plate light 163
  rear plate lamp 228
  requirement 163
  size 163, 166
  trailers 163
Registration offences 169
Registration plate suppliers 170, 171
Removal of vehicles 287, 354
Restricted speed vehicle 304–305
Restriction of right-hand lane
  on motorway (Scotland) 373
Reversing 112
Reversing alarm 55
Reversing lights 227
Road checks 286–287, 339
Road friendly suspension
  definition 28, 34
Road (Scotland)
  definition 357
  obstruction 360
  restriction on placing bridges etc 361
  deposit of mud on 362
  damage to 363
  placing ropes etc 364
Road traffic offences (Scotland)
  aiding and abetting 365
  careless driving (use of
  telephone in vehicles) 367
  taking away motor
  vehicles 366

S

Salvage operators	288
Seat belts	
adults, rear	64
application	57–61
children	65–66
definitions	57, 67
exemptions	60
fitting	59–60
minibus and coaches	62
use	61
Seat belts, appropriate, meaning	67
Seat belts, notification to bus passengers	63
Seat belts, definitions	57, 66, 67
Sidecars–fitting	43
Side marker lamps	230–231
Sideguards	107
Silencers	45
Skips (Scotland)	
control of builders	358
removal of	359
Small bus, definition	68
Small child, definition	68
Small vehicle definition	5
Special types vehicles	
additional requirements	102–103
abnormal loads	76–81
agricultural	90–91
engineering plant	85–87
excavators	92–94
experimental	94–95
general conditions	75
highway testing	101
mobile cranes	82–84
motor cutters	98–99
moveable platform	97
natural gas	101
notices	104
operational military	100
over 4.3 m wide	92
pedestrian controlled	98
recovery vehicles	88–89
straddle carriers	96
track laying	96, 100
Specified passenger seat, definition	57
Specimens	
drink/driving	
procedure	291
Speed limiters	304
plates	304
Speed limits	300–303
general	300
road	300–301
special types of vehicles	300–301
Speedometer	56
Spray suppression	109
Stop and search	340
Stop lamps	222–223
Stopping distances	349
Stopping engine	110
Straddle carriers	96

T

Suspension road friendly	
definition	28, 34
Tachograph	263–278
Tachograph, driver card	272
Tachograph, workshop card	273
Tachograph card, lost, malfunctioning etc.	273
Tachograph card, unauthorised	273
Taking without authority	
Taxis (see also Hackney Carriages)	183
roof signs	190
touts	343
Television sets	112
Test	
goods vehicles	172–174
Test, other vehicles	172
Testing	
premises on	286
roads, on	
'T' forms	192
TIR carnet	192
Towing, see Trailers	
Track laying vehicles	96, 100
Trade plates	169, 181
Trailer plates triangular	239
Trailers	
description	38, 39
length	8–10
living van	8
motor cycle towing	40
number, maximum	38
PSV towing	44
reflectors	239
secondary coupling vehicle as	43
Transport, animals	331–333
Travelling height	35
Tremcard	192
Trial vehicles	101
Triangular trailer	
plates	239
Turning circles	13
Tyres	48–53

U

Unattended vehicle	112
Unlicensed vehicle	161
Urine specimens	296–299

V

Vehicle	
aggravated vehicle taking	
alarm	55
combinations, length	8
definitions	2–5
interference	290
removal of	287
taking without authority	366
Vision	74

W

Warning beacons	229
Warning instrument	36, 37, 54, 55
Weighing, police powers	19
Weight	
additional authorised weights	32
articulated vehicles	25–26
axle	18, 25, 26, 29, 30, 34
bus	20
combined transport operations	28
locomotive	20
maximum	20–28
maximum laden	20–28
notional gross	31
offences	18
plates	18
power to weigh	19
procedure	19
rigid vehicles	22–24
trailers	27
vehicles	32
vehicle combinations	33
Wide vehicles over 4.3 m	90–91
Width	
calculations	16
maximum	15
Windscreen	
washers	74
wipers	74
Working time	282

Notes

Notes

Notes

Notes